T0135182

Lecture Notes in Information Systems and Organisation

Volume 27

Lecture Notes in Information Systems and Organization—LNISO—is a series of scientific books that explore the current scenario of information systems, in particular IS and organization. The focus on the relationship between IT, IS and organization is the common thread of this collection, which aspires to provide scholars across the world with a point of reference and comparison in the study and research of information systems and organization. LNISO is the publication forum for the community of scholars investigating behavioral and design aspects of IS and organization. The series offers an integrated publication platform for high-quality conferences, symposia and workshops in this field. Materials are published upon a strictly controlled double blind peer review evaluation made by selected reviewers. LNISO is abstracted/indexed in Scopus

More information about this series at http://www.springer.com/series/11237

Alessandra Lazazzara · Raoul C. D. Nacamulli
Cecilia Rossignoli · Stefano Za
Editors

Organizing for Digital Innovation

At the Interface Between Social Media,
Human Behavior and Inclusion

 Springer

Editors
Alessandra Lazazzara
Department of Social and Political
 Sciences
University of Milan
Milan, Italy

Raoul C. D. Nacamulli
Department of Human Sciences
 for Education
University of Milano-Bicocca
Milan, Italy

Cecilia Rossignoli
Department of Business
 Administration
University of Verona
Verona, Italy

Stefano Za
LUISS Guido Carli University
Rome, Italy

ISSN 2195-4968   ISSN 2195-4976   (electronic)
Lecture Notes in Information Systems and Organisation
ISBN 978-3-319-90499-3   ISBN 978-3-319-90500-6   (eBook)
https://doi.org/10.1007/978-3-319-90500-6

Library of Congress Control Number: 2018945087

Printed on acid-free paper

This Springer imprint is published by the registered company Springer International Publishing AG
part of Springer Nature
The registered company address is: Gewerbestrasse 11, 6330 Cham, Switzerland

Preface

This book presents a collection of research papers exploring the human side of digital innovation management, with a specific focus on what people say and share on social media, how they respond to the introduction of specific IT tools, and how digital innovations are impacting sustainability and inclusion. Given the plurality of views that it offers, the book is particularly relevant for digital technology users, companies, scientists, and governments. The overall spread of digital and technological advances is enhanced or hampered by people's skills, behaviors, and attitudes. The challenge of balancing the digital dimension with humans situated in specific contexts, relations, and networks has sparked a growing interest in how people use and respond to digital innovations. The content of the book is based on a selection of the best papers—original double-blind peer-reviewed contributions—presented at the annual conference of the Italian chapter of the AIS, which was held in Milan, Italy, in October 2017.

Milan, Italy
May 2018

Alessandra Lazazzara
Raoul C. D. Nacamulli
Cecilia Rossignoli
Stefano Za

Contents

The Innovation Agency: An Overview

Alessandra Lazazzara, Raoul C. D. Nacamulli, Cecilia Rossignoli and Stefano Za

The rise of digitalization is causing disruptive changes in business models in many industries and it is radically transforming how innovation should be understood and managed by scholars and practitioners [1]. New digital infrastructures (e.g. 3D printing, cloud computing), platforms (e.g. social media, virtual world) and ways of cooperation (e.g. co-design, co-production) are reshaping the meaning of innovation and introducing new challenges related to actors' interaction within digital ecosystems. According to Nambisan et al. [1: 224], digital innovation is "the creation of (and consequent change in) market offerings, business processes, or models that result from the use of digital technology". This broad definition introduces two specific features of digital innovation. The first is related to the flexibility offered by digital technology which is expanding the innovation phenomenon by not confining it anymore within the borders of an organization. This implies an increase in the fluidity of innovation process and also a continuous flux in which innovation outcomes may continue to evolve even after their delivery. The second feature concerns the potential for innovation agency to be distributed. It exploits the different actors

A. Lazazzara (✉)
Department of Social and Political Sciences, University of Milan, Milan, Italy
e-mail: alessandra.lazazzara@unimi.it

R. C. D. Nacamulli
Department of Human Sciences, University of Milano-Bicocca, Milan, Italy
e-mail: raoul.nacamulli@unimib.it

C. Rossignoli
Department of Business Administration, University of Verona, Verona, Italy
e-mail: cecilia.rossignoli@univr.it

S. Za
LUISS University, Rome, Italy
e-mail: sza@luiss.it

© Springer International Publishing AG, part of Springer Nature 2019
A. Lazazzara et al. (eds.), *Organizing for Digital Innovation*,
Lecture Notes in Information Systems and Organisation 27,
https://doi.org/10.1007/978-3-319-90500-6_1

which are actually involved into the innovation process (e.g. individuals, organizations, customers, policymakers), underlying the paradigms' shift from the "good-dominant" to the "service-dominant" logic [2].

The book collects some of the best contributions presented to the XIV Conference of the Italian Chapter of AIS (ItAIS) which was held at the University of Milano-Bicocca, Milan, Italy, in October 2017. ItAIS is an important forum for scholars and researchers involved in the Information Systems domain and gathers national and international researchers to identify and discuss the most important trends in the IS discipline. The contributions included in this volume cover a wide variety of topics related to how individuals and organizations can successfully handle emerging challenges in new technologies implementation with a specific focus on what can be classified as human aspects of digital innovation.

Advanced technologies are permeating every aspect of people's work and life. The role of humans in such a rapidly evolving landscape is unquestionable and represents an essential driver for digital innovation. The increasing speed of digital adoption and the continuous emergence of new technologies make people's attitude towards technology a critical concern for organizations wanting to stay competitive and becomes a catalyst for innovation. Organizations who want to make the most of technology should bear in mind the attention to the "human side" or "human agency" of advanced information technology. Indeed, the relationship between individuals and technology is not unidirectional since individuals may both use the features provided by technology or try to resist or modify them in order to achieve their goals [3]. Therefore, people's skills, behaviors, attitudes, motivational traits and goals changes need to be better understood in order to innovate successfully [1, 2].

All the 21 selected papers which are reported in this volume have been evaluated through a standard blind review process in order to ensure theoretical and methodological rigor. The book has been organized into four sections covering (a) Digital innovation and its effect on individuals; (b) Digital innovation for inclusion and sustainability; (c) Innovative solutions in digital learning; (d) Organizing for digital innovation.

1 Part I: Digital Innovation and Its Effect on Individuals

The first part of the book explores the pivotal role of individuals in technology adoption and usage and the related effects on a number of important individual outcomes (e.g. job satisfaction, perceived benefits, user performance) in different kind of contexts (i.e. private and public organizations, digital service providers).

From the job design perspective, Sarti and Torre aim at disentangling the effect of ICT usage on the degree to which employees are satisfied with their current job by taking into account the moderating effect of six job dimensions. More specifically, they found evidence that three job characteristics—namely autonomy, formalization and the relational dimension of the job—significantly affect the relationship between the use of information technology and job satisfaction. This suggests that HR professionals and managers should carefully take into account the technological dimension when designing a job. The nature of the job together with other individual characteristics are also analyzed in the paper by Caldarelli, Ferri, Maffei, and Spanò which applies the Technology acceptance model (TAM) in order to investigate the existence of the differences in information systems usage between two different groups: accountant and ICT workers. The authors ask for greater emphasis on the analysis of personal and cultural variables that can affect information systems intention to use and to further consider them in the development of implementation strategies within companies.

Moving to the context of the public sector, Tursunbayeva, Bunduchi, Franco and Pagliari explore the effect of the implementation of a Human Resource Information System (HRIS) in a healthcare organization by means of a case study methodology. Interestingly, studies on HRIS benefits rarely examine the kind of expected benefits that motivate different stakeholders (e.g. hospital managers, clinicians, nurses, HR professionals) to accept new HRIS initiatives. This study develops an extended model of the expected and realized benefits of HRIS for different users and maps the interconnections between these benefits in healthcare. Moving to a specific sector of Public Administration, namely judicial system, Lepore, Pisano, Alvino and Paolone investigate the relationship between individual cultural orientation and information system's individual impact. More specifically, they highlighted how group-oriented, dynamic and entrepreneurial features in organizational cultures are successful factors in the implementation of information systems.

As a conclusion to this section, the topical theme of personal data protection is investigated by Gómez-Barroso, Feijóo and Palacios. The authors apply the theory of planned behaviour (TPB) to a representative survey of 1500 Internet users in Spain to test how users' knowledge about service providers usage of personal data influences privacy attitudes, intentions and disclosure behaviour. The study reveals that increasing users' awareness and knowledge about the mechanism of exchange of personal data for improved services can encourage control of personal data.

2 Part II: Digital Innovation for Inclusion and Sustainability

The effect of digital innovation goes beyond its role in boosting performance and productivity—both at the individual and organizational level—and it may have a huge potential in terms of addressing inclusion and sustainability challenges. However, there is also a dark side in new technology adoption such as the negative effect on specific social groups because of a distort use of social media and their role in creating and spreading specific representations of members of certain social categories. This is the focus of the study by Perna, Varriale and Ferrara which analyses how media, and more specifically social media, have contributed to the spread of distorted and stereotyped images of nurses hence negatively affecting their reputation as qualified professionals. This representation of nurses on social media has a number of negative organizational consequences such as issues in recruiting and organizational image and brand. Prejudice and discrimination affect another social group, namely women in science and technology careers. D'Agostino and De Nicola apply semantic social network analysis to gender diversity in the Italian information systems community. Although there was an overall lower participation of women in this specific community, leveraging on their analysis the authors conclude that there is no evidence of gender discrimination and that men and women have an equally relevant role in the advancement of the information system discipline. Moreover, digital innovation may play a role in solving specific social problems. This is the case of crowd funding for social causes, a phenomenon which is quickly gaining popularity. Di Pietro, Spagnoletti and Prencipe analyze donations collected by a charity-crowd funding online platform and show the negative influence of a poor technology infrastructure as well as the positive effect of individuals' digital skills and social network interactions. Those results may be useful for leading the development of successful charitable initiatives and contribute to the further development of digital social innovation.

Another important aspect of digital innovation is its role in reinventing collaboration by facilitating the participation of various actors in the innovation process and gaining sustainability. Indeed, as described by Romanelli, Metallo and Agrifoglio, participation and technologies are the key issues to be addressed for future sustainability since they enable cities to become smart cities. Their contribution presents the concept of sustainable and smart cities and describes the role of citizens' participation as a means to engage them in decision-making processes concerning the development of urban areas. In this vein, interactive technologies, platforms and tools are a crucial prerequisite in order to support cities towards a sustainable development. However, according to Spagnoli, van der Graaf and Brynskov, especially within the smart cities' context there is a plethora of definitions of service co-creation and a large number of tools and platforms taken into account from different perspectives and disciplines without any harmonizing effort. Therefore, their study analyses methods and tools adopted by different cities in order to implement co-creation processes in collaboration with different stakeholders and tries to define the methods and digital tools that cities should pursue to fully exploit the potential of these platforms in terms of enhancing global collaborations. Among the main challenges cities are facing in terms of co-creation, those related to engaging the stakeholders and organising co-creation activities with new actors around virtual communities are the biggest. The engagement of citizens in collaboration is extremely useful and provides new possibilities and advantages for complex scientific research projects such as the one described in the paper by Bolici and Colella. Their paper aims at contributing to the "open/citizen science" research domain by examining and testing public engagement activities for a robotics research project and determine a series of guidelines useful to design public-engagement initiatives. Therefore, increasing citizen participation is one of the main components of the future sustainability challenges and can help governments to be more responsive to community and scientific needs.

3   Part III: Innovative Solutions in Digital Learning

As the digital technologies are reshaping organizations and workplaces, innovations and transformations in education and learning are underway. Technology-based learning is the future of training and there is a flourish of terms and concepts referring to the new forms resulting from digital technologies applied to learning. However, the growing interest and the increase in the number of publications on this topic has led to confusion rather than more understanding of the phenomenon. On the basis of this assumption, Caporarello, Giovanazzi and Manzoni perform a content analysis on the last twenty years of research and discuss the use of the most diffused 16 learning terms in the literature. They provide a comprehensive learning model that clarifies interactions and interdependencies among the terms and offers some insights for both practitioners and scholars. The growing shift towards technology-based learning is coupled with the spread of gamification, that is, the use of game design elements in non-game contexts. Caporarello, Magni and Pennarola provide a new definition of gamification for learning and an overview of applications. Moreover, the paper presents and discusses research on the effectiveness of gamification for learning purposes, focusing on students' attitude, knowledge and behaviour, which constitutes one of the main gaps in gamification literature. Specifically related to the topic of gamification is the concept of absorption, which is a sense of high psychological involvement that someone can experience when performing a task or a game. Many previous studies consider absorption as a positive antecedent of training outcomes and in their contribution, Aliberti and Paolino address the challenges posed by technological learning environments characterized by high degree of absorption. More specifically, the two authors tried to disentangle the effect of two negative antecedents of absorption, namely distraction and boredom, on learning and training transfer by proposing a theoretical model. Furthermore, they aim at exploring the role of creative climate in these relationships.

This section presents several innovative solutions related to digital learning in the higher education scenario. In their chapter, Previtali and Scarozza focus on the changes undergoing in the Italian university sector due to the rise of online educational programs. Using a case study, the authors describe the blended learning adoption and implementation by an Italian University and identify institutional strategy, structure, and support policies that could lead to the improvement of teaching and learning conditions. Moreover, they shift from students to faculty members' perspective in disentangling factors which most likely affect satisfaction in a blended learning program. Finally, the last contribution of this section presents another very innovative blended learning form which is called e-internship. Jeske and Axtell analyze this new kind of internship which requires no or minimal in-person interaction since work and collaboration on projects are supported by online tools and software. The number of e-internship is growing across different countries and is posing new research questions about how people learn in virtual contexts and also about how higher education institutions can manage college-to-work transitions.

4 Part IV: Organizing for Digital Innovation

Companies involved in digital transformation efforts may require substantial changes in roles, routines, processes, departments and the overall organizational structure. However, there is not a one-size-fits-all solution. Rather, the design of the digital transformation journey starts with the analysis of the particular needs of the organization together with the identification of competitive advantage sources and the formulation of strategic priorities.

Although SMEs are considered to be slower than larger firms in adopting digital technologies, digital innovation may improve their competitiveness with new products, services, processes and businesses models. Therefore, in order to keep customers and expand their markets SMEs are increasingly adopting e-business. De Paoli and Za present a pragmatic approach to defining a model aiming at facilitating the design and implementation of e-business for SMEs. This is an interaction-based model which distinguishes between different levels of interaction among internal (the entrepreneur, employees) and external (clients and suppliers) actors. Indeed, understanding and engaging external and internal customers and how those relationships differ from the online ones is a central anchor of digital innovation. Adopting the external customers perspective, Pennarola, Caporarello and Magni perform a comparative study among four companies in the jeans manufacturing and retailing industry in Italy operating both in the online (e-commerce websites) and offline (stores) channels. The authors analyze how the product return strategies differ among online and offline retailers and the effect of such strategies on consumers' attitude to purchase again and to return the product. With a focus on internal customers, Galanaki, Lazazzara and Parry try to classify configurations of e-HRM actually existing at the global level. By combining the actual degree of technological presence and the degree to which the technology is used to enable HRM activities, they identify four types of e-HRM configurations named "non-usage", "HR primacy", "Integrated e-HRM", and "IT primacy". Creating value for employees and managers is one of the main drivers for new technology adoption for HR purposes but the lack of cooperation between IT and HR departments generates hybrid and unsuccessful e-HRM configurations.

Moreover, within the context of digital innovation social media constitute important platform for stakeholders' engagement and may reshape marketing and communication strategies. Metushi and Fradeani perform content analysis on social media posts by large Albanian companies in order to analyze how companies adopt social media. Although social media usage has an important role in increasing company's audience and there is a positive relationship between a company's social media activity and sales. Companies adopt social media mainly for marketing purposes but are still not considered as a communication tool able to increase firms' transparency. In the same vein, Gesuele and Celio analyze social media adoption in a specific context, namely municipality, as a means for citizen engagement. Using the case study methodology, they explored the official Facebook Municipality account activities of the City of Naples in terms of contents disclosed and impact on citizens. They reveal that through social media usage municipalities are enhancing their social image and improving the citizens' participation, but a true adoption for co-design purposes is yet to come.

Finally, we are grateful to the Authors, the Conference Chairs and Committee members, to the members of the Editorial Board and to the Reviewers for their competence and commitment. This publication would not have been possible without their active and generous contribution.

References

1. Nambisan, S., Lyytinen, K., Song, M.: Digital innovation management: reinventing innovation management in a digital world. MIS Q. **41**(1), 223–238 (2017)
2. Lusch, R.F., Nambisan, S.: Service innovation: a service-dominant-logic perspective. MIS Q. **39**, 155–175 (2015)
3. Leonardi, P.M.: When flexible routines meet flexible technologies: affordance, constraint, and the imbrication of human and material agencies. MIS Q. **35**, 147–168 (2011)

Part I
Digital Innovation and its Effect on Individuals

ICT Use and Job Satisfaction. The Moderating Role of Task Characteristics

Daria Sarti and Teresina Torre

Abstract This paper focuses on the relationship between ICT use and job satisfaction, following a classic but always relevant research stream, and analyses the role of work design in moderating this relationship. The findings of the analysis, carried out on a sample of 35,187 employees in Europe (data source: EWCS2010), demonstrate that the use of ICT is important in bolstering the individual's satisfaction about his/her own work. We also demonstrated that job design plays an important role in determining the strength and the form of the relationship between ICT use and job satisfaction. Our results offer interesting stimuli for a debate among scholars and practitioners on the management of employees in a context in which technologies represent an indispensable tool for workers, so that the role of the organization is to "design" tasks properly so as to grant them this new way of working.

1 Introduction

In the last decades, the technological revolution has deeply modified the content of work and the way in which it is performed. For example, routinized tasks, which were carried out by employees in the past, are accomplished nowadays by technological equipment. Intellectual work has been influenced by modern technologies, which are used as normal tools. In general, these technologies have enabled individual to work to achieve a higher level of potential, though at the same time some drawbacks have emerged.

Starting from this premise the aim of our work is to understand the impact of ICT use in the work context correlating it to the more traditional dimensions with

D. Sarti (✉)
Department of Economics and Management, University of Florence, Florence, Italy
e-mail: daria.sarti@unifi.it

T. Torre
Department of Economics and Business Studies, University of Genoa, Genoa, Italy
e-mail: teresina.torre@economia.unige.it

© Springer International Publishing AG, part of Springer Nature 2019   11
A. Lazazzara et al. (eds.), *Organizing for Digital Innovation*,
Lecture Notes in Information Systems and Organisation 27,
https://doi.org/10.1007/978-3-319-90500-6_2

which the organization 'manages' the work dimension. We are referring to work design, which is considered a central element in organizational issues, thereby showing its relevant connection with job satisfaction (JS). Furthermore, we are interested in analyzing whether there is an interaction between job design components and the use of ICT in favoring or disrupting JS. In our opinion, the influence of work characteristics on the relationship between ICT use and JS has been neglected, even though it might represent a useful lever to understand how it works and some of its elements might offer major support to ICT technologies.

The paper has been organized in the following manner. In the second part, the theoretical background is presented and our hypotheses are introduced; in the third section, we present the analysis and the most relevant results. Finally, some preliminary suggestions are introduced in relation to our questions and then considerations useful for future research activities are proposed.

2 Theoretical Background

2.1 Work Design and Employees' Job Satisfaction

Work design has been recognized for many decades as a prominent strategy for improving the productivity as well as 'the quality of the work experience of employees' in organizations [1: 250]. Starting from the last century, thousands of studies have been conducted that have examined work design issues and presented different complementary dimensions for the design of jobs, like the ones introduced by Mintzberg [2]: specialization (horizontal and vertical), work formalization and training. Indeed, as suggested by Morgeson and Humprey [3], work design was demonstrated as important for a range of individual, group, and organizational outcomes [4, 5].

In the table below, we refer to three pivotal studies in this field that give rise to three different diagnostic instruments useful to analyze job characteristics, these are: the Job Diagnostic Survey-JDS [1, 6], the Work Design Questionnaire-WDQ [3] and the Job Content Questionnaire-JCQ [7] (Table 1).

The precursor among the job design models, the one by Hackman and Oldham [1, 6], was born in order to suggest that job design and job re-design might represent an important foci of motivation for employees. Nowadays, this pattern represents the one most extensively used in academic literature (e.g. [8]), as well as the most popular one cited in current manuals (e.g., [9]).

According to Hackman and Oldham [6: 160] positive employees' outcomes — such as motivation, satisfaction, quality performance, low absenteeism and turnover — are achieved in a given working environment 'when three critical "psychological states" are present for an employee (experienced meaningfulness of the work, experienced responsibility for the outcomes of the work, and knowledge of the results of the work activities). […] these critical psychological states are created by the presence of five "core" job dimensions.'

Table 1 Synthesis of the pivotal studies on job characteristics (*)

Study's reference	Hackman and Oldham (1975, 1976)	Morgeson and Humprey (2006)	Karasek et al. (1998)
Validated Instrument	Job diagnostic survey (JDS)	Work Design Questionnaire (WDQ)	The Job Content Questionnaire (JCQ)
Dimensions in the theoretical model	Skill Variety Task Identity Task Significance Autonomy Feedback (*) (dealing with others, feedback from agents, feedback from the job)	Task characteristics Work scheduling autonomy Decision-making autonomy Work methods autonomy Task variety Significance Task identity Feedback from job Knowledge characteristics: Job complexity Information processing Problem solving Specialization Social characteristics Social support Initiated interdependence Received interdependence Interaction outside organization Feedback from others Work context Ergonomics Physical demands Work conditions Equipment use	Skill Discretion Decision Authority Skill Utilization Decision Latitude Psychological Job Demands Supervisor Social Support Co-worker Social Support Physical Job Demands Job Insecurity

Note Feedback which represents just one dimension in the authors' theoretical model, in the JDS was divided in three sub-variables (here in blankets)

In the same work, the Authors provide the definition of the relevant job dimensions [6: 161–162] and their theoretical model, developing the JDS as an instrument that provides measures of the core dimensions.

The job dimensions they included are reported here now. *Skill variety* means 'the degree to which a job requires a variety of different activities in carrying out the work, which involves the use of a number of different skills and talents of the employee'. *Task identity* represents 'the degree to which the job requires completion of a 'whole' and identifiable piece of work—that is, doing a job from beginning to end with a visible outcome'. *Task significance* is described as 'the degree to which the job has a substantial impact on the live or work of other people—whether in the immediate organization or in the external environment'. *Autonomy* is considered to be 'the degree to which the job provides substantial freedom, independence and discretion to the employee in scheduling the work and in determining the procedures to be used in carrying it out'. *Feedback from the job* is 'the degree to which carrying out the work activities required by the job results in the employee obtaining direct and clear information about the effectiveness of his or her performance.' [6: 161, 162].

Furthermore, two supplementary dimensions were included by scholars in the analysis. These are: *Feedback from agents,* which is described as 'the degree to which the employee receives clear information about his or her performance from supervisors or from co-workers', and *dealing with others,* which is 'the degree to which the job requires the employee to work closely with other people in carrying out the work activities' [6: 162].

Nevertheless, there are several criticisms about JDS [10]. According to Morgeson and Humprey [3], it focuses on a narrow set of motivational job characteristics whereas a number of other important work characteristics are ignored [11]. The point of view of some authors is that 'if scholars simply use the JDS without examining the larger work design literature, their research runs the risk of being deficient.' [3: 1231]. In this respect, they propose other dimensions apart from the task characteristics, such as: knowledge characteristics, social characteristics and work context.

Despite all that is stated above, only the dimension of task characteristics (as determinant of employee's positive outcomes) is considered here; in fact, in this work, our aim is to focus specifically on aspects that are more closely related to the issue of organizational design. Indeed, such an aspect, and its specific scale, have been widely used in a large number of previous studies, focusing specifically on a part directly related to the content of work in its authentic dimension of job design.

JS is typically defined as a multifaceted psychological construct that measures the degree to which employees are satisfied and happy with their current jobs [12, 13]. It is strictly related to all the characteristics of the job. Indeed, if employees are satisfied with their jobs' characteristics and the overall job it is likely that they will work harder; however, if their JS is low, this will discourage employees' commitment and may also increase their willingness to quit the organization and the job [14, 15].

The conventional approach in the literature on JS [16] assumes that utility from work depends on a number of traits of the individual, on the features of the firm and job characteristics. Furthermore, according to the JD-R model, working conditions refer to those physical, social and organizational aspects of the job, which describe the whole work context [17, 18].

In the literature, it is widely acknowledged that some characteristics of work favour the positive attitudes of workers and, at the same time, reduce counter-productive behaviours. Some studies suggest that the dimension of continuous learning activities and skills development for specific professions increases JS and retention and enables continued provision of high-quality services [19–21]. Furthermore, other researches demonstrate the importance of perceived autonomy and control on JS and the quality of care [22, 23].

Hence consistent with prior studies in this area, we posit that a statistically significant relationship exists between job characteristics and JS. Thus:

- Hp1. Task characteristics have a significant relationship with JS.

2.2 ICT Use, Work Design and Employees' Job Satisfaction

A number of studies have highlighted both beneficial and detrimental effects in the use of technologies at work. Despite this, authors claim that few studies have examined the impact of ICT on employees' well-being [24]. According to recent reviews, the use of ICT in the workplace can have both positive and negative effects on employees' work experiences [25, 26]. In other words, ICT may be perceived as both a resource and a work demand [25].

Some researchers underline the positive effect of ICT use considering it an instrument enabling individuals to be 'closer' to them, in terms of time and space, and in so feeding their social relationships. Authors highlight the positive impact of new technologies on the increase of individuals' overall job satisfaction. In particular, it has been shown that ICT use favours a growth in the rate of communications among employees, improves bottom-up flows of communication, reduces status differences and promotes equality. Furthermore, it stimulates participation in problem-solving and decision-making [27–29].

Recent literature suggests that in modern workplaces ICT use can increase job demands due to increasing expectations and employee accessibility to the workplace [26]—which in turn can have a negative impact on employees' health and well-being [25, 28, 30] and family-to-work conflict [31].

However, if we start from the pivotal study of Chester Barnard [32] and from his idea of the organization as a 'cooperative' system-, in which the satisfaction of both the organizational goals and individuals' needs have to be pursued - we can approach ICT as an 'instrument' and a 'mean' for the achievement of the above mentioned twofold goals. Thus, we believe that a conscious use of such an instrument is pursued within a context in which the social nature of the organization as a 'cooperative system' is a constitutional element.

In this vein, we posit that:

- Hp2. ICT has a positive and significant relationship with JS.

A moderation effect is assessed, wherein researchers aim to understand the role that a third variable—i.e. the moderation variable—may have on the relationship between a dependent variable and an independent one. In particular, if a moderation exists the moderator variable affects either the form or the strength of the relationship between a predictor and a criterion variable [33].

In the introduction to this paper, we mentioned that following the huge increase in ICT use at work some variance has to be included in job design. Indeed, on the one hand, personal computers (PCs) represent nowadays the principal tool for many kinds of works. They allow people to store huge amount of data and information and provide aids towards in computing, decision-making and problem-solving. This kind of support represents a useful instrument for routine activities even though it is claimed that it might fail to favour creative and intellectual tasks [34]. Furthermore, PCs are today equipped as a mass communication medium, which enables individuals to be connected with others all over the world via the world wide web. Thus, the new technology increases the democratization of communication, favours immediate feedback and reduces costs in coordination.

In this paper, our aim is to understand whether job characteristics may represent a useful lever to implement the main relationship between ICT use and JS. Therefore, an interactive effect between ICT usage and job design is hypothesized.

In their study, Day and colleagues [24] propose that: 'the extent to which ICT demands exist in organizations and elicit a strain response in employees may be influenced by the extent to which the organization frames and support employees' use of ICT' [24: 476]. In other words, authors propose a relationship between ICT and 'organization frames', thereby suggesting that the effect of ICT on employees' outcomes may also be affected by organizational elements [25]. As previously reported, a number of studies have proved the relevance of job design for employee's JS. According to this stream, we believe that an interaction exists among ICT use and task characteristics, which may have an interactive effect on job satisfaction. Hence, we suggest that:

- HP3. Task characteristics moderate the relationship between ICT use and JS.

The figure below summarizes our model of analysis (Fig. 1).

3 Empirical Analysis

3.1 Method

The empirical research was based on data gathered from the database of the fifth European Working Conditions Survey (EWCS), which was conducted in 2010 on a large sample of workers from the EU35 and which is the most recent one at disposal. Only people who declared their status of being employed were included in

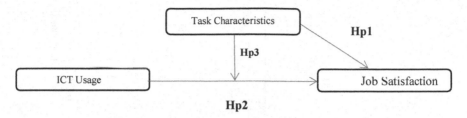

Fig. 1 The model of analysis

the analysis for the purpose of our analysis. The final sample resulted composed by 35,187 individuals. The EWCS sample is representative of those aged 15 years and over who are in employment and resident in the 35 EU countries. In each country, a multistage, stratified random sampling design was used.

3.2 Analysis and Results

In order to identify the fundamental dimensions of job design as well as the ICT use, an exploratory factor analysis (EFA) was performed on the 21 items chosen from the survey questionnaire. Factors were extracted using the principal component method. Based on previous scales validated in current literature such as JDS [35] WDQ [3] and JCQ [7], relevant items about job characteristics and ICT usage were identified among the set of questions of the EWCS.

The Keiser criterion was used to select the total number of factors (7) guaranteeing a percentage of cumulative explained variance of 59%. Bartlett's sphericity test (p-value < 0.001) and the Keiser Meyer Olkin index (KMO = 0.749) were then calculated to check the appropriateness of factor analysis and the sampling adequacy. We conclude that each of them was very good. Then, a varimax (orthogonal) factor rotation was performed to make factor interpretation more reliable. In the end, from the 21 questions, seven factors emerged. In detail, six were related to job design dimensions and one to the 'ICT use' (factor number 4, Table 2).

In order to test the hypothesis presented in this paper, an OLS regression analysis was performed among the main variables.

JS was considered as the dependent variable of the study; it was measured though a single-item-scale that is: 'On the whole, are you very satisfied, satisfied, not very satisfied or not at all satisfied with working conditions?' The responses were based on a five-point-scale ranging: 5 = Strongly agree; 4 = Agree; 3 = Neither agree nor disagree; 2 = Disagree; 1 = Strongly disagree.

Though some authors advice caution in using single-item scales in empirical research [36], others favour the use of this approach [e.g., 37]. Indeed, it has been demonstrated that 'single-item measures of overall job satisfaction correlated highly with multiple-item measures of overall job satisfaction' [37: 77] and might be used in special circumstances [36].

Table 2 Obliquely rotated component loadings for 21 survey items

	Components						
	1	2	3	4	5	6	7
Able to choose or change methods of work	0.812						
Able to choose or change order of tasks	0.786						
Able to choose or change speed or rate of work	0.783						
Able to apply own ideas in work	0.444		0.412				
The job involves complex tasks		0.663					
The job involves learning new things		0.643					
Tasks require different skills		0.599					
The job involves solving unforeseen problems on your own		0.595					
The job involves assessing the quality of own work		0.534					
Having the feeling of doing useful work			0.819				
Job gives you the feeling of work well done			0.802				
Know what is expected of you at work			0.710				
Work with computers.				0.921			
Job involve using internet/email				0.916			
Pace of work dependent on numerical production targets or performance targets					0.758		
Pace of work dependent on automatic speed of a machine or movement of a product					0.668		
Pace of work dependent on the direct control of your boss					0.601		
Pace of work dependent on direct demands from people						0.849	

(continued)

Table 2 (continued)

	Components						
	1	2	3	4	5	6	7
Job involves dealing directly with people (not employees)						0.810	
Immediate supervisor provides with feedback							0.765
Immediate supervisor is good at planning and organizing the work							0.755
Eigenvalues	2251	2091	2038	1856	1526	1484	1237
Percentage of total variance	10,718	9956	9703	8838	7268	7068	5891
Number of text measures	4	4	3	2	3	2	2

Note Loadings ≥ 0.40

The independent variables related to work design dimensions are the six factors emerging from the EFA, that was previously performed (see Table 2). These are: autonomy (AU; factor 1), skill variety (SV; factor 2), task significance (TS; factor 3), work control and formalization (WF; factor 5), dealing with others (DO; factor 6), and feedback from agents (FB; factor 7). As differently from the previous model of Hackman and Oldham [1], task identity was not identified as a factor. Instead, we recognized a fifth dimension that is 'work formalization' (factor 5) which might also be slightly related to the other dimension that is missing in this model—compared to the one by Hackman and Oldham [1]—that is feedback from the job.

The moderation variable of the model, that is 'the use of technologies' at work, emerges by the factor 4 in the CFA, as shown in Table 2.

In order to test our hypothesis, we first introduced six control variables, as they have been identified in the extant literature as relevant drivers for JS (sex and age of respondent, dimension of the firm the individual is employed in, years in the organization, the number of subordinates, average numbers of hours worked per week). In the second step of the model, the factors emerging from the job characteristics were introduced. In the third step, the 'ICT usage' was included. We later incorporated in the model the multiplicative terms computed by multiplication of all the six independent variables related to job characteristics with ICT use (Table 3).

The regression analysis first shows interesting results about the relationship between the task's characteristics and the dependent variable, i.e. JS. Indeed, a significant increase in the overall variance of the model ($R^2 = 0.137$) was found. The results show that all the factors—except dealing with others ($\beta = -0.001$; $p > 0.05$)—affect JS. A positive and significant relationship was found between autonomy ($\beta = 0.143$; $p < 0.001$), skill variety ($\beta = 0.082$; $p < 0.001$), task significance ($\beta = 0.231$; $p < 0.001$) and feedback from agents ($\beta = 0.162$; $p < 0.001$) with JS. A negative and significant relationship was found with work formalization ($\beta = -0.122$; $p < 0.001$).

Our first findings demonstrate that work characteristics have a significant and relevant role in explaining JS.

Furthermore, the positive relationship between JS and ICT use was demonstrated.

In the end, we found that a moderation effect exists for three of the six task characteristics: autonomy, work formalization and dealing with others. Hence, when ICT usage increases, the relationship between autonomy and JS becomes weaker ($\beta = -0.015$; $p < 0.05$) as well the relationship between work formalization and JS ($\beta = -0.026$; $p < 0.01$) and furthermore, when ICT use increases the relationship between dealing with others and JS becomes stronger ($\beta = 0.031$; $p < 0.001$).

In Figs. 2, 3 and 4, the results are presented through three path diagrams.

The interaction effect between variables is evident. When the variable of dealing with others is involved (see Fig. 2) we notice that the positive relationship between ICT use and JS becomes stronger when a high degree of dealing with others is considered in the job position. In this case, it might be worth for positions implying higher levels of ICT use to consider implementing the aspect of dealing with others.

Table 3 Hierarchical regression analysis for variables predicting job satisfaction (N = 35.187)

Variable	B	SE B	β	B	SE B	β	B	SE B	β	B	SE B	β
Sex	0.019	0.013	0.013	0.038	0.012	0.027 **	0.058	0.012	0.041 ***	0.060	0.012	0.042 ***
Age	0.000	0.001	−0.008	0.001	0.001	0.013	0.000	0.001	0.001	0.000	0.001	0.001
Number of people in the workplace	−0.010	0.004	−0.024 **	−0.019	0.004	−0.046 ***	−0.010	0.004	−0.024 **	−0.009	0.004	−0.021 *
Years in the organization	0.000	0.001	−0.004	0.001	0.001	0.019 .	0.002	0.001	0.027 **	0.002	0.001	0.026 **
Number of subordinates	0.000	0.000	−0.008	0.000	0.000	−0.009	0.000	0.000	−0.007	0.000	0.000	−0.007
Average hours worked per week	0.009	0.001	0.134 ***	0.008	0.001	0.117 ***	0.008	0.001	0.122 ***	0.008	0.001	0.121 ***
Autonomy (AU)				0.102	0.006	0.143 ***	0.101	0.006	0.141 ***	0.100	0.006	0.140 ***
Skill variety (SV)				0.059	0.006	0.082 ***	0.061	0.006	0.085 ***	0.061	0.006	0.085 ***
Task significance (TS)				0.165	0.006	0.231 ***	0.165	0.006	0.231 ***	0.165	0.006	0.231 ***
Work formalization (WF)				−0.087	0.006	−0.122 ***	−0.086	0.006	−0.121 ***	−0.082	0.006	−0.115 ***
Dealing with others (DO)				0.003	0.006	0.004	0.002	0.006	0.003	−0.001	0.006	−0.001
Feedback from agents (FB)				0.115	0.006	0.162 ***	0.114	0.006	0.161 ***	0.114	0.006	0.161 ***
ICT usage							0.093	0.006	0.131 ***	0.092	0.006	0.129 ***
ICT*autonomy										−0.011	0.006	−0.015 *
ICT*skill variety										−0.002	0.006	−0.002

(continued)

Table 3 (continued)

Variable	B	SE B	β	B	SE B	β	B	SE B	β	B	SE B	β
ICT*task significance										0.001	0.006	0.001
ICT*work formalization										−0.019	0.006	−0.026 **
ICT*dealing with others										0.022	0.006	0.031 ***
ICT*feedback from agents										0	0.006	0
R^2		0.018			0.137			0.154			0.155	
F		4.201	***		175.01	***		184.2	***		127.68	***

* p < 0.05, ** p < 0.01, *** p < 0.001

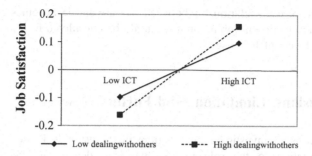

Fig. 2 The graphical representation of the moderation effect of dealing with others on the relationship between ICT usage and job satisfaction

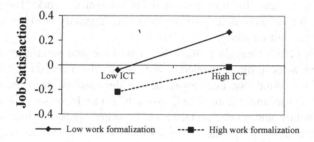

Fig. 3 The graphical representation of the moderation effect of work formalization on the relationship between ICT usage and job satisfaction

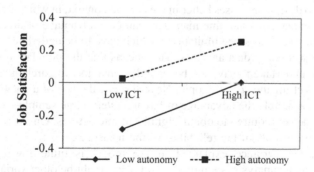

Fig. 4 The graphical representation of the moderation effect of autonomy on the relationship between ICT usage and job satisfaction

For work formalization we see a sort of 'conflict' between the two dimensions, so that when both of these—work formalization and ICT usage—have a high level there is a negative impact on JS, implying that when there is a high ICT use, it is worth reducing the work formalization. Finally, we found that when autonomy is considered, the positive relationship between ICT use and JS becomes weaker. This implies that a reduction in job autonomy should be considered for those who need to have high levels of ICT use.

4 Conclusions, Limitations and Further Research

This paper aims to investigate the relationship between ICT use and JS, with particular attention to the role played by work design in affecting such a relationship. In detail, our purpose was to prove that an interaction exists between the use of ICT and the work design dimensions and to verify whether some of them play a more relevant role. Indeed, it is acknowledged that the massive use of ICT has strong implications for the mode and the content of work. The data at our disposal offer information about two aspects of ICT, exactly working with PC and with the internet and emails.

The results of the analysis proved that a positive and significant relationship exists between work design dimensions and JS and also between ICT use and JS. Furthermore, we found that three work design dimensions affect the relationship between ICT usage and JS. In detail, when ICT use increases, the relationship between autonomy and work formalization becomes weaker, while the opposite happens with dealing with others. So, more ICT means less autonomy and, in consequence, less JS. The same is valid for work formalization. On the contrary, the relational feature of modern ICT technologies helps to strengthen the link between dealing with others and JS.

These suggestions offer some insights that would enable HR departments to manage the job design processes better in the current context, in which an even larger use of ICT is expected. Also, line managers can take advantage of this approach.

The present study has some limitations, which have to be underlined. First of all, it is based on secondary data analyses. This means that the population studied and the measures undertaken may not be exactly what the researchers might have chosen to collect for the specific topic. Nevertheless, the use of a database such as EWCS makes available the advantage of having a very large sample—which offers the statistical power required to obtain significant interactions. On the other hand, it does raise questions about the reliability of the measures.

Moreover, the variance explained in the model is quite low—so that an improvement in the analysis is required—and there might be other variables, which impacts on JS (for example, the nationality of the respondent might be considered). We are also aware of the limitations associated with the use of a single-item measure for JS as a dependent variable, even though a number of studies have done the same.

In conclusion, our work makes a contribution in getting evidence on a classic and perennially interesting topic, which is influenced by the increasing role of ICT in work and in working conditions, seeking to deepen this role and its nature. More knowledge is expected in this field.

References

1. Hackman, J.R., Oldham, G.R.: Motivation through the design of work: test of a theory. Organ. Behav. Hum. Perform. **16**(2), 250–279 (1976)
2. Mintzberg, H.: Structure in fives: designing effective organizations. NJ, Prentice-Hall Inc, Englewood Cliffs (1983)
3. Morgeson, F.P., Humphrey, S.E.: The Work Design Questionnaire (WDQ): developing and validating a comprehensive measure for assessing job design and the nature of work. J. Appl. Psychol. **91**(6), 1321–1339 (2006)
4. Morgeson, F.P., Campion, M.A.: Work design. In: Borman, D.I., Klimosky, R. (eds.) Handbook of psychology: industrial and organizational psychology, vol. 12, pp. 423–452. Hoboken, NJ, Wiley (2003)
5. Parker, S., Wall, T. D.: Job and work design: Organizing work to promote well-being and effectiveness (vol. 4). Sage, Thousand Oaks (1998)
6. Hackman, J.R., Oldham, G.R.: Development of the job diagnostic survey. J. Appl. Psychol. **60**(2), 159 (1975)
7. Karasek, R., Brisson, C., Kawakami, N., Houtman, I., Bongers, P., Amick, B.: The Job Content Questionnaire (JCQ): an instrument for internationally comparative assessments of psychosocial job characteristics. J. Occup. Health Psychol. **3**(4), 322–355 (1998)
8. Tyagi, P.K.: Relative importance of key job dimensions and leadership behaviors in motivating salesperson work performance. J. Mark. **49**(3), 76–86 (1985)
9. Ilgen, D.R., Hollenbeck, J.R.: The structure of work: job design and roles. Handbook Ind. Organ. Psychol. **2**, 165–207 (1991)
10. Hackman, J.R., Oldham, G.R.: Work redesign. Addison-Wesley, Reading, MA (1980)
11. Parker, S.K., Wall, T.D., Cordery, J.L.: Future work design research and practice: Towards an elaborated model of work design. J. Occup. Organ. Psychol. **74**(4), 413–440 (2001)
12. Christen, M., Iyer, G., Soberman, D.: Job satisfaction, job performance, and effort: a reexamination using agency theory. J. Mark. **70**(1), 137–150 (2006)
13. Dawal, S.Z., Taha, Z., Ismail, Z.: Effect of job organization on job satisfaction among shop floor employees in Automative Industries in Malaysia. Int. J. Ind. Ergon. **39**(1), 1–6 (2009)
14. Clark, A.E.: Job satisfaction and gender: why are women so happy at work? Labour Econ. **4**(4), 341–372 (1997)
15. Cohen, A., Golan, R.: Predicting absenteeism and turnover intentions by past absenteeism and work attitudes: an empirical examination of female employees in long term nursing care facilities. Career Development Int. **12**(5), 416–432 (2007)
16. Clark, A.E., Oswald, A.J.: Satisfaction and comparison income. J. Public Econ. **61**(3), 359–381 (1996)
17. Schaufeli, W.B., Bakker, A.B., Van Rhenen, W.: How changes in job demands and resources predict burnout, work engagement, and sickness absenteeism. J. Organ. Beh. **30**(7), 893–917 (2009)
18. Schaufeli, W.B., Taris, T.W.: A critical review of the Job Demands-Resources Model: Implications for improving work and health. In: Bauer, G.F., Hamming, O. (eds.) Bridging occupational, organizational and public health, pp. 43–68. Springer, Netherlands (2014)
19. Tzeng, H.M.: The influence of nurses' working motivation and job satisfaction on intention to quit: an empirical investigation in Taiwan. Int. J. Nurs. Stud. **39**(8), 867–878 (2002)
20. Yoder, L.H.: Staff nurses' career development relationships and self-reports of professionalism, job satisfaction, and intent to stay. Nurs. Res. **44**(5), 290–297 (1995)
21. Donner, G.J., Wheeler, M.: Career planning and development for nurses: the time has come. Int. Nurs. Rev. **48**(2), 79–85 (2001)
22. Rafferty, A.M., Ball, J., Aiken, L.: H: Are teamwork and professional autonomy compatible, and do they result in improved hospital care? Q. Safety Health Care **10**(suppl 2), 32–37 (2001)

23. Panari, C., Guglielmi, D., Simbula, S., Depolo, M.: Can an opportunity to learn at work reduce stress? A revisitation of the job demand-control model. J. Workplace Learn. **22**(3), 166–179 (2010)
24. Day, A., Paquet, S., Scott, N., Hambley, L.: Perceived information and communication technology (ICT) demands on employee outcomes: The moderating effect of organizational ICT support. J. Occup. Health Psychol. **17**(4), 473 (2012)
25. Day, A., Scott, N., Kelloway, E. K.: Information and communication technology: implications for job stress and employee well-being. In: Perrewe, P., Ganster, D. (eds.) New developments in theoretical and conceptual approaches to job stress, vol. 8, pp. 17–350. Emerald Group Publishing Limited (2010)
26. O'Driscoll, M. P., Brough, P., Timms, C., Sawang, S.: Engagement with information and communication technology and psychological well-being. In: New developments in theoretical and conceptual approaches to job stress, vol. 8, pp. 269–316. Emerald Group Publishing Limited (2010)
27. Kiesler, S., Siegel, J., McGuire, T.W.: Social psychological aspects of computer-mediated communication. Am. Psychol. **39**(10), 1123–1134 (1984)
28. Morgan, K., Morgan, M., Hall, J.: Psychological developments in high technology teaching and learning environments. Br. J. Edu. Technol. **31**(1), 71–79 (2000)
29. Moomal, A., Masrom, M.: ICT Development and Its Impact on e-Business and HRM Strategies in the Organizations of Pakistan. J. Adv. Manag. Sci. **3**(4), 344–349 (2015)
30. Coovert, M. D., Foster Thompson, L.: Technology and workplace health. In: Quick, J. C., L. E. Tetrick, L.E. (eds.) Handbook of Occupational Health Psychology. (pp. 221– 242). Washington, DC: American Psychological Association (2003)
31. Golden, T.D., Veiga, J.F., Simsek, Z.: Telecommuting's differential impact on work-family conflict: is there no place like home? J. Appl. Psychol. **91**(6), 1340–1350 (2006)
32. Barnard, C.I.: The functions of the executive. Harvard University, Cambridge, Massachusetts (1938)
33. Sharma, S., Durand, R. M., Gur-Arie, O.: Identification and analysis of moderator variables. J. Mark. Res. 291–300 (1981)
34. Sarti D., Torre T.: The impact of ICT on individuals' wellbeing. The role of work content. The European case. In: Harfouche, A., Cavallari, M. (eds.) The Social Relevance of the Organisation of Information Systems and ICT. Springer series. Lecture Notes in Information Systems and Organisation (LNISO) (forthcoming)
35. Agervold, M., Mikkelsen, E.G.: Relationships between bullying, psychosocial work environment and individual stress reactions. Work Stress. **18**(4), 336–351 (2004)
36. Diamantopoulos, A., Sarstedt, M., Fuchs, C., Wilczynski, P., Kaiser, S.: Guidelines for choosing between multi-item and single-item scales for construct measurement: a predictive validity perspective. J. Acad. Mark. Sci. **40**(3), 434–449 (2012)
37. Nagy, M.S.: Using a single-item approach to measure facet job satisfaction. J. Occup. Organ. Psychol. **75**(1), 77–86 (2002)

Accountants Are from Mars, ICT Practitioners Are from Venus. Predicting Technology Acceptance Between Two Groups

Adele Caldarelli, Luca Ferri, Marco Maffei and Rosanna Spanò

Abstract Several authors tried to explain the key determinants in technology acceptance using the technology acceptance model (TAM). TAM posits that ease of use and usefulness predict technology usage. Despite it strong usage there are several studies that show a lack in the model due to the absence of personal factors that should be considered. This paper aims to show the existence of significant difference in technology usage between different groups of people. Two hundred and fifty individuals responded to a survey about technology usage in their firms. Our results show that there is a statistically significant difference in ease of use and in perceived usefulness. The investigation applies TAM to help researchers, developers and managers understand antecedents to users' intention to use.

1 Introduction

Information systems researchers studied information and communication technology outcomes and ICT diffusion processes since the inception of the information systems field [1]. Many authors tried to explain the key determinants in technological acceptance in order to manage information systems change avoiding the risk of productivity paradox [2].

Nowadays, the ICT innovation-diffusion literature focused on factors such as relative advantage, complexity, ease of use, and results demonstrability in order to examine the overall impact of these variables on firms' adoption of technological innovations [1, 3]. All these factors were included in a model known as Technology Acceptance Model (TAM) and in its adapted versions [4]. TAM is the most diffused and used model in IS change field [5]. Indeed, it is considered as a good model to predict the enduring line of ICT implementation and diffusion [6]. The model posits on the idea that the key determinants of technology acceptance and usage (by the information systems actors) are the perceived ease of use (PEOU) and perceived

A. Caldarelli · L. Ferri (✉) · M. Maffei · R. Spanò
University of Naples Federico II, 80126 Naples, Italy
e-mail: luca.ferri@unina.it

© Springer International Publishing AG, part of Springer Nature 2019
A. Lazazzara et al. (eds.), *Organizing for Digital Innovation*,
Lecture Notes in Information Systems and Organisation 27,
https://doi.org/10.1007/978-3-319-90500-6_3

usefulness (PU). These theoretical constructs are strongly related with attitude toward using. Moreover, Davis et al. [4] hypothesizes that actual system use is affected by behavioral intentions, which is affected by attitudes toward use. Beliefs about the system, PU and PEOU in TAM, directly affect attitudes toward use. What should be noted is that the model was largely criticized because it does not take into account several personal variables (such as gender, education, personal values, attitude to technology, etc.) that should influence the people's decision about technology usage [7, 8].

Several studies proposed to understand how personal values, traits and experience afflict information systems adoption and technology usage. However, the effect of personal variables on information technology acceptance is still an under investigate field [5, 9, 10].

The aim of this paper is to investigate how personal differences influences the technology acceptance. To this aim we integrated the technology acceptance model with "personal variable" (such as education, age, gender) and also we divided our sample in two different groups: accountant and ICT people. What should be noted is that in this paper we consider personal education as a discriminating factor in order to understand the existence of statistically significant differences in technology acceptance.

Using the TAM proposed by Davis et al. [4] as a basis, we carried out a questionnaire to understand users' degree of technology acceptance. The questionnaire was divided into two parts. The first part covered the personal data of the participants and the second part covered the different TAM theoretical dimensions. More specifically, the questions were divided as follows: six items for perceived ease of use; six items for perceived usefulness; and one item for usage intention. All the questions of the second part were quantified using a 5-point Likert Scale set from 1 (strongly disagree) to 5 (strongly agree). The final sample was composed by 142 SMES workers: 71 accountants and 71 engineers working in ICT division. After the questionnaire validation, we processed data using simple regression on the overall sample and on the two different groups, following the approach of Gefen and Straub [1] and Pikkarainen et al. [11].

The remainder of the paper is organized as follows. Section 2 explains the TAM and the research hypothesis. Section 3 examines the research methodology and provides descriptive statistics of the sample. Section 4 presents the research findings, and Sect. 5 provides discussions and concluding remarks.

2 Theoretical Background and Model Development

2.1 Technology Acceptance Model

Several researchers conducted studies in order to examine the relationship between perceived ease of use, perceived usefulness, attitudes, and the implementation of information technologies in firms recent years [12–14]. Their research supported the technology acceptance model (TAM) as a model potentially able to predict human intention in technology usage [12–15]. TAM is based on the idea according whom perceived ease of use and perceived usefulness can predict attitudes toward technology that is the antecedent of technology usage. More specifically, according to Davis et al. [4] these two theoretical constructs represent the only variables that afflict intention to use.

More specifically, the author asserted that perceived usefulness and ease of use represent the beliefs that lead to technology acceptance. Perceived usefulness (PU) can be considered as the degree to which a person believes that a particular information system would enhance his or her job performance (i.e. by reducing the time to accomplish a task) [4]. Perceived ease of use is defined as the degree to which a person believes the use of a particular system would be free of effort. According to Davis et al. [4] and to other authors [5–8], both these constructs have a strong positive effect in people decision to accept technology.

Further studies replicated these results in different fields and countries [16–18]. In light of previous literature, we expected that both theoretical constructs have a positive effect on people's intention to use technology in Italian firms, so we can state the following hypotheses:

H.1 Perceived usefulness positively afflict intention.
H.2 Perceived ease of use positively afflict intention.

2.2   Technology Acceptance Model and Cultural Differences

TAM has attracted a growing body of research [6], however despite its strong diffusion it was widely criticized by several authors since the beginning [19]. According to Adams et al. [19] it is not possible to consider just two dimensions in technology acceptance process so the model was considered too simple. More specifically, the authors emphasize the need to introduce new theoretical constructs that push the individual towards the adoption of a particular technology and to integrate the existent model with personal and cultural variables.

Also, several authors found significant cross-cultural differences [1, 20] that should be take into account in IS study. The extant literature on information systems ignored the effects of personal attribute such as gender, age, kind of education, job relevance, etc., even though in information systems research this kind of attribute represents fundamental aspects of culture [21, 22]. Moreover, the most diffused model in information systems change and ICT acceptance do not consider personal variable such as personal education or the role covered by people in firms in the process of ICT acceptance. These variables have strong importance and should be considered because they are active parts in the decisional processes [23]. Indeed, cultural and personal variables are proposed as a cornerstone for research by Delone and McLean [23] and have also been considered as a critical element in information systems change field [24, 25]. Several authors describe this as the main

TAM limitations explaining that personal values and education are important theoretical construct in decision-making process [18, 26]. This idea was shared also by Lergis et al. [6] that discuss about the existence of several significant factors in workers technological choice. These factors are not considered in the TAM, originating a lack of completeness.

Also, other studies show the existence of several personal (i.e. training, experience, role in the company, job relevance, etc.) and sociological (i.e. the process of change, groups resistance etc.) variables that should afflict technology usage [27]. Basing on the previous literature it is possible to expect different results arising two different group of people divided by their education.

According to Laudon and Laudon [28], in each company it is possible to find different culture and different groups of people. We consider two groups divided by the personal education: accountant and ICT workers. On one hand, the ICT workers should be more focused on the usefulness of new technological systems. On the other hand, accountants should be afraid of the routine change so they should be focused on perceived ease of use. On this basis we expect the following effects:

H.1a Perceived usefulness has greater importance for engineer than accountants.
H.2a Perceived ease of use has greater importance for accountants than engineers.

Moreover, Straub et al. [16] carried out a research in order to test the TAM in different culture. They found that the model may not predict technology use across all cultures. McCoy et al. [17] tried to explain the technology prediction due to different cultures. The authors show the existence of significant differences in perception of technology usage depending by age and personal culture of the people in the sample. More specifically, the authors using the inferential statistics examinee the potential moderating effect of Hofstede's [29, 30] cultural dimensions on people technology acceptance. They reach the same conclusion of Straub et al. [16] about the effect of personal variables on the model usability. Moreover, according to Benbasat and Barki [27] in order to have a good prediction of technology acceptance factors such as the personal attribute are fundamentals and we should consider them in a technological acceptance model. Several authors show that variables such as gender, age, role in companies should have a greater impact on people acceptance of technology. For example, Gefen and Straub [1] show the existence of statistically significant differences in different gender perception of technology. The study indicates that woman and man differ in their perception but not in the final choice of technology. According to previous studies we expect the following effect of personal variables on intention to use:

H.3 Gender has a significant effect on people acceptance of technology.

With reference to other personal factors several authors found different effect on the people intention to use technology. For example, Kowalczyk [31] and Hernandez et al. [22], using a structural equation modeling based on a survey, found that the relationship between age and intention to use technology was weak or negative. Indeed, age is strongly correlated with the amount of time that users need to become familiar with new technology [22, 31–33]. However, according to the author, findings suggest that other environmental factors (such as education) could play a more important role in explaining people intention to use technology. On the basis of the previous literature it is possible to state the following hypothesis:

H.4 Age has a negative effect on people acceptance of technology.
H.5 Education has a positive effect on intention to use.

3 Research Methodology

In order to explore the existence of differences in technological perception between different group of people, we provide a regression model using as dependent variable the intention to use and as independents variables the other TAM construct. Data were collected using a Likert-based questionnaire on a sample of 250 individuals working in 125 small and medium enterprise (SMEs).

3.1 The Questionnaire

In order to test our research hypothesis, we carried out a Likert-based questionnaire [34]. The questionnaire was divided in 2 parts. The first part covered the personal data of the participants (age, gender, education, job relevance), while the second covered the TAM dimensions using 6 questions for PEOU, 6 for PU, 1 for INT. We used the questionnaire proposed by Davis et al. [4]. All the questions were quantified using a 5-point Likert Scale set from 5 (strongly agree) to 1 (strongly disagree). The questionnaire was disseminated online in order to avoid the typical problems of other dissemination methodology [35, 36]. The survey was carried out on a sample of 250 individuals (125 ICT people and 125 accountant), working in 125 different Italian SMEs. We had a final response rate of 142 individuals (56.8% of the total sample). The dissemination phase last for 60 days.

3.2 Sample

The study focused on individuals who work in firms that choose to change their information systems during the survey period. Potential individuals were selected from firms in different fields in order to avoid the risks of considering just one sector. The respondent were 142 from 71 different firms. We had a 56.7% response rate. Table 1 provides useful information for sample description.

Table 1 Sample description

Measure	Item	n	Percentage (%)
Age	18–30	38	26.76
	30–40	44	30.99
	40–50	39	27.46
	50–60	21	14.79
Gender	Male	86	60.56
	Female	56	39.44
Education	High school	21	14.79
	University degree	63	44.37
	Master	55	38.73
	Ph.D.	3	2.11

Our sample was composed by accountants and ICT workers in the same percentage

3.3 Proposed Model

The final sample of 250 individuals was divided in two groups discriminated by the job in firms (ICT people or accountant). In order to understand the effect of job difference we provided the following regression model:

$$INT = \alpha1\, PU + \alpha2\, PEOU + \alpha3\, AGE + \alpha4\, GEN + \alpha5\, EDU \tag{1}$$

where

INT   intention to use the new information system
PU   perceived usefulness of the new information systems
PEOU   perceived ease of use of the new information systems
AGE   number of years of respondents
GEN   gender of the respondents
EDU   the degree of personal education (i.e. University degree, Master, Ph.D., ECC)

The model was used three times. The first time in was used on the total sample in order to explain the general tendency in information systems intention to use, while the second time was used on two different sub-samples in order to understand the differences arising different groups using the personal education as discriminant.

4 Research Results

In order to ensure the consistency and unidimensionality of the scales, we consider a first sample of respondent in order to carry out a initial reliability studies and also an exploratory factor analyses (using PCA) [37–40]. This procedure was used to suppress indicators which displayed an item–total correlation lower than 0.3, or whose exclusion increased the Cronbach's Alpha value, which should exceed the minimum limit of 0.7 [41, 42]. No factors were eliminated after this analisys. Table 2 show the Crombach's Alpha values.

All the obtained values are over 0.8 so they are considered good. Also, we carry out an exploratory factor analyses using varimax rotation with Kaiser normalization [43–45] in order to reduce all the concepts to just one factor [46]. Finally, we carried out a first regression model on the overall sample. Table 3 provides research results.

The explanatory power of the model was examined using the resulting overall R-square. Together, perceived usefulness and perceived ease of use were able to explain 37% of the total variances observed in people's intention to use the new information systems.

Perceived usefulness contribute more to the observed explanatory power than perceived ease of use. More specifically, perceived usefulness had a significant direct positive effect on people intention to use the new information systems (co-efficient 0.33 and 0.26 both with $p < 0.05$). Our results suggest that every increment in perceived usefulness and perceived ease of use will increase the intention to use of the people in the sample. These results are compliant with those of Kim and Maholtra [47], Gangwar et al. [48] according whom the main predictor of systems intention to use is the perceived usefulness. Also, our results are compliant with Davis et al. [4], Holden and Karsh [49] and other authors [16–18], according whom there is a positive effect of PEOU on intention. As result H1 and H2 are fully supported.

With reference to gender, our result show that it does not have a significant effect on intention to use. This statement is not compliant to previous research of Gefen and Straub [1] according whom there are significative differences in technology adoption and information systems usage between woman and man. As result H3 is not supported.

Table 2 Crombach's Alpha value

Variables	Mean	S.D.	Crombach's Alpha
PU	4.33	0.28	0.93
PEOU	3.92	0.67	0.89
INT	4.55	0.12	1

Table 3 Research results of multiple regression using the overall sample

Variables	Coefficient	P-value
PU	0.33	$p < 0.05$
PEOU	0.26	$p < 0.05$
Age	−0.19	$p < 0.01$
Gender	0.02	$p < 0.01$
Education	0.08	$p < 0.05$
R-square	0.37	

With references to the age, we find a strong and negative effect of this variable on intention to use. More specifically, we find a coefficient of -0.19 (with $p < 0.1$). According to our results, it is possible to state that the age negatively affects the intention to use, so young people have greater propension to technology usage than older. This statement is compliant with the one of Diatmika et al. [50], Laudon and Laudon [28] and other authors [22, 32] according whom older people have less propension to new technology usage because they should change their routines. Also, this statement is not compliant with Kowalczyk [31] according whom age does not afflict technology usage. As result H4 is supported.

Finally, with reference to education we found a low positive effect on intention to use (coefficient 0.08 with $p < 0.05$). According to our results it is possible to state that the degree of personal education does not affect significatively the intention to use. This statement is not compliant with results of previous research, according whom the degree of education positively afflicts the technology perception and usage [22, 31–33]. As result hypothesis 5 is not supported.

After the first analysis, we carried two different regressions using the role covered in firms as discriminant following the approach of Pikkarainen et al. [11]. The following table (Table 4a, b) provides the results.

With reference to the perceived usefulness (PU) our findings reveal a strong statistical it has a high positive effect on intention to use for both sample (0.30 for accountants and 0.41 for ICT people). More specifically, PU has higher effect on ICT people's intention to use (coefficient 0.41 with $p < 0.01$) than accountants (coefficient 0.30 with $p < 0.01$). ICT people perceived technology as something important in improving firms' efficacy and their personal activity so they would be more favorable to technology adoption. As result hypothesis 1a is supported.

Table 4 Research results of multiple regression using two different sample

a	Accountants	
	Coefficient	P-value
PU	0.30	$p < 0.1$
PEOU	0.39	$p < 0.05$
Age	−0.31	$p < 0.01$
Gender	0.06	$p < 0.01$
Education	0.18	$p < 0.1$
R-square	0.16	
b	ICT people	
	Coefficient	P-value
PU	0.41	$p < 0.1$
PEOU	0.35	$p < 0.05$
Age	0.03	$p < 0.01$
Gender	−0.02	$p < 0.01$
Education	0.05	$p < 0.05$
R-square	0.20	

With reference to PEOU, it has a positive effect for both sub-samples (coefficient 0.39 with $p < 0.05$ for accountants and 0.35 with $p < 0.05$ for ICT people). What should be noted is that the PEOU has greater importance for accountants than for the ICT people. A possible explanation of this phenomenon is that accountants are more interested in improving their experience in information systems usage in order to improve their productivity. As result hypothesis 2a is confirmed.

According to these results, we can make two different statements. First of all, the perceived ease of use has strong a positive effect on perceived usefulness. This means that technology is perceived more useful if it is more ease to use. Second personal variables have a great impact on people's intention to use new technology.

5 Discussion and Conclusions

This paper aims to use technology acceptance model in order to investigate the existence of differences in information systems usage between two different groups: accountant and ICT workers. To this aim, we used a regression model on an overall sample and on two sample discriminated by the role covered in firms. Our model has a good predictive and explanatory power, confirming TAM robustness in predicting workers' intentions to use new technology. It thus helps researchers understand the relationships between ease of use and usefulness, and the acceptance of new information systems by different groups. It confirms that information systems use depends on the usefulness and ease of use. Also, it helps to understand which are the personal factors that afflict workers intention to use allowing a clear understanding of technological change phenomenon.

More specifically, our results show that there is a statistically significant effect of the personal variable in some aspects of information systems intention to use. Indeed, we show that ICT people have a stronger degree of acceptation of new technology than accountant. Also, personal formation and gender are variables with an important role in ICT acceptance process.

Our results have implications for both academic and practitioners.

From an academic point of view, our findings suggest that TAM should be integrated with personal and cultural variables that can have effects on information systems intention to use.

Moreover, with reference to practitioners' perspective, our results provide useful information in order to well manage the information systems change process. We show that managers should consider the personal dimensions of information systems final users while they decide for new technologies implementation. A complete understanding of the personal factors could help managers to develop a better implementation strategy in order to avoid problems such as productivity paradox [2, 51–53] or people resistance to information systems change [53–58].

This research has limitations. First of all, there could be few cultural and national limitations of our findings. For example, there are several cultural differences that can generate influences on how individuals respond to information systems change.

These differences make our finding not generalizable and ask for further investigation about the phenomenon. Further studies could replicate our model using a cross-cultural approach in different national cultures. Also, our conclusions are based on cross-sectional data so this is just a snapshot of this model. We should enlarge our study using a longitudinal study in the future to investigate information systems perception in different time periods (i.e. *ex ante* and *ex post* the implementation) making comparisons and providing more insight into the phenomenon. Finally, due to the structure of the questionnaire several information about the people's perception of information systems could be loss. Future research could ask individuals to respond in general about their perception of ease of use and usefulness of the new information systems in order to understand how to improve people's perception of information systems.

References

1. Gefen, D., Straub, D.W.: Gender differences in the perception and use of e-mail: an extension to the technology acceptance model. MIS Q. **21**, 389–400 (1997)
2. Van Ark, B.: The productivity paradox of the new digital economy. Int. Prod. Monit. **31**(1), 3–18 (2016)
3. Prescott, M.B., Conger, S.A.: Information technology innovations: a classification by IT locus of impact and research approach. ACM SIGMIS Database **26**(2–3), 20–41 (1995)
4. Davis, F.D., Bagozzi, R.P., Warshaw, P.R.: User acceptance of computer technology: a comparison of two theoretical models. Manage. Sci. **35**(8), 982–1003 (1989)
5. Marangunić, N., Granić, A.: Technology acceptance model: a literature review from 1986 to 2013. Univ. Acc. Inf. Soc. **14**(1), 81–95 (2015)
6. Legris, P., Ingham, J., Collerette, P.: Why do people use information technology? a critical review of the technology acceptance model. Inf. Manag. **40**(3), 191–204 (2003)
7. Lee, Y., Kozar, K.A., Larsen, K.R.: The technology acceptance model: past, present, and future. Comm. Assoc. Inf. Syst. **12**(1), 751–781 (2003)
8. Kwon, T.H., Zmud, R.W.: Unifying the fragmented models of information systems implementation. In Critical Issues in Information Systems Research, pp. 227–251. Wiley, Hoboken (1987)
9. Hu, P.J., Chau, P.Y.K., Sheng, O.R.L., Tam, K.Y.: Examining the technology acceptance model using physician acceptance of telemedicine technology. J. Manag. Inf. Syst. **16**(2), 91–112 (1999)
10. Devaraj, S., Easley, R.F., Crant, J.M.: Research note—how does personality matter? relating the five-factor model to technology acceptance and use. Inf. Syst. Res. **19**(1), 93–105 (2008)
11. Pikkarainen, T., Pikkarainen, K., Karjaluoto, H., Pahnila, S.: Consumer acceptance of online banking: an extension of the technology acceptance model. Internet Res. **14**(3), 224–235 (2004)
12. Calisir, F., Gumussoy, A.C., Bayraktaroglu, A.E., Karaali, D.: Predicting the intention to use a web-based learning system: perceived content quality, anxiety, perceived system quality, image, and the technology acceptance model. Hum. Fact. Ergon. Manufact. Serv. Ind.` **24**(5), 515–531 (2014)
13. Cheung, R., Vogel, D.: Predicting user acceptance of collaborative technologies: an extension of the technology acceptance model for e-learning. Comput. Educ. **63**(1), 160–175 (2013)
14. Kim, H.Y., Lee, J.Y., Mun, J.M., Johnson, K.K.: Consumer adoption of smart in-store technology: assessing the predictive value of attitude versus beliefs in the technology acceptance model. Int. J. Fasion Des. Technol. Educ. **10**(1), 26–36 (2017)

15. Teo, T.: Modelling Facebook usage among university students in Thailand: the role of emotional attachment in an extended technology acceptance model. Interact. Learn. Environ. **24**(4), 745–757 (2016)
16. Straub, D., Keil, M., Brenner, W.: Testing the technology acceptance model across cultures: a three country study. Inf. Manag. **33**(1), 1–11 (1997)
17. McCoy, S., Everard, A., Jones, B.M.: An examination of the technology acceptance model in Uruguay and the US: a focus on culture. J. Glob. Inf. Technol. Manag. **8**(2), 27–45 (2005)
18. Pavlou, P.A.: Consumer acceptance of electronic commerce: integrating trust and risk with the technology acceptance model. Int. J. Electron. Commer. **7**(3), 101–134 (2003)
19. Adams, D.A., Nelson, R.R., Todd, P.A.: Perceived usefulness, ease of use, and usage of information technology: a replication. MIS Q. **16**, 227–247 (1992)
20. Leidner, D.E., Kayworth, T.: Review: a review of culture in information systems research: toward a theory of information technology culture conflict. MIS Q. **30**(2), 357–399 (2006)
21. Baroudi, J.J., Igbaria, M.: An examination of gender effects on career success of information systems employees. J. Manag. Inf. Syst. **11**(3), 181–201 (1994)
22. Hernández, B., Jiménez, J., Martín, J.M.: Age, gender and income: do they really moderate online shopping behaviour? Online Inf. Rev. **35**(1), 113–133 (2011)
23. DeLone, W.H., McLean, E.R.: Information systems success: the quest for the dependent variable. Inf. Syst. Res. **3**(1), 60–95 (1992)
24. Mun, Y.Y., Hwang, Y.: Predicting the use of web-based information systems: self-efficacy, enjoyment, learning goal orientation, and the technology acceptance model. Int. J. Hum-Comput. Stud. **59**(4), 431–449 (2003)
25. Lian, J.W., Yen, D.C., Wang, Y.T.: An exploratory study to understand the critical factors affecting the decision to adopt cloud computing in Taiwan hospital. Int. J. Inf. Manag. **34**(1), 28–36 (2014)
26. Dalcher, I., Shine, J.: Extending the new technology acceptance model to measure the end user information systems satisfaction in a mandatory environment: a bank's treasury. Technol. Anal. Strateg. Manag. **15**(4), 441–455 (2003)
27. Benbasat, I., Barki, H.: Quo vadis TAM? J. Assoc. Inf. Syst. **8**(4), 211–218 (2007)
28. Laudon, K.C., Laudon, J.P.: Management information system. Pearson Education, India (2016)
29. Hofstede, G.: Motivation, leadership, and organization: do American theories apply abroad? Org. Dyn. **9**(1), 42–63 (1980)
30. Hofstede, G.: Cultural dimensions in management and planning. Asia Pac. J. Manag. **1**(2), 81–99 (1984)
31. Kowalczyk, N.: Influence of gender, age, and social norm on digital imaging use. Radiol. Technol. **83**(5), 437–446 (2012)
32. Gomez, L.M., Egan, D.E., Bowers, C.: Learning to use a text editor: some learner characteristics that predict success. Hum-Comput. Interact. **2**(1), 1–23 (1986)
33. Kirkpatrick, H., Cuban, L.: What the research says about gender differences in access, use, attitudes and achievement with computers. Educ. Technol. **38**(4), 56–61 (1998)
34. Likert, R.: A technique for the measurement of attitudes. Archives of psychology (1932)
35. Min, H., Galle, W.P.: E-purchasing: profiles of adopters and nonadopters. Ind. Mark. Manag. **32**(3), 227–233 (2003)
36. Fox, J., Murray, C., Warm, A.: Conducting research using web-based questionnaires: practical, methodological, and ethical considerations. Int. J. Soc. Res. Methodol. **6**(2), 167–180 (2003)
37. Hu, L.T., Bentler, P.M.: Evaluating model fit. In: Hoyle, R.H. (Ed.), Structural Equation Modeling: Concept, Issues and Applications. Thousand Oaks (1995)
38. Hu, L.T., Bentler, P.M.: Fit indices in covariance structure modeling: sensitivity to underparameterized model misspecification. Psychol. Methods **3**(4), 424–435 (1998)
39. Hu, L.T., Bentler, P.M.: Cutoff criteria for fit indexes in covariance structure analysis: conventional criteria versus new alternatives. Struct. Equ. Model. Multi. J. **6**(1), 1–55 (1999)
40. Byrne, B.M.: Structural equation modeling with LISREL, PRELIS, and SIMPLIS: basic concepts, applications, and programming. Psychology Press (2013)

41. Gliem, J.A., Gliem, R.R.: Calculating, interpreting, and reporting Cronbach's alpha reliability coefficient for Likert-type scales. In: Midwest Research-to-Practice Conference in Adult, Continuing, and Community Education (2003)
42. Tavakol, M., Dennick, R.:(2011) Making sense of Cronbach's alpha. Int. J. Med. Educ. 53(2)
43. Kaiser, H.F.: A second generation little jiffy. Psychometrika 35(4), 401–415 (1970)
44. McDonald, R.P.: The dimensionality of tests and items. Br. J. Math. Stat. Psyc. 34(1), 100–117 (1981)
45. Lewis, B.R., Templeton, G.F., Byrd, T.A.: A methodology for construct development. MIS Res. Eur. J. Inf. Syst. 14(4), 388–400 (2005)
46. Lederer, A.L., Maupin, D.J., Sena, M.P., Zhuang, Y.: The technology acceptance model and the World Wide Web. Decis. Support Syst. 29(3), 269–282 (2000)
47. Kim, S.S., Malhotra, N.K.: A longitudinal model of continued IS use: an integrative view of four mechanisms underlying postadoption phenomena. Manag. Sci. 51(5), 741–755 (2005)
48. Gangwar, H., Date, H., Ramaswamy, R.: Understanding determinants of cloud computing adoption using an integrated TAM-TOE model. J. Ent. Inf. Manag. 28(1), 107–130 (2015)
49. Holden, R.J., Karsh, B.T.: The technology acceptance model: its past and its future in health care. J. Biomed. Inf. 43(1), 159–172 (2010)
50. Diatmika, I.W.B., Irianto, G., Baridwan, Z.: Determinants of behavior intention of accounting information systems based information technology acceptance. Imp. J. Int. Res. 2(8), 125–138 (2016)
51. Brynjolfsson, E.: The productivity paradox of information technology. Comm. ACM. 36(12), 66–77 (1993)
52. Willcocks, L.P., Lester, S.: Beyond the IT productivity paradox. Wiley, Hoboken (1999)
53. Acemoglu, D., Dorn, D., Hanson, G.H., Price, B.: Return of the solow paradox? IT, productivity, and employment in US manufacturing. Am. Econ. Rev. 104(5), 394–399 (2014)
54. Keen, P.G.: Information systems and organizational change. Commun. ACM. 24(1), 24–33 (1981)
55. Hong, S., Thong, J.Y., Tam, K.Y.: Understanding continued information technology usage behavior: a comparison of three models in the context of mobile internet. Decis. Support Syst. 42(3), 1819–1834 (2006)
56. Hong, K.K., Kim, Y.G.: The critical success factors for ERP implementation: an organizational fit perspective. Inf. Manag. 40(1), 25–40 (2002)
57. Cassidy, A.: A practical guide to information systems strategic planning. CRC Press, Boca Raton (2016)
58. Chau, P.Y.K.: An empirical investigation on factors affecting the acceptance of CASE by systems developers. Inf. Manag. 30, 269–280 (1996)

What Kind of Benefits Different Stakeholders Can Expect and Obtain from HRIS Implementations: An Italian Case Study

Aizhan Tursunbayeva⍟, Raluca Bunduchi⍟, Massimo Franco⍟ and Claudia Pagliari⍟

Abstract Introducing IT-enabled transformational change in the public sector can be complex and challenging. Documentary analysis and in-depth interviews were used to study the introduction of a Human Resource Information System (HRIS) in one Italian regional healthcare organisation (RHO). Drawing on existing HRIS benefit models, we examined the types of benefit envisaged by different stakeholders and how these were realised in practice, along with unintended outcomes. Analysis revealed that the RHO had derived value from the implementation project, whilst demonstrating variations in expected and realised benefits between different categories of employee and co-dependencies between different types of benefit. We propose an extended and empirically-informed model of expected and realized benefits from HRIS in health organizations, which takes account of these interdependencies and differences.

1 Introduction

Over the last 30 years, considerable academic research and management effort has been devoted to understanding how best to implement Information systems (IS) in organizations and translate this to improvements in efficiency, effectiveness or

A. Tursunbayeva (✉) · R. Bunduchi · C. Pagliari
University of Edinburgh, Edinburgh, UK
e-mail: aizhan.tursunbayeva@gmail.com

R. Bunduchi
e-mail: raluca.bunduchi@ed.ac.uk

C. Pagliari
e-mail: claudia.pagliari@ed.ac.uk

M. Franco
University of Naples Federico II, Naples, Italy
e-mail: mfranco@unina.it

© Springer International Publishing AG, part of Springer Nature 2019
A. Lazazzara et al. (eds.), *Organizing for Digital Innovation*,
Lecture Notes in Information Systems and Organisation 27,
https://doi.org/10.1007/978-3-319-90500-6_4

customer satisfaction. Despite the learning that has been gained from these activities, large-scale IS projects still often struggle from problems with rollout and regularly fail to deliver their expected outcomes [1] leading to disappointing returns on investment [2]. This phenomenon has been noted both in the private and public sectors, although government-sponsored projects have arguably received the greatest scrutiny [3].

Most research on the outcomes of IS implementation focuses either on mapping their benefits (for a review see Shang and Seddon [4]), or developing recommendations for organizations on how to actively manage the benefit realization process (see Coombs [1]). While these approaches can be useful in many ways, they are inadequate for fully understanding the mediators of IS benefit. Drawing on existing HRIS research (e.g. Tursunbayeva et al. [5]), we argue that it is necessary to examine not only the stated benefits used to justify the project, but also the benefits *as anticipated and experienced* by the different stakeholders involved in the implementation process. We therefore adopted a case study approach to explore the multiple actors involved in the implementation of a HRIS in the healthcare sector, and their expected versus realized benefits.

The study reported here is part of a programme of doctoral research, which examined HRIS implementation projects in two European countries, informed by a systematic literature review on HRIS in health organizations [5]. This paper focuses on the case study of HRIS implementation in one RHO in Italy.

2 Theoretical Framework

The research examined one particular type of IS, HRIS, implemented in the specific context of a public sector, regional, healthcare organisation. Previous research has shown that the way in which organizational change is enacted during IS implementation to realize benefits [6]. Such studies also reveal how these relationships vary across organisational settings and types of IS. When studying benefits it is therefore important to consider theoretical frameworks developed in these settings.

Previous research has identified a number of specific HRIS benefits for organizations, including improvements in strategic orientation, operational efficiency, service delivery; empowerment of managers and employees to undertake HR functions [7] and standardization of HR processes within or across organizations [8]. A recent study evaluating HRIS benefits framework in ten organizations across different sectors identified a further category of improving organizational image [9].

Our recent systematic literature review of HRIS implementation studies in health contexts [5] provided support for Parry and Tyson's [9] generic HRIS benefit categories (Strategic, Operational Efficiency, Service Delivery, Empowerment, Standardization, and Organizational Image), further identifying two categories of *expected* benefits, including help in management of macro organizational changes (e.g. planned hospitals merger), and compliance with regulatory requirements (e.g. for reporting workforce information); along with four categories of *realized* benefits, including improvement in patient care (e.g. through facilitating minimum standards of nursing care), *compliance* with regulatory requirements, generation of interest from other countries, and improved IT infrastructure [5].

Studies of HRIS benefits only rarely examine how expected or realised benefits vary between types of user. For example, Lepak and Snell [7] and Ruel and colleagues [8] focused on identifying HR professionals' motives driving HRIS implementation, only briefly mentioning the benefits for other employees. Parry and Tyson [9] identified HRIS goals and outcomes at the organizational level, without distinguishing between different types of actors. In contrast, Tursunbayeva et al.'s [5] recent systematic review of HRIS in health found that HRIS users, as beneficiaries of the IS innovation, include a range of stakeholders or actors, including hospital managers, clinicians, nurses and/or HR professionals, who perform different tasks and may therefore have different expectations and perceptions of the role and benefits of a new HRIS.

Although existing HRIS research has clarified generic categories of benefit, and HRIS studies in the healthcare domain have described both expected and realized benefits, there has been little research to explore the alignments or discrepancies amongst the benefits perceived or experienced by different stakeholders [5]. Understanding this variability is important for determining what kinds of expected benefits motivate different stakeholders to accept new HRIS initiatives, and what these initiatives actually achieve for the various stakeholders involved in their implementation or adoption. The *study reported here set out to address this gap by examining the expected and realised benefits of HRIS in the context of a regional health organisation, and to understand how the alignment between these may vary between types of stakeholder.*

3 Methodology

3.1 Research Design and Setting

This research used a qualitative embedded case study approach [10], which enables the analysis of rich and detailed contextualized data. To answer the research question, HRIS implementation project was selected in one of the Italian RHOs.

In the last decade, this RHO has seen a phase of rapid growth (i.e. budget increase and 5.3% headcount increase between 2006 and 2009). This growth called for change in the organization, its processes and IS provision to ensure that the health services delivered by the RHO match citizens' growing expectations. In particular, it underlined the importance of optimizing health workforce skills in order to achieve this strategic objective. Thus, the RHO's "Strategic Development Business Plan" considered both changes to the HRM processes and introducing an IS to support them. This created the foundation for the "HR Development

Program", which included developing HRM practices, such as creating a structured system of organizational roles, improving employee development/training, and career support services. Delivering an IS to support these new practices was an important part of this HR development program. The system was procured via the EU tender process and the project was realized between 2007 and 2010.

3.2 Data Collection

Data were collected in the winter of 2016, and involved interviews and documentation. Nine semi-structured interviews with key stakeholders involved in the development and implementation of HRIS were conducted. Respondents were selected based on their knowledge of and involvement in the HRIS project, and were either recommended by project leaders, snowball sampled by asking interviewees to recommend other informed stakeholders or actively volunteered to participate in our research.

In addition, extensive documentation was collected for analysis, including internal (RHO's HR Development Program; System supplier presentation; Analysis of "As is" and "To be" HR processes; and Local implementation plan and timeline) and publicly (RHO website; (Relevant) News; Presentations about the project) available information about the history of the HRIS projects, its development, implementation process and usage of the HRIS.

3.3 Data Analysis

Data analysis included three main steps and relied on the NVivo qualitative analysis software. The first stage of data analysis involved open coding of transcripts to generate preliminary categories associated with situating the implementation of HRIS across spaces and times within the organizational context. This open coding also led to the identification of broad categories of benefits perceived at different stages during the implementation by different stakeholders. The second stage involved interpreting and mapping these broad categories of benefits into our theoretically informed categories related to HRIS Expected Benefits and Outcomes. Data that appeared not to fit were originally grouped separately, and if confirmed as the analysis progressed, these new categories were iteratively added to the original list of benefits informed by the literature review. Finally, at this stage conceptual map was created to visually explain the research findings and helped us to drive the research team's discussions.

4 Findings

The analysis demonstrates that the HRIS project was driven by a variety of expected benefits as perceived by actors at different levels. The expected and realized benefits mapped across the stakeholder groups are summarised in Fig. 1 and explained in detail in the following section.

4.1 RHO Perspective

4.1.1 Expected

The project was prompted by two *strategic* objectives incorporated into the RHO's three-year plan. First, the RHO sought to obtain European Foundation for Quality Management (EFQM) certification, in order to demonstrate the quality of its health services, which required improvements to its internal organizational processes (including those of HR department).

Second, the RHO aimed to increase the remit of its HR department, from providing administrative HR services, to comply with national requirements for public organizations and regional labour laws (e.g. monitoring of time and attendance and payroll), to performing *strategic*, objective, and transparent HRM practices (e.g. performance management process).

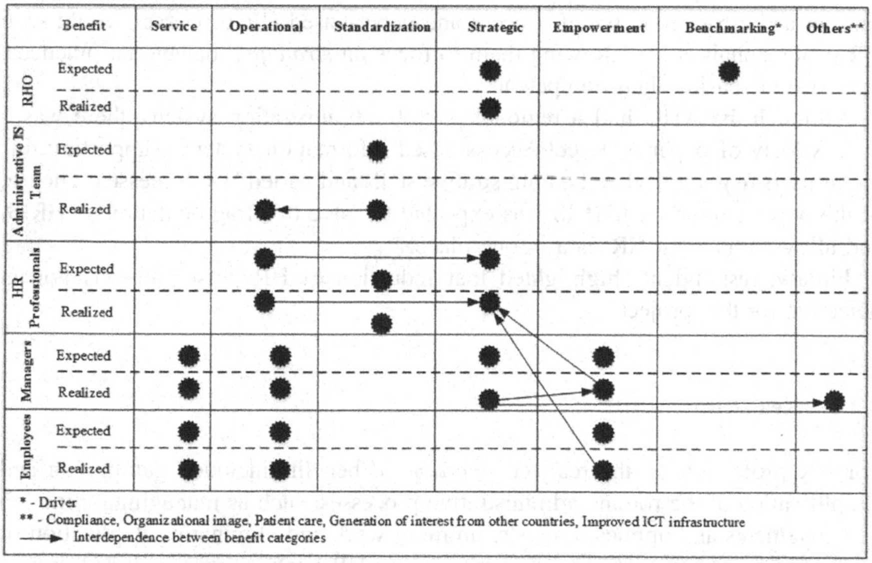

	Benefit	Service	Operational	Standardization	Strategic	Empowerment	Benchmarking*	Others**
RHO	Expected				●		●	
	Realized				●			
Administrative IS Team	Expected			●				
	Realized	●	●	●				
HR Professionals	Expected		●	●	●			
	Realized		●	●	●			
Managers	Expected	●	●		●	●		
	Realized	●	●		●	●		●
Employees	Expected	●	●			●		
	Realized	●	●			●		

* - Driver
** - Compliance, Organizational image, Patient care, Generation of interest from other countries, Improved ICT infrastructure
──► Interdependence between benefit categories

Fig. 1 Conceptual map. Benefits from HRIS and relationships between them

Our respondents also mentioned that the RHO had sought to *benchmark* itself with other RHOs in the country, as well as other large organizations already in the process of implementing large-scale HRIS. During this benchmarking exercise, it became evident that they were the first RHO within the country to implement such a comprehensive HRIS, which could support not only administrative HRM practices, but also strategic ones.

4.1.2 Realized

As envisioned, the HRIS implementation project had facilitated the RHO's EFQM certification, as well as the associated HR transformation project, through streamlining and improving the efficiency of HR processes and by launching the new strategic HRM practices (e.g. performance management).

4.2 HR Professionals Perspective

4.2.1 Expected

The main expected *operational* benefit associated with the implementation of the new HRIS here was to support the optimization and rationalization of the previously disintegrated and fragmented processes, carried out partly by HR professionals and possibly other departments.

It was also expected that the automation of previously complicated, time consuming and error-prone Excel, Access and paper-based HR processes would save HR professionals' time, allowing them to focus on *strategic*, managerial practices, thus also increasing their competence.

Although the RHO had a regional payroll administration system, there was a wide variety of paper or Excel/Access-based information systems supporting different users (e.g. clinical and administrative staff) and varied HR processes. The use of the new, standardized HRIS was expected to solve this fragmentation of HRIS, and allow to have all HR data in one place.

Finally, respondents highlighted that reduction of HR personnel was not an objective for this project.

4.2.2 Realized

For HR professionals, the realized *operational* benefits included automation and simplification of the routine administrative processes, such as managing online job advertisements and applications, streamlining work and eliminating duplication of effort. Other *operational* benefits perceived by HR professionals included greater transparency of HR processes, reduced opportunities for human error, and support for professional development of HR staff. It also enabled them to engage in *strategic* HRM practices such as performance management, and employee development.

Finally, HR professionals perceived the HRIS as an enabler of *standardization*. For example, it enabled the creation of standardized employee curriculum vitae (CV) which were previously done in different formats. These CV are legally required to be posted on RHO's website for transparency purposes.

Respondents from the *Administrative IS team, in contrast,* cautioned that opportunities to rethink HR work processes had not yet been fully exploited and that some inefficient and defragmented HR processes were still in place, despite the system having been implemented for some time. Thus, some of the benefits from the new HRIS are still to be achieved, and development of the system has continued since its deployment.

4.3 Administrative IS Team

4.3.1 Expected and Realized

Respondents from the administrative IS team reported that, as expected, the new *standardized* HRIS had either replaced or was integrated with pre-existing IS and/or Excel/Access-based systems in different parts of the RHOs, thus eliminating the need to support diverse IS and reducing maintenance costs.

4.4 Managers and Employees

4.4.1 Expected

The RHO conducted a comprehensive employee survey as part of its EFQM certification prior to the implementation of the HRIS. The results highlighted very low satisfaction level with the RHO HR services. Despite seeing the HR department as having an administrative support function, RHO staff also wanted it to deliver HRM *services* such as career development.

The expected benefit for Line Managers included having an access to accurate and up-to-date data on their teams (previously available only upon request from the HR department) which was expected to *empower* them to manage their team better, supporting *strategic* decision-making and workforce planning.

HR Professionals also envisioned that the new system would include self-service module that would not only *empower* both managers and employees to take control over some of the administrative processes previously performed by HR, but also to speed them up *(Operational efficiency)*, releasing *HR professionals'* time for *strategic* HRM activities.

4.4.2 Realized

Post HRIS-implementation, the level of RHOs satisfaction with HR processes increased significantly compared with that at the time of the original survey.

Line managers, in particular, reported being *empowered* to manage their team better (*strategic benefit*) due to automated, transparent and objective HR processes and easy access to high quality workforce data. *Empowerment* also helped Line Managers to better plan clinical (*patient care*) activities by forecasting the health workforce needed to support them.

The new system also *empowered* both *Managers* and *Employees* to update their personal employment data as necessary, without any involvement of HR professionals, thus indirectly freeing HR professionals' time to focus on *strategic* HRM practices.

5 Discussion

Drawing from previous HRIS research in healthcare [5], our research has adapted the generic model of HRIS benefits proposed by Parry and Tyson [9] to the healthcare context. The analysis identifies all benefits categories proposed by Parry & Tyson, except the expected benefit of improving *Organizational image*.

Our results indicate that, in this setting, most of the benefits expected from the HRIS implementation project were realized. However, we went further in our analysis and distinguished between the categories of benefit associated with different actors involved in IS implementation. As noted in the introduction, most HRIS studies to date have tended to focus on particular actors, e.g. HR departments [7, 8], employees and managers [8] and organizations as a whole [9]. Nevertheless, HRIS are designed for and used by a wide variety of stakeholders [5]. Our empirical analysis illustrates how the expected and realized benefits from HRIS projects may vary significantly between organizational stakeholders, thus confirming the need to include people from a range of staff categories when seeking to evaluate the benefits of new IS in complex organizations [4, 11].

Previous research also suggests that the realisation of benefits is a process that takes place during IS implementation [6], but our analysis provides clear evidence that it benefits realization continues after systems have been adopted and are being used. For example, in our case study the HRIS had already been adopted by most of the stakeholder groups. As routine HR processes were automated and end users (Employees and Managers) were *empowered* to take care of their data and/or associated HR processes via standardized IS, HR Professionals had more time to initiate or focus on *strategic* HRM practices, and IS administrators were able to focus on maintaining the new integrated HRIS instead of several separate ones. The greater efficiency arising from these changes, as well as the RHO's newly launched *strategic* HRM practices, enabled the organisation to achieve their strategic goal for HR transformation, and to obtain EFQM certification.

The case study analysed here also demonstrates that there are strong interdependencies between different categories of benefits and different actors (see Fig. 1). Thus, certain expected benefits could only be achieved for particular stakeholder groups if they had already been achieved for others; for example, strategic benefit for HR professionals could only be achieved upon the empowerment of Managers and Employees.

6 Limitations

Case studies are necessarily limited by the number of participants interviewed and the materials available for analysis. Thus, for example, the findings might not be representative for the whole population of Managers and Employees in the health organization we studied, as we had an opportunity to interview very few of them. Moreover, as the interviews depended largely on retrospective recall it is possible that post-rationalisation might have conflated expected and realised benefits. We have mitigated against this bias by drawing on extensive documentation, for example to aid the interpretation of data collected from the interviews.

7 Conclusion

The HRIS project we studied was challenging for the RHO, echoing experiences with other large-scale implementation projects involving HRIS generally [12] and HRIS in health organizations [13]. However, despite the difficulties encountered, our data suggest that it offered tremendous opportunities for the RHO to reconfigure existing HR processes, as we had also observed in study of health sector HRIS elsewhere in Europe [14], although more expected benefits were realized in this project for a number of reasons, including its smaller scale and alignment with an organizational need for accreditation.

This study builds on existing research and theory by informing the development of an extended model of the expected and realized benefits of HRIS for different stakeholders, as well as mapping the interconnections between these benefits in healthcare. We invite other researchers to evaluate its applicability to HRIS in different health organisations, public sector organizations and other industries. Governments, organisations and managers seeking to procure or implement HRIS for healthcare organisations may also gain from our delineation of expected and realized benefits and their relationships to different professional roles. The results of our case study illustrate that, although HRIS are often perceived simply as technologies for supporting HR practices, in the context of complex health organizations many different stakeholders and potential users may be involved in or affected by their implementation and their expectations, beliefs and perceptions should be taken into consideration. Doing so can not only help to inform ongoing processes of change management, audit and technology iteration, but may also ease communication between stakeholders during the often challenging experience of HRIS implementation [15]. Our study also illustrated the need to avoid conflating expected and realized benefits when assessing the success of technology implementation projects and points to the need for longer-term evaluation studies to demonstrate the true value of HRIS for strengthening the efficiency and effectiveness of healthcare systems in an environment of increasing needs and static resources.

References

1. Coombs, C.R.: When planned IS/IT project benefits are not realized: a study of inhibitors and facilitators to benefits realization. Int. J. Proj. Manag. 33, 363–379 (2015). https://doi.org/10.1016/j.ijproman.2014.06.012
2. Doherty, N., Ashurst, C., Peppard, J.: Factors affecting the successful realisation of benefits from systems development projects: findings from three case studies. J. Inf. Technol. 27(1), 1–16 (2012). https://doi.org/10.1057/jit.2011.8
3. Rajeev, S.: Abandoned NHS IT system has cost £10bn so far. In: The Guardian (2013)
4. Shang, S., Seddon, P.B.: Assessing and managing the benefits of enterprise systems: the business manager's perspective. Inf. Syst. J. 12, 271–299 (2002). https://doi.org/10.1046/j.1365-2575.2002.00132.x
5. Tursunbayeva, A., Bunduchi, R., Franco, M., Pagliari, C.: Human resource information systems in health care: a systematic evidence review. J. Am. Med. Health Inform. (2016). https://doi.org/10.1093/jamia/ocw141
6. Caldeira, M., Serrano, A., Quaresma, R., Pedrona, C., Romao, M.: Information and communication technology adoption for business benefits: a case analysis of an integrated paperless system. Int. J. Inf. Manag. 32(2), 196–202 (2012). https://doi.org/10.1016/j.ijinfomgt.2011.12.005
7. Lepak, D.P., Snell, S.A.: Virtual HR: Strategic human resource management in the 21st century. Hum. Resour. Manag. Rev. 6(3), 215–234 (1998). https://doi.org/10.1016/S1053-4822(98)90003-1
8. Ruel, H., Bondarouk, T., Looise, J.: E-HRM: Innovation or irritation. An explorative empirical study in five large companies on web-based HRM. Manag. Revue 15(3), 364–381 (2004)
9. Parry, E., Tyson, S.: Desired goals and actual outcomes of e-HRM. Hum. Resour. Manag. J. 21(3), 335–354 (2011). https://doi.org/10.1111/j.1748-8583.2010.00149.x
10. Yin, R.K.: Case Study Research: Design and Methods, 3rd edn. Thousand Oaks, CA, Sage (2003)
11. Dhillon, G.: Gaining benefits from IS/IT implementation: interpretations from case studies. Int. J. Inf. Manag. 25(6), 505–515 (2005). https://doi.org/10.1016/j.ijinfomgt.2005.08.004
12. Kavanagh, M.J.: Project management and HRM advice for HRIS implementation. In: Kavanagh, M.J., Thite, M., Johnson, R.D. (eds.) Human Resource Information Systems Basic Applications and Future Directions, 2nd edn. Sage, US (2012)
13. Thite, M., Sandhu, K.: Where is my pay? Critical success factors of a payroll system—a system life cycle approach. Australas. J. Inf. Syst. 18(2), 149–164 (2014)
14. Tursunbayeva, A., Pagliari, C., Bunduchi, R., Franco, M.: What does it take to implement human resource information system (HRIS) at scale? Analysis of the expected benefits and actual outcomes. In: Proceedings of the 31st Workshop on Strategic HRM. Segovia, Spain (2016)
15. Eden, R., Sedera, D.: The largest admitted IT project failure in the Southern Hemisphere: a teaching case. In: Proceedings of the 35th International Conference on Information Systems. Auckland, New Zealand (2014)

The Dark Side of E-justice Implementation. An Empirical Investigation of the Relation Between Cultural Orientation and Information System Success

Luigi Lepore⬚, Sabrina Pisano⬚, Federico Alvino⬚
and Francesco Paolone⬚

Abstract This paper investigates the relationship between individual cultural orientation and information system individual impact in the Court of Naples. The findings show that flexibility and discretion within courts are successful factors for implementing information systems at individual level. This study contributes to the literature on information system and organizational culture in different ways. First, we corroborate the findings that flexible organizations are a more fertile ground for Information and Communication Technologies implementation and the success of information systems or to materialize the contribution of these systems to improving individual performance. Moreover, we investigate the relationship between individual cultural orientation and information system individual impact in a specific sector of Public Administration, i.e. judicial system, that has received less attention by scholars compared to other public sectors.

1 Introduction

Over the past decades the Italian Judicial System (JS) has faced a crisis of performance, such as the unacceptable length of proceedings, a large number of both pending civil and criminal proceedings, although it has had a significant amount of money invested. As a consequence, the Italian Legislator has made efforts to realize a modernization process of the JS aimed at changing the organization of courts, at introducing management approach and performance measurement and at

---

L. Lepore · S. Pisano (✉) · F. Alvino
Department of Law, Parthenope University, Naples, Italy
e-mail: sabrina.pisano@uniparthenope.it

F. Paolone
Department of Business Administration, Parthenope University, Naples, Italy

© Springer International Publishing AG, part of Springer Nature 2019   49
A. Lazazzara et al. (eds.), *Organizing for Digital Innovation*,
Lecture Notes in Information Systems and Organisation 27,
https://doi.org/10.1007/978-3-319-90500-6_5

implementing information and communication technologies (ICT). Italy has been one of the European Countries that has invested the most in ICT to develop an "e-justice approach" to improve court performance.

Despite the modernization process and the considerable investment in e-justice, to date the results achieved have been limited and the Italian JS is still characterized by poor performance. The contribution of ICT in improving performance is still not enough sufficient, probably because the cultural background, that should favor the ICT and Information System (IS) implementation, is not adequate.

This emphasizes the relevance of the aim of our study, that investigates the relationship between individual cultural orientation and IS implementation.

The paper is organized as follows: Sect. 2 shows a literature review on cultural orientation and information system implementation; Sect. 3 describes the sample and the research model; Sect. 4 highlights the results obtained by the study and the discussion about them. Finally, Sect. 5 draws some final considerations and the main limits of this study.

2 Literature Review and Hypotheses Development

2.1 The Role of ICT Within Judicial System

The JS plays a fundamental role in the socio-economic progress of each country, a role widely recognized not only in the business administration studies [1–3], but also by legislators who have repeatedly intervened for improve their performance.

During the last years, the Italian JS has faced a dramatic performance crisis [4]. Previous studies [1, 5–9] found that the Italian JS is more inefficient and ineffective compared to that of other industrialized countries, as well as the developing ones.

In Italy, in particular, legislator started a process of modernization through numerous legislative reforms. Consistent with what happened in all the public administrations, even in the JS legislator implemented innovative organizational and management logics: the recognition of greater autonomy to executives administrative; the introduction of service monitoring tools, as well as of assessing both the costs and results; the implementation of e-justice solutions aimed at using ICT to improve efficiency and effectiveness of JS [10, 11].

The rise of digital technologies in JS augments the relevance of the IS and, in particular, of the information systems success (ISS). In fact, according to DeLone and McLean [12, p. 10], "IS success or effectiveness is critical to our understanding of the value and efficacy of IS management actions and IS investments".

IS success is a complex, interdependent, and multi-dimensional construct [13] and defining success depends on various variables, such as the setting, the objectives, and the stakeholders [14]. Previous studies developed a great number of systems success measures [e.g. 15, 16], but the DeLone and McLean [12, 17] model is the most used by researchers to investigate this issue [e.g. 18–21].

DeLone and McLean [17] classified the dimensions of IS success into six categories: (1) system quality, the measurements of IS itself; (2) information quality, the measures of IS output; (3) information use, recipient consumption of IS output; (4) user satisfaction, recipient response to the use of IS output; (5) individual impact, the effect of information on the behaviour of the recipient; and (6) organizational impact, the effect of information on organizational performance.

In this paper we focus on the fifth category, the individual impact dimension, that emphasizes the extent to which information can influence the tasks executed by user, changing work practices [22, p. 133]. More specifically, we investigate the relationship between individual cultural orientation (ICO) and information system individual impact (ISII). The ICO, in fact, is considered an important factor to perceive and achieve ISS [23].

Although numerous studies have been conducted on the relationship between organizational culture, typically focused on values, and technology, the effects of particular cultural values on differences in technology outcome, such as ISS, has been less investigated [24].

2.2 The Individual Cultural Orientation

To measure our ICO variable, we refer to the Competing Values Framework (CVF) [25], the Organizational Culture Assessment Instrument (OCAI) [26] and the Court Culture Assessment Instrument (CCAI) [27]. These models are instruments developed to assesses the overall organizational culture profile. The CVF was initially based on research to identify indicators of organizational effectiveness [25, p. 363]. Based on the CVF, Cameron and Quinn [26, 28] developed a general matched scale, the OCAI, and Ostrom and colleague [27] developed a specific scale for courts, the CCAI.

Several empirical studies in various fields have been published testing the validity and reliability of the CVF, OCAI, and CCAI in different sectors, including JS [4, 25, 27, 29, 30].

Figure 1 reports the framework we used.

Fig. 1 The framework

Our framework identifies four types of cultural orientation—clan, adhocracy, hierarchy, and market—on the basis of two dimensions: flexibility versus stability and internal orientation versus external orientation. The flexibility versus stability dimension emphasizes values as spontaneity, change and dynamism with respect to values of stability, order and control. The internal orientation versus external orientation dimension refers to the choice between focusing on internal dynamics or interacting with the external environment.

A clan culture concentrates on internal orientation and flexibility. According to Cameron and Quinn [26, p. 37], "The clan culture is typified by a friendly place to work where people share a lot about themselves. It is like an extended family". The culture of the clan is based on a family organization. Fundamental values concern the sharing of goals, cohesion, participation, and sense of community. Teamwork, staff involvement programs, sense of affinity between individuals replace hierarchical rules and procedures, as well as market orientation and profitability. The core assumptions of the clan's culture are that the environment can be best managed through teamwork and human resources development, which is crucial to develop a responsibility-based program by facilitating participation among members, affiliation and loyalty. According to CVF, a serene working environment represents the clan's culture, where collaborators share many aspects of their lives as if they were an extended family where leaders are considered mentors or parental figures. The organization is catalyzed by values such as loyalty and tradition, and affinity between people is very high. The organization promotes teamwork, participation and consensus. Success is in responding to customer needs.

The adhocracy culture focuses on external orientation and flexibility. These organizations are "characterized by a dynamic, entrepreneurial, and creative workplace" [26, p. 40]. Adhocracy orientation is based on a rather turbulent environment whose conditions are constantly changing. It represents something dynamic, temporary, and specialized where flexibility and sense of fit are the values that can adapt to uncertainty, ambiguity and lack of information. The purpose of organizations that engage in this culture is to develop products and services that are adapted to future changes or generating them. The task of managers is to promote entrepreneurship, creativity, and readiness to act. In managing relationships there is little authority, but power passes from one person to another depending on which problem is to be solved, based on assigning it to the individual or team skills. Another characteristic of adhocracy cultures is the provisionality of roles that change according to problems and needs. Effective leadership is visionary, innovative and risk-oriented. Key factors are readiness and speed in change, while goals are rapidity in long-term growth and the acquisition of new resources.

The hierarchy culture concentrates on internal orientation and stability; it is typical of organizations characterized by a clear authority, standardized rules and procedures, and control and accountability mechanisms [26]. The hierarchy culture refers to Weber's hierarchy or bureaucracy that "was the ideal form of organization, because it led to stable, efficient, and highly standardized products and services" [26, p. 34]. Hierarchical culture orientation is typical of people that perceive to work in a formalized and structured workplace, where the procedures determine the way people act. Successful leaders, in this kind of organization, are perceived as successful coordinators and organizers. The long-term goals to be pursued lie in stability, in anticipating future developments and in efficiency. Personnel management must ensure work and predictability. Large organizations are generally dominated by a hierarchical culture, due to the large number of standardized procedures, multiple hierarchical levels, and emphasis on bureaucratic rules. There is no discretion in carrying out operations to meet the required standards. The environment was considered relatively stable, the tasks and functions could be integrated and coordinated, the uniformity of the products and services was maintained, and the workers and duties were under control. The rules and procedures were standardized and the coordination mechanisms were the key to success.

The market culture is characterized by dimensions of stability and external orientation; this type of cultural orientation emphasizes transactions with external environment, highlighting a results-oriented workplace and aspects as efficiency and competitiveness [26, p. 36]. Market cultural orientation is usual for workers that consider their organization as oriented to the outside. The values on which this organizational culture is based are competitiveness and productivity, while the underlying assumptions are that the external environment is hostile, consumers have difficult expectations to meet and are interested in value. The main objective of the organization is to strengthen its competitive position. Consequently, it follows that profit maximization orientation is the main aspiration of management. Market culture takes place in a result-oriented workplace where aspiration to victory is the catalyzing element of individuals. Success is defined in terms of market share and degree of penetration. The emphasis on conquest keeps the organization together. The organizational style is based on competition.

Previous studies highlighted that flexibility generally characterizes more favorable outcomes in terms of ISS [e.g. 24, 31]. In agreement with the literature, we expect that an ICO that emphasizes flexibility values is positively associated with ISII. Therefore, we hypothesize that:

H_1 Dominant clan ICO positively influences ISII
H_2 Dominant adhocracy ICO positively influences ISII
H_3 Dominant hierarchy ICO negatively influences ISII
H_4 Dominant market ICO negatively influences ISII.

3 Method

3.1 Data Collection and Sample Analysis

Our study was conducted in the court of Naples in Campania region in Southern Italy.

The sample was selected with the deliberate aim of understanding whether the ICO of administrative staff members influences perceived individual performance improvement due to IS implementation. The court of Naples is one of the biggest Italian court. The second in terms of pending cases. The number of pending civil proceedings is 76.105 at the beginning of 2017, of which about 26% is pending for 10 years. The Clearance rate, that is the ratio between case resolved and incoming cases, is 1.06. The average number of days court takes to solve a civil dispute is 999.

We conducted a survey using a questionnaire administered to court administrative personnel between May and July 2016. The questionnaire was divided into two sections. The first one was intended for the collection of personal data and information about education, role, job placement, job experience, IS implementation and its impact on respondents' job performance. The second section, on the other hand, contains the questions necessary for the evaluation of users' cultural orientation. In particular, we conducted pre and pilot test to verify and validate the measures used, and obtained feedback from IS users and IS scholars in the first instance. Findings of the pre-test highlighted the reliability and consistency of the scales used. We administered a total of 200 questionnaires to administrative staff of the court and we received a total of 130 complete questionnaires (representing a return rate of 65.00%). To minimize data-entry errors, all the data collected were checked for consistency. This left 104 valid questionnaires.

3.2   Variable Description and Statistics

3.2.1   Dependent Variable

A specific section of the questionnaire captured information we used to assess the extent to which court users perceive IS impact on their performance within court. Our dependent variable is the ISII; it measures "the degree of success of application software in terms of (i) improving the user's quality of work, (ii) making the end user's job easier, (iii) saving the end user time, and (iv) helping fulfill the needs and requirements of the end user's job" [32, p. 66]. It was measured by adapting Etezadi-Amoli and Farhoomand's [32] user-performance four-item scale.

3.2.2   Independent Variables: Individual Cultural Orientation

Another specific part of the questionnaire was designed in accordance with the CVF, OCAI and CCAI with the aim of assessing the users' cultural orientation. We developed our scales on the basis of the above-mentioned models and instruments.

The questionnaire we used was translated into Italian and tested to ensure its comprehensibility. The CVF model is based on the assumption that human organizations are shaped by only two fundamental contradictions: the desire for flexibility, autonomy and change versus the need for control, order and stability; the focus on needs and internal issues of organization (integration and unity) versus the external focus (differentiation and rivalry).

Through these two dimensions, our version of CCAI defines four cultural orientation types (Clan Orientation, Adhocracy Orientation, Market Orientation, Hierarchy Orientation). These archetypes are also called Group, Hierarchical, Rational and Developmental.

For the assessment of the cultural orientation, the opinion of human resources, which are the "bearers" of the corporate culture, are taken into account in relation to 5 dimensions of organizational culture: (1) dominant characteristics (how is the caseflow management); (2) leadership style (paternalist, aggressive, coordinator, etc.); (3) human resources management (does judge encourages group work or individual work, or competition); (4) change management; (5) internal organization.

For each of the 5 organizational aspects mentioned above, our CCAI questionnaire offered respondents a set of 4 possible descriptions of an organization, each corresponding to a different type of culture. For each set of descriptions, respondent had to allot 100 points to the descriptions that best fitted his or her perceptions of the organization. The cultural type that received the highest score was outlined as the current dominant ICO. In the same way, we also obtained for each respondents the preferred ICO. Aggregating the scores provided by all the respondents working in the court of Naples we defined the current and preferred individual cultural type. Individual cultural type is the result of a mix of competing values of each cultural type that emerge in the current dominant and preferred cultural types.

3.2.3 Control Variables

As suggested by the IS literature, several questions were used to capture information at the individual level: age, gender, educational level, job experience and IT experience of respondents, that we used as control variables in order to better evaluate the effect of independent variables on the dependent variable.

4 Regression Analysis

4.1 Empirical Model

To assess the effects of ICO on the ISII in the court of Naples, we tested our hypotheses using single-level regressions that consider ISII as dependent variable, ICO as independent variables and several control variables (Age, Gender, Educational Level, Job experience and IT Experience).

$$ISII = \beta_0 + \beta_1 ICO + \beta_2 Control + \varepsilon \qquad (1)$$

4.2 Empirical Results

Table 1 provides the descriptive statistics for the variables we used in the models. The dominant cultural model of the Court of Naples is the Market (or Rational), as showed in Fig. 2; the second is Hierarchy. The high level of Hierarchy values is coherent with typical bureaucratic organization of Italian Public Administrations, that are often characterized by the organization of work based on control and stable bureaucratic processes and routines, by integration and unity. The highest level of Rational, instead, could be due to the reform processes that involved Italian JS in the last decade, introducing an increasing attention to performance improvement (reduction of backlog of cases, reduction of disposition time, etc.) and to stakeholders needs. The prevalence of Rational as dominant model in the court is also coherent with previous studies [30].

The preferred model is Adhocracy, followed by Clan. These results show that court administrative staff members perceive the importance of flexibility in work processes and the need for an external focus, nevertheless the internal orientation is still strong, confirming that the JS is the segment of Italian Public Administration that more slowly changes and innovates itself in the directions designed by the reform processes [33].

The overall results of the regressions consist in 4 models showed in Table 2. Regression results show the effects of four independent variables explaining the ICO (*Clan, Adhocracy, Market* and *Hierarchy*) on dependent variable ISII.

Results of Model 1 confirm hypothesis H1 that Clan orientation positively influences ISII. Similarly, Model 2 confirms H2: Adhocracy orientation positively

Table 1 Sample

Variable	Obs	Mean	Std. Dev.	Min	Max
ISII	104	5.209135	1,464,014	1	7
Clan_Orient	104	22.24038	7,928,681	2	50
Adhocracy_Orient	104	19.66731	7,671,134	4	40
Market_Orient	104	31.07692	1,235,062	10	74
Hierarchy_Orient	104	27.01538	8,637,497	10	70
Clan_Pref	104	27.18269	8.015476	10	50
Adhoc_Pref	104	28.56731	8.546576	10	58
Market_Pref	104	17.97115	8.123389	0	37
Hierarchy_Pref	104	26.27885	9.332537	10	70
Age	104	55.65385	7.800634	24	66
Gender	104	0.3173077	0.4676822	0	1
Education	104	1.326923	0.5475862	1	3
IT_exp	104	13.60096	5.931396	0.5	30
Job_exp	104	25.20192	10.65808	0.5	40

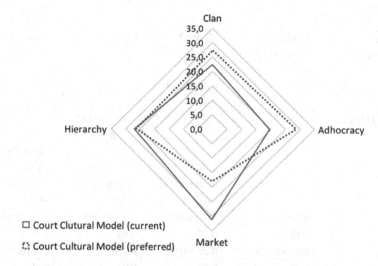

Fig. 2 Court cultural model

influences ISII. Model 3 and 4 confirm H3 and H4, showing negative and significant coefficients for Market and Hierarchy orientations. Market orientation negatively influences ISII; Hierarchical orientation, similarly, negatively influences ISII.

Our findings about the relationships between ISII and ICO corroborate the assumption that organizations characterized by strong stability, where authority, rules and procedures are the principal mechanisms of coordination, experiment much more difficulties in the implementation of new technologies, and in general in the changing or in the innovations. On the contrary, organizations characterized by flexibility are characterized by more favorable outcomes in terms of ISS [e.g. 24, 31].

In model (1), the one that uses Clan_Orient, we found a positive impact of such orientation (the coefficient is equal to 0.0664) on ISII, statistically significant at 0.1% level. By using the explanatory variable Adhocracy_Orient, the positive relation (coefficient is 0.0476) with dependent variable is less but still significant (level of 5%); Different consideration has to be made for models (3) and (4), which include Market_Orient and Hierarchy_Orient, respectively: in model (3) the relationship is negative (−0.0300) and statistically significant at 5% level. In model (4), the relationship is also negative (−0.0327) with a significance of 10% level.

In addition to explanatory variables, all the regressions were set using control variables: *Age, Gender, Education, IT_exp* and *Job_Exp*. These variables have not found to be statistically significant.

As above reported, we found two opposite and significant relationships that can be explained as follows: the cultural orientations based on Clan and Adhocracy are positively (in particular Clan) associated with the degree of success of application software at individual level (ISII).

Table 2 Results

Variable	Model_1	Model_2	Model_3	Model_4
Clan_Orient	0.06645419***			
	3.80			
Adhocracy_Orient		0.0476364*		
		2.51		
Market_Orient			−0.03009145*	
			−2.58	
Hierarchy_Orient				−0.03275016+
				−1.90
Age	−0.00620072	−0.00053567	−0.00694218	−0.00350899
	−0.26	−0.02	−0.28	−0.14
Gender	0.20088435	0.17503175	0.27097303	0.08117954
	0.68	0.57	0.88	0.26
Education	0.13346128	0.28160777	0.2647035	0.16645215
	0.48	0.97	0.91	0.56
IT_exp	0.01633745	0.02259876	0.0180641	0.01501987
	0.65	0.85	0.69	0.57
Job_exp	0.01042143	0.0118711	0.01476234	0.0123051
	0.60	0.66	0.82	0.67
_cons	3.3505817*	3.2663169*	5.4756922***	5.5281567***
	2.41	2.16	3.87	3.77
N	104	104	104	104
r2	0.14607472	0.07893594	0.08191662	0.05449599
r2_a	0.0932546	0.0219629	0.02512796	−0.00398879

T-statistics are provided under the estimated coefficient. We report the two tailed P-Value (Sig.): *** Sig. at 0.1% level, ** Sig. at 1%, * Sig. at 5%, +Sig. at 10%. Predictor variables in the multiple regression models are not highly correlated, meaning that there is no multicollinearity between variables

Thus, the family-based cultures with a focus on mentoring, nurturing, and "*doing things together*" (Clan), together with the dynamic and entrepreneurial cultures focusing on risk-taking, innovation, and "*doing things first*" (Adhocracy) have positive impact on ISII.

On the other hand, cultures with a focus on competition, achievement, and "*getting the job done*" (Market), together with more structured and controlled cultures, with a focus on efficiency, stability and "*doing things right*" (Hierarchy) have negative impact on ISII.

5 Conclusions and Limitations

The paper has investigated the relationship between ICO and ISII, giving an important contribution to an open debate started several years ago between e-justice authorities, scholars, and practitioners. This study contributes to the literature on IS and organizational culture in different ways. First, we corroborate the findings that flexible organizations are a more fertile ground for ICT implementation and the success of IS or to materialize the contribution of these systems to improving individual performance. Moreover, we investigate the relationship between ICO and ISII in a specific sector of Public Administration, i.e. JS, that has received less attention by scholars compared to other public sectors.

In particular, research findings have shown that flexibility and discretion within courts are successful factors for implementing IS at individual level. Thus, Clan and Adhocracy orientation are critical to determine success for using IS in courts, so providing interesting implications for court management literature and practitioners. Moreover, this study contributes to court management literature by emphasizing which cultural orientations have most explanatory power in the variation of the user's performance due to IS used in Italian courts.

Our findings also provide useful information for justice authorities and practitioners about IS, underlying the cultural orientations they need to consider for performance improvement. In particular, the results of this research encourage e-justice authorities to closely consider cultural variables in court systems reform design.

Considering the explorative nature of this research, some limitations need to be acknowledged and taken into account in future research. Firstly, the scales used for variables measurement are based on self-report measures and, thus, they might be subject to bias, which distorts the relationship between dependent and independent variables. However, for studies concerning employees' perceptions and feelings, data are usually based on self-assessment. Moreover, our study tests the relationship between a specific dimension of IS success and cultural orientations in just one Italian courts, without conducting a longitudinal analysis, so caution should be exercised when generalizing the results. Further research is required to test the proposed model across a representative national sample of court users.

Finally, another limitation is related to the research model, because it does not consider the effect of cultural orientation on performance of court as a whole. However, our study is aimed at understanding the effect of cultural orientation on success of IS technologies from the perspective of court administrative staff, so focusing on the user performance at individual level of analysis.

Acknowledgements The research has been published thanks to the financial support received by the Parthenope University, Naples, entitled "Bando di sostegno alla ricerca individuale per il triennio 2015–2017. Annualità 2017".

References

1. Masciandaro D.: La giustizia civile è efficiente? Primo rapporto sull'economia delle regole. Laboratorio ABI-Bocconi. Bancaria Editrice, Roma (2000)
2. Zingales L., Rajan R.G., Kumar K.: What determines firm size? Cepr Discussion Paper n. 221 (1999)
3. Bianco, M., Giacomelli, S.: Efficienza della giustizia e imprenditorialità:il caso italiano. Economia e politica industriale **124**, 89–111 (2004)
4. Lepore, L., Agrifoglio, R., Metallo, C., Alvino, F.: Un modello per la valutazione delle performance dei tribunali: un'analisi empirica. Azienda Pubblica **3**, 391–415 (2010)
5. Fabri M.: Amministrare la giustizia. Governance, organizzazione, sistemi informativi. Lexis, Bologna (2006)
6. Marchesi D.: Litiganti, avvocati e magistrati: diritto ed economia del processo civile. Il Mulino, Bologna (2003)
7. Zan, S.: Tecnologia, organizzazione e giustizia. Il Mulino, Bologna (2004)
8. CepeJ: European judicial systems, Strasbourg: CEPEJ (2016)
9. CepeJ: European judicial systems, Strasbourg: CEPEJ (2014)
10. Agrifoglio, R., Lepore, L., Metallo, C.: Measuring the success of e-justice. A validation of the DeLone and McLean model. In: Spagnoletti, P. (ed.) Organization change and information systems—working and living together in new ways. Springer, Berlin, Heidelberg, Germany (2013)
11. Lepore, L.: Efficienza, efficacia ed equità nell'amministrazione della giustizia. Azienda Pubblica. **3**, 429–448 (2009)
12. DeLone, W.H., McLean, E.R.: The DeLone and McLean model of information systems success: a ten-year update. J. Manag. Inf. Syst. **19**, 9–30 (2003)
13. Petter, S., McLean, E.R.: A meta-analytic assessment of the DeLone and McLean IS success model: an examination of IS success at the individual level. Inf. Manag. **46**(3), 159–166 (2009)
14. Van der Meijden, M.J., Tange, H.J., Troost, J., Hasman, A.: Determinants of success of inpatient clinical information systems: a literature review. J. Am. Med. Inf. Assoc. **10**(3), 235–243 (2003)
15. Bailey, J.E., Pearson, S.W.: Development of a tool for measuring and analyzing computer user satisfaction. Manag. Sci. **29**(5), 530–545 (1983)
16. Cheney, P.H., Mann, R.I., Amoroso, D.L.: Organizational factors affecting the success of end-user computing. J. Manag. Inf. Syst. **3**(1), 65–80 (1986)
17. DeLone, W.H., McLean, E.R.: Information systems success: the quest for the dependent variable. Inf. Syst. Res. **3**(1), 60–95 (1992)
18. Bernroider, E.W.N., Koch, S., Stix, V.: A comprehensive framework approach using content, context, process views to combine methods from operations research for IT assessments. Inf. Syst. Manag. **30**(1), 75–88 (2013)
19. Kaisara, G., Pather, S.: The e-government evaluation challenge: a South African batho pele-aligned service quality approach. Gov. Inf. Q. **28**(2), 211–221 (2011)
20. Wang, Y.S., Liao, Y.W.: Assessing egovernment systems success: a validation of the DeLone and McLean model of information systems success. Gov. Inf. Q. **25**, 717–733 (2008)
21. Agrifoglio, R., Metallo, C., Lepore, L.: Success factors for using case management system in Italian courts. Inf. Syst. Manag. **33**(1), 42–54 (2016)
22. Agourram, H.: Defining information system success in Germany. Int. J. Inf. Manag. **29**, 129–137 (2009)
23. Bradley, R.V., Pridmore, J.L., Byrd, T.A.: Information systems success in the context of different corporate cultural types: an empirical investigation. J. Manag. Inf. Syst. **23**(2), 267–294 (2006)
24. Leidner, D.E., Kayworth, T.: A review of culture in information systems research: toward a theory of information technology culture conflict. MIS Q. **30**(2), 357–399 (2006)

25. Quinn, R.E., Rohrbaugh, J.: A competing values approach to organizational effectiveness. Publ. Prod. Rev. 122–140 (1981)
26. Cameron, K.S., Quinn, R.E.: Diagnosing and changing organizational culture: based on the competing values framework. Reading. Addison-Wesley, MA (1999)
27. Ostrom, B., Ostrom, J.R.C., Hanson, R., Kleiman, M.: Trial Courts as organizations. Temple University Press, Philadelphia (2007)
28. Cameron K.S., Quinn R.E.: Kultura organizacyjna-diagnoza i zmiana: model wartości konkurujących. Oficyna Ekonomiczna (2006)
29. Cameron, K.S., Freeman, S.J.: Cultural congruence, strength, and type: relationships to effectiveness. Res. Organ. Change Dev. 5, 115–142 (1991)
30. Lepore, L., Metallo, C., Agrifoglio, R.: Evaluating court performance: findings from two Italian courts. Int. J. Court Adm. 4, 1–12 (2012)
31. Zammuto, R.F., O'Connor, E.J.: Gaining advanced manufacturing technologies' benefits: the role of organization design and culture. Acad. Manag. Rev. 17(4), 701–728 (1992)
32. Etezadi-Amoli, J., Farhoomand, A.F.: A structural model of end user computing satisfaction and user performance. Inf. Manag. 30(2), 65–73 (1996)
33. Lepore, L.: Il sistema giudiziario italiano nella prospettiva economico-aziendale: governance e controllo. EnzoAlbano, Napoli (2011)

Acceptance of Personalised Services and Privacy Disclosure Decisions: Results from a Representative Survey of Internet Users in Spain

José Luis Gómez-Barroso, Claudio Feijóo
and Juan Francisco Palacios

Abstract As interaction with digital providers has become a widespread practice, users are increasingly aware of the trade-off between anonymity and personalised and advantageous services. This contribution intends to ascertain whether a growing consciousness about how digital providers use personal data is having an impact in disclosure behaviour. It uses the theory of planned behaviour (TPB) and a representative survey of 1500 Internet users in Spain to test different hypotheses on how the knowledge of users about service providers usage of personal data influences privacy attitudes, intentions and disclosure behaviour. The analysis concludes that: (i) there is a direct link between privacy attitude and privacy behaviour in addition to the standard path mediated through intentions; (ii) as users become more tech savvy their behaviour regarding privacy is also enhanced except for the case of social networks, where knowledgeable individuals are less concerned; (iii) users are no longer naïve on the effects of exchanging their data for an improved provision of digital services. As a general policy result the paper argues for increasing users' awareness and knowledge as a means to encourage control of personal data.

1 Introduction

Technology offers businesses and marketing specialists the ability to collect—and, later on, to process—immense amounts of private data about individuals' interests or characteristics (whims, opinions, tastes, purchase history) as they input information

J. L. Gómez-Barroso (✉)
Universidad Nacional de Educación a Distancia (UNED), Pº Senda del Rey,
11, 28040 Madrid, Spain
e-mail: jlgomez@cee.uned.es

C. Feijóo
Tongji University/Universidad Politécnica de Madrid, Sino-Spanish Campus,
1239 Siping Road, Shanghai 200092, People's Republic of China

J. F. Palacios
Maastricht University, Tongersestraat 53, 6211 LM Maastricht, The Netherlands

© Springer International Publishing AG, part of Springer Nature 2019
A. Lazazzara et al. (eds.), *Organizing for Digital Innovation*,
Lecture Notes in Information Systems and Organisation 27,
https://doi.org/10.1007/978-3-319-90500-6_6

or just surf the Internet. A better knowledge of clients—together with the new means of contact that information and communication technologies offer—allows firms to build up new relationships with their customers and improve existing ones. Personalisation has become the key word in this new context. For already quite some time, many companies do not deal with consumers as a mass or as segments, but try to treat them as a unique and identifiable target. In this new scenario, users are not passive actors and, certainly, their response to business strategies is a fundamental element in the final result. Indeed, as personalisation has become a widespread practice, users are increasingly aware of the trade-off between anonymity and personalised, more useful, services.

Our research intends to know whether a growing consciousness about the way in which service providers use personal data—both for the worse and for the better— is having an impact in disclosure behaviour. In other words, whether the privacy calculus—understood in economical behaviour terms—plays a role in practice.

With the above research aim, the article is structured as follows. The next section describes and discusses the theory of planned behaviour (TPB) adapted to the specific framework of personal data disclosure as a basis for an integrated theoretical framework. The third section is devoted to methodology and in particular elaborates on the measurement of the different constructs in the TPB model: privacy behaviour, privacy intention, privacy attitude, privacy concerns, perceived benefits, perceived behavioural control, actual control and background factors. Results are derived from a survey that took place during at the end of 2016 with about 1500 respondents representative of the Internet population in Spain and use structural equation modelling to ascertain diverse hypotheses on the behaviour of the users regarding the trade-off between disclosure of personal information and the benefits provided by Internet firms. The paper closes with some concluding remarks and future lines of research.

2 The Model

After making a review of the theories used to frame privacy decisions, Li [1] adopts the theory of planned behaviour (TPB) as the basis for an integrated theoretical framework. TPB—first proposed in [2]—has indeed been used in a significant number of studies related to privacy [3–11].

In fact, TPB is conceivably one of the most widely endorsed social-psychological models for the prediction of behaviour. However, it has not escaped criticism. Many researchers have called for extension or expansion of the theory with additional variables in order to make it able to further improve its predictive validity, see, for all, the early contribution of Conner and Armitage [12]. A less common but substantial criticism refers to the fact that the theory is applied almost exclusively to explain a single action, being therefore not valid to comprehensively capture the essence of more general attitudinal dispositions, such as privacy behaviour. The creators of TPB suggest aggregation as a means to increase the generality of one single element. However, a compound measure of the contextual constraints and influences across a composite of actions is unachievable following the principle of aggregation [13]. Then again, control-relevant influences external to a person that affect different behaviours can be directly incorporated into a behaviour measure when this measure is based on the Rasch model [14]. Adopting such an approach breaks the TPB "principle of compatibility", which requires that all constructs be defined in terms of exactly the same elements (target, action, context, and time). Kaiser et al. [14] deliberately violate the principle of compatibility in their tests, concluding that TPB retains its explanatory power and validity, even if principle of compatibility is violated. With this modification in the criterion, the theory otherwise remains unchanged when it is applied generally to explain an entire class of behaviours, such as a person's privacy performance on different areas. Therefore, considering the type of non one-dimensional behaviour that we want to study, in this paper we keep using TPB but freed from the common implementation of the principle of compatibility. By acting this way, we are also safe from further criticism made by Kaiser et al. [14]: as the compatibility principle essentially confounds the concept definition and the measurement paradigm, it is theoretically possible that compatible measurement actually exploits common method variance, rather than elucidating true associations between concepts.

Following this line of research, in this article we use both Li [1] and Dienlin and Trepte [10] to build our model, introducing some modifications consistent with the objectives of this paper. Those modifications are in line with the latest version of TPB made by their creators [15]. Compared to this last version, the framework proposed in [10] is a simplification of TPB: they suggest that privacy concerns positively influence privacy attitudes; privacy attitudes in turn positively influence different types of privacy behaviours, both directly and indirectly through influencing privacy intentions. Li's framework [1] introduces greater detail. Firstly, attitude toward disclosure is developed from an overall assessment of privacy concerns and perceived benefits (i.e., privacy calculus), an amendment that we consider particularly appropriate for our research. Secondly, intention is positively influenced by attitude but also by subjective norm for disclosure, and by perceived behavioural control.

Considering the scenario we want to analyse, we do not see a key role for subjective norms—contrarily to what happens, very saliently, in social network sites. In our view, privacy intention is mediated by attitudes and also for perceived control, which integrates factors such as perceived risks and trust. Additionally, we recover from TPB the idea that it is not only the perceived but the actual control over performing original intentions (capacity and environment) what influences final behaviour.

Figure 1 shows the final model designed.

Formally, the model includes the following hypotheses to be tested through the survey and data analysis (see Fig. 1):

H1: There is user awareness on the trade-off between personal information disclosure and benefits in the shape of personalised services, this is, users conduct some type of privacy calculus.

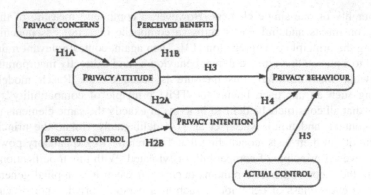

Fig. 1 TPB model in a context of personalised services and hypotheses to be tested

This is a foundational hypothesis since the model is based on the existence of this subjective awareness on concerns and benefits on the side of users. In terms of results it is expected to observe that the perceived benefits influence positively the privacy attitude and, on the contrary, that privacy concerns influence negatively the privacy attitude. Both effects are expected to be not too dissimilar in absolute value so as to trigger the need for some type of subjective cost-benefit analysis on personal data disclosure, at least for some types of users.

H2: Informational privacy attitudes (A) together with perceived control (B) are related with informational privacy intentions.

This is part of the basic mechanism of the TPB. It is expected that attitudes positively influence intention and as well self-trust (perceived control) positively affect intention

H3: Informational privacy attitudes are also significantly related to informational privacy behaviours.

This hypothesis departs from the original model of Ajzen [2] where intention always mediates between attitude and behaviour. Here, both the result of the privacy calculus and the general attitude towards privacy are supposed to directly affect privacy behaviour. This is to say that general privacy attitude is to a certain extent independent of the particular features of the provider and the privacy risk attached to it. This direct effect of attitude on behaviour is expected to be significantly large and, as a manifestation of the privacy paradox, of the same magnitude that the effect on behaviour mediated by intention.

H4: Informational privacy intentions influence informational privacy behaviours.

This is the other core assumption of the standard TPB model: from attitudes to intention and, in turn, intention is expected to positively induce behaviour as well as actual capacity (control).

H5: Capacity influence informational privacy behaviours.

The original control element in Ajzen's theory [2] has been divided in two parts: perceived control linked to intention and actual control influencing behaviour. This is a consequence of breaking the principle of compatibility. TPB retains its explanatory power and validity but since all constructs might not refer to the same action, context and time, the perceived behavioural control direct influence on behaviour can not be expected.

3 Methodology—Measures, Survey and Data Analysis

3.1 Measures

The questionnaire includes separate measures for all the elements in the model.

Privacy behaviour

General privacy behaviour was measured with different types of particular privacy behaviours. The compound of all behaviours can be used as a one-dimensional privacy performance measure. Replicating the General Ecological Behaviour scale [16], we term our one-dimensional measure as the General Online Privacy Behaviour [GOPB] scale. The set of questions is new except for some of them inspired from [17], where a set of questions measuring privacy-related activities were validated.

Privacy intention

It is a new scale that measures the intention of not being identifiable in a search engine activity in different domains increasingly more private: from travels, shopping, interests and hobbies to financial and job matters and to health, religion, political and sex issues. Three final questions measure the intention of controlling privacy features in general, and search history and location in particular.

Privacy attitude

Dienlin and Trepte [10] asked the same question six times, with six different scales. We do not see respondents being able to clearly move through all those options. Instead, we reduce the questions from six to two (not useful/very useful; worrying/ not worrying) but repeat them for several types of information. This "multidimensionality" of privacy is brought to light in [18], where was found that participants make a clear distinction between contact info and all other privacy-related data.

Privacy concerns

In our model, privacy concerns have to be understood as quite generic and not bound to any specific context. We use the scale proposed in [18], based on previous scales in [3, 19].

Perceived benefits

Measure of perceived benefits is another main novelty in this paper. We have used a compilation of the benefits promoted and promised by online firms: personalized services and offers, free and additional services, convenience, rewards, price reductions and a final encompassing question about an enhanced online experience.

Perceived behavioural control

We use perceived information control from [20]. Anonimity/secrecy is adapted from [4]. Trust is a new scale specifically designed for this study.

Actual control

Shih et al. [21] introduce four questions for computer self-efficacy and Knijnenburg et al. [15] have a section on tech-savvyness. However, questions sound outdated considering the present activity of a regular online user. Therefore, we build a new item pool with an updated version for current users.

Background factors

In addition to the usual personal and social traits, online activity is a new item pool except for the Internet/mobile phone addiction that is built taking some selected questions from both the Internet addiction test [21] and the test of mobile phone dependence [22].

3.2   Participants and Procedure

The questionnaire was conducted in September 2016. Individuals over age 16 were recruited from a general-population panel operated by a professional survey research firm to complete the online survey administered through Qualtrics, a major online survey research service. Three quota samplings were used: sex, age, and region of residence. Data for quotas were taken from the last available "Survey on Equipment and Use of Information and Communication Technologies in Households" published by INE (the Spanish National Statistics Institute).

The total sample consisted of 1661 participants. Eleven reported not using Google regularly (filter question) and were redirected to the end of the survey. Of the 1650 remaining answers, sex distribution is exactly 50% and age distribution is as follows: 12.97% under 24, 21.52% from 25 to 34, 27.27% from 35 to 44, 21.27% from 45 to 54, 12.36% from 55 to 64, 4.60% over 64. Criteria to identify low-quality responses were strictly applied, resulting in a total of 1502 valid answers.

The questionnaire was composed of seven blocks, amounting to 114 questions, from which 44 were used to complete the so-called General Online Privacy Behaviour. 57 additional questions served to define the socioeconomic and online profile of respondents. Their real knowledge of the researched topic was assessed through a true/false test of 10 questions. Mean time of completion was 23 min.

3.3 Data Analysis

The results of the Cronbach's test for independent and dependent variables show that all selected constructs had satisfactory internal consistency. Note that items with high correlation have been suppressed.

The hypotheses were analysed with structural equation models (SEM). H1, H2 and H3 were analysed together in a single SEM. However, as there are three types of online privacy behaviour, there are results for three different models: browsing behaviour, social networks behaviour, and fighting against collection of personal data, respectively SEM_{BRO}, SEM_{SNS} and SEM_{FGT}. Hypotheses were tested at 0.1, 0.05 and 0.01 levels of significance.

To estimate effect sizes, in SEM beta coefficients can be interpreted as correlation coefficients [23]. Values exceeding 0.5 were considered large effects, with values around 0.3 as medium effects and around 0.1 as small effects.

4 Results and Discussion

The three SEMs were first tested regarding model fit. Table 1 shows the resulting values. They show some reasonable model fit with root mean square of approximation (RMSEA) not exceeding the recommended threshold of 0.08, while values for standardized root mean square residual (SRMR), comparative fit index (CFI), Tucker-Lewis coefficient (TLI), and Chi2 divided by degrees of freedom lie not far of their recommended values at 0.06, 0.9, 0.9 and 5, respectively.

Table 2 shows the SEMs measurement model. All items are significant at the 0.01 level. Also all items, except AC3 (actual control—understanding of cookies) and AC6 (actual control—sharing location with applications), exceed a threshold of 0.5, implying adequate overall model fit.

H1A/B—Privacy calculus

Hypothesis 1 stated that there is user awareness on the trade-off between personal information disclosure and benefits in the shape of personalised services, this is, users conduct some type of privacy calculus. Results indicate, see Table 3, that in fact users conduct some type of analysis and as expected the magnitude of both, concerns and benefits, is not dissimilar with opposite influence on privacy attitudes. Therefore the hypothesis of privacy calculus is confirmed. However both effects, although highly significant, are relatively small. This privacy calculus is similar across browsing/searching, fighting convert collection of data and social networks scenarios of usage, with slightly less important effects for the benefits attached to the browsing/search scenario.

H2A—Attitudes influence on privacy intentions

The hypothesis of the influence of privacy attitudes on intentions is fully confirmed by the experiment across the three scenarios of privacy behaviour, see Table 3.

Table 1 Tests of model fit

	SEM$_{BRO}$	SEM$_{FGT}$	SEM$_{SNS}$
Observations	1499	1500	1502
Chi2	5381.873	4848.131	4908.588
Degrees of freedom (df)	652	581	581
Chi2/df	8.25	8.34	8.45
Log likelihood	−68487.804	−62178.757	−63031.846
df_m	127.000	121.000	121.000
RMSEA	0.070	0.070	0.070
CFI	0.826	0.800	0.795
TLI	0.812	0.783	0.777
SRMR	0.097	0.092	0.094

Table 2 SEMs measurement model

	SEM$_{BRO}$	SEM$_{FGT}$	SEM$_{SNS}$
Attitudes—Being identified is worrying when			
AW1—Search info on travels and shopping (reference category)	1.000	1.000	1.000
AW2—Search info on interests and hobbies	1.818*** (0.30)	1.733*** (0.27)	1.716*** (0.26)
AW4—Search info on health status	1.316*** (0.24)	1.289*** (0.23)	1.288*** (0.22)
AW7—Remembers info on search history	0.921*** (0.18)	0.912*** (0.17)	0.917*** (0.17)
Attitudes—Being identified is useful when			
AU2—Search info on interests and hobbies	−4.770*** (0.71)	−4.527*** (0.64)	−4.373*** (0.60)
AU3—Search info on work and financials	−4.831*** (0.72)	−4.616*** (0.65)	−4.452*** (0.61)
AU4—Search info on health status	−4.114*** (0.62)	−3.876*** (0.55)	−3.763*** (0.52)
Privacy concerns			
CN21—Bothers me when services ask for info (reference category)	1.000	1.000	1.000
CN22—Think twice before providing info	1.022*** (0.09)	1.023*** (0.09)	1.022*** (0.09)
CN24—Services collecting too much info	1.106*** (0.10)	1.112*** (0.10)	1.106*** (0.10)
CN41—Should never share info unless authorised	1.753*** (0.13)	1.750*** (0.13)	1.754*** (0.13)
CN42—Should not use info unless authorised	1.765*** (0.13)	1.762*** (0.13)	1.766*** (0.13)
CN43—Never sell info to other companies	1.785*** (0.13)	1.784*** (0.13)	1.786*** (0.13)
CN51—Unauthorised access	0.847*** (0.08)	0.843*** (0.08)	0.845*** (0.08)

(continued)

Table 2 (continued)

	SEM$_{BRO}$	SEM$_{FGT}$	SEM$_{SNS}$
Perceived benefits			
PB1—Service adapted to needs (reference category)	1.000	1.000	1.000
PB3—Save time for next visit	0.901*** (0.03)	0.901*** (0.03)	0.900*** (0.03)
PB4—Personalised commercial offers	0.966*** (0.03)	0.965*** (0.03)	0.964*** (0.03)
PB6—Additional services and/or content	0.955*** (0.03)	0.953*** (0.03)	0.953*** (0.03)
PB7—Online experience enhanced	0.944*** (0.03)	0.944*** (0.03)	0.943*** (0.03)
Privacy Intentions—Actions for not being identifiable in future searches on			
PI1—Travels and shopping (reference category)	1.000	1.000	1.000
PI3—Work and financials	1.076*** (0.04)	1.096*** (0.04)	1.094*** (0.04)
PI4—Health status	1.190*** (0.04)	1.197*** (0.04)	1.199*** (0.04)
PI6—Sex-related matters	1.000*** (0.04)	1.006*** (0.04)	1.007*** (0.04)
Actual Control—Able to			
AC2—Customise settings and toolbars (reference category)	1.000	1.000	1.000
AC3—Understand what cookies are and what are they for	0.381*** (0.03)	0.377*** (0.03)	0.380*** (0.03)
AC4—Change privacy preferences	0.553*** (0.04)	0.492*** (0.03)	0.547*** (0.04)
AC6—Know whether you are sharing location with applications	0.439*** (0.04)	0.397*** (0.03)	0.445*** (0.04)
Perceived Control—I am confident on			
PC23—Keep my info anonymous (reference category)	1.000	1.000	1.000
PC31—Providers collect info just because it is necessary for their services	1.913*** (0.12)	1.915*** (0.12)	1.914*** (0.12)
PC32—Collected info remains confidential	1.952*** (0.12)	1.955*** (0.12)	1.953*** (0.12)
PC33—Providers prevent unauthorized access	1.687*** (0.10)	1.690*** (0.10)	1.688*** (0.10)
PC34—Providers manage info in a fair way	1.854*** (0.11)	1.858*** (0.11)	1.855*** (0.11)
Privacy Behaviour when Browsing—Do you take any action to be unidentifiable when searching for			
BR4—Travels and shopping (reference category)	1.000		
BR5—Interests and hobbies	1.029*** (0.03)		
BR6—Work and financials	1.005*** (0.03)		

(continued)

Table 2 (continued)

	SEM$_{BRO}$	SEM$_{FGT}$	SEM$_{SNS}$
BR7—Health status	1.108*** (0.03)		
BR8—Religion-related matters	1.046*** (0.03)		
BR9—Sex-related matters	0.959*** (0.03)		
Privacy Behaviour to Fight Covert Collection of Personal Data			
FC2—Turn-off location tracking because of being worried (reference category)		1.000	
FC3—Use of ad/popup windows blocker		1.391*** (0.11)	
FC4—Install a cookies controller		1.283*** (0.10)	
FC5—Check your computer for spyware		1.222*** (0.10)	
Privacy Behaviour when using Social networks			
SN1—Use real name (reference category)			1.000
SN2—Use an identifiable picture as profile picture			1.704*** (0.14)
SN5—Picture with your partner or family			0.839*** (0.08)
SN9—Allow geo-tagging and location			1.882*** (0.19)

($*p < 0.10$, $**p < 0.05$, $***p < 0.01$, standard errors in parentheses)

In addition it is also worth to highlight that the effect is rather strong. This is an indication on how the user acknowledgement of the ability of providers to identify individuals when looking for different types of information is a main determinant of his/her intentions regarding privacy.

H2B—Perceived control influence on privacy intentions

The hypothesis of the influence of perceived control on intentions is not confirmed by the experiment for any of the three scenarios of privacy behaviour, see Table 3. This result calls for further analysis to examine whether perceived control directly influences behaviour and not intentions as it was proposed in the original Ajzen's model [2] and not in its later adaptations to privacy scenarios.

H3: Privacy attitudes influence on behaviours.

This hypothesis is a novelty compared with the original model of Ajzen [2] where intention always mediates between attitude and behaviour. The hypothesis is confirmed in two of the three scenarios: browsing and using social networks. However it cannot be ascertained in the scenario related with fighting covert collection of data. In addition the effect is large—as expected- in both confirmed scenarios but with

Table 3 Estimates of effects for privacy concerns and benefits, privacy attitudes, perceived control and actual control on privacy intentions and privacy behaviour for the three TPB models on browsing (SEM_{BRO}), fighting covert collection of data (SEM_{FGT}) and social networks (SEM_{SNS})

	SEM_{BRO}	SEM_{FGT}	SEM_{SNS}
H1A—Privacy Concerns on Attitude	0.141*** (0.03)	0.141*** (0.03)	0.146*** (0.03)
H1B—Privacy Benefits on Attitude	−0.095*** (0.02)	−0.100*** (0.02)	−0.106*** (0.02)
H2A—Privacy Attitude on Intentions	0.655*** (0.17)	0.632*** (0.15)	0.619*** (0.15)
H2B—Perceived Control on Intentions	0.096 (0.06)	0.093 (0.06)	0.091 (0.06)
H3—Privacy Attitude on Behaviour	−1.298*** (0.24)	−0.044 (0.04)	0.495*** (0.09)
H4—Privacy Intentions on Behaviour	0.541*** (0.03)	0.031** (0.01)	0.026* (0.01)
H5—Actual Control on Behaviour	0.297*** (0.06)	0.396*** (0.03)	−0.076*** (0.02)

(*$p < 0.10$, **$p < 0.05$, ***$p < 0.01$, standard errors in parentheses)

opposite sign: when browsing the attitude contributes to actual usage (it is negative with regard to privacy) while when using social networks privacy attitude influences positively privacy behaviour. See Table 3 for results. The differences between the three scenarios call for a separate analysis of each of them.

In the browsing scenario the questions in the experiment were posed in a negative format, this is, the user was mainly asked about actions for *not* being identifiable when browsing the Internet for different types of information; thus, the negative sign in the influence on privacy behaviour. The large effect indicates that the a priori attitude directly influences behaviour irrespective of the privacy intentions. It is, therefore, a manifestation of the privacy paradox where the user behaviour is to a large extent independent of the possible measures to protect privacy in online media -in spite of the declarations of the user—but predominantly dependent on his/her a priori attitude.

In the social networks scenario the direct effect from privacy attitude into behaviour is also large but less than half than in the browsing scenario, displaying a lesser influence of the a priori disposition of the user towards privacy. This indicates also a manifestation of the privacy paradox but here the direct effect of attitude into behaviour and the effect mediated through intentions are of about the same magnitude as it was hypothesized.

Regarding the scenario about fighting covert collection of data the hypothesis on the direct influence of privacy attitude into behaviour is not confirmed by the experiment. However the conventional effect on behaviour mediated through intentions is present. Therefore we can conclude that in this scenario we cannot disregard that the selection of provider does have an effect on the overall privacy behaviour.

H4: Privacy intentions influence on behaviours.

The core assumption of the standard TPB model: from attitudes to intention and, in turn, from intention to behaviour is confirmed in the experiment. However the level of significance and the size of the effect is rather different across scenarios.

For browsing the effect is large and significant. For the other two scenarios the effect is small and less significant (at 5 and 10% levels, respectively). The interpretation of these results is similar to the previous hypothesis: for users search intentions are directly related with browsing behaviour but not so strongly and immediately with social networks and covert collection of data.

H5: Capacity influence on behaviours.

The experiment confirms the novelty of introducing an element of actual control in the TPB model. In the case of browsing and covert collection of data the effect is of medium size, while for social networks is small and negative.

For browsing and covert collection of data, these results indicate that as the users become more technical savvy their level of privacy-prone behaviour increases. However in the case of the social networks scenario, the actual knowledge about technology makes them less concerned about privacy.

5 Conclusions

The findings of the experiment present in this paper suggest the following.

First they confirm the general applicability of the TPB model in a set of privacy behaviour scenarios.

Second, they also confirm that alterations in the standard TPB model rightly accommodate a direct link between privacy attitude and privacy behaviour in addition to the TPB standard path mediated through intentions. We can say with Dienlin and Trepte [10] that the privacy paradox is dissolved when the user is confronted to browsing in a search scenario. However still the direct influence of attitude on privacy behaviour is notorious. When the user moves from search attitude to privacy behaviour in social networks the two paths also coexist providing again an explanation for the privacy paradox. But here the difference is even greater in favour of the direct influence of attitude on behaviour: the privacy paradox is still clarified but the intentions are not a very good predictor of behaviour compared to attitude. In the covert collection of data we have an opposite scenario: we can also say that intentions explain behaviour but in this scenario the attitude regarding the usage of search engines appears irrelevant. It seems that users are unable to relate their privacy attitude when using a search provider with their actual level of privacy behaviour as if they belong to different domains.

Third, the modification of the privacy TPB model to recover from the original TPB model the actual control influence on final behaviour has also been confirmed.

As users become more tech savvy their behaviour regarding privacy is also enhanced except for the case of the link between search and social networks, where knowledgeable individuals are less concerned.

Fourth, and not less important, the influence of privacy calculus on attitude has been also confirmed across the three scenarios. The authors consider that the existence of such a concern (cost)-benefit analysis performed by the users is a cornerstone for any future {policy, economic, research} approach to privacy. It tells that users are no longer naïve on the effects of exchanging their data for an enhanced provision of digital services. It also tells that they are able to valuate the benefits in terms of convenience and price of such enhanced services against their costs in terms of personal data.

However, this research has limitations and should be understood as a first step in the direction of analysing a rich and rather complete survey. Specifically, the authors acknowledge that a next line of research should consider the link across new latent constructs, stated privacy attitudes, intentions and actual behaviour—see [24] for an example of this type of analysis—looking for the influence of past experiences in privacy frustrations, the users' real tech savviness, their level of Internet addiction or the intensity of their online purchases, just to name some of the more promising items.

As a summary, reading these conclusions together, the authors consider that the practical implications of these results mainly consists of new and important pieces of evidence to support the interest in increasing users' awareness and knowledge as a means to encourage control of personal data. In particular, elaborating from the model validated in this paper a surge in the consumers' understanding of the rules of the game in the exchange of personal data for improved services would mean that: (i) privacy calculus will be enhanced with additional insights on concerns and benefits that users are already able to balance; (ii) the privacy paradox will be more exposed through the double path of attitude direct influence on behaviour and indirect mediation of intentions; and (iii) the actual control will positively influence privacy behaviour and/or reduce concern.

References

1. Li, Y.: Theories in online information privacy research: a critical review and an integrated framework. Decis. Support Syst. **54**(1), 471–481 (2012)
2. Ajzen, I.: The theory of planned behavior. Organ. Behav. Human Decis. Process. **50**(2), 179–211 (1991)
3. Malhotra, N.K., Kim, S.S., Agarwal, J.: Internet users' information privacy concerns (IUIPC): the construct, the scale, and a causal model. Inf. Syst. Res. **15**(4), 336–355 (2004)
4. Dinev, T., Xu, H., Smith, J., Hart, P.: Information privacy and correlates: an empirical attempt to bridge and distinguish privacy-related concepts. Eur. J. Inf. Syst. **22**(3), 295–316 (2013)
5. Kim, D.J.: Self-perception-based versus transference-based trust determinants in computer-mediated transactions: a cross-cultural comparison study. J. Manage. Inf. Syst. **24**(4), 13–45 (2008)

6. Lee, K., Song, I.Y.: An influence of self-evaluated gender role on the privacy management behavior in online social networks. In: Marinos, L., Askoxylakis, I. (eds.) Human Aspects of Information Security, Privacy, and Trust—Proceedings of the First International Conference, HAS 2013, pp. 135–144. Springer, Heidelberg (2013)

7. Burns, S., Roberts, L.: Applying the theory of planned behaviour to predicting online safety behaviour. Crime Prev. Community Safety **15**(1), 48–64 (2013)

8. Saeri, A., Ogilvie, C., La Macchia, S., Smith, J., Louis, W.: Predicting Facebook users' online privacy protection: risk, trust, norm focus theory, and the theory of planned behavior. J. Soc. Psychol. **154**(4), 352–369 (2014)

9. Hughes-Roberts, T.: Privacy as a secondary goal problem: an experiment examining control. Inf. Comput. Secur. **23**(4), 382–393 (2015)

10. Dienlin, T., Trepte, S.: Is the privacy paradox a relic of the past? An in-depth analysis of privacy attitudes and privacy behaviors. Eur. J. Soc. Psychol. **45**(3), 285–297 (2015)

11. Awad, N.F., Krishnan, M.S.: The personalization privacy paradox: an empirical evaluation of information transparency and the willingness to be profiled online for personalization. MIS Q. **30**(1), 13–28 (2006)

12. Conner, M., Armitage, C.J.: Extending the theory of planned behavior: a review and avenues for further research. J. Appl. Soc. Psychol. **28**(15), 1429–1464 (1998)

13. Kaiser, F.G., Gutscher, H.: The proposition of a general version of the theory of planned behavior: predicting ecological behavior. J. Appl. Soc. Psychol. **33**(3), 586–603 (2003)

14. Kaiser, F.G., Schultz, P.W., Scheuthle, H.: The theory of planned behavior without compatibility? Beyond method bias and past trivial associations. J. Appl. Soc. Psychol. **37**(7), 1522–1544 (2007)

15. Fishbein, M., Ajzen, I.: Predicting and changing behavior. The reasoned action approach. Psychology Press, New York (2010)

16. Kaiser, F.G.: A general measure of ecological behavior. J. Appl. Soc. Psychol. **28**(5), 395–422 (1998)

17. Buchanan, T., Paine, C., Joinson, A.N., Reips, U.D.: Development of measures of online privacy concern and protection for use on the Internet. J. Am. Soc. Inf. Sci. Technol. **58**(2), 154–165 (2007)

18. Knijnenburg, B., Kobsa, A., Jin, H.: Dimensionality of information disclosure behavior. Int. J. Human-Comput. Stud. **71**(12), 1144–1162 (2013)

19. Smith, H.J., Milberg, S.J., Burke, S.J.: Information privacy: measuring individuals' concerns about organizational practices. MIS Q. **20**(2), 167–196 (1996)

20. Shih, D., Hsu, S., Yen, D., Lin, C.: Exploring the individual's behavior on self-disclosure online. Int. J. Human-Comput. Interact. **28**(10), 627–645 (2012)

21. Young, K.S.: Caught in the Net: How to Recognize the Signs of Internet Addiction and a Winning Strategy for Recovery. Wiley, Nueva York (1998)

22. Chóliz, M.: Mobile-phone addiction in adolescence: the test of mobile phone dependence. Prog. Health Sci. **2**(1), 33–44 (2012)

23. Field, A.: Discovering statistics using SPSS, 3rd edn. Sage Publications, Los Angeles (USA) (2009)

24. Potoglou, D., Palacios, J.F., Feijóo, C.: An integrated latent variable and choice model to explore the role of privacy concern on stated behavioural intentions in e-commerce. J. Choice Model. **17**, 10–27 (2015)

Part II
Digital Innovation for Inclusion and Sustainability

The Role of Communication in Stereotypes, Prejudices and Professional Identity: The Case of Nurses

Giuseppe Perna, Luisa Varriale and Maria Ferrara

Abstract Nursing, conceived as a daily professional service aimed at *"taking care of"*, *"satisfying the needs"*, *"the well-being of the assisted person"*, has a very recent history compared to other disciplines in the field of medicine and further professional fields. Nurses have found their affirmation for a long time as well as an obvious prestige and social recognition. Over recent decades, despite the deep evolution of the nurses' figure, the public opinion is still anchored to an image of them, heavily influenced by stereotypes and prejudices fuelled above all by mass media (and new media). Indeed, media contribute to provide a professional portrait that mostly corresponds to the old role, duties and composition of this professional category, with limited skills, working in the shadow of physicians to whom only clinical knowledge belongs. The aim of this paper is to define the portrait of this professional figure and how it is altered by means of communication and, thus, transmitted to public opinion. Adopting a qualitative methodology, using text analysis technique, we investigate and represent through images 50 articles published on web (blog, social media, specialized nursing websites) in the period 2008–2016, evidencing the main role and functions attributed to nurses still deeply affected by stereotypes and prejudices and the related professional identity.

1 Introduction

In contemporary society the care and support of sick people is deeply institutionalized and entrusted to skills and technical abilities of various professional figures, such as, physicians, nurses, psychologists and so forth. In this wide professional

G. Perna · L. Varriale (✉) · M. Ferrara
University of Naples "Parthenope", Naples, Italy
e-mail: luisa.varriale@uniparthenope.it

G. Perna
e-mail: giuseppe.perna@uniparthenope.it

M. Ferrara
e-mail: maria.ferrara@uniparthenope.it

© Springer International Publishing AG, part of Springer Nature 2019
A. Lazazzara et al. (eds.), *Organizing for Digital Innovation*,
Lecture Notes in Information Systems and Organisation 27,
https://doi.org/10.1007/978-3-319-90500-6_7

health care category, nurses represent the health professional working in the field of: prevention (informing, educating and supporting the citizen, the family and the community about the correct lifestyles and respect for the life), care (with diagnosis, treatment and rehabilitation), assistance (identifying and managing the needs of patients and family) and rehabilitation (promoting and supporting the recovery and maintenance of the greatest possible autonomy, particularly in chronic diseases, and educating the individual and his/her relatives with reference to self-care and appropriate lifestyles) [1]. The crucial area of the nursing profession concerns assistance, conceived as the ability to respond, on scientific basis, to the needs of people with health problems; it is the activity that all nurses share, whatever their field of work.

However, today the role and activity of nurses are perceived inadequately: there are distorted and stereotyped images spread by the media, traditional and new media, which threaten nursing autonomy and professionalism. In fact, there exist still stereotypes and prejudices linked to nurses who do not receive the right merit and social recognition for their profession, although they play a key role in the optimal functioning of the healthcare system.

Generally, the determinants of stereotypes and prejudices can be traced in most cases to ignorance, the lack of knowledge, and the strong communicative barriers among those people oriented to create negative meanings of diversity [2]. These factors affect the thinking of individuals regardless of their will and awareness, especially, when they are deeply rooted in the concerned cultural, organizational and social patterns.

Although during the last years the profession of nurses has undergone a significant ever-growing evolution, the main traditional media, cinema and television, have spread an image of nurses often approximate and far from the reality. Indeed, the big and small screen over the years have represented a stereotyped figure, that is the result of the collective imagination and unconnected from any real foundation. Stereotypes and prejudices are aspects that can hinder relationships between nurses and patients and convince them to believe that they are not receiving proper care [3]. These media often distort the concept of nursing and put society in the condition of not recognizing the very important mission of nurses; they have an immutable validity which also resists when nurses present positive features that respond to people's expectations [4]. In this regard, the wider knowledge of others and the ability to critically review their convictions are two fundamental elements to overcome distrust and prejudices.

Some research suggests that media play an important role in the spread of stereotypes and prejudices related to the nursing profession (such as stereotypes and prejudices recognize the lack of responsibilities for nurses because of doctors) and to favor an image of the category that does not faithfully correspond to current reality [5]. Therefore, professionals and trade associations should require greater respect from the mass media for more accurate and truthful information to citizens.

According to prevalent studies, the influence of mass media on public opinion is mediated by reference groups and the cultural substrate of subjects. About this, Katz and Lazarsfeld, in their critical review, emphasize that "*an attempt to change an opinion or individual attitude can not be successful if the subject shares his opinion with others*" and add that "*it is all the more likely that an attempt to change an individual's opinion or attitude is as effective as it is the opinion or attitude shared by others*" [6: p. 52]. Thus, it is evident that the group is essentially an anchor point in which individuals act, change or reinforce their opinion. Mass media reinforce a stereotyped and old image of the nursing profession in the culture and the feeling of the majority of people exposed to the message. Mass media are significantly able to influence culture and collective thinking and, therefore, news and stories reported by newspapers and television programs can affect and enhance the image that people have about nurses, their professionalism and the structures in which they operate [7].

The study of the image and nursing identity presented by media allows to describe and understand the way this profession is perceived by the population, and, hence, how it is possible nurses see themselves [8]. The professional identity desired by nurses, unfortunately, is something only theoretically existing. The reason for this uncertainty of nurses role is also related to the changes occurred in their training and specialization process; there was not enough time to promote and make the cultural and professional revolution [9] in the collective imagination, thus, promoting a disagreement in the social vision of this figure: One profession does not live unless if it is not socially visible [10].

In the international literature the belief, that the nurses' image is significantly influenced by the culture of belonging to individuals, varies according to the socio-cultural context and the prevailing health policies [11]. Therefore, individuals have an inadequate perception of the role and activity of nurses, because of existing limited thoughts difficult to decay, despite the constant growth of this profession.

When citizens report their disappointment to healthcare organizations, they often claim the little expertise of hospitals, referring primarily to nurses. Most individuals consider nurses to be mere perpetrators of medical decisions and just like operators able to practically provide services ignoring their knowledge of medicine and the fact that they actively participate into the process of care, medical innovation, diagnosis and treatment [1]. It is clear that the term professionalism is not voluntarily associated to nursing, which is still seen as a vocation to which people must devote themselves to satisfy the primary needs of patients, such as hygiene and nutrition, forgetting everything concerning the care plan.

In this complex and infinite struggle between what nurses are and are not, it is crucial that the real image about nurses can be spread from ensuring that nursing professionalism can be recognized overcoming any stereotypes and prejudices often linked to cultural traditions or origins of the profession [12].

This paper aims to identify the stereotypes most commonly associated with the figure of nurses and to what extent the current media, which play an incisive role in the image of professions. In particular, we want to see if new media have contributed and still do so to nurses' image usually far from the reality. Internet images have become more and more important in recent years due to the growing use of this form of media by the public (particularly young adults and teens) to obtain information and learn about the world. The choice to analyze this professional category is related to the fact that its image affects on: recruitment into the profession; the decisions of policy makers who enact legislation that defines the scope and financing of nursing services; the use of nursing services by consumers; and the self-image of the nurse. We firstly conducted a review of the literature on the issues investigated, that is social categorization, stereotypes and prejudices related to nursing, as well as the ability of the media, especially the Internet, to influence the perception of social reality. Also, we evidence what the image is about nurses, often approximate and far from reality, which derives by the traditional mass media, that is cinema and television. Then, we conducted a qualitative study through text analysis technique, where we illustrate the image of nurses thanks to a statistical analysis of nursing image data based on nursing articles collected on various internet sites. Indeed, 50 articles in italian language published on web (blog, social media, specialized nursing websites) in the period 2008–2016, have been analyzed with the purpose tooutline the main role and functions attributed to nurses still deeply affected by stereotypes and prejudices and the related professional identity.

2 Social Categorization, Stereotypes and Prejudices

Most social systems are characterized by the sense of belonging to a set of collective values, which contribute to the specific identity of those who are involved. The fundamental characteristic of human subjectivity is its social nature, so it builds its identity by using society as a mirror. According to this theory, each action of people depends on their interactions with other individuals and environments. A key point for understanding this phenomenon and the dynamics between social groups is the theme of *social categorization* [13]. Social categorization represents the cognitive process that divides the social world into categories to which it belongs or does not belong, which accentuates the perception of similarities and differences between the different categories and produces differentiations on the assessment and at behavioral level.

Social categorization is an useful mechanism that allows us to control our social environment and to have proper behavior within the society. However, it has also negative effects: social categorization, in fact, makes members of one group more similar to each other than they are and it exaggerates the differences between groups [14]. More specifically, categorization favors categorical differentiation, that is, the process by which the differences between the elements belonging to different groups are maximized and the differences between the elements belonging to the same group are minimized. This process helps to discriminate class members from those who are not part of the same class. To judge the value of one's own group, then, individuals are compared to other groups and the outcome of that assessment directly affects their self-esteem. For this reason, it tends to alter the comparison in an attempt to create a positive outlook for one's own group or to positively differentiate one's own group from others. This phenomenon was explained by Tajfel through the notion of social identity: "*an individual's social identity is linked to the knowledge of his belonging to certain social groups and to the emotional and appreciative meaning that comes from that belonging"* [15: 31]. Given that one of the fundamental needs for individuals is to obtain a positive self-assessment, and since membership of a group is part of our identity, then favoritism towards members of our own group can be considered in relation to strive to distinguish their group in positive terms compared to others [16].

As a consequence of categorization, individuals implement a process that in social psychology is called explanation or inference. In other words, they attribute the causes of a person's behavior to the fact that this is part of a specific category [16]. In addition, another effect of social categorization is that it, along with social identity, is strongly involved in the formation of stereotypes and prejudices. In particular, studies on group relationships have largely focused on the relationship between categorization, stereotype and prejudice.

In summary, social categorization is the basis for the stereotypes that individuals and groups tend to develop [17]. The term stereotype is used to indicate *"a pre-conception, an image of reality that is created in the mind and that determines the perception of people and events, creating a coherent and fairly rigid set of negative beliefs that some group shares with respect to Another group or social category"* [18: 5–9]. The stereotype is based on preconceived beliefs and opinions that are not verified, arise from sedentary habits and expectations systems, rely on entirely relative points of view that are considered absolute. The concept of stereotype was introduced in the social sciences by a journalist, Walter Lippman, interested in interpreting the mechanisms of formation of public opinion; in his view, *"the relationship that social actors have with external reality is mediated through the mental images that they form, especially through the media"* [18: 5–9]. The functions performed by stereotypes are manifold, as besides facilitating social assessments, they also have a psychological relevance as they provide a coherent worldview and event that can make us feel the right one. The stereotype also has the function of identifying the social object on which to discharge the responsibility of situations of collective discomfort caused by natural calamities, famines, or diseases of some members of the group [19].

From a sociocultural point of view, stereotypes reinforce the homogeneity of a group. In order to understand how stereotypes are formed, we can also consider the concept of social representation as a form of knowledge typical of modern societies that overlaps or equates to the myths of traditional societies [19], consisting of a set of values, ideas and practices that fulfill the dual function of guidance and control of the world and foster communication among members of a community as it provides a code of exchange and classification for the social, individual and group world. Social actors tend to convey the dominant collective representations in a conforming way, often welcoming stereotypical forms, aligning them with attitudes, motivations, and behavior. Social representations, therefore, rather than forms of knowledge of social systems that are elaborated by individuals transforming into individual social representations, tend to become stereotypical mental forms and as such to be assimilated [17].

The psychological explanations of stereotype development argue that social actors tend to establish illusory correlations between group membership and undesirable behaviors, tending to recall anti-social behaviors committed by members of minorities rather than acts similar items made by members of the majority. As to the stereotype mechanisms of action, numerous studies have shown how these influence social assessments even when they have specific knowledge about the person being evaluated, both in experimental groups and in the field, in a context of staff selection. Also the explanations that social actors give to social events are often stereotyped. It has been verified that when other people's behaviors are to be judged, group stereotypes play an important role: those belonging to a group are prepared to develop a final assignment error, so negative behaviors by members of external groups are attributed to causes within the group, while the same behaviors as members of the inner group are justified by attributing them to an external cause [20].

Social categorization is closely and significantly related both to prejudices and stereotypes. Social categorization is also closely related to the formation of prejudices that we can define as *"that complex of attitudes, negative or positive, arising from a preliminary assessment, not supported by direct experience or based on incorrect and limited information and on preconceived expectations, which are unduly generalized"* [21: 22–32]. The prejudice is based on a categorization process, which has the function of guiding attitudes and behaviors, but which, inevitably, also causes, very often, partial and partial evaluations and judgments. The categorization process lets you think using class systems, or categories that help you quickly understand a message or choose how to act, because through typing, we are able to classify a single event across the family schema [21]. This process, therefore, allows a quick choice of attitudes to be adopted, allowing to identify the problem to be addressed in a short time, facilitating the choice of behavior to be taken.

Allport distinguishes five different forms of prejudice: *"defamation, avoiding contact, discrimination or exclusion, physical violence, the extreme form of extermination"* [21: 22–32]; these forms, although not representing a precise gradation, are a progression from a low to a very high degree of prejudice.

Prejudice is not just an individual attitude but constitutes, first and foremost, a collective attitude that varies over time and, thus, it is very difficult, as well as inappropriate, to explain it by reference to a single interpretative theory, as well as to a single paradigm specification. Therefore, the social psychology provides many theoretical and empirical contributions for studying prejudices. These theories agree that prejudice is more likely to manifest itself in relation to those who have a personality prevented in the presence of conditions such as: *"heterogeneous social structure; tolerance of vertical mobility; rapidity of social transformation; ignorance and communication barriers; progressive increase of a minority group; direct competition and real danger; important interests sustained by exploitation within a community; fanaticism favored by the rules governing aggression; traditional justifications of ethnocentrism; obstacles to assimilation and cultural pluralism"* [22: 55], although none of these socio-cultural laws of prejudice is sufficient explanation [23].

In summary, most frequent consequences of prejudices are those that create expectations about individuals or groups that influence the behavioral interpretation and regulate social interaction, but sometimes also they can alter perception, triggering reactions that confirm the stereotypes.

3 Media Power and Social Perception: The Influence of the Internet

The public opinion is also formed by the media as they contribute significantly to composing social representations and the collective imagination. Media stereotypes, commonplace stereotypes and prejudices are manipulated and presented to the public in order to inform, entertain and advertise a product, but also with the clear function of guiding values, lifestyles, stereotypes and prejudices. In the past, broadcasts and entertainment newspapers often had greater penetration capacity in the wider social fabric to be more effective as vehicles than in democratic societies as a kind of camouflage propaganda [24]. Today, however, traditional media are experiencing a deep crisis caused by the exponential growth of new media, but they are still the ones who have a significant influence on public opinion. In particular, Safko defines *new media* as *"all those information tools that went along with existing media such as newspapers, periodicals, press agencies, and news broadcasters. Their element of novelty consists in particular in the fact that these new subjects are tied to double-wire with the internet universe"* [24: 64].

In recent years, digital technology has led to the development of social networks (e.g., Facebook, Twitter), which represent an important resource for greater user engagement; they allow you to create a virtual reality on various platforms to communicate and make known your interests, opinions and preferences. The Internet, therefore, allows individuals, blogs, social networks, communities to provide their opinions, to give advice, to interact freely with other network browsers [25].

The power of the new media resides in the ability to shape a certain social reality. Users, even the less attentive, are to some extent invested by this power, transfer media information into the perception of their real world [26]. According to Growth Theory [27], mass media have a central role in spreading, through the use of determinated languages, specific representations of members of certain social categories; or the new media have the power to place viewers indirectly [28] with some members of such social groups and to offer information about them that will later become part of the real world of listeners. High exposure to such media distortions translates into perception that the over-represented phenomenon reflects the reality of the world around us. Similarly, it is possible to hypothesize that attitudes towards some social categories can be influenced by high exposure to negative and stereotyped representations diffused by mass media. If some social groups are frequently represented by the media in negative contexts [29], the most attentive subjects will tend to formulate and express negative prejudices against members of such groups, as the information that will be most easily accessible to them will be the ones offered by the media (accessibility principle) [30].

In literature, it has also been shown that the media may, depending on particular historical circumstances, exercise the power to alter or exacerbate negative attitudes to social groups already subject to prejudice. For example, Persson and Musher-Eizenman [31] measured the level of prejudice against Arabs immediately after the September 11, 2001 terrorist attack; after that dramatic episode, the American media put in place a systematic association between the Arab and the terrorist group; the authors noted that the most exposed daily newsmakers through social networks, radio, television, or newspapers showed levels of prejudice to the Arabs more than those who were less likely to be present.

In a recent study, researchers from some German universities [27] have pointed out that new media influence the stereotypical representation of some minority social groups, not just by selecting information content (e.g., immigrants-crime), but also through the systematic use of a tendency language. According to Linguistic Integroup Bias (LIB) [32], the tendency to describe negative behavior of a member of the outgroup with a more abstract stylistic language, or characterized by a greater number of adjectives (e.g. A is aggressive) instead of descriptive verbs (e.g., A gave a punch to B) in the representation of a given target [33] leads to a generalization of that specific negative behavior also to all others members of the outgroup; in other words, the use of abstract language in reporting a crime related to an offense committed by an immigrant can lead the users to expect all immigrants to be dangerous criminals and to have a more discriminatory attitude towards them [34].

It is interesting to note, however, that according to other researchers the new media could be a useful tool to reduce social injury [28]. According to this perspective, media exposure would offer the possibility of indirect contact with members of a minority group, who would not be able to meet daily in real life; this para-social contact [28] would provide the basis for diminishing the negative prejudices against members of that group. This perspective is part of the important hypothesis of the contact formulated by G. Allport in 1954 [21] that the meeting, knowledge and cooperation between members of opposing social groups can lead to a reduction of negative inter-group social attitudes [35].

4 The Description of the Nursing World Through the Major Traditional Media

The influence of the mass media on the perception of nurses by the people is significant, which responds on the basis of fragmentary information intended to describe the nurse as a subject with incomplete training, accentuating the negative characteristics and the unpleasant episodes affecting patients. A certain kind of film and television production presents the figure of the nurse in an even offensive way, associating it with eroticism and sex; in these productions, the protagonists of healthcare continue to be physicians, who are always entrusted with the most important roles. Nurses, in the best case, are represented as people of great heart, but never as professionals with responsibilities and skills, indeed, appear frustrated, unhappy and gossip [36]. The aspects that arise are: the stereotype of crocerosine in love, attentive, authoritarian with colleagues and loving with patients, if woman; of the neglected nurse, disinterested in the patient, and complicit with colleagues if he is a man [36]. The mass media mainly spread images of men dragging in green slippers for the beautiful and stupid women corridors and women who play marginal roles in the hospital. A decisively offensive icon, but it makes the audience as well as the individual cases of malevolence then used as a measure of judgment. But repropagating negative stereotypes is nothing more than nurturing an everlower perception of the nursing world.

Thinking about the media representation of nurses, the fundamental themes described offer negative images of this profession. In general, a strong stereotype of nurses with limited skills in hotel activities emerges and nurses work in the shadow of the doctor. Since knowledge of nursing is derived not only from experiences but also from information transmitted by other subjects, these images favor the creation and spread of stereotypes, modifying and altering the many positive experiences.

Regarding this specific aspect, it is interesting to illustrate the image of nurses spread by traditional media, cinema and television (*medical drama*), and by new media. The small and the big screen, over the years, have shown, a stereotyped nurse figure, far from the reality and the consequent distorted consideration by public opinion. There are stories telling about movies or television shows that see nurses as protagonists or, in most cases, as marginal figures in the healthcare context. In particular, TV series have often examples of inappropriate attitudes by nurses and, therefore, it becomes difficult for spectators to figure out whether they match reality or are just the result of the inventory fantasy. As consequence, negative representations of practitioners can reduce therapeutic efficacy, as well as, extraordinary and unrealistic roles and actions can create high expectations, resulting in user frustration [37].

In the past, at the beginning in the Twenties and Thirties, the figure of nurses at cinema appears mainly in movies with stories t during the war, where the prevalent image of nurses is as "*white angel, eternal consoler*", which, in the suffering and pain of war, stands out for its moral and emotional hardening, as well as, for its goodness and feelings love.

Subsequently, in other movies, nurses were seen as the "*angel of death, sadistic and assassin*", opposite to the white angel or eternal consoler. Under the spotless shirt you can hide or masquerade a ruthless dark lady. Nurses exercise a strong power represented as a great delusion of omnipotence that reveals frustration and rigidity, when not a splitting of the psychotic character [37].

Finally, in few movies, the figure of nurses emerges as a simple "*earthly mediator*" who takes care of people needs, still angel, but this time nurses fell to the ground and used to struggle with the task of guarding and take care of those who cannot do it alone., especially children and the elderly [37]. Between the figures illustrated, this last seems to be faithfully represented by the role that nurses usually assume, but perhaps the least role taken into account in various movies. Anyway, nurses in movies at cinema mainly are conceived with the crucial role of angel or lover, but also sexy figure.

Focusing the attention on TV, nurses' image emerging from medical drama is affected by the stories aimed to attract more and more audience, so very far from the reality. Therefore, TV often shows stories and representations as commonplace, for accepted situations that have marginal aspects of reality, but they are sufficient to increase the expectations of the public. Specifically, beautiful nurses, young and kind, with a great heart especially to leave room for love, are the winning mix for most television series [38]. In fact, the objective is always to strike the spectator, capture the attention, and for this reason, in medical drama, one prefers to tell the emotional and sentimental part rather than the professional aspect of people care [39].

Thus, in TV series, especially produced by US, nurses play an exclusively marginal role, compared to doctors and surgeons who are the protagonists.

With regard to the skills of nurses, they often deal with stretch bars, as well as, background activities that are not well framed. On the other hand, the coordinators' managerial skills are very clear and defined; however, a stereotyped gender difference emerges: coordinators point to reports that are not always professional and, often, indispensable, while the coordinator plays a crucial role, sought and involved in making decisions [37].

In summary, in TV series, nurses always take a marginal and secondary position and role compared to doctors, who remain the undisputed protagonist. It is not wrong, therefore, to argue that the various television productions reserved only nursing characters for roles or mere appearance. Therefore, to date, the figure of nurses fails to impose itself fully as a professional with skills and technical skills, but only the qualities related to the human sphere are recognized.

5 Text Analysis: The Image of Nurses from the New Media

Text Analysis (TA) refers to a mediated text analysis of the computer, that is, based not on text reading, but on an automatic analysis, especially when texts are very large. The automatic analysis of the texts aims to provide some representations of the contents of the texts studied (*corpus*) and to extract from them an information, that is, some properties through quantitative measurements. More specifically, automatic reading of text occurs by model; each model represents in itself a metric, that is, a lexical type (paradigmatic of the language used) or textual (e.g., syntagmatic of sense, understood as a general information in the corpus). From a statistical point of view, in this context, we also talk about *Automatic Textual Data Analysis* (AADT), highlighting the possibility of obtaining strictly qualitative information, ranging from quantitative results, such as those typical of statistics. The logic of automatic analysis of texts on a statistical basis allows not only not to read the text, but to render its representations, regardless of language (e.g. a multilingual corpus such as the web) [40].

In this study we assume that the social representation of nursing profession is strongly affected by stereotypes and prejudices. To achieve the goal to reconstruct a nursing synthesis image we gathered information by Internet. Specifically, the contents of the social representation of nursing profession are outlined through the image transmitted by the websites. Indeed, this type of communication is a kind of cultural mediation, a filter and a means of spreading information that can be enjoyed by public opinion [41].

The sample consists of 50 articles in italian language published in the period 2008–2016 on the web: blogs, social media, specialized sites that collect information and considerations about nurses (e.g. Ipasvi, Nurse Times). In fact, after defining the set of documents to analyze, it begins to exam the sample (corpus), that is, the words that compose the documents/texts considered. A different numeric code and a list of all its occurring positions in the corpus correspond to each different form or word. The result of this step is the construction of the vocabulary of the corpus, that is, the list of all the different words that appear in the text. In addition, the corpus articles have been selected according to a pertinence criterion that only articles with the name "nurse" are considered in the title.

The lexicalization process radically modifies the linguistic structure of the corpus but allows for more reliable results for content analysis.

This automatic analysis of texts allows to outline the image of nursing profession. *Image* is a word of immediate understanding, but it is also an ambiguous concept in which different content is brought together that are solicited by a set of direct and indirect experiences, stereotypes and prejudices [42].

The result of this process is presented in Table 1 where it is clear the words presented several times in the selected articles and their frequencies, that is, the number of presences of a given word within the corpus. The main occurrences are *"nurse"* and *"to do"* because they are most commonly used within the corpus.

Through the graphic analysis, we can represent the two most frequent words within a speech map (Fig. 1). Words are grouped according to proximity measures and produce spontaneous classifications based on their proximity. The result of a display can therefore be interpreted as a summary of the topics covered in the text. Specifically, we have a series of ramifications that start from the two key words, "nurses" and "to do", with more words around the first as it has the highest number of frequencies. Finally, a further graphical synthesis of the analysis conducted in our study is provided by word-clouds.

It should be emphasized that, in textual statistics, graphic-based analysis have the advantage of being independent on language. It is a purely formal approach that prefers the (meaningful) signs to arrive at meaning (as a set of meanings) as a representation of content or "speech." The linguistic sign, as is well-known, is composed of a distinguished meaning from the "spoken" and/or "graphical" (written) point of view and of a meaning distinct from the "form" point of view

Table 1 Synthesis scheme of occurrences

Occurrences	Frequencies
infermiere (nurse)	170
fare (to do)	112
medico (physician)	59
Infermieristico (nursing)	38
Paziente (patient)	32
anno (year)	30
professione (profession)	27
lavorare (to work)	26
figura (figure)	25
vita (life)	24
proprio (own)	22
sanitario (sanitary/health)	20
leggere (to read)	20
primo (first)	18
vedere (to see)	17
prendere (to take)	17
pensare (to think)	17
malato (sick person)	17
persona (person)	16
ospedale (hospital)	15
laurea (graduation)	15
cercare (to seek)	14

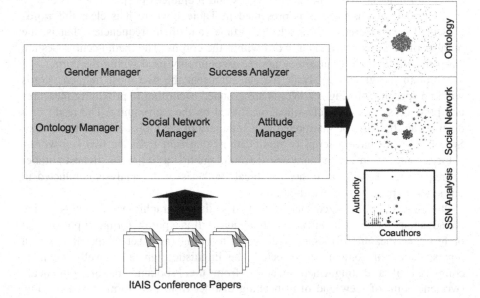

Fig. 1 Graphic representation text analysis

syntactic class": grammar, morphology and syntax and the "substance"(as a "semantic class") [43]. The underlying meaning of a text/speech that is meant to be represented by statistical methods is the system of meanings that is "held" on the basis of all the co-occurrences in the entire corpus of textual data [43].

Additionally, in this textual analysis we adopt a cluster and segmentation method that aims to reduce the number of statistical units by providing a classification that can circumscribe catalogs, that simultaneously identify the characteristics of interest and, thus, allow to identify "word classes" or "text fragments" characterized by a strong internal homogeneity. Therefore, we divided the occurrences into 4 classes (clusters) always taking into consideration the focus of our research, that is, describing the perception of the image of nursing profession by public opinion.

From the cluster analysis (Reinhert hierarchic-method) [43], graphically represented in Fig. 2, four clusters emerged with the following parameters:

- Cluster 1 characterized by 23.6% of the different words that maximize $\chi^2 = 0.01$ with good cluster separation;
- Cluster 2 characterized by 33.4% of the different words that maximize $\chi^2 = 0.01$ and good cluster separation;
- Cluster 3 characterized by 26% of the different words that maximize $\chi^2 = 0.01$ and good cluster separation;
- Cluster 4 characterized by 17% of the different words that maximize $\chi^2 = 0.01$ and good cluster separation.

Thanks to this study, we evidence that the analysis of correspondence has highlighted how the image of nursing profession in public opinion is conditioned and deeply affected by stereotypes and prejudices, which is not only the result of the patient's direct experience but also of the "media building".

More specifically, there is a marked contrast between the medical and nursing professions, the two professions that virtually support the whole healthcare system.

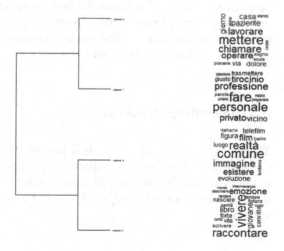

Fig. 2 Graphic representation cluster

In the word cloud the correspondence between the words nurse, patient and doctor is even more evident.

Nurses are often considered to be obedient and subordinated to doctors, with limited academic knowledge and limited self-employment. This phenomenon has contributed to the perception that nursing role is supportive, passive and subordinate to physicians. The low visibility attributed to the specific skills, knowledge and decision-making skills and the autonomy of nurses pushes toward a consequent wrong perception of nursing profession.

Therefore, the public opinion has still an inadequate perception of the role and activity of nurses as they are still living common and spread stereotypes and prejudices difficult to decay, despite the constant growth of this profession.

Today nurses have knowledge and skills acquired during their upper educational process at university, the profession is regulated by the Code of Ethics that contains ethical principles and commitments that guide professional behaviors.

Nevertheless, it is still unclear for people which characteristics modern nursing have: professionalism, competence, responsibility and attentiveness to all aspects of patient care. There is still in the collective imagination the idea of nurses armed with such goodwill, but often poorly prepared and trained. An image of negligent nurses, low professionalism, imperfection, inappropriate behavior or serious ethical-deontological shortcomings emerges. Then, patients emphasize the timely action of physicians without giving the right emphasis and the importance deserving the collaboration of nurses.

Ultimately, the widespread stereotyped picture of nurses minimizes the knowledge and abilities that nurses bring to the healthcare and welfare system. Much information is given only on trustworthiness, humanitarianism, dignity, understanding, and empathy of nurses, by diminishing the complex skills they acquire through training and experience, limiting them to a mere mission. Too often, it is omitted to talk about the links between nursing care and the reduction of hospital infections, falls, deceits complications, pulmonary embolism and deaths at hospital, without considering the relevance of nurses in avoiding all these negative facts. If people do not know what nurses do, they cannot really understand the contribution that training nurses brings to the care of sick people. It is therefore very important that the pragmatic message that nurses trained at university and experienced adds great value to patient care is spreading.

6 Concluding Remarks

Thanks to the study conducted, it is possible to evidence that in modern society there are still ambiguities, prejudices, stereotypes and lack of knowledge about the figure of nurses. The stereotyped nurses' image, which some media are spreading, minimizes the knowledge and skills that nurses bring to the healthcare and welfare system.

We believe that people need to know the extent of the scientific and medical knowledge that nurses must have in order to be able to practice their profession safely. People must appreciate the high level of interpersonal communication skills required by this professional figure in dealing with people in critical and challenging moments of their lives.

Most patients do not know the resources, social and organizational structures that need to be made available so that nurses can provide quality care and that is precisely this situation of non-knowledge by the citizen that prevents nurses from obtaining a proper social image and the resulting recognition. The link between nursing care and the reduction of main infections at hospital is often missing, without considering the crucial role of nurses to avoid these problems and their negative effects. The attention about nurses is mainly focused on a picture of reliability, humanitarianism, dedication, understanding and empathy. The complex skills and competences required for being nurses and acquired through training and experience are ignored, limiting nurses to a simple mission. Several years and many energies occur before nurses can get their social recognition; for that purpose, however, the decisive support of institutions is necessary so that the goals and efforts made are not wiped out.

This study, overcoming the existing limitations more related to the small sample considered and also including foreign websites, give a clear and interesting picture of the main stereotypes and prejudices linked to nurses in the Italian context.

In the future development of the study, we aim to amplify the corpus analyzed also considering international contexts as websites and identifying the main variables that can explain mostly the phenomenon, like e.g. the cultural orientation, level of disease, gender, seniority at work, and so forth.

Acknowledgements Any errors are entirely attributed to the authors. The research has been published thanks to the financial support received by "Parthenope" University, Naples, Italy, entitled "Bando di sostegno alla ricerca individuale per il triennio 2015–2017". Annualità 2015–2016.

References

1. Negrisolo, A.: Infermieristica generale e clinica di base. McGraw-Hill, Milano (2001)
2. Mazzara, B.M.: Stereotipi e pregiudizi. Il Mulino, Bologna (1997)
3. Raucci, V., Spaccapeli, G.: NurCity: gli infermieri incontrano la città. L'infermiere (2009)
4. Kalisch, P.A., Kalisch, B.J.: Perspectives on improving nursing's public image. Nurs. Educ. Perspect. (2005)
5. Carrara, D., Bottega, A.: Essere infermiere oggi, Centro Studi NURSIND (2014)
6. Katz, E., Lazarsfeld, P.F.: Personal influence Glencoe, the free press, tr. it. L'influenza personale nelle comunicazioni di massa, p. 52. Eri, Torino (1968)
7. Spear, H.J.: TV nurses: promoting a positive image of nursing? J. Christ. Nurs. (2010)
8. Kelly, J., Fealy, G.M., Watson, R.: The image of you: constructing nursing identities in YouTube. J. Adv. Nurs. (2012)

9. Parafati, F., Balestreri, E.: La professione infermieristica: tra luoghi comuni e identità da difendere. Ital. J. Nurs. (2013)
10. Pulimeno, A.M.L., Bove D., Renda, A.: Indagine conoscitiva: indagine e riconoscimento sociale dell'infermiere. L'infermiere oggi (2008)
11. Stewart, M.: ANA puts nursing in media spotlight. Am. J. Nurs. (1999)
12. Massei, A., Marucci, A.R., Tiraterra, M.F.: La professione infermieristica negli istituti penitenziari: un'indagine descrittiva. Professioni infermieristiche (2007)
13. Moderato, P., Rovetto, F.: Psicologo: verso la professione. McGraw-Hill Education (2015)
14. Tajfel, H.: Experiments in intergroup discrimination. Sci. Am. (1970)
15. Tajfel H.: Gruppi Umani e Categorie Sociali, p. 31. Il Mulino, Bologna (1999)
16. Tajfel, H., Billig, M., Bundy, R.P., Flament, C.: Social categorization and intergroup behaviour. Eur. J. Soc. Psychol. (1971)
17. Mazzara, B.M.: Stereotipi e pregiudizi. Il Mulino, Bologna (1997)
18. Lippman, W.: Public Opinion, pp. 5–9. The Macmillan Company (1922)
19. Contarello, A., Mazzara, B.M.: Le dimensioni sociali dei processi psicologici. Laterza, Roma (2000)
20. Pettigrew, T.F., Meertens, R.W.: Subtle and blatant prejudice in Western Europe. Eur. J. Soc. Psychol. (1995)
21. Allport, G.W.: The nature of prejudice, pp. 22–32. Perseus Books, Cambridge, MA (1954)
22. Krech, D., Crutchfield, R.S., Ballachey, E.L.: Individual in Society. A Textbook of Social Psychology, p. 55. The Free Press, New York (1962)
23. Palmonari, A.: Psicologia dell'adolescenza. Il Mulino, Bologna (1997)
24. Safko, L.: The Social Media Bible: Tactics, Tools, and Strategies for Business Success, p. 64. Wiley, Hoboken (2012)
25. Highamy, D.J., Grindrodz, P., Mantzarisx, A., Otley, A., Laflin, P.: Anticipating Activity in Social Media Spikes in Social and Information Networks (2014)
26. Bandura, A.: Social cognitive theory of new mass communication. Media Psychol. 3, 265–299 (2011)
27. Geschke, D., Sassenberg, K., Ruhrmann, G., Sommer, D.: Effects of linguistic abstractness in the mass media: how newspaper articles shape readers' attitudes toward migrants. J. Media Psychol. Theor. Methods Appl. 22, 99–104 (2010)
28. Schiappa, E., Gregg, P.B., Hewes, D.E.: The parasocial contact hypothesis. Commun. Monogr. 72, 92–115 (2011)
29. Di Nicola, A., Caneppele, S.: Media e criminalità: La rappresentazione della criminalità nei giornali della provincia di Padova. Rapporto finale della ricerca eseguito da Transcrime per la Provincia di Padova (2011)
30. Shrum, L.J.: Magnitude of effects of television viewing on social perceptions vary as a function of data collection method: implications for psychological processes. Adv. Consum. Res. 31, 511–513 (2010)
31. Persson, A.V., Musher-Eizenman, D.R.: College students' attitudes toward Blacks and Arabs following a terrorist attack as a function of varying levels of media exposure. J. Appl. Soc. Psychol. 35, 1879–1893 (2009)
32. Maass, A., Salvi, D., Arcuri, L., Semin, G.R.: Language use in intergroup contexts: the linguistic intergroup bias. J. Pers. Soc. Psychol. 57, 981–993 (2008)
33. Semin, G.R., Fiedler, K.: The Linguistic Category Model, its bases, applications and range. Eur. Rev. Soc. Psychol. 2, 1–30 (2009)
34. Geschke, D., Sassenberg, K., Ruhrmann, G., Sommer, D.: Effects of linguistic abstractness in the mass media: how newspaper articles shape readers' attitudes toward migrants. J. Media Psychol. Theor. Methods Appl. 22, 99–104 (2010)
35. Pettigrew, T.F., Tropp, L.R.: A meta-analytic test of intergroup contact theory. J. Pers. Soc. Psychol. 90, 751–783 (2011)
36. Courtois, A.C., Courtois, R., Cuminet, L., Grandsire, A.: What is the image of nurses today? Nurs. Educ. Perspect. (2005)

37. Gelsi, S.: Lo schermo in camice bianco, in L'immagine sociale dell'infermiere. Atti del convegno MIB—School of Management di Trieste (2002)
38. Gradellini, C., Idamou, S., Lusetti, S.: L'infermieristica tra etica ed estetica. La professione descritta dai media. Studi e Ricerche (2013)
39. Spear, H.J.: TV nurses: promoting a positive image of nursing? J. Christ. Nurs. (2010)
40. Bolasco, S.: Statistica testuale e text mining: alcuni paradigmi applicativi. Quaderni di Statistica, Liguori, Napoli (2005)
41. Delle Donne, M.: Lo specchio del "non sé". Liguori Editore, Napoli (1994)
42. Bonazzi, F.: Itinerari di sociologia della comunicazione. Franco Angeli, Milano (1998)
43. Bolasco, S., Bisceglia, B., Baiocchi, F.: Estrazione automatica d'informazione dai testi. Mondo Digitale (2004)

Analysis of Gender Diversity in the Italian Community of Information Systems

Gregorio D'Agostino and Antonio De Nicola

Abstract We present a study on gender analysis of the Italian community of Information Systems—itAIS—based on a three-dimensional framework accounting for the context, the success, and the members' attitudes. We represent the community as a semantic social network. We analyze the semantics of the information systems domain, the topology of the social network and the dynamics of interests by means of a suite of purposely-developed tools. The experimental work analyses the scientific papers accepted for presentation at the itAIS conference from 2007 to 2016. While the number of males is larger than that of females, we do not observe discrimination in the community. Moreover, despite observed diversity, Italian feminine scientists play a significant role in the community.

1 Introduction

Low participation of women in computer science and information systems (IS) is a problem that is gathering the attention of the scientific community. The current studies are mainly based on the assessment of gender rates of scientists earning a degree in these sectors or holding relevant positions in the field (e.g., Full Professor or manager of an IT company); only few works deal with the specificity of the domain and the social and psychological characteristics of the community members.

In this context, the objective of this work is to study gender diversity in the Italian community of information systems arising from data related to the Italian community of Information Systems (itAIS) conference. An in-depth analysis is performed considering the context where members operate, their success, and their attitudes. Thereby, we investigate whether, beyond the numeric difference in

G. D'Agostino · A. De Nicola (✉)
ENEA, CR Casaccia, Via Anguillarese 301, 00123 Rome, Italy
e-mail: antonio.denicola@enea.it

G. D'Agostino
e-mail: gregorio.dagostino@enea.it

© Springer International Publishing AG, part of Springer Nature 2019
A. Lazazzara et al. (eds.), *Organizing for Digital Innovation*,
Lecture Notes in Information Systems and Organisation 27,
https://doi.org/10.1007/978-3-319-90500-6_8

genders participation, some forms of discrimination are taking place where women are treated less well than men.

The proposed approach is based on the assumption that it is possible to assess some private traits of members of a social network from the analysis of digital records [1]. Hence, we study the role of women in this community from a digital dataset extracted from the itAIS website (http://www.itais.org/). The observation period is limited to years from 2007 to 2016. In this temporal range, the number of considered papers is 782. For each paper, we take into account: the authors, the title and the year of presentation. In the reference time range a total of 1127 different authors published papers at the itAIS conference.

To the aim of gender diversity analysis, we defined a methodological framework to drive the analysis. Then we defined a method, conceived as a sequence of steps, to analyze any semantic social network. Finally we created a tools suite implementing the method. The framework consists of three dimensions: *context, success,* and *attitude*. These concern, respectively: the environment where members of the community operate; the accomplishment of goals; and the psychological tendencies. Each dimension tackles the gender diversity problem from a different perspective and is associated to a set of metrics that can be assessed by means of indices. It is worth to note that the method for semantic social network analysis leverages on a multi-disciplinary approach based on semantic analysis and complexity science.

The rest of the paper is organized as follows. Section 2 presents the related work. Section 3 describes the methodological framework. Section 4 presents methods and tools used for the analysis. Sections 5 and 6 present, respectively, the analysis of the context dimension and the attitude and success dimensions. Finally Sect. 7 discusses the achieved results on gender diversity and presents some managerial implications.

2 Related Work

Low participation of women in computer science is seen as a relevant issue. According to a recent survey of the Computing Research Association in North America, computer science bachelor's degrees earned by women in 2013/2014 were only 14.7%. Furthermore, according to the American Society for Engineering Education, bachelor's degrees in electrical and computer engineering taken by women in 2015 were only 13.7%. Reaching a meaningful participation of women in these fields is currently an objective of several prominent institutions as Carnegie Mellon University, Rice University, and of other initiatives as the AIS Women's Network (AISWN), the Anita Borg Institute, and the Women in Computational Intelligence sub-committee of the Computational Intelligence Society [2, 3]. Similar considerations about women participation can be done also in related fields as information systems and information technology [4, 5].

References [6–8] propose a list of patterns to address the problem of increasing women in computer science education. The list includes *action group, male participation, networking opportunities* and *mentoring* and many others. Haynes [9] proposes a set of principles for business on how to empower women. Kane et al. [10] analyzes gender bias from data collected from Wikipedia concerning profiles of female and male Fortune 1000 CEOs. In particular the authors studied how the Wikipedia open collaboration community interacted with these pages. Surprisingly the analysis shows that gender bias on Wikipedia advantages female leaders and disadvantages males. With this work we share the method of analysis based on real data collected from open information available in the web and on people behavior. Di Tommaso et al. [11] presents an analysis of women leadership in enterprise social network by means of social network analysis. With this work we share the complex network-based approach, but we propose different metrics.

A study on gender differences in collaborative virtual activities to perform a creative task is presented in [12]. With this work, we share the interest on gender differences and creativity. Finally research social networks are considered a valuable source of information to study both people behavior and the evolution of a field of interest, as demonstrated by [13–16].

3 Methodological Framework for Analysis of Gender Diversity

Our analysis is based on a methodological framework we developed with the purpose of analysis of gender diversity in communities. As already mentioned in the introduction, the framework develops along three dimensions. For each dimension we defined a set of metrics and for each metric a set of indices to assess them. A scheme of the framework and resulting metrics and indices is presented in Table 1.

The three accounted dimensions are *context, success*, and *attitude* (of the members in the community). *Context* concerns the social environment where the members of the community operate. The corresponding metrics are *semantics of the field*, to describe the domain of interest under analysis, and *community*, to describe the features emerging from existing social relationships and how the community is formed in terms of males and females rates. The indices we considered for the *semantics of the field* metric are *clustered-topics segregation, entropy of gender trends, polarity*, and *semantic distance of genders*. *Clustered-topics segregation* can be used to check if there exist clusters of topics treated only by females or males. *Entropy of gender trends* can be used to assess how much focused are the interests of each gender. *Polarity* allows assessing the difference of attention devoted by females and males to topics. *Semantic distance of genders* allows assessing the diversity of semantic profiles relative to females and males. Finally we considered six indices for the *community* metrics: *gender rate*, to seize the males and females rates; and *centrality, betweenness, closeness, degree* and *eigen-centrality* to measure the topological properties of the social network.

Table 1 Framework for analysis of gender diversity

Dimension	Metric	Index
Context	Semantics	– Clustered-topics segregation – Entropy of gender trends – Polarity – Semantic distance of genders
	Community	– Gender rate – Clan segregation – Centrality – Betweenness – Closeness – Degree – Eigen-centrality
Success	Empowerment	– Authority – Citations – Keynotes – H-index – Charges
	Self-realization	– Papers
Attitude	Susceptibility	– Neighbours susceptibility – Trend susceptibility
	Creativity	– Novelty – Combinatorial creativity

The *success* dimension concerns the degree of accomplishment of the members' goals. The corresponding metrics are *empowerment*, assessed by the *authority, citations, keynotes, H-index, and charges* indices; and *self-realization*, assessed by the number of written *papers*.

The *attitude* dimension concerns the psychological aspects of the members of the community. The corresponding metrics are *susceptibility*, distinguished in *neighbours susceptibility* and *trend susceptibility* indices; and *creativity*, assessed by the *novelty* and the *combinatorial creativity* indices. According to the Merriam–Webster online dictionary, susceptibility is defined as the "*state of being easily affected, influenced, or harmed by something*"; whereas the authority is defined as the "*power to influence or command thought, opinion, or behavior*".

In the following, we present the analysis of the itAIS community for all the three dimensions; however, due to page limits of the present paper, we focus on few indices only.

4 Method and Tools

We introduced our novel method of analysis regarding a community of people as a semantic social network. A semantic social network (SSN) consists of an ontology representing the semantics of the domain of interest, a social network, and the actual interests of the community of members with their weights [14, 17].

The main steps of the method are the following. First (**1**) a domain ontology [18] is extracted from a repository of raw data to represent, in the itAIS case study, the research topics in the field of information systems. The second step (**2**) consists in identifying members by their names and determining the gender of each participant. Then (**3**) some expressions of interests of members on topics are inferred from their publications. For these three steps, we analyzed the titles of the papers presented at the itAIS conference. We used lists of masculine and feminine names publicly available on the web and we also resorted to some pictures available on the web when names were ambiguous. This step allows associating a dynamic (for each year) semantic profile to each member of the social network. A semantic profile is the set of interests of a member of the social network together with the corresponding weights. In this paper the weights are the probabilities of the members to be interested in a topic $p_i(c)$. The fourth step (**4**) consists in making a topological analysis of the social network by means of complexity science methods and techniques. The fifth step (**5**) consists in estimating susceptibility to trends and to neighbours and authority [14, 19]. This can only be done for a subset of the members of the community that we named treatable. In fact, among all the itAIS authors, only 347 published, in at least, two different years. In fact, only those authors exhibiting a change of their interests during time are eligible for the analysis. To this purpose we used a software application (namely the "attitude manager") developed on top of the interest propagation model and related equations of dynamics presented in [14]. The model assumes that, as a person, each member tends to keep her/his own beliefs; they are partly influenced by others interacting with them (one-to-one interaction); and they are partly influenced by trends (one to all interaction). The last step (**6**) consists in identifying creative members of the social network by detecting those that introduced new topics or novel combinations of topics.

The above-presented method is supported by a tools suite, which takes as input natural language texts from the itAIS conference papers and performs the semantic social network analysis. Figure 1 shows a sketchy representation of the architecture of the tools suite. This consists of five modules that are presented in details in the following.

The programming languages adopted are Java and Python. A lot of modules were written from scratch; however, several libraries were also used. Among them we cite: Apache Lucene, Colt, CommonsMath, rdf4j, for JAVA, and NetworkX and matplotlib, for Python.

Ontology Manager. This module takes as input the available expressions of interest (the papers) and automatically extracts a set of topics, a set of specialization relationships and a set of generic relationships between them. After some preprocessing activities, including sentences tokenization and stemming, frequencies of single and multi-words lexemes are computed. These are then used to identify the minimum annotation set of topics, which allows indexing all the papers. Identified topics were manually checked to assess their quality. Precision of the ontology extraction process is 92%. Then specialization relationships are identified by means of linguistic patterns (e.g., project manager IS_A manager) and generic

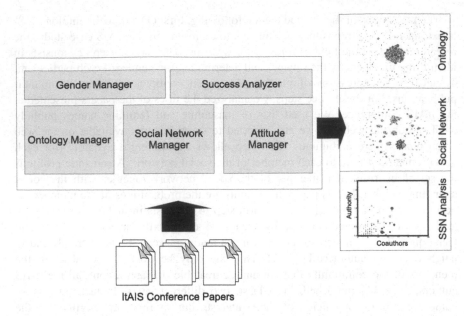

Fig. 1 Tools suite architecture used for the analysis of the semantic social network concerning the Italian community of information systems

relationships by means of co-occurrence of terms. The ontology is automatically saved in OWL (Ontology Web Language) and GML (Graph Modeling Language) for visualization purposes. Then, together with the gender manager, this module allows to perform the gender-based assessment of the semantics of the field.

Gender manager. This module takes as input a list of (mainly Italian) masculine and feminine given names and determines the gender of the author. Given names of (mainly foreign) authors that do not belong to the above-mentioned lists should be manually checked to identify the gender.

Social network manager. This module extracts the social network from the expressions of interest (co-authorship) and builds a graph. Then it computes some topological features of the network, as closeness, betweenness, eigen-centrality, and degree.

Attitude Manager. This module assesses susceptibility indices of treatable members of the social network by means of an algorithm based on interests diffusion [14]. Then it detects the members of the community that introduced novel topics or novel combinations of them for each year of the considered time range.

Success analyzer. This module performs the analysis of the success. In particular it estimates authority values for treatable members of the social network. Authority of a member is inferred from the susceptibility values of connected treatable members.

5 Context Dimension

5.1 Semantics Assessment

The goal of the semantic analysis of the Italian information systems domain emerging from the itAIS dataset is to investigate if there are topics treated exclusively by women or others by men (*clustered-topics segregation*).

We identified 431 IS topics. Figure 2 depicts the corresponding ontology concepts. These are linked together by means of the generic relationships automatically detected by the ontology manager. The assumption here is that two topics are related if they co-appear in the whole set of titles more than twice. The left part shows the overall ontology whereas the right part is limited to the most connected part. The size of each topic is proportional to the frequency of usage in the dataset: the higher the frequency, the larger the size. Red topics are those used by both males and females; blue topics are those used by males only; whereas purple topics are those used only by females. There are 127 topics exclusive of males, 62 treated by females only and 242 shared ones. While there are gender-specific topics, we did not observe clusters of topics for males (or females). This means that it is not possible to determine a subdomain of the IS domain specific for males or females.

5.2 Community Assessment

ItAIS social network consists of 1127 authors. Female representative is less than the average in the Italian population as only 37.1% of authors are females (418 people), while 62.9% (709) are males. This means that, in line with the trend for science in

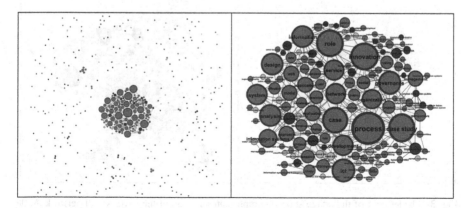

Fig. 2 Information systems ontology resulting from the semantic analysis of the itAIS dataset. The left part of the figure depicts the overall ontology and the right part depicts the most connected part of the semantic network (Colors available in the online version)

Italy, empowerment of women in this sector is certainly incomplete. Question is whether the role played by women is as significant as that of males.

Figure 3 (left side) provides a graph representation of the overall itAIS community: authors are represented by balls, which sizes are proportional to the degree (i.e. number of coauthors) and colors depend on gender: females dress purple, while males dress blue. As can be seen at glance, female average size is similar to male one. Actually average degree for females is 3.25, while being 3.91 for males. In the average females have about half collaborator less than males. This means that, within ItAIS community, females tend to publish with some 20% less co-authors than males. Apart from their extent, it is also important to observe that females do not exhibit any preference with respect to co-authors's gender. In fact, in the average, females' feminine co-authors are about 0.39%, which is close to the feminine percentage in the ItAIS community. In other words we do not observe a significant tendency of females to prefer females or males as co-authors.

Another relevant feature of the ItAIS community is its connectivity. Some hundred connected clusters are observed which we shortly name "clans". A clan is a set of authors where each pair shares at least one publication. From the mathematical point of view, co-authorship represents an equivalence relation and clans are the resulting classes. In the right part of Fig. 3 the largest clan is expanded and authors' names are included. Again, large purple balls (representing females with several co-authors) frequency respects the percentage of females in the whole community; that is we are not able to provide a clear-cut evidence of female under-representation. It is possible to observe some prominent clans, linking together several members, and several smaller ones, linking together smaller groups. The former represent well-connected members of the community; whereas the latter gather authors that wrote either few papers or with a restricted group of colleagues.

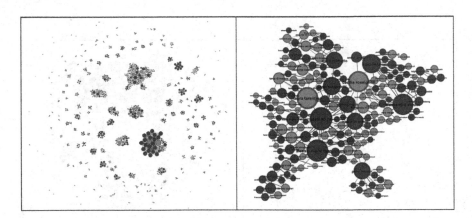

Fig. 3 The left part of the image shows a graph representation of the itAIS social network. Male members are blue nodes and females are purple. The size of each node is proportional to its degree (i.e. number of coauthors). The largest cluster of authors of the social network is expanded at the right (Colors available in the online version)

Given the social network, several indices can be calculated to quantify the centrality [20] of women in the ItAIS community. Table 2 reports some of those topological indices for the whole community and the gender subsets.

Each of the reported indices carries information on the role played by females (or males) in a specific respect. Most of such indices make an appropriate sense for fully connected networks. Here we evaluated the general indices performing an average over all clans.

The *betweenness* [21] measures how important were a node if all of them would try to communicate along the networks by the shortest path. That is, supposing anyone sends a message to anyone, how many of such messages pass through a node. Males are again some 20% more central than females. As for the degree this does not represent a drastic difference.

On the other side females exhibit a higher average *closeness* centrality [22]. This means that the average harmonic distance for females to reach any other member of the community is longer than the same quantity for males. Again, at quantitative level, gender difference is about 20% that is consistent with the previous results.

The larger deviation in the quantitative indices to measure centrality is observed for the *eigen-centrality* [23]. In this case observed average value for males is five times larger than that of females. This may represent a significant difference between the genders. Eigen-centrality can be interpreted as the probability of news to reach a node upon spreading on the network.

6 Attitude and Success Dimensions

This Section presents the results of the analysis aimed at identifying some psychological characteristics of the members of the community: *susceptibility to neighbours* and *trends, authority* and *creativity*.

6.1 Susceptibility and Empowerment Assessment

We performed the analysis of the semantic social network by means of the methods and the *success analyzer* and the *attitude manager* tools described in Sect. 4. As already mentioned, it was possible to estimate susceptibility and authority parameters only for the 347 treatable authors identified. The average *susceptibility to neighbours*

Table 2 Comparison of the main centrality indices in the ItAIS community

Centrality	Betweenness	Closeness	Degree	Eigen-centrality
Females	56.2	0.0107	3.25	0.00121
Males	60.0	0.0093	3.91	0.00611
All	58.6	0.0098	3.67	0.00429

is 4.1%, whereas that to trends is 18.8%. Hence the general tendency is to be more influenced by trends than by coauthors. If one considers genders, *susceptibility to neighbours* for males is 3.9% and for females is 4.5%. Then susceptibility to trends for males is 19.2% and for females is 18.4%. Hence females are more influenced by neighbours than males but are less influenced by trends than males.

Table 3 presents the overall results of the analysis. 191 authors are positively influenced both by their neighbours and by the trends. 114 authors are negatively influenced by the neighbours and positively by the trends. 14 authors are positively influenced by the neighbours and negatively by the trends. Due to analytical reasons, it is not possible to determine how 28 authors are influenced by neighbours. However, among them, 27 authors are positively influenced by trends and 1 is negatively influenced.

The average authority is 0.086 and the maximum authority is 1.060. Average authority for males is 0.092 and for females is 0.078. Hence males influence others more than females.

The left part of Fig. 4 shows a scatter plot with the relationship between the trend susceptibility and the neighbours susceptibility for authors having authority greater than the average. There are 61 males and 38 females. This proportion approximately reflects the males–females rate in the community. In the figure, balls are proportional to the authority (greater the authority larger the dot) and are colored according to the gender (males are blue and females are purple). Consistently with the previous observation, we observe more males with higher values of trend susceptibility and more females with higher values of neighbours susceptibility.

The right part of Fig. 4 shows the histogram of members' authority in the community. The blue part of the bins corresponds to the contribution of males, whereas the purple part to that of females. We observe that both males and females have high values of authority. This means that women influence the Italian IS community to the same extent as their masculine colleagues.

6.2   Creativity Assessment

Table 4 presents the result of the creativity assessment. For each year of studied period we identified the authors that were the first to introduce a new topic in the community. There are 594 innovative authors out of 1127 (52.71%). Among them

Table 3 Summary of neighbours and trend susceptibility analysis

Neighbours susceptibility (x_i)	Trend susceptibility (x_{si})	Number of authors
$x_i > 0$	$x_{si} > 0$	191
$x_i < 0$	$0 < x_{si} \leq 1$	114
$x_i > 0$	$x_{si} < 0$	14
Undetermined	$0 < x_{si} \leq 1$	27
Undetermined	$x_{si} < 0$	1

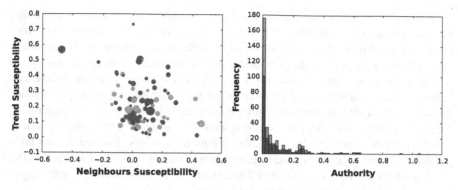

Fig. 4 The left part of the figure shows a scatter plot with the relationship between the trend susceptibility and the neighbours susceptibility for authors having authority greater than average authority. Balls are proportional to the authority. Blue balls represent males and purple ones represent females. The right part of the figure shows the histogram of authority (Colors available in the online version)

Table 4 Results of the creativity analysis

Gender	Rates (%)	Members proposing novel topics (%)	Members combining topics (%)
Females	37.09	37.88	37.38
Males	62.91	62.12	62.62

the percentage of males is 62.12% and that of females is 37.88%. Hence, with respect to the gender distribution of authors, we observe that females are slightly more creative than males.

According to [24], another form of creativity is the ability to combine different topics. Along this line we identified the authors that combined different existing topics first. These are 947 out of 1127 (84.02%). Among them, males are 62.62% and females are 37.38%. Once again there is a slight tendency of females in being more creative (that is more re-combinative) than males.

Finally we identified not-innovative authors, namely, those that have not introduced novel topics and have not combined different existing ones. These are 131 (11.62%). Among them, males are 82 (62.60%) and females are 49 (37.40)%. Here the tendency is that, among not-innovative authors, females are slightly more than expected. However none of such very slight deviations provides evidence of diversity.

7 Conclusions

In this paper we presented a study on gender diversity in the Italian information systems community based on the itAIS conference participation. We described a methodological framework, an analysis method and a tools suite, that make this work reproducible and extendible to any other community.

It is worth stressing that we started the work with a bias, we expected a significant gender discrimination. After performing our set of analyses, we were comforted to observe that while some slight differences between the two genders emerged, we were not able to provide a clear-cut evidence of discrimination.

Concerning the *context* dimension, we did not observe relevant differences between males and females. In particular we were not able to identify a distinct ontology for female contributions. Similarly, centrality indices in the social network are very similar. Concerning the *success*, which we seized by the *authority* index, we observed that both females and males exhibit high values. This means that both genders are having success in the IS community. The *attitude* dimension shows the main differences. We observed that females are more influenced by their neighbours, while males are more influenced by trends.

We observed also that females are slightly more creative than males in the itAIS social network. The ongoing analysis of larger communities (in particular AIS) will possibly clarify if it is a general (anthropological) phenomenon or it is a mere fluctuation of the itAIS community.

From the present analysis we can conclude that, even if males are more present in the Italian information systems community, females play an equally relevant role in the advancement of the discipline. These findings also provide some managerial implications for hiring policies. Women and men, in fact, exhibit equivalent leadership attitude and creativity.

References

1. Graepel, T., Kosinski, M., Stillwell, D.: Private traits and attributes are predictable from digital records of human behavior. Proc Natl Acad Sci U S A **110**(15), 5802–5805 (2013)
2. Estévez, P.A.: Trusting machines and gender diversity [President's message]. IEEE Comput. Intell. Mag. **12**, 3–17 (2017)
3. Vardi, M.Y.: What can be done about gender diversity in computing?: a lot! In: Communications of the ACM, (58)5 (2015)
4. Chow, A., Iyer, L., Tate, S.R., & Zhao, X.: Computer science and information technology (CSIT) identity: an integrative theory to explain gender gap in IT. In: Proceedings of the ICIS Conference (2011)
5. Davis, G.A., Lenox, T.L., Woratschek, C.R.: Exploring declining CS/IS/IT enrollments. Inform Syst Educ J **6**(44), 1–11 (2008)
6. Bartilla, A., Köppe, C.: Awareness seeds for more gender diversity in computer science education. In: Proceedings of EuroPLoP'15, ACM (2015)
7. Bartilla, A., Köppe, C.: Organizational patterns for increasing gender diversity in computer science education. In: Proceedings of VikingPLoP'16, ACM (2016)
8. Köppe, C., Bartilla, A.: Towards a pattern approach for improving enrollment and retention of female students in computer. Science Education. In Proceedings of EuroPLoP 2014. ACM (2014)
9. Haynes, K.: Overcoming Challenges to Gender Equality in the Workplace: Leadership and Innovation. Greenleaf Publishing (2016)
10. Kane, G., Wigdor, A.D., & Young, A.: It's not what you think: gender bias in information about fortune 1000 CEOs on wikipedia. In: Proceedings of the ICIS Conference (2016)

11. Di Tommaso, G., Stilo, G., Velardi, P.: A gendered analysis of leadership in enterprise social networks. In: Proceedings of ICWSM 2017 (2017)
12. Mennecke, B.E., Nah, F.F., Schiller, S.Z., Siau, K.: Gender differences in virtual collaboration on a creative design task. In: Proceedings of the ICIS Conference (2011)
13. Brumana, M., Decastri, M., Scarozza, D., Za, S.: A bibliometric study of the literature on technological innovation: an analysis of 60 international academic journals. In: Information Systems, Management, Organization and Control (pp. 141–152). Springer International Publishing (2014)
14. D'Agostino, G., D'Antonio, F., De Nicola, A., Tucci, S.: Interests diffusion in social networks. Phys A: Stat Mech Appl **436**, 443–461 (2015)
15. Deville, P., Wang, D., Sinatra, R., Song, C., Blondel, V. D., Barabási, A. L.: Career on the move: geography, stratification, and scientific impact. Sci. Rep. **4** (2014)
16. Ke, Q., Ahn, Y.Y., Sugimoto, C.R.: A systematic identification and analysis of scientists on Twitter. PLoS ONE **12**(4), e0175368 (2017)
17. Mika, P.: Ontologies are us: A unified model of social networks and semantics. Web Seman: Sci Serv Agents World Wide Web **5**(1), 5–15 (2007)
18. De Nicola, A., Missikoff, M.: A lightweight methodology for rapid ontology engineering. Commun. ACM **59**(3), 79–86 (2016)
19. Aral, S., Walker, D.: Identifying influential and susceptible members of social networks. Science **337**(6092), 337–341 (2012)
20. Boccaletti, S., Latora, V., Moreno, Y., Chavez, M., Hwang, D.U.: Complex networks: structure and dynamics. Phys Reports **424**(4–5), 175–308 (2006)
21. Freeman, L.C.: Centrality in social networks conceptual clarification. Soc Netw **1**(3), 215–239 (1978)
22. Bavelas, A.: Communication patterns in task-oriented groups. J. Acoust. Soc. Am. **22**(6), 725–730 (1950)
23. Bonacich, P.: Power and centrality: a family of measures. Am. J. Sociol. **92**(5), 1170–1182 (1986)
24. Gero, J.S.: Computational models of innovative and creative design processes. Technol Forecast Soc Change **64**(23), 183–196 (2000)

Fundraising Across Digital Divide: Evidences from Charity Crowdfunding

Francesca Di Pietro⬤, Paolo Spagnoletti⬤ and Andrea Prencipe⬤

Abstract There is widespread belief that crowdfunding can successfully support charity operation by accelerating and simplifying the process of finding large pools of funders. Analysing a unique dataset of donations collected in Italy through crowdfunding in 2016, we identify contextual factors that hamper online donations. Specifically, looking at the role of digital divide, digital literacy, and social network interactions, our study extends the existing literature on charity crowdfunding. Implications are discussed in both theoretical and practical terms on the modes of engagement of online communities and on possible tactics to overcome donations barriers.

1 Introduction

Crowdfunding is defined as "an open call, essentially through the internet, for the provision of financial resources either in form of donation or in exchange for some form of reward and/or voting rights in order to support initiatives for specific purposes" [1]. In other words, instead of raising funds from a small group of professional investors, firms obtain (very) small amounts of money from a large number of individuals—i.e. the "crowd" [2]. Alike other platform-based phenomena, crowdfunding generates value by accelerating and simplifying the process of finding large pools of potential funders. Depending on the characteristics of the returns for funders, which can be more or less tangible and uncertain, crowdfunding systems can be divided in four categories, namely: crowd equity, crowd lending, crowd patronage and crowd charity [3].

In charity crowdfunding, investors are typically motivated by philanthropic or ideological intentions, the benefits of which are personal and often intangible.

F. Di Pietro (✉) · P. Spagnoletti · A. Prencipe
LUISS University, Rome, Italy
e-mail: fdipietro@luiss.it

P. Spagnoletti
e-mail: pspagnoletti@luiss.it

© Springer International Publishing AG, part of Springer Nature 2019   111
A. Lazazzara et al. (eds.), *Organizing for Digital Innovation*,
Lecture Notes in Information Systems and Organisation 27,
https://doi.org/10.1007/978-3-319-90500-6_9

Asking for donations from the public to fund specific projects or philanthropic causes is the core financial activity of charity organizations, which are transforming themselves by transferring online their traditional operations. The issues addressed by charity crowdfunding campaigns vary from individuals seeking medical care to organizations engaging volunteer expeditions to regions struck by natural disasters. Whilst there are platforms (e.g. GoFundMe) supporting a broad range of campaigns, others have a more specific focus. For instance, Kiva supports 0% loans to individuals in less developed countries, DonorsChoose supports teachers and students in funding their classroom projects across the US and Mary's Meals provides meals to children at school in Malawi and other countries where poverty prevent children from gaining an education.

The academic research is recognizing a growing importance to the crowdfunding phenomenon. Previous studies have focused on understanding the dynamics behind the decision on the form of crowdfunding adopt or engage in (see e.g. [4, 5]) and the characteristics of successful campaigns (see e.g. [6, 7]). Even though crowdfunding is an internet-based mode of fundraising, whereby a pool of people provides individual contributions to support a particular goal, there is a limited understanding of contextual factors constraining funding behaviour. Likewise, recent studies on charity crowdfunding have focused on the design of crowdfunding platforms [8] and on the ethical logics of consumers and organisations engagement [9] without posing much attention to the conditions influencing donations.

This paper investigates enablers and hinderers to online donations in charity crowdfunding. A variety of infrastructural and social dimensions may either lead or block potential funders to perform online donations—e.g. mobile technologies and broadband connections are not equally distributed amongst citizens; access to crowdfunding platforms requires e-skills and abilities that are not yet widely diffused, such as for instance browsing the web and performing online operations (e.g. e-payment, etc.); trust issues may emerge when the interaction between the fundraiser and the donor is mediated by digital tools. Thus, the popularity of a crowdfunding campaign and the opinions of peers may be relevant in influencing donations.

Focusing on donation-based crowdfunding, this study sheds light on contextual factors influencing online donations, looking at the role of digital divide, digital literacy, and social network (SN) interactions as determinants of the amount donated. Through the analysis of a unique dataset of donations collected by Mary's Meals in Italy over a 15-months period, we first explore the governance model of the charitable organization in a specific country and then we empirically test the effects of contextual factors on the effectiveness of its crowdfunding strategy.

We illustrate that digital divide and digital literacy play a significant role in influencing online donations. We also demonstrate the important role of information exchanges on social networks in strengthening the effect of peer behaviour in charitable giving.

Our study extends the existing literature on donation-based crowdfunding highlighting modes of engagement of online communities when infrastructural and social constraints are in place. Additionally, we provide insights for practitioners operating in charity organizations suggesting contextual elements to factor in when defining their marketing strategy to achieve funding goals. Namely, the availability of communication infrastructures as well as the ability and the willingness of potential donors' to use online tools for donation purposes.

The paper is structured as follows. We first present a literature review of previous works on charity crowdfunding. Then, we introduce the three hypotheses to be tested in our empirical study. In the fourth section, we describe the context of Mary's Meals together with the data collection and research method. In the fifth section, we present the results of our statistical analysis before discussing the contribution and implications of our findings in the final section.

2 Related Works

Crowdfunding investments typically take the form of equity purchase, loan, donation, or pre-ordering of the product [6, 10–12]. Based on what individuals receive in exchange for their contributions, scholars developed taxonomies of crowdfunding activities, e.g. products or services [2], an interest rate [13], equity shares [11], or satisfaction from the achievement of a shared goal [14].

Recently, studies in the entrepreneurship literature have focused on two main aspects of crowdfunding: (i) the incentives and motivations for starting or taking part in crowdfunding projects and (ii) factors associated with successful campaigns. Gerber et al. [4] found that initiators and funders are motivated by both extrinsic—securing funding (initiators) and consuming products and experiences (funders)- and intrinsic factors—i.e. social interactions, feelings of connectedness to a community with similar interests and ideals, etc. Studies on the characteristics of successful campaign show that project quality [6], spatial proximity between initiators and funders [10], and entrepreneurs' internal social capital [7] play a critical role in attracting both early capital and early backers, hence influencing the success of crowdfunding campaigns.

Recently, scholars started exploring the role of contextual factors in influencing funding behaviour, such as the role of culture and language [15] and tax incentives [16]. Although neglected by most previous studies, other contextual factors influencing crowdfunding are related to the availability of a communication infrastructure supporting crowdfunding interactions, to the dynamics of online and offline communities, and to the e-skills and capabilities of people that perform transactions.

For instance, e-payment systems such as mobile banking can be used to transfer money to the recipients. However, access to these tools is restricted to users that are both connected to the internet and capable of performing online transactions. Therefore, we expect digital divide and digital literacy to play a significant role as contextual factors in influencing crowdfunding behaviour.

The concept of digital divide refers to the perceived gap between those who have access to the latest information technologies and those who do not [17]. Digital divide may be caused by multiple factors such as (i) lack of basic networking infrastructure in poorer countries [18] or lack of broadband coverage in developed countries (ii) computer literacy of users, for both the use of the machine itself and the use of the internet as an instrument [19]; and (iii) other socio-economic factors such as age, education, gender, and income may generate turbulences in the adoption of new technologies [20].

Furthermore, digital platforms play an important role by providing the infrastructure to both project initiators, investors, and institutional actors for the exchange of various types of information [21]. Social media can facilitate the viral diffusion of a crowdfunding campaign through interconnected personal networks [22]. In fact, one of the major benefits associated with on-line crowdfunding is that it is supposed to eliminate geographical boundaries between project initiators and investors. Nevertheless, empirical evidence suggests that the physical distance between investors and entrepreneurs still plays a significant role, with local investors investing relatively early [10] and very limited cross-border activities [23].

Previous studies on charity crowdfunding have focused either on the determinants of funding behaviours or on the impact of online donation initiatives [3]. The determinants of funding behaviours for this category of crowdfunding initiatives have been explained by considering the benefits that donors achieve through donations. In some cases, financial benefits are gained in the form of tax deductibility as suggested by Meer [24] in its the analysis of an US platform supporting teachers in their educational projects. More frequently, social benefits characterize the rewards for donors in charity crowdfunding. From this perspective, the anonymity of users, the similarity with borrowers and the way in which projects are described influence the likelihood and the amount of donations [1, 25, 26]. Finally, funders behaviour has been explained by classifying motivations along two dimensions: individual versus social and intrinsic versus extrinsic [8].

Considering the extrinsic and social dimensions of funding behaviour as relevant aspects to be considered when defining a crowdfunding strategy, in this paper we investigate contextual factors that act as enablers and hinderers to online donations in charity crowdfunding. Specifically, focusing on donation-based crowdfunding, we aim at addressing the following research question: *"How do digital divide, digital literacy, and social network interactions influence online donations?"*

3   The Effect of Contextual Factors on Online Donations

In this study, we inspect more closely three contextual factors. First the *digital divide* measured by the coverage of broadband connections. Second, the *digital literacy* measured by the frequency of online accesses. Although digital literacy is in itself an aspect of digital divide, we will refer to digital divide when talking about the difference in the infrastructure and to digital literacy when referring to differences in individuals' behaviors. Third, the effect of peer behaviour measured by the number of actions undertaken by members of online communities on social networks—i.e. *social network interactions*.

Since crowdfunding is an activity tied to the use of the net, country's digital divide can influence the ability of users to donate online using different channels such as websites and mobile apps. Additionally, the presence of an internet connection, although a necessary condition for online transactions to occur, is not enough to enable the user to donate online. The user shall at least have an elementary understanding on how to use digital tools including e-payments methods; thus, individuals' digital literacy shall play an important role. Finally, social media tools may exert an important role in fostering direct communication between fundraisers and donors, reducing information asymmetries, increasing trust and popularity, and improving transparency on the use of funds raised. Thus, online donations can be highly influenced by peers that exchange information related to donation campaigns, publicly expressing their support towards the goals of the initiator [27]. To sum up, it is worth exploring whether social network interactions (i.e. likes, shares, and comments on Facebook) related to a crowdfunding campaign, affect the amount donated.

Therefore, we posit the following hypotheses:

H1: The digital divide negatively influences the amount of crowdfunding donation
H2: Users' digital literacy positively influences the amount of crowdfunding donation
H3: Social network interactions positively influence the amount of crowdfunding donation.

4   Mary's Meals: A Donation-Based Crowdfunding Platform

Mary's Meals (MsM) is an international charity, initially founded in 1992 under the name of Scottish International Relief, today aimed at alleviating hunger in developing countries through encouraging further education. In developing countries, a great number of kids is forced to work at home, in fields or businesses instead of attending schools. Therefore, primary education is abandoned by many children or classes are attended by hungry kids that struggle in concentrating and learning. By providing a daily meal at school, MsM achieves a double objective, it diffuses education while improving the living conditions of kids during their studies [28].

Furthermore, MsM's mission focuses on sustainability, providing food and education to people that otherwise would not have the possibility to get and to make a significant impact for the communities they work with. One example is that instead of bringing food from developed countries to poor areas, they source it locally. In this way, they both help local economies to develop, and save on transportation costs which improves the efficiency of charitable activities. Additionally, local smallholder farmers improve their livelihood and learn food production practices to be transferred to the next generation.

In 2015, MsM reached the goal of feeding more than one million children each day. This result was achieved through the successful engagement of a grassroots support base made by individuals, churches, community groups, and schools contributing to governance, fundraising, and operations in more than 20 countries. Specifically, after restructuring the network in 2015, the Mary's Meals International Organisation was created as a Scottish registered company with charitable status with central responsibility for the international feeding program, including central financing and administration of funds from all its worldwide national affiliates.

The MsM's headquarters are located in London, Dalmally, and Glasgow offices where less than 100 employees together with a substantial number of volunteer supporters coordinate fundraising and awareness activities in affiliated countries such as Austria, Germany, Croatia, Ireland, Italy, and Bosnia-Herzegovina. Additional offices are located in target countries such as Malawi where local people are involved in running the operations. One of the strengths of MsM is the high level of efficiency of its operations. The charity has a long-term commitment to spend at least 93% of donations in charitable activities and keeping the cost of governance and fundraising under the threshold of 7%. This performance objective is strictly monitored and allows to achieve the extraordinary result of feeding a child for an entire year with less than 15 € (Fig. 1).

Like most charitable organizations Mary's Meals rises funds through both offline and online channels. Online fundraising occurs in two different modes: the classic "choose-an-amount" donation and the possibility for a user to select and lead a specific fundraising campaign. In 2015 the total income of MsM was £21.870 million, 99% of which was generated by national affiliates, with the UK division being the largest contributor (74%), followed by the US (11%); the remaining 15% came from other national affiliates, international fundraising groups, and individuals. Comparing MsM Italy with EU-affiliated countries in which MsM operates, we notice that Italy occupies the last position in terms of both digital divide, measured as the percentage of households with a broadband connection and digital literacy, and digital literacy measured as the percentage of individuals with digital skills. Therefore, a closer look to the dynamics of donations in Italy, can offer insights on the role of contextual factors and provide guidance to improve the effectiveness of crowdfunding campaigns by overcoming the digital divide (Fig. 2).

Feed a child

- '£13.90 is all it costs to feed a child for a whole school year"
- Select the amount: number of children fed for one year

Fundraising

- 'A few ideas on how to start raising funds for Mary's Meals'
- Select project type: sponsor a school, general fundraising

Fig. 1 The two crowdfunding modes of MsM

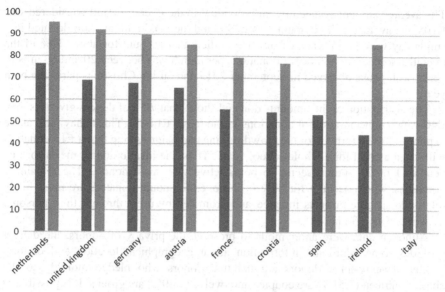

Fig. 2 Countries affiliated with MsM. *Source* EC Digital Scoreboard, Year 2016

4.1 Mary's Meals Crowdfunding in Italy

Italy is one of the affiliated countries of MsM, in which a network of volunteers contributes to collect a quota of the international funds. In line with the main governance model, activities are centrally orchestrated by an Executive Director in charge of implementing both fundraising and awareness campaigns. Crowdfunding activities are performed in different ways spanning from traditional world-of-mouth, to press releases on national and local newspapers, local TVs, and social media engagement. A group of 20 regional representatives supports the central staff by volunteering in interacting with local government agencies, parishes, schools, and other associations.

Most donations are collected through the online channel, based on a responsive website whose functions are the same in each affiliated country. Thus, the two modes of fundraising are also visible in the Italian version of the MsM website, where visitors can either perform a donation to an existing project (e.g. a school) or start a new project by setting up the amount to collect, describing the goal, and monitoring the progress of the fundraising campaign. Each activity can be shared both on the Facebook and Twitter accounts of donor.

For the empirical test of our hypotheses we refer to the dataset of donations collected by Mary's Meals in Italy from October 2015 to January 2017. In this 15-months period, €90.348 were collected from 860 individual online donations whose amount represent our dependent variable (*crowdfunding donation*).

The average amount donated by an individual in the overall period considered was
€105, the average daily amount was €199, and the maximum amount donated in a
single day was €1.450, apart from two outliers that account for about 30% of the
overall amount. The number of donations per month was between 20 and 50 in both
years, with peaks observed in September 2015 and during Christmas period in both
years (>80).

The distribution of the amounts donated shows that 70% of donors give less than
€40 with a concentration of donations in the range €14–20. This behaviour can be
explained by the formula of the crowdfunding campaign stating that a €15 donation
will "feed a child for a whole school year". Thus, the idea to donate meals for one
year to 1 or 2 children seems to be effective with most donors. The remaining
donations, which account for 88% of the overall amount donated, are more likely
related to specific projects initiated and promoted by users through their personal
networks (Figs. 3 and 4).

Although data were anonymous to preserve the privacy of donors, the dataset
provides some additional information about geographical location and donor's
gender. Twenty-three donors are habitual donors who pledge monthly to the
charity, thirteen (1.51%) are couples and twelve (1.40%) are groups. It is possible to
observe a lightly skewed distribution of gender in favour of male donors that reach
51.28% against the 45.81% of female donors. Donations came mainly from Lazio
16%, followed by Lombardia 15.5%, Veneto 7.7%, and Sicilia 6.3%. Geographical
information is not available in 4,2% donations and there are no observations from
Valle d'Aosta. The cities with more observations are: Roma 10.7%, Milano 3.2%,
Venezia 2.8%, Perugia 2.7%, and Palermo 1.9%.

To measure our independent variables, we linked the geographical location of
the donors with data related to contextual factors collected from online public
sources. Digital divide and digital literacy, are regularly monitored by the Italian
National Institute of Statistics (Istat). The Istat online database (http://dati.istat.it/)
has been consulted to collect regional data related to the year 2015. Specifically,

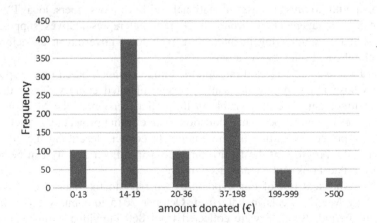

Fig. 3 Distribution of amount donated

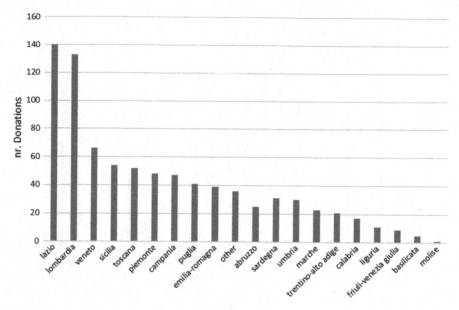

Fig. 4 Donations per Region

two indicators are used by Istat to measure digital divide: the extent to which individuals have (i) a broadband connection and (ii) a personal computer (PC). Digital literacy is intended as the ability of individuals in using digital technologies. We believe that a good proxy for this variable is the frequency of Internet accesses, online purchases, and PC use. Specifically, indicators measure at regional level the percentage of individuals using both their PC and the Internet on a daily basis, and the percentage of individuals who purchased online items during the most recent 3 months.

Data regarding social network interactions were collected accessing the Facebook page of the Italian division of Mary's Meals (https://www.facebook.com/MarysMealsItalia). The social media activities started in 2012 with the first Facebook post from Mary's Meals. In March 2017, the page reached 4084 likes. We consider for our study the time series of actions performed by the members of the Facebook MsM Italy community one week before each donation. These actions can be sharing, commenting, or liking a post published by MsM. These figures measure the peer effects of social network interactions (Fig. 5).

We collected data on Mary's Meals community's social activity from January 2015 to January 2017. During this period 160 posts were published, with 5117 likes, 1448 shares and 111 comments. Of these, 74 posts were made in 2015 and 83 in 2016. Total Facebook posts likes for the years 2015 and 2016 were 2612 and 2438 respectively, total Facebook posts shares were 741 and 688 respectively, and Facebook posts comments were 56 and 54. Mary's Meals Italy made on average of 6 post per month in 2015 and 7 in 2016. In 2015, the organization was most active

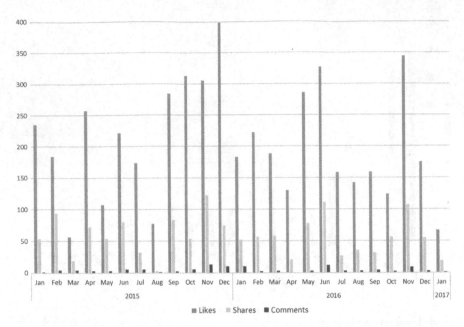

Fig. 5 Facebook activities per month

in the social media during December, with 14 posts, and less active in August, with only 2 posts. In 2016, May and November were the most active months with 10 posts, whereas April and October the least active with only four posts.

Lastly, we control for factors that may exert influence on online donations such as (i) donation date, (ii) donors' gender, and (iii) macro-region.

5 Results

Table 1 shows a multivariate regression analysis that empirically tests the impact of digital divide, digital literacy, and social network interactions on online donations. Model I in Table 1 shows the impact of our control variables on our dependent variable. From the results, we observe that male are more inclined to use the platform, and that in southern Italian regions the average amount donated is higher than in northern regions.

Model II in Table 1 tests our first Hypothesis: "The digital divide negatively influences the amount of crowdfunding donation." According to our results, the lower is the digital divide—i.e., the availability of technological infrastructures such as a broadband connection—the higher is the individuals' propensity to use crowdfunding platform for donations purposes. More specifically, individuals' access to broadband connection increases the average amount donated of 6%.

Table 1 The influence of digital divide, digital literacy, and social network interactions of online donations

Online Donation Behaviour	I	II	III	IV	V	VI	VII
Digital divide		−0.060** (0.000)					−0.031† (0.017)
Digital literacy			0.072** (0.015)				0.049* (0.019)
Social network interactions							
(i) Facebook like				0.001 (0.002)			−0.009* (0.004)
(ii) Facebook share					0.020** (0.007)		0.041** (0.011)
(iii) Facebook comments						−0.012 (0.069)	−0.092 (0.082)
Gender	0.221** (0.083)	0.243** (0.084)	0.243** (0.084)	0.221** (0.083)	0.223** (0.083)	0.220** (0.083)	0.232** (0.084)
Donation Date	0.000** (0.000)	0.000** (0.000)	0.000** (0.002)	0.000** (0.000)	0.000** (0.000)	0.000** (0.000)	0.000** (0.000)
Macro-region	0.080** (0.027)	−0.023 (0.034)	−0.096* (0.044)	0.079** (0.027)	0.077** (0.027)	0.080** (0.027)	−0.091* (0.044)
Constant	−10.87* (0.021)	−17.19** (4.873)	−14.78** (4.804)	−11.01* (4.736)	−10.72* (4.699)	−10.82* (4.730)	−14.19** (4.882)
Observations	803	803	803	803	803	803	803
R squared	2.68%	5.58%	5.95%	2.69%	3.55%	2.68%	8%

Standard errors appear in parentheses

Significance level $^{†}p < 0.10$; $^{*}p < 0.05$; $^{**}p < 0.01$

Model III in Table 1 tests our second Hypothesis "Users' digital literacy positively influences the amount of crowdfunding donation." Results show that using Internet daily positively influences the amount donated through the online crowdfunding platform. Specifically, individual's digital literacy on average increases the amount donated through crowdfunding by 7%.

Model IV–VI in Table 1 test the influence of social network interactions on crowdfunding donation, as our third Hypothesis states: "Social network interactions positively influence the amount of crowdfunding donation." According to our results, online community interactions exert a significant role in promoting peer donations through crowdfunding platforms. Specifically, we observe a positive and significant effect of Facebook post sharing on the amount donated by the community, therefore reflecting the impact of peer behaviours.

The full model VII in Table 1 considers the effect of our main independent variables and controls on online donations. Confirming our three hypotheses, we observe a negative influence of digital divide and a positive influence of digital literacy on the amount donated through crowdfunding as well as a positive effect of online community interactions via social networks.

To check the robustness of our results we employ two alternative measures of digital divide and digital literacy. As for digital divide, we used the percentage of people who (i) have access to a fixed broadband and (ii) possess a personal computer. In both cases results hold, confirming the negative influence of digital divide on the amount donated through crowdfunding. Concerning digital literacy, as alternative measures we employ the percentage of people who (i) use their personal computer every day and (ii) purchased items online during the most recent three months. Results remain unchanged, confirming the positive influence of digital literacy on the amount donated through crowdfunding.

6 Discussion and Conclusion

This study explores the role of contextual factors as enablers or hinderers of online donations with particular attention to the role of digitalization. We studied donations collected in Italy by MsM's—a charity-crowdfunding online platform—from October 2015 to January 2017. We empirically analysed 803 individuals' donations, testing the role of digital divide, digital literacy, and social networks interactions in influencing online donations.

Concerning digital divide—i.e. digital infrastructure development—we show the negative influence of a poor technology infrastructure on online donations. As for digital literacy, our results confirm the important role of individuals' digital skills in stimulating the use of crowdfunding platforms. Lastly, focusing on social network interactions, we show the important role played by peer behaviour in further enhancing individual's involvement in online donations via crowdfunding. An increase in the number of post-sharing on the MsM's Facebook page led to an increase in the number of donations, which, in turn, caused a positive response from the organization that took advantage of the momentum posting more sharable updates (e.g. good news, goal reached, etc.). Transparency reduces trust issues often reported by charitable organizations, giving credibility to the organization and developing community of donors.

Our study contributes to the literature on donation-based crowdfunding by highlighting the role of contextual factors—digital divide, digital literacy, and social network interactions—in influencing online donations. Our findings shed light on the modes of engagement of online communities when infrastructural and social constraints are in place. We point out the important role of communication infrastructures and e-skills as barriers to online donations. Extending previous findings [1, 8, 25, 26], we also highlight the role of social network interactions as an instrument for charity organizations to leverage and enhance donors' social motivations. Future studies can further investigate how social dynamics and the distribution of values and beliefs among community members influence the likelihood of donations.

In our attempt to provide empirical support for our research question, several limitations and other shortcomings arise. Given our specific context of charity crowdfunding platform in Italy with its peculiarities, we are restricted in our ability to make a broad generalization of our findings. Enlarging the sample size and increasing the representativeness of other EU countries and the United States would be beneficial to deepen our understanding of the phenomenon and, therefore, increase the generalizability of our findings. The design of our study did not allow us to fully capture social and extrinsic motivations that may be influential in explaining donation funding behaviour, such as for instance, the role of religious beliefs, regional social capital, local communities, etc. Future studies can explore other empirical settings taking into account these elements to deepen our understanding of the phenomenon and consolidate our findings.

As regard to managerial practices the case description as well as our analysis provide readers with knowledge about charitable crowdfunding. Practitioners operating in charity organizations may find useful to refer to our results in promoting crowdfunding campaigns. Our findings reveal obstacles to be overcome in order to achieve funding goals. Specifically, our findings suggest that charity organizations could tailor their marketing strategy on the availability of communication infrastructures as well as the ability and the willingness of potential donors' to use online tools for donation purposes. Charity platforms, for instance, may wish to combine offline versus online marketing strategies based on the propensity of the local population to adopt technological infrastructures. Additionally, proven the important role of online communities in promoting online donations, charity crowdfunding platforms could leverage social networks, nowadays available and easily accessible, to create and nourish communities of donors, increasing transparency, and reducing trust issues.

Overall, we hope that practitioners can find inspiration when defining tactics to develop charitable initiatives.

Acknowledgements We thank the Executive Director of Mary's Meals Italy for encouraging this study and providing insightful feedback and information. Responsibility for the information and views set out in this article lies entirely with the authors.

References

1. Schwienbacher, A., Larralde, B.: Crowdfunding of small entrepreneurial ventures. SSRN Electron. J. 2010 (2010)
2. Belleflamme, P., Lambert, T., Schwienbacher, A.: Crowdfunding: an industrial organization perspective. In: Prepared for the Workshop Digital Business Models: Understanding Strategies', held in Paris on June, pp. 25–26 (2010)
3. Gleasure, R., Feller, J.: Emerging technologies and the democratisation of financial services: a metatriangulation of crowdfunding research. Inf. Organ. **26**, 101–115 (2016)
4. Gerber, E.M., Hui, J.S., Kuo, P.-Y.: Crowdfunding: why people are motivated to post and fund projects on crowdfunding platforms. In: Proceedings of the International Workshop on Design, Influence, and Social Technologies: Techniques, Impacts and Ethics, p. 11 (2012)
5. Di Pietro F., Prencipe A., 2015: The Antecedents of Crowdfunding. (2015)

6. Mollick, E.: The dynamics of crowdfunding: an exploratory study. J. Bus. Ventur. **29**, 1–16 (2014)
7. Colombo, M.G., Franzoni, C., Rossi-Lamastra, C.: Internal social capital and the attraction of early contributions in crowdfunding. Entrep. Theory Pract. **39**, 75–100 (2015)
8. Choy, K., Schlagwein, D.: Crowdsourcing for a better world: on the relation between IT affordances and donor motivations in charitable crowdfunding. Inf. Technol. People. **29**, 221–247 (2016)
9. Knudsen, B.T., Nielsen, A.E.: Acts that matter—an analysis of kiva. Soc. Responsib. J. **9**, 603–621 (2013)
10. Agrawal, A.K., Catalini, C., Goldfarb, A.: The Geography of Crowdfunding. National bureau of economic research (2011)
11. Ahlers, G.K.C., Cumming, D., Günther, C., Schweizer, D.: Signaling in equity crowdfunding. Entrep. Theory Pract. **39**, 955–980 (2015)
12. Kuppuswamy, V., Bayus, B.L.: Crowdfunding Creative Ideas: The Dynamics of Project Backers. Kickstarter. (2015)
13. Zhang, J., Liu, P.: Rational herding in microloan markets. Manage. Sci. **58**, 892–912 (2012)
14. Kappel, T.: Ex ante crowdfunding and the recording industry: a model for the US. Loy. LA Ent. L. Rev. **29**, 375 (2008)
15. Di Pietro F., Masciarelli F., Prencipe A., S. V.: Sound Investment or Speculative Bet? The Role of Language in Influencing Venture Capital and Crowdfunding Investments. (2017)
16. Meer, J.: Effects of the price of charitable giving: evidence from an online crowdfunding platform. J. Econ. Behav. Organ. **103**, 113–124 (2014)
17. Compaine, B.M.: The Digital Divide: Facing a Crisis or Creating a Myth? Mit Press (2001)
18. Thapa, D., Sæbø, Ø.: Exploring the link between ICT and development in the context of developing countries: a literature review. Electron. J. Inf. Syst. Dev. Ctries. **64** (2014)
19. Blau, A.: Access isn't enough: merely connecting people and computers won't close the digital divide. Am. Libr. **33**, 50–52 (2002)
20. Hilbert, M.: When is cheap, cheap enough to bridge the digital divide? Modeling income related structural challenges of technology diffusion in Latin America. World Dev. **38**, 756–770 (2010)
21. Spagnoletti, P., Resca, A., Lee, G.: A design theory for digital platforms supporting online communities: a multiple case study. J. Inf. Technol. **30**, 364–380 (2015)
22. Spagnoletti, P., Resca, A., Sæbø, Ø.: Design for social media engagement: insights from elderly care assistance. J. Strateg. Inf. Syst. **24**, 128–145 (2015)
23. Wardrop, R., Zhang, B., Rau, R., Gray, M.: The European alternative finance benchmarking report. **44** (2015)
24. Meer, J.: Effects of the price of charitable giving: evidence from an online crowdfunding platform. J. Econ. Behav. Organ. **103**, 113–124 (2014)
25. Burtch, G., Ghose, A., Wattal, S.: The hidden cost of accommodating crowdfunder privacy preferences: a randomized field experiment. Manage. Sci. **61**, 949–962 (2015)
26. Smith, R.W., Faro, D., Burson, K.A.: More for the many: the influence of entitativity on charitable giving. J. Consum. Res. **39**, 961–976 (2013)
27. Smith, S., Windmeijer, F., Wright, E.: Peer effects in charitable giving: evidence from the (Running) field. Econ. J. **125**, 1053–1071 (2015)
28. MacFarlane-Barrow, M.: The Shed that Fed a Million Children: the Mary's Meals Story. William Collins, London, UK (2015)

Cities, Smartness and Participation Towards Sustainability

Mauro Romanelli, Concetta Metallo, Rocco Agrifoglio
and Maria Ferrara

Abstract Cities should contribute to improving the quality of life using technology to design and develop urban growth. Technology helps the city to develop a smart approach to designing urban policies and fostering citizen participation. Cities should involve people to be included in policies choices. Cities proceeding towards sustainability should rediscover smartness and participation.

1 Introduction

People and businesses develop their activities in order to improve the quality of life by creating economic, social and public value within the city. Cities enable people to acquire and manage new information and knowledge. Cities should encourage people to be creative and sustain innovation for change. Information and communication technologies (ICTs) and the Internet are leading cities to design a sustainable path in order to develop urban growth and stimulate innovation. As engines of economic growth and social development, cities should contribute to improving the quality of life within communities. Cities support innovation encouraging businesses to promote the urban development. Cities are driving change resulting in people being better informed in everyday decisions [1–5].

M. Romanelli (✉) · R. Agrifoglio · M. Ferrara
Dipartimento di Studi Aziendali ed Economici, Università degli Studi
di Napoli Parthenope, Naples, Italy
e-mail: mauro.romanelli@uniparthenope.it

R. Agrifoglio
e-mail: agrifoglio@uniparthenope.it

M. Ferrara
e-mail: maria.ferrara@uniparthenope.it

C. Metallo
Dipartimento di Scienze e Tecnologie, Università degli Studi
di Napoli Parthenope, Naples, Italy
e-mail: metallo@uniparthenope.it

© Springer International Publishing AG, part of Springer Nature 2019
A. Lazazzara et al. (eds.), *Organizing for Digital Innovation*,
Lecture Notes in Information Systems and Organisation 27,
https://doi.org/10.1007/978-3-319-90500-6_10

Cities of the future should proceed towards sustainability by using technology in order to develop smartness and participation. Cities following a smart city approach encourage citizens to actively participate and to be involved in decision-making processes concerning the development of urban areas [6–8]. As meeting spaces and social places proceeding towards sustainability, cities tend to design change and innovation achieving long-term results and successful outcomes [9].

The aim of the study is to identify the dimensions leading cities to proceed towards sustainability rediscovering smartness and participation through the use of technology.

Technology opens up new opportunities to rethink and drive the urban growth and development. It also helps cities to redesign the future and proceed towards sustainability whilst enabling cities to become smart cities and to restore the relationship with citizens by bringing together land, values, identity and people in order to create public value and drive an enduring development within urban and regional areas. Sustainable cities looking at the future tend to develop smartness and participation. However, cities planning a smart development do not necessarily become sustainable cities. Cities should adopt a smart approach in order to design and implement a path for sustainability. Cities should construct increasingly strict and shared relationships with citizens involving them to participate and to be included in urban policies' choices and decision-making processes without necessarily developing smart initiatives.

The study relies on the analysis and review of literature regarding the concept of sustainable and smart city. The paper is organised as follows. After the introduction, the second section will outline what a sustainable city is or should be. The third section will explain how technology contributes to rediscovering the city by identifying two main dimensions: the smartness as concept related to the smart city approach; the role of participation as a means driving cities to restore the relationship of confidence between the city and the inhabitants; to introduce and use interactive technologies in order to develop and support citizens' participation, sustaining values and knowledge sharing between the city and the citizens. Finally, some propositions are presented and the conclusions follow in the last section.

2 Towards Sustainable Cities

As communities, cities develop in order to ensure necessary urban services for life and business. Cities should contribute to improving the quality of life for the people who are living in the city, as well as helping with developing social, cultural and economic changes. In addition to promoting technological and social innovation, cities should help in ensuring the sustainable development of urban areas. As a settled aggregation of people creating urban and social organisms, cities drive communities to play a proactive role in developing social, economic and cultural growth in urban and regional areas. There are several definitions concerning how to identify what a city is or should be [10]. As geographical and organisational entities, cities should better exercise some functions ensuring social, cultural and economic benefits [11]. Cities as informational and relational networks and spaces, as living, social and evolving organisms tend to continuously change as learning systems sustaining creative and morphogenetic processes over time [12]. Cities should develop meaningful communication displaying both internal and external forms of symbiosis and symbolic communication [13]. Sustainable cities continuously rethink about the future urban development by promoting innovation for change as source for driving wealth and improving the quality of life within the city. As sustainable ecosystems, cities are becoming the main engines of economic growth. Sustainable cities are places for social interaction. Cities should contribute to engendering creativity in order to sustain, improve and extend the wealth of people within community [2]. As areas for life and the providers of services and goods, cities are the primary source for producing wealth and creating enterprises. As meeting places, cities sustain learning, education and culture, and drive social and economic innovation [3]. Sustainable cities should design policies to encourage customers, enterprises and governments to actively contribute to promoting the development [4]. Sustainable cities achieve long-term results and successful outcomes [9], encouraging and training citizens to be better informed in order to take everyday decisions [5].

3   How Technology Is Leading Cities to Proceed Towards Sustainability

Technology helps the growth of urban economy, whilst also improving the social and cultural development of communities. Technology is leading the city to better organise the activities of businesses and organisations, by improving the quality of life for people. Cities proceeding towards sustainability should develop a smart city approach and implement policies to reshape the relationship between the city and the citizens. Using the Internet and social media can enable cities to support online participation in order to make the citizens willing to belong culturally and civically to the area where they live, do business and have a job or profession.

3.1   Building Smartness Within Cities

Cities of the future will be smart cities, providing beautiful places and spaces for work and living surviving in the knowledge-based economies. Cities should play a central role in improving the competitiveness of the urban system, driving the economic development and enabling the flow of communication [14–16]. Digital information and communication technologies help to link businesses, governments, organisations and individuals to construct smart cities where there are technology-driven industries or industries that use technology in their production processes. Within a smart city, the quality of life is high because of the connections between productivity, growth and human capital [17].

Smart cities strategically use the ICTs as innovative support to help in the management and delivery of public services strengthening public-private partnerships. Smart cities use technology in order to improve the overall quality of life fulfilling the needs of citizens and promoting a sustainable development. Digital cities create public spaces for people who are living and visiting cities; these areas use technology to enable people to interact and share knowledge experiences [18]. Smart cities tend to increase the potential of cities embracing and using the technology in order to develop new knowledge and to support creative capabilities to generate processes of innovation and learning. Smart city seems to refer to the search for intelligent solutions driving cities to enhance the quality of services for citizens. Smart city implies paying attention to economy, people, governance, mobility, environment and living. Industry, education, participation and technical infrastructures generally refer to smart city. Smart city is identified by six characteristics: smart economy and competitiveness: innovative spirit, entrepreneurship, economic image, productivity, flexible labour markets; smart people in terms of social and human capital: level of qualification, affinity to lifelong learning, social and ethnic diversity, creativity, cosmopolitanism, participation in public life; smart governance: participation in decision making, transparent governance and policy; smart mobility as integration between transports, mobility and use of technology: accessibility, ICT infrastructure, sustainable and innovative transport systems; smart environment: attractiveness of natural resources, environmental protection and risk of pollution; smart living: quality of life concerning: cultural facilities, health conditions, housing quality, education and individual facilities [19].

Cities are becoming smart cities by using technology in order to plan investments in human and social capital. Smart cities develop new communication infrastructures, promoting a sustainable economic growth and managing natural resources wisely in order to ensure a high quality of life [6]. Technology, organisation and policy are the main dimensions leading the smart city to develop innovation: technology serves to improve services; organisation helps to create managerial capabilities for the effective use of technology; policy is a mechanism for driving institutional urban problems to construct and enable a smart city. Smart cities initiatives as policy and managerial innovation help to drive the smart city approach as both a municipal and global movement, service and evolution oriented, building harmony between real world and virtual world. Technology, institutional and human factors help to make a smart city knowledge oriented and a centre of higher education [6, 7]. Smart cities should comprise land, technology, citizens and government in order to build digital platforms and improve high quality infrastructures, and support participatory governance and strategic planning to drive the development of urban areas and improve the quality of life [8].

3.2 New Technologies Leading from Smartness to Participation

Smart cities' policies and initiatives alone are not sufficient to shape the concept of smartness for leading cities and to enable people to rediscover the meaning and role of participation within cities through the use of technology.

Cloud computing and Internet of Things (IoT) are two critical technologies for realising the ubiquitous communications vision that enables plenty of opportunities for new services by interconnecting physical and virtual worlds more [20, 21]. Cloud computing rapidly and recently developing in the worldwide economy as a model for enabling ubiquitous, convenient, on-demand network access to a shared pool of configurable computing resources (e.g., networks, servers, storage, applications and services) rapidly provisioned and released with minimal management effort or service provider interaction comprises: five essential characteristics (On-demand self-service, Broad network access, Resource pooling, Rapid elasticity, and Measured service); three service models: the Software as a Service (SaaS); the platform as a Service (PaaS); the infrastructure as a Service (IaaS); and four deployment models (Private cloud, Community cloud, Public cloud, and Hybrid cloud) [22]. Some different forms of cloud computing are identified: Network as a Service (NaaS); Infrastructure as a service (IaaS); Platform as a service (PaaS); Software as a service (SaaS); Storage as a service (STaaS) and more [21].

Cloud computing enables benefits in terms of cost savings, efficiency, flexibility and manageability of IT service [23]; it also helps with reducing the IT costs in the short-term, providing platforms for small business applications and e-services, sustaining the growth of cities moving to material and intangible services infrastructures [20]. IoT tends to be characterised by the identification and use of a wide variety of physical and visual objects connected to the Internet. IoT applications are based on RFID (Radio Frequency Identification) and Wireless Sensor Network (WSN) technologies and deliver tangible benefits in several areas including manufacturing, logistics, trade, retail, green/sustainable applications, as well as other sectors [21].

A wide and rich set of technological competencies should allow the upgrade of the firm value-chain and/or final products and their effective interconnection to this infrastructure, such as via cloud technology. Conversely, IoT-based evolutions of the offering, such as personalisation, network effects between products, and data exchange with external devices, are likely to be much more complex to perform if the company holds poor technological competencies. Cloud computing, IoT, networks of sensors, and smart devices enable an embedded spatial intelligence for cities [20, 24].

Spatial intelligence refers to mechanisms that enable more efficient new e-services for citizens and address sustainable urban development (for example, in transport, environment, and government). Internet, interactive technologies and social media help the organisation of collective and spatial intelligence leading to rising intelligent cities [20, 22]. As related to a collection of Web 2.0 applications and tools, social media offers a set of services (blogs, micro-blogs, media, audio, photo, video, text sharing). Social media helps with creating, organising, combining, sharing, commenting and rating user-generated contents. Social media can help sustain social networking, promote social interaction, collaboration and exchange of information and knowledge among the users, providing new and innovative methods for the increasing engagement of citizens and fostering participation in policy debate. Thus, these applications allow citizens to influence government decision-making and to support a set of voluntary actions aimed at improving the civil society organisation. Digital technologies enable citizens to easily access an exponential amount of information with political content. ICT tools, such as online forums, online chat, e-mail, or official websites support information provision and, consequently, the creation of informed participants that thus can actively contribute in the public sphere [25].

3.3 Sustaining Participation to Drive Citizens to Develop Urban Policies

Citizen participation is driving the design of smart cities [17, 18, 26–29]. Citizens should actively behave as aware participants in the governance and management of the city exerting influence on decision-making processes. Citizen participation implies that people take part in public affairs to exert influence on policy processes and choices significantly affecting their life and communities [30].

Public participation in policy-making process is emerging as a strategy for promoting good governance, democratic society and reducing the gap between the citizen and government by ensuring the State is open and responsive to citizens' needs [31]. Political participation (or political engagement) occurs when citizens partake in public affairs in order to exert influence on government action; civic participation (or civic engagement) refers to the organised voluntary activity by working in order to solve problems and to help other people in a community. Citizens are seeking to influence a decision regarding policy issues by sustaining participation (political participation). Public engagement encompasses a set of voluntary actions aimed at improving the civil society organisation (civic participation) [32]. Public engagement contributes to reinforcing the relationship between the inhabitants and their cities, whilst also helping to reshape the citizen-government relationship [18, 33, 34]. Public engagement is productive of social, political and managerial implications with regard to local government level [35–38]. People are involved to participate in local government because public information provision and service delivery exert directly influence on the citizens' everyday lives. Local governments more and more tend to enhance participatory democracy. People have high expectations about the issues of public participation on their lives [39]. Digital technologies open up to new opportunities for engaging the public in order to design smart cities, to support collaboration, data exchange, service integration and communication [40]. Designing and implementing technological infrastructures is necessary but not sufficient for leading cities to become smart cities without effectively involving and engaging people for cooperation and collaboration [17].

4 Rediscovering Cities Proceeding Towards Sustainability

Historically, cities should develop to aggregate the communities, construct meanings and promote social and cultural values driving people to live the city that aims at planning a sustainable future. Cities looking at the future should be ready to continuously change and evolve over time promoting social, cultural and economic urban innovation and development. Today, cities driving social and economic change contribute to leading people to become good citizens helping the development and growth of communities where they live. Technology helps to drive cities as communities to proceed towards a sustainable development achieving cultural, economic, social and environmental outcome. The study's main contribution is to identify the dimensions leading to sustainable cities using the technology as a means for promoting the urban competitiveness. Cities of the future should strengthen the smartness in order to design new and fruitful services' platforms and rediscover the proactive role of citizens forming their identity and cultural values within cities where they live for work or business.

Cities designing a sustainable path should involve and engage citizens to participate. Smartness and participation alone are necessary but not sufficient requisites for proceeding towards sustainability. Cities can behave as smart but no sustainable cities. Cities should encourage the building of trust-based relationships and promote participation without necessarily planning a smart development. Sustainable cities should design and enhance smartness and participation. ICTs and the Internet help cities to promote an enduring urban development over time. Sustainable cities contribute to fostering continuous change and innovation developing policies and searching for a dialogue with community constructing roles and mechanism of participation and governance. Sustainable cities tend to continuously rethink the development by promoting innovation for change as a source for driving wealth and improving the quality of life within the city.

Cities should empower the citizens as people living within the city. Cities should invest in human capital and lead citizens to actively participate and contribute to developing sustainable urban policies. Citizens living in the city are the key source for driving cities towards sustainability as a principle of governance guiding actions and policies. Technology helps to promote innovation and enables the city to drive change within urban and regional areas to develop the city as a community. Cities surviving in the long-term in order to communicate meanings, values, identity and citizenship should rethink how to design a sustainable development that is future-oriented. Future research should investigate how technology helps citizens' involvement and participation in urban policy processes and choices. It is interesting to understand how technology helps citizens to exert influence on city governments to improve urban policy choices.

References

1. Newman, P., Jennings. J.: Cities as Sustainable Ecosystems. Principles and Practices. Island Press, Washington DC (2008)
2. Camagni, R.: Economia e pianificazione della città sostenibile. IlMulino, Bologna (1996)
3. Evans, B., Joas, S., Sundback, S., Theobald, K.: Governing Sustainable Cities. Earthscan, London (2005)
4. Satterthwaite, D.: Sustainable cities or cities that contribute to sustainable development? Urban Stud. **34**, 1667–1691 (1997)
5. Haughton, G.: Developing sustainable urban development models. Cities **14**, 189–195 (1997)
6. Nam, T., Pardo, T.A.: Smart city as urban innovation with dimensions of technology, people and institutions. In: Proceedings of the 5th International Conference on Theory And Practice Of Electronic Governance (pp. 185–194). ACM (2011)
7. Nam, T., Pardo, T.A.: Conceptualizing smart city with dimensions of technology, people and institutions. In: Proceedings of the 12th Annual International Digital Government Research Conference: Digital Government Innovation in Challenging Times (pp. 282–291). ACM (2011)
8. Dameri, R.: Searching for smart city definition: a comprehensive proposal. Int. J. Comput. Technol. **11**, 2544–2551 (2013)
9. Czarniawska, B.: Remembering while forgetting: the role of automorphism in city management in Warsaw. Public Adm. **62**, 163–173 (2002)
10. Bourne, L.S.: Internal Structure of the City. Readings on Space and Environment. Oxford University Press, New York (1971)
11. Tinacci Mossello, M.: Geografia economica. IlMulino, Bologna (1990)
12. Camagni, R.: Economia urbana. Principi, concetti e metodi. La Nuova Italia Scientifica, Roma (1992)
13. Schnore, L.F.: The city as a social organism. In: Bourne, L.S. (ed.) Internal Structure of the City. Readings on Space and Environment (pp. 32–39). Oxford University Press, New York (1971)
14. Begg, I.: Cities and competitiveness. Urban Stud. **36**, 785–809 (1999)
15. Eger, J.M.: Smart growth, smart cities, and the crisis at the pump. A worldwide phenomenon. I-Ways J. E-Gov. Policy Regul. **32**, 47–53 (2009)
16. Castells, M.: The Informational City: Information Technology, Economic Restructuring, and the Urban Regional Process. Blackwell Publishers, Oxford, Cambridge (1989)
17. Shapiro, J.M.: Smart cities: quality of life, productivity and the growth. Effects of human capital. Rev. Econ. Stat. **88**, 324–335 (2006)
18. Ishida, T.: Digital city Kyoto. Commun. ACM **45**, 76–81 (2002)
19. Caragliu, A., Del Bo, C., Nijkamp, P.: Smart cities in Europe. J. Urban Technol. **18**, 65–82 (2011)
20. Komninos, N., Schaffers, H., Pallot, M.: Developing a policy roadmap for smart cities and the future internet. In: eChallenges e-2011 Conference Proceedings, IIMC International Information Management Corporation (2011)
21. Suciu, G., Vulpe, A., Halunga, S., Fratu, O., Todoran, G., Suciu, V.: Smart cities built on resilient cloud computing and secure internet of things. In: 19th International Conference on Control Systems and Computer Science (CSCS), (pp. 513–518). IEEE (2013)

22. Komninos, N.: Smart cities and the future internet: innovation ecosystems of embedded spatial intelligence. In: Proceedings of International Conference for Entrepreneurship, Innovation and Regional Development, ICEIRD (2013)

23. Mell, P., Grance, T.: The NIST Definition of Cloud Computing. Recommendations of the National Institute of Standards and Technology, pp. 1–3. NIST Special Publications Gaithersburg, MD (2011)

24. Dahlberg, T., Kivijärvi, H., Saarinen, T.: Longitudinal study on the expectations of cloud computing benefits and an integrative multilevel model for understanding cloud computing performance. In: Proceedings of the 50th Hawaii International Conference on System Science (HICSS), pp. 4251–4260 (2017)

25. Mitchell, W.: Intelligent cities. e-J. Knowl Soc (2007)

26. Breindl, Y., Francq, P.: Can Web 2.0 applications save e-democracy? A study of how new Internet applications may enhance citizen participation in the political process online. Int. J. Electron. Democracy 1, 14–31 (2008)

27. Glaeser, E.L., Berry, C.R.: Why are smart places getting smarter? Taubman Center Policy Briefs, PB-2006-2. Available at http://www.hks.harvard.edu/rappaport/downloads/policybriefs/brief_divergence.pdf (2006)

28. Giffinger, R., Gudrun, H.: Smart cities ranking: an effective instrument for the positioning of cities? ACE Architect City Environ. 4(12), 7–25. http://upcommons.upc.edu/revistes/bitstream/2099/8550/7/ACE_12_SA_10.pdf (2010)

29. Giffinger, R., Fertner, C., Kramar, H., Kalasek, R., Pichler-Milanović, N., Meijers, E.: Smart Cities: Ranking of European Medium-Sized Cities. Centre of Regional Science (SRF), Vienna University of Technology, Vienna, Austria. Available from http://www.smart-cities.eu/download/smart_cities_final_report.pdf (2007)

30. Chourabi, H., Nam, T., Walker, S., Gil-Garcia, J.R., Mellouli, S., Nahon, K., Scholl, H.J.: Understanding smart cities: an integrative framework. In: 45th Hawaii International Conference on System Science (HICSS), pp. 2289–2297. IEEE (2012)

31. André, P., Martin, P., Lanmafankpotin, G.: Citizen participation. In: Côté, L., J.-F. Savard (eds.), Encyclopedic Dictionary of Public Administration, [online]. www.dictionnaire.enap.ca (2012)

32. OECD.: Citizens as Partners: Information, Consultation, and Public Partnerships in Policy Making. OECD, Paris, France (2001)

33. Verba S., Schlozman K.L., Brady H.E.: Voice and Equality: Civic Voluntarism in American Politics. Harvard University Press, Cambridge (1995)

34. La Porte, T.M.: Being good and doing well: organizational openness and government effectiveness on the World Wide Web. Bull. Am. Soc. Inf. Sci. Technol. 31, 23–27 (2005)

35. Torres, L., Pina, V., Acerete, B.: E-governance developments in EU cities: reshaping government's relationship with citizens. Governance 19, 272–302 (2006)

36. Fung, A., Wright, E.O.: Deepening democracy: innovations in empowered participatory governance. Polit. Soc. 29, 5–42 (2001)

37. Irvin, R.A., Stansbury, J.: Citizen participation in decision making: is it worth the effort? Public Adm. Rev. 64, 55–65 (2004)

38. Yetano, A., Royo, S., Acerete, B.: What is driving the increasing presence of citizen participation initiatives? Environ. Plann. C: Gov. Policy 28, 783–802 (2010)

39. van Veenstra, A.F., Janssen, M., Boon, A.: Measure to improve: a study of eParticipation in frontrunner Dutch municipalities. In: International Conference on Electronic Participation, pp. 157–168. Springer, Germany (2011)

40. Odendaal, N.: Information and communication technology and local governance: understanding the difference between cities in developed and emerging economies. Comput. Environ. Urban Syst. 27, 585–607 (2003)

The Paradigm Shift of Living Labs in Service Co-creation for Smart Cities: SynchroniCity Validation

Francesca Spagnoli, Shenja van der Graaf and Martin Brynskov

Abstract In the literature there are many definitions of co-creation and several disciplines are involved within this approach, especially co-design, participatory design and open innovation. Co-creation has been linked with many tools and platforms, without a coherent framework and specific guiding principles to follow, especially within the smart cities' context for developing new services. For this reason, it is required to clearly define which are the methods and digital tools that cities should pursue to fully exploit the potential of these platforms in terms of enhancing global collaborations. Starting from the review of the literature on participatory design, co-creation and open innovation, the paper aims to discuss the role of Living Labs in supporting service design for smart cities, by providing an effective approach for involving stakeholders in real life experimentation through digital platforms. The evaluation has taken into account the current use of co-creation approaches by eight smart cities involved in the SynchroniCity project, and considered as the current best practices in Europe. The analysis focused on timing, stakeholders, activities for involving citizens, rewarding systems, tools and metrics used to investigate the success of their implementation. Ten methods and twelve tools have been selected as the one best supporting smart cities in service design and their real application has been investigated through an online questionnaire and in depth interviews to the cities. As a result of the study, Living Lab has resulted as the most used and effective method for the smart cities in the EU for service design.

F. Spagnoli (✉) · S. van der Graaf
imec-SMIT-VUB, Pleinlaan 9, 1050 Brussels, Belgium
e-mail: francesca.spagnoli@imec.be

S. van der Graaf
e-mail: shenja.vandergraaf@imec.be

M. Brynskov
Department of Digital Design and Information Studies,
Aarhus University, Helsingforsgade 14, 8200 Aarhus, Denmark
e-mail: brynskov@cavi.au.dk

© Springer International Publishing AG, part of Springer Nature 2019
A. Lazazzara et al. (eds.), *Organizing for Digital Innovation*,
Lecture Notes in Information Systems and Organisation 27,
https://doi.org/10.1007/978-3-319-90500-6_11

1   Definition of Central Concepts

1.1   Co-creation for the Smart Cities

Originally, co-creation has been defined as the participation of end-users in the process of developing a product or a service [1]. Co-creation has been linked with many applications, without a coherent framework to follow [2, 3]. De Koning et al. [4] have provided an analysis of 50 co-creation methods and definitions, presenting a first comprehensive framework. According to the authors, in literature the co-creation term has been approached by following four different models, which are: the co-creation spectrum, the co-creation types, the co-creation steps and the joint space of co-creation. The types of co-creation define the process by identifying three criteria: when the co-creation happens, the amount of direct benefit or change produced, and the level of collaboration among the parties. What is clear and commonly agreed upon in the analysis of the literature, is that co-creation tends to refer to the active involvement of end-users sharing ideas with firms at various stages of the production process [5]. The core principle of co-creation is engaging people to create valuable experiences together, while enhancing network economics [6]. A central element of the transition to co-creation is the ability to effectively develop and manage two-way communications and information systems [7]. In the literature, authors have been provided three different definitions of the co-creation term according to the perspective of involving citizens in the process [8]: citizens as co-implementers of public services, they only perform some implementation tasks; citizens as co-designers, they decide how a service should be designed; and citizens as initiators, they trigger themselves an initiative and the government follows their approach. Within the context of smart cities and IoT projects, we support that these definitions are not representing the active role assigned to the citizens and the complex set of stakeholders usually involved. Hence, we prefer to apply the definition provided by Leading Cities [9], which sees co-creation as: *"an active flow of information and ideas among five sectors of society: government, academia, business, non-profits and citizens—the Quintuple Helix—which allows for participation, engagement, and empowerment in, developing policy, creating programs, improving services and tackling systemic change with each dimension of society represented from the beginning"*.

By taking into account these approaches and the specificities of smart cities activities, the following steps have been here defined as complementary for the effective implementation of co-creation practices in smart cities:

- *Step 1: Co-analysis*: defines the objectives to be achieved, including the approach to select the group that should be involved in co-creation and also the tools to put in place, considering stakeholders' needs.
- *Step 2: Co-design*: citizens generate new ideas to reshape or improve existing services. Within smart cities, co-design can be horizontal, engaging different municipalities in a city and in different regions; or vertical, when stakeholders are involved in both ways from up and down the service chain.

- *Step 4: Co-evaluation*: it aims to assess the efficacy and effectiveness of the proposed solutions by evaluating its potential socio-economic impacts. This phase includes also testing with stakeholders.
- *Step 5: Co-implementation*: the project takes its final shape and real results are occurring. By co-evaluating the products/services with current stakeholders, it is necessary to ensure the real usage and impact of the solutions.

1.2 Participatory Design Versus Co-creation

Participatory design is a process focused on the definition of a service idea implemented together with stakeholders to provide a service ready to be used. In more traditional views on participatory design, stakeholders tend to be involved in the process only as testers during the prototype phase. This process has been evolved since 80s, from customers to users in 90s, from participants to co-creators until today. The participatory design theory has then advanced thanks to the Scandinavian School, supporting the idea that through a participatory design approach we do not design things as objects, but socio-material assemblies, real things [10–12]. Co-creation has emerged for sure in connection with the participatory and human centred design approaches, where the attention was focused on empowering people for decision making processes and working practices. In participatory design, people contributes to the design processes, for this reason the connection with co-creation is strong and sometimes misleading. However, within the participatory design approach, co-creation is only seen as one of the strategies that can be applied to increase effectiveness, especially within social innovation contexts [13], rather than an autonomous process. Moreover, often in the participatory approach, co-creation is subordinated to co-design, to which a more relevant role is assigned, representing the collaboration process. By applying co-creative techniques, the focus should be on people as proactive citizens, rather than as consumers of services. The process is more related to the engagement of different communities, rather than only to some users in a group [9]. In this context, co-creation is seen as the only effective way to support governments to be more responsive to citizens' needs and to increase effectiveness and efficiency of cities [14]. In contrast, participatory design is managed by design experts acting as facilitators, rather than empowering citizens to make decisions for governments in the first place and be active contributors in the service development process [15].

1.3 Philosophy of Open Innovation in Smart Cities

Open innovation is a widely accepted concept both in academic and in business contexts. This is confirmed by the fact that searching the term in Google Scholar it shows 1.490.000 results. The topic has been one of the most discussed, especially in relation to economics, psychology, sociology and culture [16]. The first definition of open innovation has been provided by Chesbrough [17], however, the concept is not totally new, it is derived from the 70s' literature on customer and user-driven innovation, open systems and open paradigms [18, 19]. The open innovation concept has been applied to smart cities only recently to be closely linked to innovation systems at national and regional level [20], as an application to open innovation platforms and for public policies. From this first analysis, Open Innovation has been continuously investigated also referred to the capability of generating public policies for governments implementing open source software as a strategy to create socio-economic value for citizens. However, implementing open data policies requires to adopt also transparency and accountability. Indeed, according to the European Commission [21], within smart cities, open innovation can only be realised if the prerequisites of innovation are taken into account and if open knowledge, data, access and connectivity are implemented in the cities.

2   Social Transformation of Citizens in Adopting Co-creation Platforms

The analysis of the basic concepts about co-creation and participatory design clears the need of changing the usual engagement perspective provided by governments in the past twenty years. Indeed, using digital tools to gather feedback from citizens requires specific actions to them. According to the survey submitted by the Intelligence Unit of The Economist [22] to 1950 citizens and 615 business executives in 12 cities around the world, the majority of citizens (51%) requires a wider access to digital platforms enabling them to communicate with governments, but only a small part of them (32%) is actively providing feedback on local issues. Citizens and business both share the need to find new communication channels and processes to enable them to participate in Smart City initiatives. Transparency and trust are generally still considered to be the main concerns slowing the engagement process. Within the Smart City context, is clear that empowering citizens can contribute to concretely solve this issue, who should not be only seen as real time data providers; instead, they can really provide added value from data for improving decision making processes and governmental digital services. The concept of *Smart Citizenship* is also relevant to be analysed, as it assigns the capability of smart cities to support the citizens to recognise their position not only in a community (as in the traditional framework), but also in a network through digital platforms. This process requires the citizens to provide feedback and establish different connections in this complex context [23]. However, to enable them to activate this bidirectional approach and create new services, cities should yield them all the necessary tools. Within this framework, the smart citizenship approach focuses on the power of citizens, rather than on the impact of technologies, which are then seen only as an instrument for allowing them to shape new urban environments, defining policy and development processes, to take positive actions for an effective change of the society. According to the smart citizens' manifesto, the most relevant role of citizens is in supporting cities to improve their quality of life by refusing to be mere consumers or informers to decision makers [24]. The manifesto recognises the usual scepticism of citizens to implement collaborative and co-creation practices with municipalities. In contrast, the Director of the Waag Society, the first promoter of the manifesto, supports the need to implement this change. The manifesto upholds a previous study introducing the *"citizensourcing"* concept defined as a process originally performed by a public agent and now outsourced to large groups of people through open calls within the whole lifecycle of an initiative [25]. Citizens are acting as policy makers, often providing ideas that really improve the governmental policies. Citizensourcing has been also seen in the literature as a process called *e-participation* and enabled by the new technologies for improving deliberative democracy and increasing government transparency [26].

2.1 The Role of Living Labs in the Innovation Process for Smart Cities

The Living Lab term has emerged in the beginning of 2000 [27]. Originally the concept of Living Labs has been arisen in USA within the artificial lab context to describe a research facility implemented as a real home with the objective to provide observations of individuals [28]. In Europe, the concept is often connected to both open innovation and user innovation. The dynamics of the everyday life are part of the innovation experiment to co-create new products and services in a real life environment. Living Labs usually exploit a four steps approach based on contextualisation, concretisation, implementation and feedback gathering. The first phase aims to describe the framework and identify the group of users to involve in the analysis. The concretisation step is defined by the users' perception and their behaviour. During the implementation phase, the users are involved in the co-creation process. In the last step, users are requested to provide their opinions on the experience, in order to evaluate the change of attitudes and perceptions in relation to the products and services developed. Within smart cities and IoT projects, Living Lab strategies can be implemented to enable users to deploy real-life experiments involving large scale panels, including both the public and private sector. This approach has a huge impact in terms of acceptance and adoption of the solutions proposed and consequently aims to stimulate a more accurate market potential by exploiting the full potential of local innovation opportunities. Five key principles guide Living Labs: continuity, openness, realism, empowerment of users and spontaneity [29]. Empowerment of users is confirmed to be one of the most relevant, together with realism, as the main objective of Living Labs is to involve its users to participate in a real process of adding value to existing technologies or exploiting new products and services. This is mostly important in the context of smart cities and it is strictly connected to participatory design.

3 The SyncroniCity Project

SynchroniCity [30] represents the first attempt to deliver a Single Digital City Market for Europe by piloting its foundations at scale in reference zones across 8 European cities, involving also other cities globally. It addresses how to incentivise and build trust for companies and citizens to actively participate, in finding common co-created IoT solutions for cities that meet citizen needs and to create an environment of evidence-based solutions that can easily be replicated in other regions. The project moves from observing that the digital transformation of cities has been on the agenda of the R&I community and technology vendors for more than a decade. SynchroniCity aims to synchronize existing IoT-enabled smart city ecosystems in Europe by removing barriers of fragmentation and misalignment that currently sets them apart. It will pilot the necessary building blocks and drivers for change to foster an environment that will contribute towards technical, legal and socio-economic harmonization of the European smart city market. For *European citizens*, the resulting environment will create a richer choice of affordable citizen-centric services that meet their needs and expectations through increased market competition and co-creation opportunities. It will also provide them with new opportunities to participate in active policy-making. Indeed, in cases where IoT interventions are expected to drive human behavior change or disrupts existing business practice, the right legal and policy framework must be in place to incentivise stakeholders' participation and/or buy-in. Current environments are too constrained and rigid to experiment with such new opportunities and SynchroniCity in this sense aims to overcome this issue.

4 Co-creation Methods and Tools in Smart Cities

Starting from a systematic review of the literature, including the analysis of 89 papers on co-creation and on participatory design in Living Labs, smart cities and in contexts applying Open Innovation (both used as specific keywords for the search), ten methods and twelve tools have been identified to be specifically applied to smart cities, since the analysis of this particular environment is still scarce in the literature. This study has been developed taking into account the characteristics of the services and products that can be generated by implementing IoT infrastructures, considering also the specificities of the SynchroniCity project. A series of 'factsheets' have been provided to the reader to identify the approach implemented by each method, the context, reasons to apply it and the process to follow. The guiding principles have been selected and presented to the cities involved in SynchroniCity through an online questionnaire and in depth interviews, to support them to implement the methods and tools best supporting the cities to achieve their objectives. It is relevant to clearly define what is a method and what is a tool in the co-creation process. Indeed, a *method* is the systematic and theoretical framework guiding the whole co-creation approach. A *tool* is the instrument used to practically exploit the co-creation process within different phases. The methods and tools for co-creation in smart cities have been chosen by taking into account the specific needs of the cities involved in SynchroniCity and they are currently used in the whole co-creation process (as explained in Sect. 1.1). The following tables provide a brief description of each method and tool selected. The application of each tool has then been linked to the different co-creation methods to support the smart cities to identify which ones have been effectively put in place for service design (Tables 1 and 2).

5 Results from the Questionnaire and Interviews

The questionnaire has been available online for the smart cities involved in the SynchroniCity project at the following link https://www.surveymonkey.com/r/5D2T3V3 from May 2, 2017 until June 6, 2017 and it has been sent to eight cities' leads (Antwerp, Carouge, Eindhoven, Helsinki, Manchester, Milan, Porto and Santander). The questionnaire has been based on eleven open and close questions.

Table 1 Methods for co-creation in smart cities

Method	Description
Personas	A method using the everyday experiences and needs of representations of the users to identify their perspectives in all aspects of the design process
Lego serious Play™	A method for positioning a service offer in a team and to dialogue on the potential exploitation of a service at early stages of development
Gamification	A process of enhancing a service through gameful experiences supporting users' value creation, by bringing implicit knowledge and maintaining engagement over time
Bodystorming	A technique to physically experience a situation and deriving new ideas. It requires setting up an experience and physically implementing it, by providing feedback
Appraisal interviews	A method to evaluate past performances of an activity developed within a group and identify areas of further improvement
Basis SWOT workshops	A method used in bottom-up strategy development with different and heterogeneous stakeholder groups, to collect and visualise data describing the actual situation of a group
Strategic roadmaps	A method to gather insights on knowledge management processes and on indicators to increase benefits
Social network analysis	A method to support knowledge sharing in social networks, providing suggestions to influence relationships among network actors
Role play	A method to involve customers to perform a hypothetic service experience and build a potential journey on functionalities
Living lab	A method to implement real-life experimentation processes where stakeholders co-design innovative products and services

Table 2 Tools for co-creation in smart cities

Tool	Description
Social media	A set of online tools for gathering feedback during to generate public values about services entering the market
Mobile contribution (apps)	A mobile tool to collaboratively share open data and create innovative products/services, by incubating innovation capacity
Visual collaboration maps and mindmaps	A set of maps to visualise information during brainstorming processes with large groups of actors, and quickly exploit a topic
Toolkits (sensors, pictures and sharing results, etc.)	A set of instruments for providing data, presenting images and concepts relevant for the brainstorming process in co-design
Crowdmapping	A map for crowd-generated contents in a social media platform. It is useful to provide information on real-time data and connections
Rating and voting	A system to evaluate actual or potential services/products designed in the co-analysis and co-design phase
Mock-ups	A replica of a product/service, providing mainly information on its structure, used for instructional or experimental purposes
Issue cards	A physical instrument to show a picture of the current situation and to express users' different viewpoints and provide solutions
Affinity diagram	A brainstorming tool presenting a series of facts on a general theme and organizing it into clusters by natural relationship or affinity
Character profiles	An instrument for describing the personality of a potential user of the services and listing activities and fears in adopting such services
Storyboard	A graphic representation of the final product, to share the user's vision behind the result of co-design
Motivation matrix	A tool to focus on the motivations of the users when making a purchasing decision. It requires a clear understanding of the market

The theoretical implications of this study are derived from the literature review and the main objective of the questionnaire was first to provide an understanding of the cities on previous experiences with co-creation; then to investigate the effective application and relevance of the methods and tools proposed within the SynchroniCity project. This approach has helped us to better refine the co-creation methodology for the cities, and to identify the relevant topics to further investigate within the in-depth interviews. All the cities have replied to the questionnaire, by providing relevant information in terms of previous involvement in co-creation practices and methods. The results from the online questionnaire have been useful for better understanding at what stage of the project cities are using co-creation and what methods are already in place, their objectives, the tools and the rewarding systems used, and the current phases of development. However, several cities have declared to use some methods that in the literature do not apply to a specific phase (e.g. appraisal interviews during co-analysis, which indeed should be applied during co-evaluation and co-implementation) or have not considered other ones that can best serve their co-creation needs. Through these in depth interviews, we have discussed with the cities the replies to the questionnaire and proposed them to apply other methods. The results from the questionnaire have clearly shown a *medium to high level* of experience on co-creation. All the cities have already put in place at least one co-creation activity. Indeed, cities have very different experiences and knowledge about co-creation and this should be carefully taken into account to provide the right support to everyone. Specifically, Antwerpen, Eindhoven, Porto, Milan and Santander use co-creation often, not only for involving the citizens, but also all the stakeholders involved in the process, such as public and private companies, academia, suppliers, utilities, service providers and so on. Helsinki implements co-creation approaches all the time for developing digital services and for urban planning. Carouge and Manchester have less experience, but are both very interested in exploiting more co-creation methods for their use cases within the SynchroniCity project. All the cities have declared to use co-creation mainly to *engage their stakeholders*, including not only citizens but also public and private companies, start-ups and academia to develop innovative action plans and solutions. This result confirms the theoretical implication included in our definition of co-creation, that the cities are concretely implementing a *"quintuple helix approach"*. Seven out of the eight cities have declared co-creation is important also for *creating new services* and *increasing the efficiency* of already existing products. Co-creation is mostly implemented in the *co-design* phase and this reflects their need to implement such processes for digital service development. *Citizens* and *industry* are always engaged in co-creation activities organised by the cities, but also **utilities** are often the main stakeholders, especially in terms of urban planning, and this is an interesting result, as from the review of the literature there is no reference on the involvement of this actor for co-creating smart cities. All the cities use co-creation for *brainstorming processes,* and six out of the eight cities, implement these approaches to generate ideas on novel solutions, evaluate new concepts and improve the governance framework within their municipalities. It is then clear that even if the cities do not recognise it, co-creation is used by them mostly within the *co-analysis* phase; hence, the activities declared to be implemented by them are mainly used in the first stages of co-creation. As emerged from the analysis of the literature, more work has to be put in place to fully support smart cities around Europe to include co-creation activities within the co-evaluation and co-implementation phases. It is therefore very important to have all the stakeholders on board to assess the potential impact of the services developed on the market and to efficiently deploy the *"smart citizenship"* concept. Currently, the definitions provided by the authors on the role of the citizens on co-creation, represents only them as co-initiators and co-designers, but not as *co-implementers*. In terms of rewarding systems, by analysing the results from the questionnaire, it is evident that cities favour *community recognition* to reward their stakeholders to participate in co-creation activities, together with *virtual prizes*. This result clearly confirms the need of the cities to engage real communities of stakeholders bounded around the co-creation process to increase *e-participation* for improving deliberative democracy and increasing government transparency. This scope can only be achieved by using the a single digital effective platform. Offering new jobs or providing monetary prizes are not very applied as rewarding systems, as the real value for the stakeholders relies on sharing good practices in the community and stand out on the activities developed among the different users for each city. With reference to the co-creation methods used, it is impressive to detect that all the cities are currently exploiting **Living lab** as the main method. Five cities are also implementing Personas, Gamification, Appraisal interviews, Basis SWOT workshops and Strategic roadmaps. This result reflects the need of the cities to benefit from a method that can be applied both in co-analysis, co-design and co-evaluation phases, especially for implementing brainstorming processes, and this is a theoretical implication confirmed both by the questionnaire and by the interviews with the cities. In this sense, Living lab is a more effective holistic approach in considering the whole value chain and to mix in a rational way all the ingredients needed for service design, provide a succeeding story and build the smart cities' ecosystem. With reference to Bodystorming, it has not been applied by the cities involved in the study, even if it is usually implemented in the co-analysis phase, which is relevant for mostly of them, but it requires a lot of efforts from governments to physically engage the stakeholders to experience and implement service processes. Moreover, the stakeholders involved are mainly using virtual communities and it would be very difficult to involve them in real word activities. On the contrary, it has been detected the importance of **Hackathons**, already used by Helsinki, to be implemented later on by Manchester, which are more successful for enabling service development based on actual technologies and they require less psychological and personal involvement in the co-creation process. In terms of tools applied, even if Social Network Analysis as a co-creation method is only used by one city, seven out of eight cities have declared to use *social media* as a main tool for co-creating with their users. *Apps* and specific *toolkits* implemented by the cities (including sensors) are also put in place. This result confirm the theoretical implication related to the need of the smart cities to work alongside with their stakeholders in virtual communities through digital platforms. The main metrics to evaluate the success of co-creation activities are related to *increase the number of people participating* in these processes (mostly achievable thanks to the use of online communities) and *improve innovation capabilities*. Six cities have also declared to assess the impacts of co-creation approaches against *improving sustainability* of products and services, by confirming that co-creation is relevant for improving the co-implementation phase and should be further exploited in all smart cities around the world.

6 Conclusions and Next Steps

The online questionnaire and the in-depth interviews have shown the ten methods presented in this document have been effectively used by the cities to implement co-creation processes in close collaboration with their stakeholders. Indeed, as a result of the study, the *main challenges* for the cities in terms of co-creation, are related to engage the stakeholders in the first place and organise co-creation activities with new actors around virtual communities, to effectively deliver what is designed or agreed with them. To have a digital platform which can really incentivise the third parties to be involved in the co-creation activities, it is the most urgent issue to enable the smart cities to select the right tools to be used by the different categories of stakeholders involved every time in a co-creation approach. This platform can also be relevant for building a co-creation community and constantly engaging the actors in the process, within the whole co-creation lifecycle, thus providing the right methods to keep the stakeholders interested over time and to address their needs. Finally, the platform should make clear to the different stakeholders what is in it for them, considering the different level of knowledge provided by them.

Therefore, as a result of the study, **Living Labs** can play a relevant role in the smart cities framework. However, to achieve this goal, legal requirements should be clear and shared with all the stakeholders, open data should be automatically collected and available online for all the citizens through the digital platform. Online community building methods should further exploited, taking into account the relevance of such communities to develop services, which are useful for them. In terms of infrastructure development, this should be interoperable and value-added services should be implemented. In order to generate concrete innovation outcomes, the target market has to be specified and IPR principles should be established. SMEs potentially relevant for the co-creation process should also be engaged and business models have to be identified. As Living Labs are predominant for the smart cities' service design process, SynchroniCity should connect possible users and co-creators involved in each cities' activities through them. The next steps of the study will be to analyse the results and issues faced by the cities in applying co-creation methods proposed and to provide a final set to be used throughout the whole lifecycle of the project, by discussing these directly with the cities.

Acknowledgements

Funding This work has been supported by the European Union's Horizon 2020 research and innovation programme under grant agreements no 732240, 2017.

References

1. Von Hippel, E.: Cooperation between rivals: informal know-how trading. Res. Policy **16**(6), 291–302 (1987)
2. Payne, A.F., Storbacka, K., Frow, P.: Managing the co-creation value. J. Acad. Mark. Sci. **36**, 83–96 (2007). https://doi.org/10.1007/s11747-007-0070-0
3. Roser, T., Samson, A., Humphreys, P., Cruz-Valdivieso, E.: Co-creation: New Pathways to Value (White Paper). Promise/LSE Enterprise, London (2009)
4. De Koning, I.J.C., Crul, R. M., Wever, R.: Models of co-creation, Paper No. 31, TU Delft, The Netherlands (2016)
5. Prahalad, C.K.; Ramaswamy, V.: Co-creation experiences: the next practice in value creation. J. Interact. Mark. **18**(3) (2004)
6. Ramaswamy, V., Gouillart, F.: The power of co-creation: built it with them, boost growth, productivity and profits. Free Press, New York (2010)
7. Leavy, B.: Collaborative innovation as the new imperative-design thinking, value creation and the power of "pull". Strategy Leadersh. **40**(2), 25–34 (2012)
8. Voorberg, W. H., Bekkers, V.J.J.M. & Tummers, L. G.: A systematic review of co-creation and co-production: embarking on the social innovation journey. Public Manage Rev **17**(9), 1333–1357 (2014). https://doi.org/10.1080/14719037.2014.930505
9. Leading Cities.: Co-creating cities. Defining co-creation as a mean of citizen engagement, https://leadingcities2014.files.wordpress.com/2014/02/co-creation-formatted-draft-6.pdf (2012)
10. Ehn, P.: Participation in design things. In: Proceedings of the 10th PDC 2008, Indiana, USA (2008)
11. Björgvinsson, E., Ehn, P., Hillgren, PA.: Participatory design and democratizing innovation. In: Proceedings of PDC 2010, Sydney, Australia (2010)
12. Emilson, A., Seravalli, A., Hillgren, P.A.: Dealing with dilemmas: participatory approaches in design for social innovation. Swed. Des. Res. J. **1**, 23–29, Malmo, Sweden (2011)
13. Cantù, D. & Selloni, D.: From engaging to empowering people, a set of co-design experiments with a service design perspective, POLIMI DESIS, social frontiers, the next edge of social innovation research, p. 4, Milan, Italy (2013)
14. Percy, S.L.: Citizen participation in the coproduction of urban services. Urban Aff. Rev. **19**(4), 431–446 (1984)
15. Langley, J.: Participatory design: co-creation|co-production|co-design combining imaging and knowledge. In: Knowledge Utilisation Colloquium, Llandudno, Wales (2016)
16. Huizingh, E.: Open innovation: state of the art and future perspectives. Technovation **31**(1), 2–9 (2011)
17. Chesbrough, H.: Open Innovation: The New Imperative for Creating and Profiting from Technology, p. 43. Boston: Harvard Business School Press (2003)
18. Von Hippel, E.: Democritizing Innovation. The MIT Press, Cambridge, Massachussets. ISBN: 0-262-00274-4 (2005)
19. Selden, L. & MacMillan, I.: Manage customer-centric innovation systematically. Harvard Bus. Rev. Financ. Manag (2006)
20. Savitskaya, I., Torkkeli, M.: A framework for comparing regional open innovation systems in Russia. Int. J. Bus. Innov. Res. **5**(3), 332–346 (2011)
21. European Commission.: Open innovation 2.0 yearbook 2016, DG communications networks, contents and technology. https://www.researchgate.net/profile/Rianne_Valkeburg/publication/303822705_Open_Innovation_20_Yearbook_2016/links/57566c9cae10c72b66f315/Open-Innovation-20-Yearbook-2016.pdf (2016)
22. The Economist Intelligence Unit.: Empowering cities. The real story of how citizens and businesses are driving smart cities. http://empoweringcities.eiu.com/ (2016)
23. Martelli C.: A Point of View on New Education for Smart Citizenship. Future Internet Journal, MDPI, Firenze, Italy (2017)

24. Hemment, D., Townsend, A.: Smart citizens. Future everything publications, Manchester, UK, http://futureeverything.org/wp-content/uploads/2014/03/smartcitizens1.pdf (2013)
25. Hilgers, D., Ihl, C.: Citizensourcing: applying the concept of open innovation to the public sector. Int. J. Public Participation 4(1), 67–88 (2010)
26. Preston, E.: Citizensourcing: Harnessing the Power of the Crowds to Monitor Public Services. CEU eTD Collection (2012)
27. Markopoulos, P., Rauterberg, G.W.M.: Living lab: a white paper. In: IPO Annual Progress Report (2000)
28. Intille, S.S., Larson, K., Beaudin, J.S., Nawyn, J., Tapia, E.M., Kaushik, P.: A living laboratory for the design and evaluation of ubiquitous computing technologies. In: CHI'05 Extended Abstracts on Human Factors in Computing Systems—CHI'05, p. 1941. ACM Press, New York, USA (2005)
29. CoreLabs.: Living labs roadmap 2007–2010: recommendations on networked systems for open user-driven research, development and innovation. In: Open Document. Luleå University of Technology, Centrum for Distance Spanning Technology, Luleå (2007)
30. http://cordis.europa.eu/project/rcn/206511_en.html

How to Design Citizen-Science Activities: A Framework for Implementing Public Engagement Strategies in a Research Project

Francesco Bolici and Nello Augusto Colella

Abstract Many studies have shown that volunteers have the potential to provide a valuable contribution to complex research projects. To reach this outcome, the environment in which contributors are engaged has to be carefully configured to foster collaboration while designing tasks with low interdependence. The broad term defining this integration of external contributions in scientific research is "open/citizen science". Being this phenomenon relatively innovative in its capillary applications, theoretical frameworks and operative guidelines are still evolving. Our paper aims to contribute to this research field, examining and testing public engagement activities for a robotics research project, HeritageBot (HB). In detail, our paper explores the process of developing collaborative initiatives involving external actors in a set of HB's scientific research tasks through a set of public engagement, "open", activities. First, we will propose a theoretical framework that we designed to support our activities, and then, we will compare and select a set of methodologies for designing open/citizen-science strategies. Subsequently, we will focus on empirical episodes in which we were involved while developing HB's public engagement solutions. Finally, we will introduce the experimental validation process of the identified solutions, showing also a summary of preliminary results.

1 Introduction

The capillary diffusion of Information and Communication Technology have enabled the emergence of open collaborative models which have provided new possibilities and advantages for complex scientific research projects. This process of opening the solution of a problem also to individuals not formally involved in the work is a well-known phenomenon in other sectors, as for example the case of open

F. Bolici (✉) · N. A. Colella
OrgLab, University of Cassino and Southern Latium, Cassino, Italy
e-mail: f.bolici@unicas.it

N. A. Colella
e-mail: nellocolella@gmail.com

© Springer International Publishing AG, part of Springer Nature 2019   149
A. Lazazzara et al. (eds.), *Organizing for Digital Innovation*,
Lecture Notes in Information Systems and Organisation 27,
https://doi.org/10.1007/978-3-319-90500-6_12

source projects in the software industry [1, 2]. Different movements (e.g. open access, open science, crowdsourcing) have recently emerged, rising the interest on the concept of a broader scientific process, where everybody can access and contribute according to her/his own skills and abilities. To reach a meaningful level of public involvement, scientific projects have to design "spaces" of interactions and experiments where the volunteers' contributions can be valuable. Many scientific research projects have indeed successfully designed virtual participatory spaces, being able to benefit from the potentialities of distributed knowledge and at the same time disseminating scientific results to the public.[1] There are, in fact, many well-known benefits of opening up research projects to external contributions: i. the access to a large human computational power (e.g. through the so called crowdsourcing initiatives); ii. the possibility of raising a broader awareness and knowledge on scientific topics; iii. an early understanding of the market needs and expectations; iv. a large number of users testing early versions of the research outcomes.

This research will address the design and implementation of a citizen science process as part of a robotics research project. Even considering the mentioned potential benefits of an open approach to this field of research, cutting-edge robotics technologies are still generally hidden from the common citizen eye [3, 4]. There are several reasons for the existence of these participation barriers between scientists and citizens, ranging from the complexity of the specific research topic, to the tools and means needed to design and implement a robotic solution, till the time and effort needed to effectively open up the research to external contributions. The design and implementation of open—citizen science based public engagement activities in this type of projects presents a set of specific challenges, as for example: an adequate coordination and alignment of open-citizen science principles, with the projects' long term objectives (e.g. concerning intellectual property rights and sensitiveness of research issues); the nature of the products and the processes involving the scientific activities have to be diluted and divulged in a simplified manner, to overcome motivational and knowledge gaps between researchers and public; and goals, methodologies and protocols of such initiatives have to be clearly defined ex-ante. Such conditions make the whole process time consuming and represent a strong disincentive to researchers to open their project to external actors. There are however, projects that successfully integrated external actors in their innovation processes: Inmoov[2] and iCub.[3]

In this work, we will present the experience of designing a set of activities for public engagement to be integrated within the research activities of HeritageBot, a

---

[1]Notable example is the "Galaxy Zoo" project which, through the contribution of hundreds of thousands of volunteers categorized more than 50 million galaxies (www.galaxyzoo.org). Gravity Spy is another successful participatory initiative, counting more 8000 volunteers and more than 2 million classifications of gravitational waves detectors' outputs (https://www.zooniverse.org/projects/zooniverse/gravity-spy).

[2]Project's website: http://inmoov.fr/.

[3]Project's website: http://www.icub.org/.

market-aimed robotics development project. We will first provide an overview of the project and of the developed methodology's theoretical foundations. Then, we will systematize, through empirical episodes, our action research-based approach to public engagement strategy development. Finally, we will introduce our work-in-progress experimental methodology, instrumental to the validation of the developed strategy.

2 Literature Review

Many scholars have investigated feasibility and best practices of research approaches based on "open" principles. Most of the literature on the topic evidences the increasing popularity of research initiative aiming at directly involving also amateurs and volunteer scientists into the discovery process. This phenomenon is summarized by the words "open science", defined as the "umbrella term encompassing the multitude of assumptions about the future of knowledge creation and dissemination" [5]. Open science scholars focus on proposing shared and multidisciplinary principles aiming at developing ethics, tools and workflows to promote transparency, reproducibility, dissemination and transfer of new knowledge [6]. The demand for a more participative—"open"—vision of science is driven by numerous factors. Among the most discussed drivers of openness, the increasing complexity of problems to be investigated by scientists, together with the exponential growth of data to be analyzed and the commitment to better understand society's needs and expectations, are generating the need of exploiting the potentialities of distributed human computational power [7]. Integrating citizens into research processes, has been proved to not only facilitate awareness and diffusion of the research-produced knowledge, but also to empower researchers themselves providing additional research possibilities [7, 8]. Nonetheless, the connotations of the term have raised debates regarding its benefits, limits, applicability and goals. Part of the literature perceives openness as an opportunity to dramatically increase the range of available expertise, thus expanding the spectrum of solvable problems [9, 10]. In other instances, openness is viewed as a democratization of knowledge, addressing the fact that scientific data, methodologies and findings are often unequally distributed. The latter picture in particular keeps up the barriers for: first, generating trust, legitimacy and funding for research projects [11, 12]; second, for promoting communication and collaboration between researchers [13–15]. Additionally, citizens' engagement with science, together with the dissemination of knowledge and benefits derived from research to the society as a whole, may also be hindered by not pursuing an "open" vision [16, 17]. Open-citizen science principles, however, are not without criticism. Some scholars have displayed concern about the facts that the incentives of doing research, and the control over the quality and utilization of the produced science, may as well be reduced [18–20].

Others argue that the design of open initiatives may take a level of effort and time (for example: to prepare and release data and documentation, to train citizen scientists, to set up an adequate communication infrastructure), that may surpass their potential benefits. Addressing this problem, Bonney [21] developed a series of citizen science projects design guidelines, but their application is mostly limited to environmental research. In the fields of technology science and robotics, exploiting the interests and curiosity of the people, may represent a promising opportunity to crowdsource data, ideas and solutions [3]. In fact, open-citizen science solutions share similarities with the open innovation concept [22], as they may "accelerate internal innovation and expand the market for external use of innovation". Is also evident that open science principles carry strong analogies with the open source movement, for which the convergence of means, benefits, limitations and methodologies have been documented in literature [e.g. 23]. However, the process of introducing the "open" formulas into market oriented research is complicated, as evidenced also by the lack of shared methodologies in this regard. By showing pre-production prototypes, or releasing sensible data regarding innovative products to the public, the risks of sensible information spillovers may increase, potentially reducing research products' value. This condition raises the strategic dilemma of how to open up to distributed knowledge while maximizing research products' security.

3 The Case: HeritageBot

The context of our research is a publicly funded, multidisciplinary, robotics research project, aimed at cultural heritage valorization and conservation: HeritageBot (HB). The objective is to develop a hybrid multifunctional modular, remotely controlled robotic device. HB is specifically conceived to be used in cultural patrimony preservation, valorization and fruition. Its innovative drone—walker configuration is particularly useful for architectural and archeological applications. In fact, the device is being designed to be extremely versatile and to allow to remotely obtain an optimal quantity of visual data and metrics from locations needing to be explored or visited. HB's research team is multidisciplinary. Together with the engineering sub-team (in charge of designing and assembling the robot) there are also researchers from economics, business, architecture, finance, legal and organizational studies. This integration of multiple research fields was motivated by the aim of producing a research product with a clear and immediate value for the market. In particular, our research laboratory leads the activities focused on studying and developing an open-citizen science framework to facilitate the integration of external actors in the project's workflow.

4 Developing Public Engagement Initiatives

Approaching the problem of developing public engagement strategies in the context of a robotics research project was not without issues. The aim to bring to the market HB product, together with the complicated nature of the device, challenges the design method to follow for an open—citizen science solution. Therefore, in order to face the complexity of the task, we developed a hybrid methodological approach [24] (Table 1). We build on the general citizen science guidelines defined by Bonney [21], integrated with the principles of action research methodology, as proposed by [25], to define a set of HB contextualized operative steps. In our case, the first step was coincident with the *diagnostic* phase of the AR methodology, functional *"to the identification of the primary problems that are the underlying causes of the organization's desire for change"* [26]. This was the most challenging stage of our research because the team was multidisciplinary and we, as organizational specialists, had very limited knowledge on some of the other fields, as for example robotics and mechatronics. In order to share the different perspectives and knowledge bases a series of collective meetings and private interviews with the various sub-teams from the different fields involved were conducted. During the meetings, we gathered also an extensive quantity of documentation and audio-visual material regarding the device, including pre-production blueprints, 3D renders and work-in-progress photos. Additionally, thanks to valuable ideas coming from all the other team members, we defined a set of initial goals for our specific research goal: I. Promote the awareness on the project. II. Facilitate knowledge dissemination. III. Attract and valorize the distributed knowledge of extra-organizational actors.

The following step, coinciding with the action planning phase, involved the identification of activities that were compatible with both the market-aimed nature of project and the defined public engagement goals. Many potential activities were identified, including a parallel incubator based on open hardware and open source principles, a gamified virtual 3D robot configurator and a series of robotics

Table 1 Hybrid methodological approach: citizen science—Action research

Citizen science Bonney et al.	Action research Susman and Evered	HeritageBot research project
Choose a scientific question	Diagnosis	Meetings – Interviews with research team
Form scientist/evaluator team	Action planning	Identification of compatible initiatives
Develop, test, refine protocols		Pilot testing
Recruit participants	Action taking	Launch initiatives and experiments
Train participants		
Accept, edit, and display data	Evaluating	Analysis of the metrics and KPIs
Analyze and interpret data		
Disseminate results	Specifying learning	Tweaking
Measure outcomes		

workshops. However, only two of the identified activities were, at the same time feasible in terms of time and cost, fully compatible with the project's market-aimed nature, and representative of the proposed public engagement goals.

4.1 The Social Micro-Blogging Initiative

The first of the conducted activities, also encompassing the widest audience, regards the utilization of social media platforms—specifically Facebook, Instagram and Twitter—to periodically publish project-related content. All the content was presented in the form of micro-blog entries [12, 27] as news, updates, curiosities and insights regarding the HB project were regularly proposed to the public. The different social platforms were used according to their peculiarities, to develop a cross promotional, informative online space. Since the launch of the social initiatives, the published content has covered all the main activities and shareable results of the research team. Given that "science is by nature complicated, making it all the more important that good science writing should be simple, clean and clear" [28], all the information and material collected during previous team-wide meetings was accurately diluted, reformulated, and posted on each social platform in an easy to read and "appealing" form. After iteratively adjusting the type and presentation of the content, following the AR cycle, the social strategy was ultimately a success in terms of visibility growth and knowledge diffusion, also considering that the profiles' promotion was strictly organic (non-paid). In particular, the initiative provided satisfactory results on facebook (with an average reach of 793 users for videos, 186 users for pictures and 46 followers) and Instagram (averaging 13 likes per post and 34 followers). The social activities also provided insights on the preferences of the public in regards of content typology. The most liked posts were the ones containing videos, animations or pictures of the various phases of the prototypes' construction, accompanied by brief, simple descriptions. The least liked posts were those proposing technical content such as diagrams and simulation videos. In any case, the social approach failed to incentivize public active participation, as comments were rare.

4.2 The HeritageBot Seminar Survey

The second activity concerns the inclusion of a public engagement experiment in the context of a project-related seminar. This was organized by the HeritageBot's business development team and was aimed at students of a start-upping course (organized by ImprendiLab). During the seminar, both the business and technological aspects of HB were introduced. The capabilities and functionalities of the robot were thoroughly explained as so were its potential fields of application. At the end of the seminar, after introducing the project's public engagement goals, a public engagement survey was administered to the students (23 respondents). The survey questions aimed at obtaining feedback on specific aspects of the device that were still in progress (for example: how should the robot be named; how could it be improved) and especially at identifying the participation drivers. The results showed that the seminar was welcomed by the students with interest and enthusiasm as 87% of them answered "Yes, I would like to know more" to the question "would you like to participate in additional seminars regarding HeritageBot?". Further proof of the interest on the project was the fact that the attending students also raised numerous questions and generated debates about the device and the project. The students' reaction and the survey's results evidenced a potential willingness to contribute to the development of the device. Additionally, 95% of the students enjoyed the seminar experience, 91% liked the HeritageBot idea, and some also started following the project's social profiles. The seminar survey activity evidenced the need to make the participation experience simple, non-linear (allowing the users to ask questions regarding what they are interested in), rewarding and entertaining (interactive). However, as pointed by all the research team members, it would be an impractical and costly solution to organize a series of seminars to engage a wider audience.

5 Developing and Validating the *Ad Hoc* 3D Simulator

On the basis of the previously cited two experiences we developed a public engagement solution for the project by combining the identified positive aspects of both social and seminar activities. In particular, we developed a system that combines the potential online visibility and low cost of social media with, to some extent, the interactive, nonlinear and rewarding experience of a workshop (Fig. 1). The solution takes the form of an *ad hoc* 3D simulator aimed at: i. Allowing potential volunteers to autonomously obtain information about the project and participate, reducing the interdependencies between non-expert actors and the research team, typical in workshops and seminars; ii. Providing an online space, an interface, capable of attracting the user's attention by making the project interesting; iii. Proposing a rewarding experience, adding 3D exploration sections, to let the user "play" with the device under development, interactive videos and non-linear navigation of the interface.

Specifically, the solution consists in an interactive animated infographic containing information about the device presented in a simple, non-technical manner (Fig. 2). The interested user will be able to navigate the platform at will, exploring the different sections as he prefers. The presented content, extrapolated in part from the most popular posts shared on social media, and in part based on the topics that gathered higher participation during the survey experiment, ranges from explanations of the different parts of the robot to the presentation of the different participation channels.

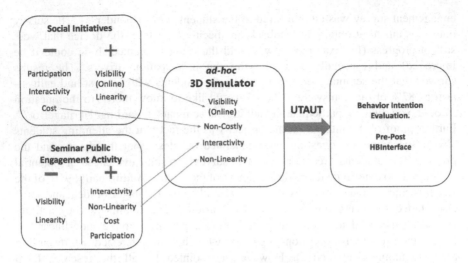

Fig. 1 From the initial activities to the *ad hoc* 3D simulator

Fig. 2 HeritageBot *ad hoc* 3D simulator, alpha version, screenshot (in Italian)—Selection of the part of the device to explore

These informative sections are enriched with a significant number of interactive audio-visual content including a 3D device visualization section. The content was provided by the HeritageBot team over the course of the team wide meetings. In order to validate this solution, we constructed a pilot experiment. The validation process involved two questionnaires, based on the Unified Theory of technology

Acceptance and Use of Technology (UTAUT) [29], as we find some of its constructs to be compatible with open—citizen science goals. In particular, the pilot experiment aimed at measuring if the subjects' behavior intention regarding actively participating in a research project was influenced by the availability of an interactive online interface simulating some characteristics of the final research product. As for today, the UTAUT based experimental methodology was tested with a group of economics students. These students were selected based on availability and willingness to participate. The experiment itself was configured as follows: The sampled students were asked to complete a preliminary questionnaire, with minimum information about the HeritageBot project provided by the experiment coordinators, aimed at gathering demographic data, information regarding their knowledge of robots and their opinion on different public engagement initiatives. The subsequent phase involved the exploration of the *ad hoc* 3D simulator: the students were allowed to navigate the demonstrative interface freely in order to evaluate its informative power. At the end of this phase the students were asked to answer a final questionnaire aimed at collecting their opinions on the demo platform and measuring their willingness to participate in the research project. The test was executed in two separate instances with two different groups, and received a total of 43 valid responses. The first test involved 20 undergraduate students. From these, only 50% completed the experiment correctly, hinting that the experimental methodology had to be made simpler and more straight forward for respondents. Following some improvements to the protocol, the test was repeated with a second group of students. This time the completion rate was way higher, as about 90% of the students (33) provided valid responses. Demographic composition of respondents is summarized in Table 2.

Table 2 Respondents demographic data

Character		Frequency	Percentage (%)
Gender	Male	16	37.2
	Female	27	62.8
Age	<20	1	2.3
	20 < X < 25	24	55.8
	25 < X < 30	12	27.9
	>30	6	14
Education	University degree	14	32.5
	High school	29	67.5
Declared level of knowledge about robots	Low	26	60.5
	Medium	14	32.5
	High	3	7

6 Preliminary Results

The number of valid responses collected, as for today, is insufficient to perform an in-depth analysis of the scale reliability and internal constructs' consistency [30]. However, we were able to obtain some interesting insights on the perception of proposed solutions' validity in incentivizing public engagement for the HB project. As previously explained, in the first questionnaire students were asked to provide information on their interest in participating, on their perceived difficulty involved in contributing to the project and their opinion on the usefulness of some proposed initiatives.

Questions regarding the students' opinion on the project were structured in a 6 point Likert scale, to avoid central tendency. Results for the first questionnaire (in Table 3) showed that there is a widespread perception (mean over 3.5), among

Table 3 Descriptive statistics of first questionnaire—6 point Likert scale

Indicator	Scale	Mean	Std. deviation	N.
How difficult do you think it is to contribute to the project in a useful way?	1—Very Easy 6—Very Hard	4.02	1.471772046	43
How much would you be interested in participating in the project? (available only if answered "Yes" to "Would you like to participate in the HeritageBot Project?")	1—Not Interested 6—Very Interested	3.75	1.040833	28
How difficult do you think it would be for you to contribute? (available only if answered "Yes" to "Do you feel capable of contributing to the HeritageBot Project?")	1—Very Easy 6—Very Hard	4.21	1.100745298	28
How much would you be interested in contributing to the project if you felt capable? (available only if answered "Yes" to "Do you feel capable of contributing to the HeritageBot Project?")	1—Not Interested 6—Very Interested	4.06	1.032795559	15
How much time do you think it would take you to obtain the knowledge necessary to become capable of contributing? (available only if answered "Yes" to "Do you feel capable of contributing to the HeritageBot Project?")	1—Not much time 6—A lot of time	4.4	0.632455532	15
How useful do you think a series of robotics workshops would be in disseminating the knowledge needed to contribute to the project in a useful way?	1—Not useful 6—Very useful	4.333	1.161720059	43
How useful do you think an online demo platform would be in incentivizing public participation in the project?	1—Not useful 6—Very useful	4.761	1.007521078	43

Meaning of values in the "scale" column

students of a high difficulty, level of effort and time needed in obtaining the knowledge to usefully participate in the project. However, interest in participating was also noticeable both among those who felt capable (63% of respondents) and those who didn't (37% of respondents). The proposed idea of an online demo platform was also considered very useful in the preliminary questionnaire.

The second questionnaire provided some interesting insights on the usefulness of the 3D simulator platform—social initiatives approach. A summary of questions and responses can be found in Table 4. All answers for the proposed questions were again configured as a 6 point Likert scale where 1 meant "strongly disagree" and 6 "strongly agree". The UTAUT constructs used as base for the proposed questions are: Performance Expectancy (PE), Effort Expectancy (EE), Facilitating Conditions (FC) and behavior intention (BI). PE is intended as the perceived effectiveness of the 3D simulator platform in providing the information needed to usefully contribute to the project. EE is intended as the perceived effort needed to navigate the platform and to obtain desired information. FC measures the perception of effectiveness of the demo platform and the social profiles, in facilitating the user participation. BI represents the intention of the respondent in participating to the project. Results (Table 4) indicate that the sample of students, on average, moderately agrees with the statements proposed for PE1 and PE2. In regards of EE, in all four questions, the students involved in the tests agrees that the platform

Table 4 Descriptive statistics for second questionnaire—Answers in 6 point Likert scale where 1 meant "strongly disagree" and 6 "strongly agree"

UTAUT construct	Indicator	Mean	Std. deviation	N.
PE1	After using the demo platform, I feel I can contribute usefully to the project	3.48837	1.054967682	43
PE2	I think the demo platform can be useful to provide necessary information to non-experts interested in contributing, usefully, to the project	3.79069	1.059158236	43
EE1	I think the demo platform provides information in an easy to understand, to non-experts, manner	4.09302	1.15085793	43
EE2	I believe the demo platform is easy to navigate	4.20930	1.186393887	43
EE3	I think the 3D explorative sections made the demo experience more rewarding	4.60465	1.094130115	43
EE4	I think the interactivity of the demo platform makes the project more interesting	4.53488	1.076786162	43
FC1	I think the social—demo approach is useful to facilitate a public participation in the HeritageBot research	4	1.133893419	43
FC2	I think is easy to contribute to the project through the demo and the social platforms	3.81395	1.052340112	43
BI1	I am interested in participating in the HeritageBot project	3.67441	1.128018284	43
BI2	I intend to participate actively through the social platforms	3.37209	1.291423279	43

provides an easy to access and to navigate mean to obtain information on the project and on the participation channels. The most appreciated features were the 3D exploration sections and the interface's interactivity. The sample also agrees on the validity of the social media and the demo platform as facilitating solutions for public participation (FC1 and FC2). For the BI construct, the students declared a moderate intention of contributing to the project and actively participating through dedicated social media profiles. Overall these preliminary results are satisfactory, indicating an effectiveness of the proposed solutions in terms of knowledge dissemination, ease of access to information and facilitating solution for the participation of external volunteers in the HB research.

7 Conclusions

We addressed the case of designing and introducing public engagement initiatives in the research process of a robotics research project (HB). We found that the market oriented nature of HB, together with the complex nature of the device, challenges the introduction of traditional open—citizen science propositions. We started assessing the problem of determining an appropriate methodology by analyzing the open and citizen science related literature, as well as by exploring successful initiatives based on these principles. A lack of well-established theoretical frameworks, compatible with the characteristics of the HB project, emerged by our literature review. Thus, we worked to fill this gap, developing a hybrid methodological approach to determine a series of guidelines useful to design public-engagement initiatives. By combining the traditional citizen science process with AR methodology, we identified two initial activities fully compatible with the project's characteristics and objectives: social network micro blogging and seminar public engagement survey. From the results of these two experiences, we recognized the need of creating an online space aimed at reducing the interdependence between potential volunteers and research team, providing easy to access information about the project and facilitating the participation through the social channels. We, therefore, developed *ad hoc* 3D Simulator combining the positive elements observed during the social and seminar initiatives into one comprehensive and interactive interface. The UTAUT-based validation experiment for this solution provided positive preliminary results. The group of students involved in the validation process agreed, on average, on the informative power of the solution. In particular, the most appreciated features were the 3D exploration sections and the interface's interactivity. The sample also on average agrees on the validity of social media and demo platform as solutions for facilitating public participation. Even if these results suggest an actual effectiveness of the identified solutions, a broader scale experiment will be needed in order to allow more in depth analyses. These will be especially aimed at confirming the validity of the solutions identified and of the proposed methodology for developing public engagement activities in highly complex scientific research projects.

References

1. von Krogh, G., Spaeth, S.: The open source software phenomenon: characteristics that promote research. J. Strateg. Inf. Syst. **16**(3), 236–253 (2007). https://doi.org/10.1016/j.jsis.2007.06.001
2. Hippel, E. von, Krogh, G. von.: Open source software and the "Private-Collective" innovation model: issues for organization science. Organ. Sci. **14**(2), 209–223 (2003). https://doi.org/10.1287/orsc.14.2.209.14992
3. Wilkinson, C., Bultitude, K., Dawson, E.: "Oh Yes, Robots! People Like Robots; the robot people should do something": perspectives and prospects in public engagement with robotics. Sci. Commun. **33**(3), 367–397 (2011)
4. Special Eurobarometer 382. (2012) Retrieved on http://ec.europa.eu/public_opinion/archives/ebs/ebs_382_en.pdf
5. Fecher, B., Friesike, S.: Open science: one term, five schools of thought. In S. Bartling & S. Friesike (eds.), Opening Science, pp. 17–47 (2014)
6. Grigorov I.: FOSTER Open Science Learning Objectives. Zenodo (2015)
7. Hand, E.: Citizen science: people power. Nature **466**(7307), 685–687 (2010)
8. Brossard, D., Lewenstein, B., Bonney, R.: Scientific knowledge and attitude change: the impact of a citizen science project. Int. J. Sci. Educ. **27**(9), 1099–1121 (2005)
9. Nielsen, M.: Doing science in the open. Phys. World **22**(5), 30 (2009)
10. Nielsen, M.: Reinventing Discovery: the New Era of Networked Science. Princeton University Press, Princeton, N.J (2012)
11. Grand, A., Wilkinson, C., Bultitude, K., Winfield, A.F.: Open science a new, "Trust Technology"? Sci. Commun. **34**(5), 679–689 (2012)
12. Puschmann, C.: (Micro) blogging science? Notes on potentials and constraints of new forms of scholarly communication. In: S. Bartling & S. Friesike (eds.), Opening Science, pp. 89–106 (2014)
13. Tacke, O.: Open Science 2.0: how research and education can benefit from open innovation and Web 2.0. In T. J. Bastiaens (2010)
14. Vision, T.J.: Open data and the social contract of scientific publishing. Bioscience **60**(5), 330–331 (2010)
15. Gowers, T., Nielsen, M.: Massively collaborative mathematics. Nature **461**(7266), 879–881 (2009)
16. Whyte A., Pryor G.: Open science in practice: researcher perspectives and participation. International Journal of Digital Curation (2011)
17. Royal Society (Great Britain) and policy studies unit: "Science as an open enterprise". (2012)
18. Gezelter, J. D.: Open science and verifiability. The Open Science Project, 5 (2011)
19. Friesike, S., & Schildhauer, T. Open science: many good resolutions, very few incentives, yet. In Incentives and Performance, pp. 277–289. Springer (2015)
20. Goldman, G.: Cautiously open to open science—The equation. Retrieved from ucsusa.org/gretchen-goldman/cautiously-open-to-open-science-138. (2013)
21. Bonney, R., Cooper, C.B., Dickinson, J., Kelling, S., Phillips, T., Rosenberg, K.V., Shirk, J.: Citizen science: a developing tool for expanding science knowledge and scientific literacy. Bioscience **59**(11), 977–984 (2009)
22. Chesbrough, H.: From open science to open innovation. Institute for Innovation and Knowledge Management, ESADE (2015)
23. J. Willinsky: The unacknowledged convergence of open source, open access, and open science. First Monday. **10**(8) (2005)
24. N.A. Colella, F. Bolici. Public engagement in a research project: designing citizen science activities as a part of its business model. IEEE Global Wireless Summit (2016)
25. Susman, G., Evered, R.: An assessment of the scientific merits of action research. Adm. Sci. Q. **23**, 582–603 (1978)

26. Baskerville, R.L.: Investigating information systems with action research. Commun. AIS. **2** (3es) (1999)
27. Ebner, M., Maurer, H.: Can weblogs and microblogs change traditional scientific writing? Future Internet **1**(1), 47–58 (2009)
28. Cribb, J., Sari, T.: Open Science: Sharing Knowledge in the Global Century. CSIRO Publishing, Collingwood (2010)
29. Venkatesh, V., Morris, M. G., Davis, G. B., & Davis, F. D.: User acceptance of information technology: Toward a unified view. MIS Q. 425–478 (2003)
30. Yurdugul, H.: Minimum sample size for Cronbach's coefficient alpha: A Monte-Carlo study. Hacettepe Univ. J. Educ. **35**, 397–405 (2008)

Part III
Innovative Solutions in Digital Learning

(E)Learning and What Else? Looking Back to Move Forwards

Leonardo Caporarello, Alessandro Giovanazzi and Beatrice Manzoni

Abstract In recent years, there has been a growing debate and rise in publications about learning in its multiple forms. This variety has contributed to the richness of existing research but it has also increased, rather than reduced, the need for more clarity to advance further. Through a content analysis performed on the last twenty years of research, we aim at providing clarity about the complex definitions landscape of the most diffused 16 learning terms in the literature. We discuss their use over the years and we depict some trends. We conclude by providing a comprehensive learning model that clarifies interactions and interdependencies among the terms. The framework classifies the terms into models, modes and methodologies.

1 Introduction

In recent years, we witnessed a sharp rise in publications, as well as conference sessions, research reports and working papers related to the concept of learning [1]. The growing number of publications may imply that a greater understanding of the learning phenomenon is in act, but it is not always the case. There is a variety of conceptualizations and interpretations of learning, which occurs in multiple forms. On the one hand this variety has contributed to the richness of existing research, on the other hand it has increased, rather than reduced, the need for more clarity to advance further [2].

This increase is particularly boosted by a technological shift which is occurring in the learning landscape [3, 4]. Indeed, technology has determined the rise of a number of learning methodologies and processes. Among these, the most explored one is "E-learning" [5], whose meaning is quickly evolving over time [6].

L. Caporarello (✉) · B. Manzoni
SDA Bocconi School of Management, and Department of Management
and Technology, Bocconi University, Milan 20136, Italy
e-mail: leonardo.caporarello@unibocconi.it

A. Giovanazzi
Bocconi University, Milan 20136, Italy

© Springer International Publishing AG, part of Springer Nature 2019
A. Lazazzara et al. (eds.), *Organizing for Digital Innovation*,
Lecture Notes in Information Systems and Organisation 27,
https://doi.org/10.1007/978-3-319-90500-6_13

Apart from a few exceptions, which however adopted a more narrow scope on blended learning [7] and online learning [5], there is a lack of contributions providing a comprehensive overview of the phenomenon.

In this article, we take on the challenge of giving order to the multiplicity of terms and definitions around some concepts related to learning over the last twenty years with the purpose to provide clarity among the different definitions and to propose a fruitful agenda for future research.

The remainder of this article is organized as follows. The first paragraph describes the method we used to select and filter the most cited article related to the concept of learning. In the second paragraph we provide clarity about the complex definitions landscape of the most cited learning terms in the literature. In the third paragraph we discuss the use of these terms over the years and we depict some trends. In the fourth paragraph we propose a framework for a learning model, which organizes the terms into models, modes and methodologies and which clarifies interactions and interdependencies among them. Finally we conclude with some implications for future research.

1.1   Content Analysis: Overview of the Method

To ensure theoretical transparency, reliability, and validity, we followed a structured content analysis process [8]. We developed the sample by searching for "learning" on Google Scholar over a time frame of the last twenty years, and then listing what terms were used in combination with it. We sampled articles, books, book chapters and conference proceedings. We did not take into considerations theses and unpublished materials. Although some authors argue that highly cited papers are not always indicative of impactful research [9], it is reasonable to consider that high citation rates do reflect a certain level of quality [10], thus we filtered for those cited at least 20 times. This resulted in 3616 publications from 1997 to 2016, including 2874 articles, 229 books, 56 book chapters and 457 conference proceedings.

1.2   Shedding Light on Multiple Ways of Learning

Based on the results of the literature review, as described in the previous paragraph, we then conducted a content analysis [8] about the following learning terms: active learning, asynchronous learning, blended learning, cooperative learning, distance learning, e-learning, face-to-face learning, game-based learning, informal learning, mobile learning, non-formal learning, online learning, personalized learning, problem-based learning, project-based learning and synchronous learning.

Our analysis reveals a complex variety of conceptual definitions around learning. As Table 1 shows, the 16 selected learning terms have different meanings but they also present an unfocused richness in the sense that definitions are sometimes confused [7, 11, 12], in overlap [13, 14] or combinable [15, 16].

First, confusion exists about many terms that remain "ill-defined" [28]. Several authors point out that there is "either no clear definition or a very vague reference to [...] terms such as online course/learning, web-based learning, web-based training, learning objects or distance learning believing that the term can be used synonymously" [2]. For example problem-based learning has been described both as a method [86] and as an educational strategy [11]. This lack of clarity is particularly evident for all the tech-based learning terms: confusion persists about blended learning [28], online learning [7], mobile learning [65] and e-learning [12]. For example, with regard to e-learning "although [it] has become a hot topic in training and education organizations around the globe, there is considerable variance in opinion about just what it is" [1]. Mobile learning is interpreted as either the learner or the device being mobile [65].

Secondly, overlap in terms of meaning is evident across different concepts. For example cooperative learning and game-based learning are sometimes described similarly, in the sense that authors stress the fact of working together to accomplish goals or to develop an end product within a play framework [13, 14, 37, 54]. Mobile learning is seen as a more recent version of distance learning [2]. Online learning is also seen as a form of distance education where technology mediates the process [7]. E-learning often overlaps with most of the other learning terms here studied [1, 30, 78].

Finally, combinations occur with many terms. For example, blended learning is often combined with synchronous learning [15], mobile learning with synchronous learning [16], informal learning [67] or game-based one [57]; distance learning with synchronous learning [16], cooperative learning with distance learning [34]. Problem-based learning is frequently addressed as a specific type of active learning [22], as well as project-based learning [87]. With regard to E-learning specifically, the term is often combined with personalized learning [78], mobile learning [16], synchronous learning [16], online learning [30], distance learning [30], and asynchronous learning [1].

1.3   The Use of Learning Terms Over Time

In this section we discuss how the 16 learning terms have been used and researched from 1997 onwards. In particular we discuss how learning trends developed over fifteen years, what are the most recent trends and how tech-based learning terms progressively became more debated.

Table 1 Exemplary definitions of learning concepts

Learning concepts	Exemplary quotations	Exemplary references[a]
Active learning	"Any instructional method that engages students in the learning process" [17] "In active learning, the processing of knowledge also requires a problem solving orientation, a critical approach and an evaluation of knowledge" [18]	[17–21]
Asynchronous learning	"The use of the Internet to deliver anytime, anywhere" [22] "In asynchronous settings, learning is self-paced, and users have access to previous activities contributed by others from the same group" [23]	[22–25]
Blended learning	"A learning program where more than one delivery mode is being used with the objective of optimizing the learning outcome and cost of program delivery" [26] "The thoughtful integration of classroom face-to-face learning experiences with online learning experiences" [27] "A description of particular forms of teaching with technology. However, […] it remains ill-defined" [28]	[2, 28–32]
Cooperative learning	"A "catch all "phrase for group learning" [33] "A structured form of group work where students pursue common goals while being assessed individually" [17] "Distance learning has made possible several innovative means to include Cooperative learning in virtual pedagogical settings" [34]	[13, 17, 33–37]
Distance learning	"Some authors will provide either no clear definition or a very vague reference to other terms such as online course/learning, web-based learning, web-based training, learning objects or distance learning believing that the term can be used synonymously" [2] "[It] can be integrated into different learning situations, where distance equals either space or time; it can be a complement or a supplement to non-remote situations such as classroom or regular campus situations" [38]	[38–44]
E-learning	"Technology-based learning in which learning materials are delivered electronically to remote learners via a computer network [45] "People now think of e-learning as an instructional approach, whereas e-learning is actually a delivery platform with an interesting set of capabilities" [12] "All forms of electronically supported or mediated learning and teaching" [30]	[4, 12, 42, 46–48]
Face-to-face learning	"A learning process where learners and experts are present physically in same place at same time" [49]	[25, 49–52]

(continued)

(E)Learning and What Else? Looking Back to Move Forwards

169

Table 1 (continued)

Learning concepts	Exemplary quotations	Exemplary references[a]
Game-based learning	"[It] refers to the borrowing of certain gaming principles and applying them to real-life settings to engage users" [53] "[It] is similar to problem based learning (PBL), wherein specific problem scenarios are placed within a play framework" [54]	[14, 54–58]
Informal learning	"It is learning that rests primarily in the hands of the learner and happens through observation, trial and error, asking for help, conversing with others, listening to stories, reflecting on a day's events, or stimulated by general interests" [59] "All learning that occurs outside the curriculum of formal and non-formal educational institutions and programs" [60]	[61–64]
Mobile learning	"Exactly what we mean by mobile learning is the subject of some debate. Does mobile learning refer to the mobility of learners—the idea that one can learn anytime and anywhere—or to the portability/mobility of mobile devices themselves?" [65] "Learning across multiple contexts, through social and content interactions, using personal electronic devices" [66] "[It] can emphasize those unique attributes that position it within informal learning, rather than formal" [67]	[65, 67–70]
Non-formal learning	"An umbrella that gather corresponding theories on activity and inherent concepts related to ludic activities motivated by curiosity, exploration, play and aesthetics rather than externally defined tasks" [71] "[It] encompasses informal learning which can be described as unplanned learning in work situations and elsewhere, but also includes planned and explicit approaches to learning introduced in work organisations and elsewhere, not recognised within the formal education and training system" [72] "Out-of-school learning that is unstructured and does not follow a specific curriculum, such as a visit to a museum or science exhibit. [...] has a specific structure and is connected to some kind of a syllabus or curriculum" [73]	[71–75]
Online learning	"Online and traditional distance education approaches do share common attributes, including the emphasis on "any time—any place" learning" [7] "A form of distance education where technology mediates the learning process, teaching is delivered completely using the Internet, and students and instructors are not required to be available at the same time and place" [7] "A more recent version of distance learning" [42]	[7, 42, 76, 77]

(continued)

Table 1 (continued)

Learning concepts	Exemplary quotations	Exemplary references[a]
Personalized learning	"Personalized learning aims to develop individualized learning programs for each student with the intent to engage him/her in the learning process to optimize each child's learning potential and success". [78] "It advocates that instruction should not be restricted by time, place or any other barriers, and should be tailored to the continuously modified individual learner's requirements, abilities, preferences, background knowledge, interests, skills, etc." [79]	[78–83]
Problem-based learning	"A student-centred approach to learning which enables the students to work cooperatively in small groups for seeking solutions to situations/problems" [84] "Problem based learning is an educational strategy. A method to organize the learning process in such a manner that the students are actively engaged in finding answers by themselves" [11]	[11, 84–86]
Project-based learning	"The theory and practice of utilizing real-world work assignments on time-limited projects to achieve mandated performance objectives and to facilitate individual and collective learning" [87] "A student-driven, teacher-facilitated approach to learning. Learners pursue knowledge by asking questions that have piqued their natural curiosity. The genesis of a project is an inquiry. Students develop a question and are guided through research under the teacher's supervision. Discoveries are illustrated by creating a project to share with a select audience" [88]	[11, 87–89]
Synchronous learning	"Learning and teaching where remote students participate in face-to-face classes by means of rich-media synchronous technologies such as video conferencing, web conferencing, or virtual worlds" [15] "[It] requires teachers and students to work together, albeit at a specific time, and focuses on reconstructing the traditional in-class learning environment over the Internet" [16]	[15, 16, 90, 91]

[a]The complete list of references is available upon request by contacting the corresponding author

Blended learning, online learning but especially e-learning are the mainstream learning terms of the past fifteen years (see Fig. 1[1]). E-learning is the top trend learning term, but instead of growing up, it is decreasing in use suggesting that it will not be probably on the edge in the future. Online learning increased a lot, reaching stability in the period 2009–2012. Finally, distance learning, that was the

---

[1]We do not include citations after 2012 here because the number of citations drops not as a matter of less interest in the topic but as a matter of shorter time available for citations.

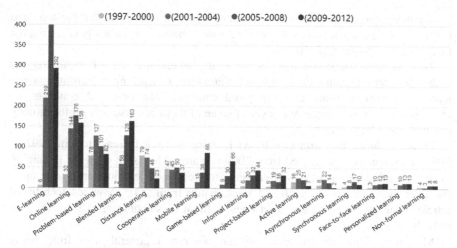

Fig. 1 The use of learning terms over the years (1997–2012)

top mainstream learning term of the last years of the nineties, and according to many expected to grow [43], has been clearly replaced by the rapid growth of informal learning, game-based learning, mobile learning and, above all, blended learning.

The past four years (2013–2016) show similarities as well as differences with the previous ones (Fig. 2). E-learning remains the top first topic. Blended learning and online learning trends are growing fast, and also mobile learning is gaining interest. Game based, problem based and informal learning are also debated terms in the literature and this possibly suggest the importance of providing learning experiences which "solve" real problems.

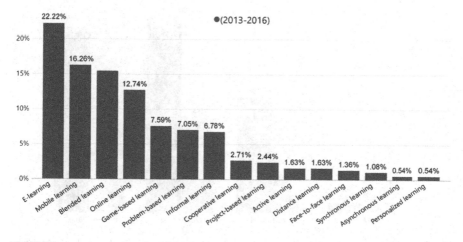

Fig. 2 The most recent trends (2013–2016)

Another interesting trend in the literature is related to the fact that the top cited learning concepts are tech-based, showing how technology is radically changing the face of organizations [24, 50, 64].

Tech-based learning includes those terms where the use of technology is embedded and inevitable. Given this definition blended learning, e-learning, mobile learning, Online learning are tech-based concepts. The other 12 concepts are classified as non tech-based ones even if some of them can also rely on technology but it is not a "must have".

Figure 3 shows that non tech-based learning has not increased from 1997 to 2008 and it has even decreased from 2009 onwards. Moreover, until the beginning of the new millennium, articles discussing non tech-based learning terms were up to six time more than the tech-based ones, while from 2005 onwards tech-based articles doubled the non tech-based ones, with an outstanding growth of 641% in only 10 years.

Moreover, from our analysis we can observe a general shift from being instructor-centred to being student-centred [7] but also from being learning-driven to technology-driven [67, 82]. This last shift needs to be however carefully managed to maintain the learner at the centre and to avoid that technology becomes the fulcrum of the learning experience.

1.4 A Proposed Framework for a Comprehensive Learning Model

In this section we intend to provide an answer to the following two questions: "Why is confusion and overlap about learning terms still in place?"; "Why can we

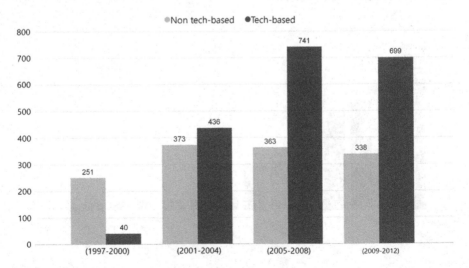

Fig. 3 Trends in using non tech-based and tech-based learning terms in the academic literature (1997–2012)

combine some learning terms and not others?". Referring to the first question, we argue that terms mean different things and that they are not all at the same level, even if they all include learning in their definition. Referring to the second question, we argue that we can combine terms across different levels and not within levels.

Thus, we intend to propose a learning framework (Fig. 4) that organizes the different learning concepts into different levels.

The first level is one of the learning model is the set of general principles based on which an entire course is built upon. According to our interpretation of the literature, it is an exclusive choice between an online, blended and traditional learning.

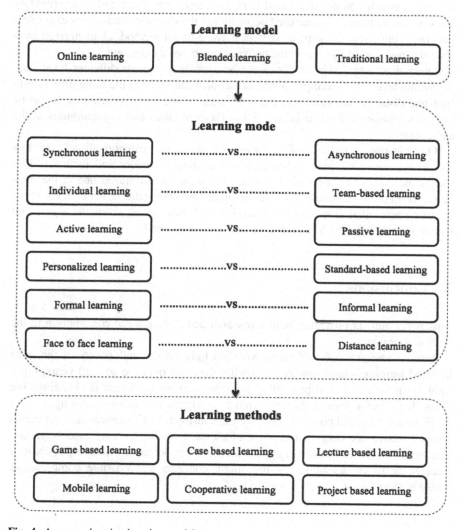

Fig. 4 A comprehensive learning model

The second level is the one of the modes which is composed by at least six couple of terms: synchronous versus asynchronous, individual versus team based, active versus passive, personalized versus standardized, face-to-face versus distance, formal versus informal learning. Modes are dichotomies in the sense that either we choose one or another. The real difference between a model and a mode is that a course can be composed by only one model but multiple modes. For example in a blended learning course there are parts that are based on distance learning and other parts that are face to face. Another course may provide a mix of active and passive engagement.

The final level is the one of methods where we can have at least six concepts. Differently from the modes, the methods are a list of options among which we can choose. A course can be subdivided in one or more parts. Each part is described by one specific method and structured according to the different modes. For example a part of a course can be structured with a game-based method, characterized by a specific spectrum of synchronous, active, team-based modes, etc.

Interactions and combinations occur between terms across different levels and not within levels. For example, a part of a course cannot be at the same time face-to face and distance, but can be at the same time online and synchronous; it can be also synchronous and game-based, but not synchronous and asynchronous at the same time.

One learning concept—E-learning—eludes this categorization. In fact E-learning can result from different mixes of models, modes and methods. This makes the concept of E-learning, which is also the most diffused one in the literature, much more pervasive in the model than any other term. In the end, could we possibly argue that E-learning is Learning and vice versa, given the significant technological shift which occurred in the past few years?

2 Conclusions

This paper aims at providing both a research and a managerial contribution in the field of learning.

From a research point of view, we shed light on the multiplicity of the most diffused learning-related concepts showing their use over the past 20 years, highlighting major trends and presenting how the learning landscape is changing. We show that a technological shift occurred in academic research on learning.

From a managerial point of view, we offer instructional designers and lecturers a comprehensive and detailed overview of all the available learning models, modes and methods they can use to design a course. We make these different possibilities clear in terms of definitions of the single concepts and possible combinations between them.

References

1. Fallon, C., Brown, S.: E-Learning Standards: A Guide to Purchasing, Developing, and Deploying Standards-Conformant E-Learning. CRC Press (2016)
2. Moore, N., Gilmartin, M.: Teaching for better learning: a blended learning pilot project with first-year geography undergraduates. J. Geogr. High. Educ. **34**, 327–344 (2010)
3. Garrison, DR.: E-learning in the 21st Century: A Framework for Research and Practice. Taylor & Francis (2011)
4. Welsh, E.T., Wanberg, C.R., Brown, K.G., Simmering, M.J.: E-learning: emerging uses, empirical results and future directions. Int. J. Train (2003)
5. Siemens, G., Gasevic, D., Dawson, S.: Preparing for the digital university (2015). Available on June 6 2018, online at http://linkresearchlab.org/PreparingDigitalUniversity.pdf
6. Caporarello, L., Iñesta, A.: Make blended learning happen: conditions for a successful change process in higher education institutions. EAI Endorsed Trans. e-Learning **3**(16) (2016)
7. Joksimović, S., Kovanović, V., Skrypnyk, O.: The history and state of online learning. Prep. Digit. Univ 93–122 (2015)
8. Krippendorff, K.: Content Analysis: An Introduction to Its Methodology. SAGE (2012)
9. Waltman, L., Van Eck, N.J., Wouters, P.: Counting publications and citations: is more always better? J. Informetr. **7**, 635–641 (2013)
10. White, H.D.: Author co-citation analysis: overview and defense. Sch. Commun. Bibliometr. **84**, 106 (1990)
11. Kolmos, A.: Problem-based and project-based learning. In: Skovsmose, O., Valero, P., Christensen, O.R. (eds.) University Science and Mathematics Education in Transition, pp. 261–280. Springer, US (2009)
12. Allen, M.W.: Michael Allen's Guide to e-Learning: Building Interactive, Fun, and Effective Learning Programs for Any Company. Wiley (2016)
13. Johnson, D.W., Johnson R.T., Stanne, M.B.: Cooperative learning methods: a meta-analysis (2000)
14. Sung, H.-Y., Hwang, G.-J.: A collaborative game-based learning approach to improving students' learning performance in science courses. Comput. Educ. **63**, 43–51 (2013)
15. Bower, M., Dalgarno, B., Kennedy, G.E.: Design and implementation factors in blended synchronous learning environments: outcomes from a cross-case analysis. Comput. Educ. **86**, 1–17 (2015)
16. Huang, Y.-M., Kuo, Y.-H., Lin, Y.-T., Cheng, S.-C.: Toward interactive mobile synchronous learning environment with context-awareness service. Comput. Educ. **51**, 1205–1226 (2008)
17. Prince, M.: Does active learning work? A review of the research. J. Eng. Educ. **93**, 223–231 (2004)
18. Niemi, H.: Active learning—a cultural change needed in teacher education and schools. Teach. Teach. Educ. **18**, 763–780 (2002)
19. Jensen, J.L., Kummer, T.A., Godoy, P.D.: Improvements from a flipped classroom may simply be the fruits of active learning. CBE-Life Sci. Educ, **14**, ar5 (2015)
20. Roach, T.: Student perceptions toward flipped learning: new methods to increase interaction and active learning in economics. Int. Rev. Econ. Educ. **17**, 74–84 (2014)
21. Michael, J.: Where's the evidence that active learning works? Adv. Physiol. Educ. **30**, 159–167 (2006)
22. Hiltz, S.R.: Impacts of college-level courses via asynchronous learning networks: some preliminary results. J. Asynchronous Learn. Netw. **1**, 1–19 (1997)
23. Northey, G., Bucic, T., Chylinski, M., Govind, R.: Increasing student engagement using asynchronous learning. J. Mark. Educ. **37**, 171–180 (2015)
24. Rovai, A.P.: Building and sustaining community in asynchronous learning networks. Internet High. Educ. **3**, 285–297 (2000)

25. Ocker, R.J., Yaverbaum, G.J.: Asynchronous computer-mediated communication versus face-to-face collaboration: results on student learning, quality and satisfaction. Group. Decis. Negot. **8**, 427–440 (1999)
26. Singh, H., Reed, C.: A white paper: achieving success with blended learning. Cent. Softw. **1**, 1–11 (2001)
27. Garrison, D.R., Kanuka, H.: Blended learning: uncovering its transformative potential in higher education. Internet High. Educ. **7**, 95–105 (2004)
28. Oliver, M., Trigwell, K.: Can "blended learning" be redeemed? E-Learn. Digit. Media **2**, 17–26 (2005)
29. Porter, W.W., Graham, C.R., Spring, K.A., Welch, K.R.: Blended learning in higher education: institutional adoption and implementation. Comput. Educ. **75**, 185–195 (2014)
30. Al-Qahtani, A.A., Higgins, S.E.: Effects of traditional, blended and e-learning on students' achievement in higher education. J. Comput. Assist. Learn. **29**, 220–234 (2013)
31. Moore, M.G.: Editorial: blended learning. Am. J. Distance Educ. **19**, 129–132 (2005)
32. Graham, C.R.: Emerging practice and research in blended learning. Handb. Distance Educ. **3** (2013)
33. Pedersen, J.E., Digby, A.D.: Secondary Schools and Cooperative Learning: Theories, Models, and Strategies. Routledge (2014)
34. Kupczynski, L., Mundy, M.A., Goswami, J., Meling, V.: Cooperative learning in distance learning: a mixed methods study. Online Submiss. **5**, 81–90 (2012)
35. Capar, G., Tarim, K.: Efficacy of the cooperative learning method on mathematics achievement and attitude: a meta-analysis research. Educ. Sci. Theory Pract. **15**, 553–559 (2015)
36. Millis, B.J., Cottell, P.G.: Cooperative Learning for Higher Education Faculty. Series on Higher Education. Oryx Press (1997)
37. Panitz, T.: Collaborative versus cooperative learning: a comparison of the two concepts which will help us understand the underlying nature of interactive learning (1999)
38. Dijkstra, S.: Instructional Design: International Perspectives II: Volume I: Theory, Research, and Models: Volume Ii: Solving Instructional Design Problems. Routledge (2014)
39. Shukla, N., Hassani, H., Casleton, R.: A Comparison of Delivery Methods for Distance Learning Mathematics Courses. In: SoTL Commons Conference (2014)
40. Simpson, O.: Supporting Students in Online Open and Distance Learning. Routledge (2013)
41. Lockwood, F.: Open and Distance Learning Today. Routledge (2013)
42. Moore, M.G., Kearsley, G.: Distance Education: A Systems View of Online Learning. Cengage Learning (2011)
43. Galusha, J.M.: Barriers to learning in distance education (1998)
44. Porter, L.R.: Creating the Virtual Classroom: Distance Learning with the Internet. Wiley (1997)
45. Zhang, D.: Interactive multimedia-based e-learning: a study of effectiveness. Am. J. Distance Educ. **19**, 149–162 (2005)
46. McCutcheon, K., Lohan, M., Traynor, M., Martin, D.: A systematic review evaluating the impact of online or blended learning vs. face-to-face learning of clinical skills in undergraduate nurse education. J. Adv. Nurs. **71**, 255–270 (2015)
47. Tavangarian, D., Leypold, M.E., Nölting, K.: Is e-learning the solution for individual learning? Electron. J. E-Learn. **2**, 273–280 (2004)
48. Govindasamy, T.: Successful implementation of e-learning: pedagogical considerations. Internet High. Educ. **4**, 287–299 (2001)
49. Singh, A.K., Yusoff, M.A., Oo, N.: A comparative study between traditional learning and e-learning. In: Proceedings of Teaching and Learning Open Forum 2009. CSM, Sarawak, pp. 1–7 (2009)
50. Castaño-Muñoz, J., Duart, J.M., Sancho-Vinuesa, T.: The Internet in face-to-face higher education: can interactive learning improve academic achievement? Br. J. Educ. Technol. **45**, 149–159 (2014)

51. Clegg, T., Yip, JC., Ahn, J.: When face-to-face fails: opportunities for social media to foster collaborative learning. In: Tenth International Conference on Computer Supported Collaborative Learning (2013)
52. Artino, A.R.: Online or face-to-face learning? Exploring the personal factors that predict students' choice of instructional format. Internet High. Educ. **13**, 272–276 (2010)
53. Pho, A., Dinscore, A.: Game-based learning. Tips Trends (2015)
54. Ebner, M., Holzinger, A.: Successful implementation of user-centered game based learning in higher education: an example from civil engineering. Comput. Educ. **49**, 873–890 (2007)
55. Hamari, J., Shernoff, D.J., Rowe, E.: Challenging games help students learn: an empirical study on engagement, flow and immersion in game-based learning. Comput. Hum. Behav. **54**, 170–179 (2016)
56. Tobias, S., Fletcher, J.D., Wind, A.P.: Game-based learning. In: Handbook of Research on Educational Communications and Technology. Springer, pp 485–503 (2014)
57. Huizenga, J., Admiraal, W., Akkerman, S., Dam, G.: Mobile game-based learning in secondary education: engagement, motivation and learning in a mobile city game. J. Comput. Assist. Learn. **25**, 332–344 (2009)
58. Papastergiou, M.: Digital game-based learning in high school computer science education: impact on educational effectiveness and student motivation. Comput. Educ. **52**, 1–12 (2009)
59. Dabbagh, N., Kitsantas, A.: Personal learning environments, social media, and self-regulated learning: a natural formula for connecting formal and informal learning. Internet High. Educ. **15**, 3–8 (2012)
60. Schugurensky, D.: The forms of informal learning: towards a conceptualization of the field (2000)
61. Kukenberger, M.R., Mathieu, J.E., Ruddy, T.: A cross-level test of empowerment and process influences on members' informal learning and team commitment. J. Manag. **41**, 987–1016 (2015)
62. García-Peñalvo, F.J., Conde, M.Á.: Using informal learning for business decision making and knowledge management. J. Bus. Res. **67**, 686–691 (2014)
63. Cox, M.J.: Formal to informal learning with IT: research challenges and issues for e-learning. J. Comput. Assist. Learn. **29**, 85–105 (2013)
64. Marsick, V.J., Watkins, K.E.: Informal and incidental learning. New Dir. Adult Contin. Educ. **2001**, 25–34 (2001)
65. Hockly, N.: Mobile learning. ELT J. **67**, 80–84 (2013)
66. Crompton, H.: A diachronic overview of technology contributing to mobile learning: a shift towards student-centred pedagogies. Increasing Access. **7** (2014)
67. Traxler, J.: Current state of mobile learning. Mob. Learn. Transform. Deliv. Educ. Train. **1**, 9–24 (2009)
68. Sharples, M., Spikol, D.: Mobile learning. In: Duval, E., Sharples, M., Sutherland, R. (eds.) Technology Enhanced Learning, pp. 89–96. Springer International Publishing (2017)
69. Jones, A.C., Scanlon, E., Clough, G.: Mobile learning: two case studies of supporting inquiry learning in informal and semiformal settings. Comput. Educ. **61**, 21–32 (2013)
70. Martin, F., Ertzberger, J.: Here and now mobile learning: an experimental study on the use of mobile technology. Comput. Educ. **68**, 76–85 (2013)
71. Petersson, E.: Non-formal learning through ludic engagement within interactive environments. Malmö högskola, Lärarutbildningen (2006)
72. Bjornavold, J.: Making Learning Visible: Identification, Assessment and Recognition of Non-Formal Learning in Europe. ERIC (2000)
73. Garner, N., Hayes, S.M., Eilks, I.: Linking formal and non-formal learning in science education—a reflection from two cases in Ireland and Germany. Sisyphus J. Educ. **2**, 10–31 (2014)
74. Gallacher, J., Feutrie, M.: Recognising and accrediting informal and non-formal learning in higher education: an analysis of the issues emerging from a study of France and Scotland. Eur. J. Educ. **38**, 71–83 (2003)

75. Colley, H., Hodkinson, P., Malcolm, J.: Non-formal learning: mapping the conceptual terrain, a consultation report (2002)
76. Shea, P., Bidjerano, T.: Does online learning impede degree completion? A national study of community college students. Comput. Educ. **75**, 103–111 (2014)
77. Huang, H.-M.: Toward constructivism for adult learners in online learning environments. Br. J. Educ. Technol. **33**, 27–37 (2002)
78. Lin, C.F., Yeh, Y., Hung, Y.H., Chang, R.I.: Data mining for providing a personalized learning path in creativity: an application of decision trees. Comput. Educ. **68**, 199–210 (2013)
79. Sampson, D., Karagiannidis, C., Cardinali, F.: An architecture for web-based e-learning promoting re-usable adaptive educational e-content. Educ. Technol. Soc. **5**, 27–37 (2002)
80. Kong, S.C., Song, Y.: An experience of personalized learning hub initiative embedding BYOD for reflective engagement in higher education. Comput. Educ. **88**, 227–240 (2015)
81. Huang, Y.-M., Liang, T.-H., Su, Y.-N., Chen, N.-S.: Empowering personalized learning with an interactive e-book learning system for elementary school students. Educ. Technol. Res. Dev. **60**, 703–722 (2012)
82. Song, Y., Wong, L.-H., Looi, C.-K.: Fostering personalized learning in science inquiry supported by mobile technologies. Educ. Technol. Res. Dev. **60**, 679–701 (2012)
83. Chen, C.-M.: Intelligent web-based learning system with personalized learning path guidance. Comput. Educ. **51**, 787–814 (2008)
84. Kong, L.-N., Qin, B., Zhou, Y.: The effectiveness of problem-based learning on development of nursing students' critical thinking: a systematic review and meta-analysis. Int. J. Nurs. Stud. **51**, 458–469 (2014)
85. Walker, A.E., Leary, H., Hmelo-Silver, C.E., Ertmer, P.A.: Essential Readings in Problem-Based Learning. Purdue University Press (2015)
86. Wood, D.F.: Problem based learning. BMJ **336**, 971 (2008)
87. DeFillippi, R.J.: Introduction: Project-Based Learning, Reflective Practices and Learning. Manage. Learn. **32**, 5–10 (2001)
88. Bell, S.: Project-based learning for the 21st century: skills for the future. Clear House J. Educ. Strateg. Issues Ideas **83**, 39–43 (2010)
89. Boss, S., Krauss, J.: Reinventing project-based learning: your field guide to real-world projects in the digital age. Int. Soc. Technol. Educ. (2014)
90. Young, T.P., Bailey, C.J., Guptill, M.: The flipped classroom: a modality for mixed asynchronous and synchronous learning in a residency program. West. J. Emerg. Med. **15** (2014)
91. Warden, C.A., Stanworth, J.O., Ren, J.B., Warden, A.R.: Synchronous learning best practices: an action research study. Comput. Educ. **63**, 197–207 (2013)

One Game Does not Fit All. Gamification and Learning: Overview and Future Directions

Leonardo Caporarello, Massimo Magni and Ferdinando Pennarola

Abstract One of the most interesting and disruptive trends in the current elearning scenario is gamification, that is, the use of game design elements in non-game contexts. This paper provides a definition of gamification in the educational field and an overview of its applications. It then discusses the existing studies on the effectiveness of gamifiction for learning purposes, focusing on their impact on students' attitude, knowledge and behavior. Finally, it highlights the main gaps in the current literature, pointing to new directions of research.

1 Introduction

Learning is one of the most relevant evolutionary and development processes of human beings, which has been studied and modeled by a wide number of different theories and approaches. In the last decades, the overall learning scenario has seen a disruption due to the digital revolution started in the latter half of the 20th century. Digital innovation has indeed brought to an expansion of the learning scenario towards e-learning, both vertically and horizontally. This shift has been pushed further by the increased connection of younger generations of learners to the digital world.

Among the other digital tools, videogames have aroused particular interest due to their diffusion among the younger generations. As a result, e-learning has paid increasing attention to the gaming universe, from the first attempts to the most sophisticated systems. One of the most appropriate definitions for this trend is Game Based Learning (GBL)[1]: with Game Based Learning, it is addressed the use

---

[1]For the purposes of this paper the term "Game Based Learning" will be used as a comprehensive label that includes all the learning techniques using digital games and game mechanics.

L. Caporarello (✉) · M. Magni · F. Pennarola
SDA Bocconi School of Management, Department of Management
and Technology, Bocconi University, Milan, Italy
e-mail: leonardo.caporarello@unibocconi.it

© Springer International Publishing AG, part of Springer Nature 2019   179
A. Lazazzara et al. (eds.), *Organizing for Digital Innovation*,
Lecture Notes in Information Systems and Organisation 27,
https://doi.org/10.1007/978-3-319-90500-6_14

of educational-related digital games that allow learners to play and experience situations that, otherwise, would have been impossible for cost, time, logistical or safety issues.

One of the most interesting and disruptive GBL trends is the gamification one due to its complexity, its completeness and versatility. Although until now literature does not provide a standard definition of gamification, maybe one of the simplest but more appropriate definitions is the one by Deterding et al. [1] describing it as *the use of game design elements in non-game contexts*; therefore, gamification represents the use of game mechanics, dynamics, and frameworks not just in education, but potentially in any field, from retail to behavioral change.

In this paper, we shall first provide an overview and a definition of gamification in the educational field, at all levels; we shall then review the studies on the effectiveness of gamification for learning purposes, and discuss them critically; and finally, we shall point to new directions of research in the field.

2 Gamification in Learning

Applications of gamification to products and services have been used from the very beginning in several industries (from retail to government) and processes (from marketing to HR). Indeed, the more the different fields evolved, the more their characteristics changed and differentiated the ones from the others, although some general trends can be observed (e.g. a shift in game design towards a more implicit and deep level).

When talking about gamification of learning processes, the spectrum of possible applications is extremely wide and diversified. In fact, gamified learning systems are used in different contexts (work, school or personal life) with different aims (initiation, engagement and evaluation of the learning process). When talking about the use of gamification at school, several applications can be seen, from first-grade school to executive education and MBA programs. Indeed, solutions differ deeply the ones from the others according to the target audience and to the quality of information transferred. An example of gamification applied to a first level classroom is the teaching of mathematical principles through the filling of puzzles and quizzes. When talking about learning in a business context, instead, the target audience is just adults. Also here solutions are several, even if less diversified in terms of game thinking than the schooling ones. An example of gamified learning applied to the work environment is the one of change management. Thanks to desktop or mobile games, employees can be involved in learning activities through games crafted to overcome their hostility towards changes or their low proactive attitude. Together with the other traditional activities, games can make it fun to learn new information about subject matters, languages, organization, processes, technologies, products and services.

In gamification applications, each functionality has got a doubled soul. On the one hand, there is the "gaming" part of the process, the one that allows users to interact with the system. On the other, there is the specific subject's part. This should never be just considered as the filling content of the system, because it represents the core of the learning activity itself and gives to the entire process the theoretical validation and justification. Each valuable gamified process, in fact, should be designed accordingly to specific aims supported by field's previous research and experience.

3 Theoretical Framework

When talking about gamification for learning the whole phenomenon can't be reduced nor to just one learning theory, nor to a single design and development strategy [2]. Implications aroused by gamification of learning processes can be summarized in two main groups of theories explaining the learning dimension of gamification:

- how learning occurs on networks by connection (Connectivism approach to knowledge transfer) or collaboration (Constructivism approach to knowledge transfer);
- how the learning activity can be enhanced through immersion and experience in a process of continuous learning through actions (Self-Determination theory and related sub-theories).

In addition to this, researchers focused on the support dimension of gamification:

- how people accept multimedia and interactive delivery methods (gamification is here considered as an evolutional step of the Digitization of learning trend)
- how people perceive games both as entertainment and in their application to the learning dimension (gamification as a Game Based Learning trend).

These dimensions, moreover, are strictly interconnected and an appropriate comprehension of the topic is possible just through its complete overview. Nevertheless, we shall provide a brief outline of gamification characteristics, means and aims when applied to education, based on the gamification literature addressing its definition [1, 3–5] through the various learning and gaming frameworks.

In this view, a new definition of gamification for learning, summarizing the related literature, can be the following:

> Gamification of learning consists in the use of game logics [6] (components, mechanics and dynamics) and game aesthetics [7] designed with the aim to promote and enhance learning through motivation [8–10] (seen as the combination of the elements of attention, relevance, confidence and satisfaction).[2]

---

[2]Among the different theories on the motivational dimension on learning, one of the most complete is the so-called ARCS model of motivational design [11].

Learning is the final outcome of a complex process entirely *studied for* and *performed by* the user. The stimuli of the gamified system, according to literature, leverage on its interest curve [3], connection and collaboration among participants [12], feedbacks and rewards [13], freedom to fail [3], storytelling, problem solving challenges and emotional engagement [14].

In this perspective, a definition of the system allowing the enhancing of the learning activity through gamification can be stated as:

> A gamified system is a digital structure built on game logics [6] and game aesthetics [7] to create student-centered learning experience [15] in order to enhance it in a self-determination perspective [16].

A schematization of the gamification of learning process as analyzed until now is provided in Fig. 1.

4 Studies on Effectiveness

A whole branch of studies analyzed gamification performances as a learning tool through experiments with students. Indeed, several gamified systems were ad hoc created to test whether they were effective. For others, instead, existing gamified tools or game-based-learning tools were tested on individuals to study which dimensions of learning experience were impacted. Indeed, studies on the enhancement of the learning processes through gamification can be split into three inter-connected sub-categories, defined by outcome measure:

Fig. 1 The gamificaiton for learning framework: from the game design to the learning experience

Table 1 Study on gamification effectiveness in changes in attitude, behavior and knowledge acquisition

	Change in attitude	Change in behavior	Change in knowledge
Positive	15	8	10
Negative	0	1	0
Neutral	6	12	11

- Change in attitude;
- Change in behavior;
- Change in knowledge.

For the purposes of this paper, a consolidation of the results was carried out based on this three-dimensional perspective of effectiveness.

Evidences from the analyzed studies showed that the most frequently occurring outcomes are positive changes in attitude towards learning (more than 70% of the analyzed studies), followed by changes in knowledge/content understanding (almost 50% of the analyzed studies) (Table 1). This reflects the parallel interests in the engaging features of games as an entertainment medium and increasingly also their use for learning. Evidences in behavioral changes are instead less strong, where most of the studies (almost 60% of them) didn't notice any change in users' behavior [17].[3]

Some studies appeared effective in every dimension. One example is the contribution of Fujimoto et al. [18], who conducted an experiment using a card game called JobStar. The results of a pre- and post-survey for participants indicated that the game offered an engaging opportunity that enhanced social interactions and facilitated participants' learning. Participants gained a positive attitude regarding their future paths and experiencing with the game made them more confident about their competence in choosing their future occupations.

Another example is the study of Morrison [19] that ran an experiment on students with BrainPlay, an artefact designed to teach and practice primary school subjects and test explicit memory acquisition. The research showed that games are useful above all to represent complexity. Indeed, they often possess mechanisms that make learning more effective through mimicking behaviors required for study (call to focus, increasing levels of difficulty of skill, repetition and the need for players to regularly remember elements such as rules or previous moves). In the repetition of the learning activity, these elements have a positive effect on learners' attitude towards school as well.

Another interesting result about how gamified systems are able to impact on people's behavior, is the study of Przybylski et al. [20]. The study is based on the motivational model associated to videogames and proves that videogames are a key

---

[3]For accuracy in reporting, it should be mentioned that most of the times changes in behaviors were out of scope of the analyzed papers. This means that evidences were not found, sometimes also because not specifically addressed.

tool for influencing cognitive evaluation. Indeed, the findings showed that different games are able to induce different decisions. That means, they change users' behaviors. Deep immersion in natural environments resulted positively correlated with more prosocial goals and decision-making, whereas high levels of immersion in less natural contexts produced more self-interested orientations.

These are among the best representative outcomes for highly effectiveness gamification systems. A complete overview of the studies, nevertheless, highlights that results appear overall highly heterogeneous. Indeed, a deeper analysis of the studies' characteristics could explain why the outcomes are not uniform. First, every gamified system is different from the others. A direct comparison among different systems, due to the importance of game logic design and desired aesthetics, wouldn't be reliable. Second, studies differed for learning topics and objectives. This is for sure a further obstacle in the comparison of different research works, since the effectiveness of knowledge acquisition doesn't just depend on the means involved, but also on the complexity of what is taught/learned. Last but not least, some differences concern the target users involved in the gamified experiences. Indeed, almost every study devoted some effort to the definition of the target users. As mentioned before, in fact, the personal background of learners is fundamental both during the game play and in its approach.

5 Discussion

As emerged in the screening of the literature on gamification, until now researchers have mostly focused especially on the definition and evaluation of two aspects of gamification for education: its design and its educational effectiveness.

As far as the design of gamified systems and their relative definition and classification are concerned, a branch of the studies aimed to create a systematic review of all the gamification theorization attempts, based on its frameworks. Indeed, they suggested specific definitions and evaluation criteria starting from the educational and gaming literature.

As far as the measure of effectiveness is concerned, instead, literature focused on the three dimensions of possible change induced by gamification: changes in attitude, in behavior and in knowledge. Indeed, the vast majority of the studies on gamification applications to learning provided positive or neutral results. Gamification resulted to be at least not significantly correlated to student's performances in everyone of the case studies. This is not a minor outcome. Indeed, negative effects of both digital learning systems and gaming tools have been found. As far as digital learning is concerned, for example, Sereetrakul [21] tested Facebook as a facilitator of connection among people to enhance a learning goal. Nevertheless, they found that it had a negative impact on students' performance, due to its distracting potential.

Most of the empirical studies on gamified systems focused on during-the-experience evaluation and after-the-experience evaluation. Indeed, just a very limited number of studies focused consistently on before-the-experience evaluation. The dimension, nevertheless, is far from being easy to address. Expectations towards gamified learning systems, in fact, involve both elements coming from the socio-demographic background and from the personal learning, gaming and ICT perception. Moreover, expectations appear to be fundamental in order to predict the motivation to use a gamified system and, indeed, the intention to use it.

In particular, people's expectations towards gamification should not be underestimated due to two main reasons regarding both the first adoption and the iteration in using gamified systems. First of all, expectations are crucial when evaluating the intention of people to start using a gamification method for the first time. Indeed, the choosing process of whether put effort in a new activity or not was theorized by the so-called *Expectancy Theory of Motivation* [22]. This model is based on the concept of scarcity, and proposes that individuals are motivated to choose a certain behavior over others, based on what they expect the result of that behavior will be [23]. Indeed, people would be motivated to choose gamification over other learning methods just if their expectations towards gamification will be higher than the ones towards traditional learning. According to this theory, underestimating or overestimating the evaluation of people's expectations would lead to a misrepresentation of their motivation to take part in the gamified experience. That means, consequently, an erroneous prediction of prospect users' intention to participate.

Another support to the importance of expectations not just in the phase of first adoption of the gamified system, but also in its further iterated use, is the expectation disconfirmation theory (EDT) [24]. In IT context, EDT explains how technology satisfaction is created as users form initial expectations of the technology, use it and compare technology performance against initial expectations. Indeed, expectations are seen as user's anticipated perceptions of the future experience itself. Although apparently self-explaining, the results of the model are far from being obvious, especially if combined with the *Expectancy Theory of Motivation's* ones.

For example, according to the *Expectations Disconfirmation Theory*, higher satisfaction is easier to reach when expectations are low, and *vice versa*. When pre-test expectations are extremely high, it is harder to overcome them and consequently the post-test evaluation is more likely to show a medium-low satisfaction. Nevertheless, low expectations are not always a good index at all. Without a reasonably high level of expectations, in fact, according to the *Expectancy Theory of Motivation* people will not be motivated enough to live the experience itself.

Indeed, it is due to the fundamental role of motivation in gamification literature that a study wholly devoted to its connection to expectations is needed. Motivation, in fact, is important in gamification for more than one reason: on the one hand, it allows users to play the gamified system action after action, enacting, one step after the other, the whole learning path. On the other hand, as mentioned before, the motivational incentive is critical in the approach to the gamified system itself.

Despite the rich theoretical evidence for the importance of expectations and motivation of prospect users towards gamified learning systems, just a very limited number of studies focused on the before-the-experience moment. Moreover, none of the investigated studies went deeper in the analysis of general expectations towards gamified learning systems, and of the intention whether to use them. Most of the studies testing expectations and perceptions of gamified systems, in fact, were conducted in already existing classes. Even though different studies were conducted in classes differing for both dimension and school grade, any comparison among results of the existing literature appears to be difficult run due to several reasons.

First, most of the times results show per se a scarce significance. At first, this limit may be explained because the topic is almost never the main research purpose. A deeper analysis of the reasons behind a low significance of results shows that students in the same class tend to have a similar background. Analyzed records, in fact, will be likely to be really close to each other, representing a poor estimation model not able to predict expected behaviors. What could happen is that apparently identical children under the considered dimensions would take opposite decisions without apparent reason.

A practical example of this limitation was described in the research of Cheong et al. [6] that focused on the perception of gamified learning in a group of 51 undergraduate IT students. The study consisted in a before-the-experience evaluation and was centered on the perception of game elements. Indeed, among the limitations of the study the researchers reported the extremely similar background of participants that did not allow researchers to specifically find some significant trends. In literature, the fact that gamified experiences are usually offered to homogeneous classes leads to both a scarce consistency of the tested model and a low representativeness of the results for a wider public.

Second, experiments are hard to compare since students living in-class experiences are really likely to be influenced by contingent extra-experiment interactions. Indeed, this could happen in both the instructor-student relationship and the student-student one. As far as the first kind of connection is concerned, studies are not comparable since the personality of the instructors and their relationship with the class (which usually fall outside the scope of gamifications studies) is a potentially extremely high bias in expectations' measurement. Whether a teacher is considered reliable by his students, for example, could significantly influence learners' expectations.

As far as the relationship among classmates is concerned, instead, the bias stems from the different nature of classmates' relationships in different classes (e.g. relationships among primary school children *vs.* relationships among MBA students). It should also be considered that in almost every study, interactions happened both online and offline. Indeed, a further problem concerns the tracking of interactions in order to measure their relevance and relative influence in the measured outputs. Once again, the heterogeneity of the samples, even if potentially positive for its broad spectrum, does not allow an effective comparison of results. Last but not least, it should be mentioned that the analyzed studies don't even share a common definition of gamification: as it has been seen, in fact, definitions substantially differ the ones from the others.

6   Research Proposition

What appears to be useful in order to overcome all of these limits is *a cross-sectional study on the topic*. Indeed, an ad hoc designed cross-sectional study may help investigate different people's expectations and motivation to take part in a gamified learning system. A deeper analysis of literature in this direction showed that some cross-sectional surveys have already being carried out with the aim to investigate the willingness to use gamification. A meaningful example is the study of Hamari and Koivisto [25], which focused on the social factors predicting attitudes towards gamification and intention to continue using a gamified service (Fitocracy) for physical exercise. As it can be easily argued, nevertheless, the study is not related to learning at all. Other studies have been carried out but none of them specifically addressed gamification for learning. Indeed, these studies could not be significant for this purpose for two reasons. First, the personal background of individuals involved in the learning experience is not accounted for. Second, the expectations towards the effectiveness of gamification as a learning tool are totally missing. Moreover, none of them adopted the aforementioned theoretical framework connecting expectations towards gamification to motivation and, in the end, the intention to really use it.

Indeed, this is why further study on the topic is needed. In particular, it could be interesting to examine which aspects of the personal background majorly impact on prospect users' expectations. Moreover, the expectation dimension could be analyzed taking into account both the learning aspect and the interactive and connecting one. Indeed, assumed that the final aim of the gamified experience is the acquisition of knowledge through a non-conventional method, this study might also help understand how different dimensions of expectations affect people's motivation to take part in the process. These findings, in the end, may be a significant addition to gaming and learning literature, not just towards designing successful gamified systems, but also towards properly tailoring them to their prospect users' background and expectations.

References

1. Deterding, S., Dixon, D., Khaled, R., Nacke, L.: From Game Design Elements to Gamefulness: Defining "Gamification". In: MindTrek 11. Tampere, Finland (2011)
2. Bozkurt, A., Akgun-Ozbek, E., Yilmazel, S., Erdogdu, E., Ucar, H., Gule, E., Aydin, C.H.: Trends in distance education research: A content analysis of journals 2009–2013. Int. Rev. Res. Open Distributed Learn. 330–363 (2015)
3. Kapp, K.: Games, gamification, and the quest for learner engagement. T+D Magazine Am. Soc. Training Develop. 64–68 (2012)
4. Kapp, K.: The Gamification of Learning and Instruction: Game-Based Methods and Strategies for Training and Education. Pleiffer, San Francisco (2012)
5. Zichermann, G., Linder, J.: Game-Based Marketing: Inspire Customer Loyalty though Rewards, Challenges and Contests. Wiley, Hoboken, NJ (2010)

6. Cheong, C., Filippou, J., Cheong, F.: Towards the gamification of learning: investigating student perceptions of game elements. J. Info. Syst. Edu. (2014)
7. Hunicke, R., LeBlanc, M., Zubek, R.: MDA: A formal approach to game design and game research. In: Game Design and Tuning Workshop at the Game Developers Conference. San Jose (2004)
8. Zichermann, G., Cunningham, C.: Gamification by Design: Implementing Game Mechanics in Web and Mobile Apps. O'Reilly Media, Inc. (2011)
9. Rubin, K., Fein, G.G., Vandenberg, B.: Handbook of Child Psychology: Vol 4. Socialization, Personality, and Social Development. In: E.M. Hetherington (Ed.), New York(1983)
10. Dörnyei, Z., Ushioda, E.: Teaching and Researching: Motivation. Longman Publishing Group, UK (2010)
11. Hamzah, W.A., Haji Ali, N., Saman, M.M., Yusoff, M.H., Yacob, A.: Influence of gamification on students' motivation in using e-learning applications based on the motivational design model. Int. J. Emerging Technol. Learn. 30–34 (2015)
12. Romero, M., Ott, M., de Freitas, S., Earp, J.: Learning through playing for or against each other? Promoting collaborative learning in digital game based learning. In: European Conference on Information Systems (ECIS). Association for Information Systems AIS Electronic Library (AISeL) (2012)
13. Raymer, R.L Gamification: Using game mechanics to enhance elearning elearn magazine. eLearning Magazine (2013)
14. Connolly, T.M., Boyle, E.A., MacArthur, E., Hainey, T., Boyle, J.M.: A systematic literature review of empirical evidence on computer games and serious games. Comput. Edu. 661–686 (2012)
15. Nicholson, S.L.: A user-centred theoretical framework for meaningful gamification. In: Proceedings of Games+Learning+Society 8.0. Madison, WI (2012)
16. Aparicio, A.F., Vela, F.L., Sànchez, J., Montes, J.: Analysis and application of gamification. In: Proceedings of the 13th International Conference on Interacciòn Persona-Ordenador (p. 17). Elche, Interacion (2012)
17. Bahji, S.E., Lefdaoui, Y., El Alami, J.: S2P learning model for combining game-based learning and text-based learning. In: 5th Guide International Conference 2011 E-learning innovative models for the integration of education, technology and research. Rome, Italy (2011)
18. Fujimoto, T., Fukuyama, Y., Azami, T.: Game-based learning for youth career education with the card game 'JobStar'. In: Conference: The 9th European Conference on Games Based Learning (p. 203). Steinkjer, Norway; Nord-Trondelag University College (2011)
19. Morrison, G.: BrainPlay: Serious game, serious learning? In: European Conference on Games Based Learning (pp. 680–686). Reading: Academic Conferences International Limited (2015)
20. Przybylski, A., Rigby, C. S., Ryan, R.M.: A motivational model of video game engagement. *Review of General Psychology American Psychological Association*, 154–166 (2010)
21. Sereetrakul, W.: Students' Facebook usage and academic achievement: A case study of private university in Thailand. In: IADIS International Conference con Cognition and Exploratory Learning in the Digital Age (pp. 40–56). Unt University of Noth Texas, Fort Worth, Texas (2013)
22. Vroom, V.H.: Work and motivation, (p. 196). Wiley, New York (1964)
23. Oliver, R.L.: Expectancy theory predictions of salesmen's performance. J. Market. Res. 243–253 (1974)
24. Lankton, N.K., McKnight, H.D.: Examining two expectation disconfirmation heory models: Assimilation and asymmetry effect. J. Assoc. Info. Syst. 88–115 (2012)
25. Hamari, J., Koivisto, J.: Social motivations to use gamification: an empirical study on gamified exercise. In: Proceedings of the 21st European Conference on Information Systems. Association for Information Systems AIS Electronic Library (2013)

Being Absorbed in Technological Learning Environments: Distraction, Boredom and the Effects of a Creative Climate on Learning and Training Transfer

Daniela Aliberti and Chiara Paolino

Abstract The gap this study addresses is the relationship between absorption, its negative antecedents—distraction and boredom—and its outcomes on learning and training transfer in environments characterized by technological learning. To address this research goal, the purpose of this study is to develop a theoretical model to explain these relationships, in order to understand the role of absorption to shape different training outcomes. While some research has emphasized the positive antecedents of absorption, we focus on the drawbacks of distraction and boredom. In addition, we theorize how creative climate moderates the link between distraction, boredom, absorption and training outcomes.

1 Introduction

In the recent decades, there has been a shift to technology in all aspects of organizational life. To invest in information technology constitutes a significant aspect of organizational work and it potentially contributes to the strategic and operational goals of a firm. Most importantly, it has been acknowledged that information technology is particularly effective for organizational learning as it can enable the application of constructive, cognitive, collaborative and sociocultural ways of learning [27], together with intentional changes in teaching and learning processes. Furthermore, previous studies have addressed the application of IT support to the processes of organizational learning and knowledge management, identifying technology as an infrastructure for sharing, accessing and revising elements of organizational memory [34]. The use of IT has become a major trend in manage-

D. Aliberti (✉) · C. Paolino (✉)
Università Cattolica del Sacro Cuore, Milan, Italy
e-mail: daniela.aliberti@unicatt.it

C. Paolino
e-mail: Chiara.Paolino@unicatt.it

© Springer International Publishing AG, part of Springer Nature 2019   189
A. Lazazzara et al. (eds.), *Organizing for Digital Innovation*,
Lecture Notes in Information Systems and Organisation 27,
https://doi.org/10.1007/978-3-319-90500-6_15

ment education and it is has been recognized as a key resource in enabling innovative and enhanced learning [2].

For the aim of this research, we focus on technological environments characterized by a high degree of absorption, as they appear to be particularly effective for learning. Previous studies have already observed the role of absorption in enhancing learning process in technological environments [1, 28]. Motivated by a need to examine further the negative antecedents of absorption, in this paper we focus on distraction and boredom [5, 7] and we aim to understand how they negatively affect different training outcomes, specifically learning and training transfer, through the mechanism of absorption itself.

Furthermore, we aim at exploring the role of creative climate in these relationships. Research has widely focused on climate as a training dimension to investigate in order to understand training outcomes, focusing on several dimensions such as learning climate and error climate. We believe that creative climate is particularly interesting to be analyzed as a boundary condition when exploring negative antecedents and training consequences of absorption.

Thus, in this paper, we develop a theoretical model and related testable propositions about the relationship between absorption and its negative antecedents, distraction and boredom; the role of absorption to shape different training outcomes; and we will focus on the role of creative climate as a moderator of these relationships (see Fig. 1). Therefore, the paper aims to provide a theoretical framework on the role of absorption in the context of technology mediated learning. In addition, it offers testable propositions about absorption's antecedents and the boundary conditions for their links to training outcomes.

The propositions offered in this paper can be tested in a learning setting that is designed with the goal to use technology to develop engaging environments that may favor learning. From such a perspective, the ideal setting for testing our propositions is within a managerial classroom on organizational behavior topics and that relies on a computer-based simulation as a metaphorical context to transfer the

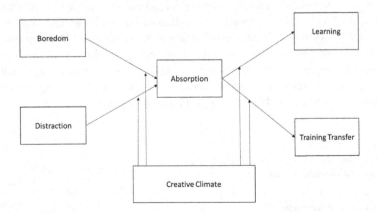

Fig. 1 *Research* model

content of the class. More specifically, in order to outline the role of the climate, the most suitable simulations are those developed to be played in-group settings (e.g. classes or teams).

2   Concepts and Propositions

Absorption is a state of intense psychological involvement in an activity, which helps a mechanism of total immersion in this given activity [13]. It has been acknowledged that, through this mechanism, people enjoy themselves and are able to intensively focus on a task [1]. The concept of absorption is often linked to what researchers have called a state of flow—which represents the mechanisms through which it is potentially able to influence individual learning. The state of flow can be described through the following dimensions: intense concentration, sense of being in control, a loss of self-consciousness and transformation of time dimension. Csikszentmihalyi [13] argues that these elements are able to build an optimal experience of learning, especially in the interaction with symbolic systems—like mathematics and computer language, which characterizes computer-based simulations.

On the one side, the concept of absorption is pivotal to understand and measure the interaction human-technology and its potential in terms of training outcomes [40]. The positive effect of absorption on learning has been investigated by several studies in the training domain—as they show that high absorption is critical to effective training because it is able to leverage on individual intrinsic motivation, involvement and enjoyment during a learning experience [24, 29, 38, 39]. However, there are studies that have questioned this positive effect of absorption on training outcomes, implying a more complex relationship. For this reason, in this study, we want to better explore this link, by theorizing a different relationship between absorption and learning, and absorption and training transfer. We argue that, not only the relationship between absorption and learning is not linear, in accordance to previous research, but also that this relationship is differently shaped if we consider more long term outcomes, with respect to learning, such as the transfer on the job.

On the other side, it is interesting to analyze the negative antecedents of absorption and how it is a mediating mechanism between these antecedents and training outcomes. While extant research on how to enforce absorption in technology based learning environment is wide, the dark side of these learning experiences on absorption is not fully developed from a theoretical and empirical standpoint. This is especially true if we consider both shorter and longer-term outcomes, such as learning and transfer. Consequently, there is the need to study what would be the effect of distraction and boredom on absorption and to understand how absorption, as influenced by distraction and boredom, can influence learning and training transfer.

According to this analysis, the state of the art on absorption makes it worthy to argue about the boundary conditions for its link with training outcomes and its less explored antecedents. In particular, as noted above, we focus on creative climate as a meaningful moderator of the links among boredom, distraction, and absorption and training outcomes. Creative climate enhances not only the traditional perception of resources, but also the perception of freedom and challenge [16]. In this way, creative climate can be assumed to interact and to compensate the effect of distraction and boredom to shape absorption, and with absorption to shape training outcomes.

In the following paragraphs, the concepts of analysis and their relationships will be illustrated. A final section is dedicated to the contribution and the next steps of this research.

2.1 Distraction, Boredom and Absorption

We look at distraction as a given aspect of a repetitive, routinary activity involving the use of technology. Distractions are stimuli that direct attention away from the ongoing activity and they are caused, for example, by information overload [30]. Previous literature in this area describes a variety of causes of information overload associated with the use of information technology. The characteristics of information technology, such as the ability of IT to push information at a user—for example through e-mail [8, 37], incoming text messages, or data verification pop-up notifications in tax preparation software—have the potential to induce information overload in the recipient. Studies have shown that while multitasking may increase productivity up to a certain point, after that threshold is reached workers face diminishing marginal returns [4]. It is argued that the higher the rate of multitasking, the higher the cognitive switching costs between tasks. As a result, due to distraction, cognitive load increases and the ability to stay focused and to acquire knowledge decreases.

Boredom happens to influence cognition and deep learning [13, 31] and it is often preceded by a sense of frustration about one's own work [33]. Previous research has focused on detecting frustration in human-computer interaction [20, 26]. Recent research considers boredom as a primary cognitive-affective state [5], which shows its significance with respect to the negative correlation to learning [5, 12, 18]. It has a negative valence and low level of arousal [5], according to the core-affect framework built by Russell [35]; in particular, as re-adapted by Baker et al. [5], boredom can be placed between the senses of displeasure and deactivation (re-adaptation of the learning-centered cognitive-affective states mapped by Russel [35], by Baker et al. [5]). Csikszentmihalyi [13] argues that flow incorporates the concept of concentration, but boredom may represent a persistent element able to influence this state [5]—here is the negative potential of boredom with respect to concentration, to flow and, as a consequence, to absorption.

According to the above mentioned arguments, we develop the following propositions:

Proposition 1: distraction will have a negative effect on absorption
Proposition 2: boredom will have a negative effect on absorption.

2.2 Absorption, Learning and Training Transfer

The effects of absorption have been investigated in several educational and learning-oriented settings, such as higher education [17, 25], foreign language studies [15], and music education [14]. Research has explored the positive influence of absorption, and many studies have yielded support for the positive impact of cognitive absorption on learning in various educational situations. As above stated, when people are in a state of absorption, they undertake tasks with attentiveness and vigor, which have the potential to improve training outcomes in classroom environments [13]. Indeed, the flow experience increases individual concentration, the sense of control, and personal enjoyment [19], and in doing so, it positively affects the individual's perception of self-efficacy and motivation to learn [13].

Nonetheless, we argue that absorption might also have negative and differential effects on training outcomes, depending on the result we are investigating [10, 23]. Magni et al. [28] state that individual learning will be most effective when there are moderate levels of cognitive absorption. In this light, training participants who reach a balance between immersion and reflection in an engaging training experience are better poised to transform their experience into learning [9]. Along with these studies, we aim at replicating that there is a curvilinear relationship between absorption and learning outcomes. In addition, given this questioned effect of absorption on learning, we aim at extending previous research by comparing the effect of absorption on learning and on training transfer.

In particular, for transfer to occur "a learned behavior must be generalized to the job context and maintained over a period of time on the job" [6]. Given this more durable behavioral transformation implied in the concept of transfer, we argue that the relationship between absorption and transfer is still curvilinear, but that it is weaker than the one between absorption and learning. This is because the detachment caused by too high level of absorption can produce a weaker result on a behavioral application on the job, since the transfer activity is temporarily, physically and cognitively separated from the training moment and from the experience of absorption. Thus, transfer implies for the trainee the additional effort of connecting to the job an experience of full concentration, enjoyment in a training experience carried out through technology in a completely different and detached setting from the job one. We argue that this distance implies a weaker curvilinear relationship between absorption and transfer than between absorption and learning.

On the basis of the previous arguments, we formulate the following propositions.

Proposition 3: absorption will have an inverted u-shaped effect on learning
Proposition 4: absorption will have an inverted u-shaped effect on training transfer
Proposition 5: absorption has a stronger effect on learning than on training transfer.

2.3   Creative Climate

People's perceptions and beliefs of environmental attributes shape expectations about outcomes, contingencies, requirements and interactions in the work environment [22, 32, 36]. They have a localized nature that communicates these expectations at an individual and at a group level [11], which we consider as able to moderate the effects of absorption on learning processes and training transfer. A number of different theoretical frames have been built to specify which climate variables define a creative one [3, 21, 41]. We consider the creative climate definition that recalls the conditions useful to make learning through technology effective, focusing on the creative climate questionnaires (CCQs) by Ekvall [16]. The CCQ instrument covers ten dimensions: challenge, freedom, idea support, trust/openness, dynamism/liveliness, playfulness/humor, debates, conflicts, risk taking and idea time.

Theoretically, there are two mechanisms through which a creative climate may enhance the effect of absorption on learning and training transfer, while reducing the negative outcomes of boredom and distraction. As stated above, a creative climate enhances innovation through the perception of playfulness; therefore, it enhances enjoyment, the emergence of new ideas, and the challenge. In this way, it is able to weaken the negative effect of distraction and boredom on absorption. For what concerns learning outcomes, a creative climate is able to allow the re-focus on the task and to give people the perception of having intrinsic resources at their disposal to cope with the learning task. All of these elements would contribute to the creation of a context that potentially becomes more effective for leveraging the impact of absorption on learning and transfer, while weakening the negative effect of distraction and boredom.

On the basis of the above reported arguments we develop the following propositions:

Proposition 6a: creative climate will moderate the relationship between boredom and absorption
Proposition 6b: creative climate will moderate the relationship between distraction and absorption
Proposition 7a: creative climate will moderate the relationship between absorption and learning
Proposition 7b: creative climate will moderate the relationship between absorption and training transfer

As follows, we provide a table depicting all the variables included in our theoretical model. In Table 1, we also suggest the measures that should be adopted; all of them rely on scales validated in previous established studies and they should be adapted for the training environment. Beyond the perceptual approach, when possible according to extant literature, we indicate objective measures of the listed variables.

3 Contribution

The above-mentioned propositions contribute to the state of research of absorption in technological learning environments, by clarifying how distraction and boredom affect absorption and how absorption influences in different ways learning and training transfer. We enrich in this way the debate around absorption as the process through which learning and transfer occur in the technological training environment, by illustrating its mediating role in the link between negative aspects of this environment, boredom and distraction, and training results.

In addition, this study can contribute to theoretically discuss and set the boundaries among boredom, distraction and absorption, clarifying the nature of absorption itself as the process that can foster learning but at the same time harmed by the sources of distraction and boredom.

Table 1 Variables and measures

Variables	Sample items and objective measurement approach
Absorption (14-items scale)	Sample items: 'Time appeared to go by very fast during the training; Sometimes I lost track of time during the training; Time flied doing the tasks/during the training'
Learning (5-items scale)	Sample items: 'I was able to acquire important know-how through this training; I learned important lessons from this training; This training improved my professional knowledge' Objective measure: multiple-choice test on the concepts and relationships explored during the training
Training Transfer (9-items scales)	Sample item: 'My productivity has improved due to the skills that I learned during the training'
Distraction (8-items)	Sample items: 'other participants' laptop interfered with my attention to the training; other participants talking interfered with my attention to the training; other participants coming and going' Objective measure: observation of how many times participants checked emails, surfed the web, lost track of what the instructor was saying
Boredom (17-items)	Sample items: 'the training was monotonous; I got apathetic during the training; I often got bored during the training'
Creative Climate (10 dimensions)	Sample items: 'many different points of view were shared during the training; differences of opinion were frequently expressed during the training; people often exchanged opposing viewpoints during the training'

Data is going to be collected through a survey administrated to a sample of executive master participants enrolled in a management program, according to at least two waves of data collection, in order to gather independent, mediator and dependent variables at different times.

References

1. Agarwal, R., Karahanna, E.: Time flies when you're having fun: Cognitive absorption and beliefs about information technology usage. MIS Q. **24**, 665–694 (2000)
2. Alavi M., Gallupe R.B.: Using Information Technology in Learning: Case Studies in Business and Management Education Programs; Academy of Management Learning & Education, (Vol. 2, No. 2, pp. 139–153) (2003)
3. Amabile, T.M., Conti, R.: Changes in the work environment for creativity during downsizing. Acad. Manag. J. **42**, 630–641 (1999)
4. Aral S, Brynjolfsson E, Van Alstyne M.: Information, technology and information worker productivity: task level evidence. In: Proceedings of the 27th Annual International Conference on Information Systems, 2006, Milwaukee, Wisconsin (2006)
5. Baker, R.S.J., D'Mello, S.K., Rodrigo, M.M.T., Graesser, A.C.: Better to be frustrated than bored: The incidence, persistence, and impact of learners' cognitive–affective states during interactions with three different computer-based learning environments. Int. J. Human-Computer Studies **68**(2010), 223–241 (2010)
6. Baldwin T.T., Ford J.K.: Transfer of Training: A Review and Directions for future research. Person. Psychol., 41 (1988)
7. Basoglu, K.A., Fuller, M.A., Sweeney, J.T.: Investigating the effects of computer mediated interruptions: An analysis of task characteristics and interruption frequency on financial performance. Int. J. Account. Inf. Syst. **10**, 177–189 (2009)
8. Bawden, D.: Information Overload. British Library Research and Development Department, London (2001)
9. Carver, L., Turoff, M.: Human computer interaction: The human and computer as a group in emergency management information systems. Commun. ACM **50**, 33–38 (2007)
10. Chou, C., Condron, L., Belland, J.C.: A review of the review on internet addiction. Educ. Psychol. Rev. **17**, 363–368 (2005)
11. Cooke, R.A., Rousseau, D.M.: Behavioral norms and expectations: A quantitative approach to the assessment of organizational culture. Group Organ. Stud. **13**, 245–273 (1988)
12. Craig, S.D., Graesser, A.C., Sullins, J., Gholson, B.: Affect and learning: an exploratory look into the role of affect in learning with AutoTutor. J. Educ. Media **29**(3), 241–250 (2004)
13. Csikszentmihalyi, M.: Flow: The psychology of optimal experience. HarperCollins, New York (1990)
14. Custodero, L.A.: Seeking challenge, finding skill: Flow experience and music education. Arts Educ. Policy Rev. **103**, 3–9 (2002)
15. Egbert, J.: A study of flow theory in the foreign language classroom. Modern Language J. **87**, 499–518 (2003)
16. Ekvall, G.: Organizational climate for creativity and innovation. Euro. J. Work Organ. Psychol. **5**, 105–124 (1996)
17. Ghani, J.A.: Flow in human-computer interactions: Test of a model. In: Carey, J.M. (ed.) Human/actors in information systems: Emerging theoretical bases, pp. 291–309. Ablex, Norwood, NJ (1995)
18. Graesser, A.C., Rus, V., D'Mello, S., Jackson, G.T.: AutoTutor: learning through natural language dialogue that adapts to the cognitive and affective states of the learner Current Perspectives on Cognition. In: Robinson, D.H., Schraw, G. (eds.) Learning and Instruction:

Recent Innovations in Educational Technology that Facilitate Student Learning, pp. 95–125. Information Age Publishing, USA (2008)

19. Guo, Y., Ro, Y.: Capturing flow in the business classroom. Decis. Sci. **6**, 437–462 (2008)
20. Hone, K.: Empathic agents to reduce user frustration: the effects of varying agent characteristics. Interact. Comput. **18**, 227–245 (2006)
21. Isaksen, S.G., Lauer, K.L.: The climate for creativity and change in teams. Creativ. Inno. Management. **11**, 74–86 (2002)
22. James, L.R., James, L.A., Ashe, D.K.: The meaning of organizations: The role of cognition and values. In: Schneider, B. (ed.) Organizational climate and culture, pp. 40–84. Jossey-Bass, San Francisco (1990)
23. Jia, R., Hartke, H., Pearson, J.: Can computer playfulness and cognitive absorption lead to Problematic technology usage? In: Proceedings of the 28th International Conference on Information Systems (ICIS) (2007)
24. Keys, B., Wolfe, J.: The role of management games and simulations in education and research. J. Manag. **16**, 307–336 (1990)
25. Kiili, K.: Content creation challenges and flow experience in educational games: The IT-Emperor case. Int. Higher Educ. **8**, 183–198 (2005)
26. Klein, J., Moon, Y., Picard, R.: This computer responds to user frustration—theory, design, and results. Interact. Comput. **14**(2), 119–140 (2002)
27. Leidner, D.E., Jarvenpaa, S.L.: The use of information technology to enhance management school education: A theoretical view. MIS Q. **19**, 265–291 (1995)
28. Magni, M., Paolino, C., Cappetta, R.: (2013); Diving too Deep: How Cognitive Absorption and Group Learning Behavior affect Individual Learning. Acad. Manage. Learn. Educ. **12**(1), 51–69 (2013)
29. Mathieu, J.E., Martineau, J.W.: Individual and situational influences on training motivation. In: Ford, J.K., Kozlowski, S., Kraiger, K., Salas, E., Teachout, M. (eds.) Improving training effectiveness in work organizations, pp. 193–221. Erlbaum, Mahwah, NJ (1997)
30. Milford, J.T., Perry, R.P.: A methodological study of overload. J. Gen. Psych. **97**, 131–137 (1977)
31. Miserandino, M.: Children who do well in school: individual differences in perceived competence and autonomy in above-average children. J. Educ. Psychol. **88**, 203–214 (1996)
32. Parker, C.P., Baltes, B.B., Young, S.A., Huff, J.W.: Relationships between psychological climate perceptions and work outcomes: a meta-analytic review. J. Organ. Beh. **24**(4), 389–416 (2003)
33. Perkins, R.E., Hill, A.B.: Cognitive and affective aspects of boredom. Br. J. Psychol. **76**(2), 221–234 (1985)
34. Robey, D., Boudreau, M.C., Rose, G.M.: Information Technology and organizational learning: a review and assessment of research. Account. Manage. Info. Technol. **10**(2), 125–155 (2000)
35. Russell, J.: Core affect and the psychological construction of emotion. Psychol. Rev. **110**, 145–172 (2003)
36. Schneider, B., Reichers, A.E.: On the Etiology of Climates. Pers. Psychol. **36**(1), 19–39 (1983)
37. Schultze, U., Vandenbosch, B.: Information overload in a groupware environment: now you see it, now you don't. J. Organ. Comput. Electron. Commer. **8**, 127–148 (1998)
38. Tannenbaum, S., Yukl, G.: Training and development in work organizations. Annu. Rev. Psychol. **43**, 399–441 (1992)
39. Tharenou, P. 2001. The relationship of training motivation to participation in training and development. J. Occup. Organ. Psychol. **74**r, 599–621
40. Trevino, L.K., Webster, J.: Flow in computer- mediated communication: electronic mail and voice mail evaluation and impacts. Commun. Res. **19**(5), 539–573 (1992)
41. West, M.A., Borrill, C.S., Dawson, J.F., Brodbeck, F.C., Shapiro, D.A., Howard, B.: Leadership clarity and team innovation in health care. Leadersh. Quart. **14**, 393–410 (2003)

Discovering Blended Learning Adoption: An Italian Case Study in Higher Education

Pietro Previtali and Danila Scarozza

Abstract In the last decade, online education has become a fast-growing delivery method in higher education in Italy. According to data provided by the Italian Ministry of Education, Universities and Research during the academic year 2014–2015, 60,000 students were enrolled in a Telematic University, experiencing a 60% growth rate in the last five years. In this frame it is important to inquire about blended learning adoption and implementation in order to assist University leaders in changing policies that will lead to improvement of teaching and learning conditions. Using a case study and conducting a survey on online structure this paper aims: (a) to identify institutional strategy, structure, and support markers that would allow administrators to determine their progress in transitioning exploration of blended learning to implementation; (b) to understand what are the main factors affecting satisfaction of faculty involved in a blended learning experience.

1 Introduction

The progression of information technology such as internet surged the growth of online educational programs that change the traditional system of education [1, 2]. Also in Italy, in the last decade, online education has become a fast-growing delivery method in higher education [3, 4]. Evidence of the embracement of online education is provided through the analysis of trends over the last decade. According to data provided by the Italian Ministry of Education, Universities and Research during the academic year 2014–2015, 60,000 students were enrolled in a Telematic University, experiencing a 60% growth rate in the last five years. The current economic downturn has increased demand for both online courses and programs it is expected that this trend will continue. Maeroff [5] maintained that developments

P. Previtali · D. Scarozza (✉)
University of Pavia, Via San Felice 5, 27100 Pavia, Italy
e-mail: danila.scarozza@uniov.it

© Springer International Publishing AG, part of Springer Nature 2019
A. Lazazzara et al. (eds.), *Organizing for Digital Innovation*,
Lecture Notes in Information Systems and Organisation 27,
https://doi.org/10.1007/978-3-319-90500-6_16

in online education are not "just a fad" but a "sea change" (p. 2). The amalgamation of knowledge and technology permits higher education to provide learning anytime, anyplace, and to anyone [6, 7]. Today, online education represents a firmly embedded part of the higher education landscape: the use of information and communications technologies (ICT) has facilitated an explosive growth in this relatively new method of teaching. Moreover, the emergence of technology has become a competitive advantage for higher education institutions as it can provide an alternative approach in providing better quality of learning.

According to several scholars [8–11], the "blended learning" represents one of the most recurrent approach to deliver course content. Probably its features contribute to the diffusion of this approach since it combines traditional face-to-face teaching, typically with the use of online teaching resources and materials. Concurrent with the phenomenal growth in blended learning, stakeholders in education continue to demand greater accountability and evidence of effectiveness in teaching [12, 13]. One of the ways to evaluate the effectiveness of blended learning is through the satisfaction of its users [14]. Wu and Liu [15] revealed several studies that consider student satisfaction as a crucial parameter to evaluate and assess the learning effectiveness specifically in academic institution.

However, along with students' satisfaction, also faculty's satisfaction is a critical building block of quality [16–18] in online education. Faculty's satisfaction is quite important, given that it affects faculty's motivation, which, in turn, contributes to enhancing students' learning experience. Webster and Hackley [19] stated that the positive attitude by e-learning instructors toward technology, interactive teaching style, and control over technology contributed to some of the success of effective learning.

Even though many studies have been conducted on online learning, studies specifically on blended learning are still scarce [14]. Relatively little research on blended learning addresses institutional adoption, although such research would benefit institutions of higher education in strategically adopting and implementing blended learning [20]. Moreover, as factors that would influence satisfaction towards blended learning are still explored. Thus it would be interesting to identify the issue. In this frame, it would be interesting to identify both the issues. Without faculty engagement, in fact, any initiative to adopt a blended learning approach is likely to fail [21]. After all, faculty members are the primary decision-makers in their courses [22]. Research involving distance education has recognized the importance of considering faculty members' attitudes and experiences but existing literature has often neglected the faculty perspective.

Using a case study to describe the implementation of a blended learning approach involving today 2200 students and approximately 50 teachers at the University of Pavia (Italy) (UNIPV), this paper has a twofold purpose:

1. on the one hand, the aim is to analyze the adoption of a blended learning approach in an Italian University identifying institutional strategy, structure, and

support markers that would allow administrators to determine their progress in transitioning from awareness and exploration of blended learning to adoption and implementation;

2. on the other hand, the goal is understand what are the main factors affecting satisfaction of faculty involved in a blended learning experience.

2 Understanding Blended Learning

Blended learning is the combination of two words: blend and learning. *Blend* means combining things and *learning* can be defined as the acquisition of new knowledge [23]. Even if there is not a commonly accepted definition of blended learning [23], it is usually defined as "the mix of traditional methods of teaching, such as face-to-face teaching and online teaching" [11, 24: p. 233, 25–28]. Due to its features, this is perhaps the most common meaning of blended learning used in a higher education context. However, it is not clear as to how much, or how little, online learning is inherent to blended learning since several degree of blending may occur within these two approaches. According to some scholars, in fact, it is important to distinguish blended learning from other forms of learning that incorporate online opportunities. Jones and colleagues [29, 30]. suggest a continuum of blended learning, which begins with no ICT use, then progresses through the most basic level of ICT used to support face-to-face teaching, to intensive use, whereby the whole course is delivered online with minimal or no face-to-face interaction.

In order to understand the degree of blended the real test is represented by the effective integration of the two main components (face-to-face and online technology) such that we are not just adding on to the existing dominant approach or method. This holds true whether it be a face-to-face or a fully online-based learning experience. A blended learning design represents a significant departure from either of these approaches. It represents a fundamental reconceptualization and reorganization of the teaching and learning dynamic, starting with various specific contextual needs and. For this reasons, despite some researchers define blended learning as a simplex approach [11] it is possible to introduce the great complexity of blended learning. In this respect, no two blended learning designs are identical. Following this assumption, also the analysis of a single experience can be very useful to understand the several patterns followed during the implementation of a blended learning approach.

In higher education, this way to intend blended learning is often referred to as a hybrid model. Hybrids are course in which a significant portion of the learning activities have been moved online, and time traditionally spent in the classroom is reduced but not eliminated. The goal of this hybrid courses is to join the best features of online learning to promote active, self-directed learning opportunities for students with added flexibility [31]. Italy has moved in the same direction.

Following the Ministerial Decree n. 47/2013 and according to the Guidelines provide by the National Agency for the Evaluation of Universities and Research Institute (ANVUR) [32] the course of studies could be defined:

- *Telematics (or online)* if they are provided by a Telematic Universities or when the didactic activities involve the support of ICT technologies for a CFU number greater than 75% of total CFUs;
- *Blended (or hybrid)* when the didactic activities involves the support of ICT technologies for a CFU number not less than 30% and not more than 75% of total CFUs.

Many higher education institutions—also in Italy—are systematically trailing various forms of blended learning in order to improve their student learning experience. There are many advantages over traditional teaching methods. For example, there is greater flexibility and students can download learning materials at their convenience, independent of location, time or physical attendance at the traditional lessons. Many students have the opportunity to balance work and study commitments. In addition, there is increasing evidence that students now use technology effectively in conjunction with workshops and lessons because they are more active and can prepare in greater detail for class when they do attend. The perceptions of faculty teaching blended learning courses have also been studied. On the one hand, the blended learning model provides some advantages: a high quality teaching experience, higher quality interaction between faculty and students compared to traditional in-person courses, and a "community of inquiry" through flexible course design [33, 34]. The high quality teaching experience comes from the ability of blended courses to provide opportunities for increased interaction between the students and faculty. On the other, instructors teaching a blended learning course can expect to invest more time becoming familiar with available technology, creating in-class activities, and reflecting on overall course structure [35, 36]. In addition, instructors need to consider ongoing classroom assessment. Because of these time-consuming tasks, some advise that faculty receive additional support and resources when teaching blended learning courses for the first time [37].

3   The Conceptual Framework

Previous literature have studied the adoption of various types of educational technology used for online learning in higher education institutions [38–40]: open educational resources [41, 42], a university's learning management system [43], an e-portfolio system [44], or an e-assessment system [45]. Many studies examined the role of ICT as an agent of change in learning identifying both the constraints and the factors enabling faculty technology adoption. Buchanan and colleagues [46] discovered that in a British University the issue related to the availability of technology and represented the most important barriers to technology adoption. One year later, the results of the research conducted by Lin et al. [47] showed that the greatest barriers, preventing the adoption of ICT included insufficient support and insufficient time for developing technology driven activities. Some other studies tried to understand both factors promoting the adoption and the use of ICT by faculty and the factors perceived as barriers. On the one hand, the improved student learning, the advantages over traditional teaching, the tools availability and the ease of their use and, finally, the student interest represent—according to Beggs [38]—some of the factors that facilitate technology use. Furthermore, Butler and Sellbom [48] asked to faculty which factors could influence the decision whether to adopt technology: technology reliability, the knowledge about the way to use technology or the difficulty using it and the technical support are identified as the most critical factors. On the other hand, Humbert [49] discovered that the decreasing in student-teacher interaction, the lack of time to prepare online content and activities are the main barriers in a French university; heavy workloads, lack of motivation, and lack of financial support are, instead, the barriers to blended learning adoption identified in the research conducted by Oh and Park in 2009 [50].

Despite these studies aiming to identify determinants and barriers to blended learning adoption, very little is known about the extent to which blended learning been adopted in universities [51–53].

Probably in many cases, a blended learning approach has been adopted without a strategic intention or without assuming an institutional perspective. In this frame and considering the relevance that blended learning approach has gained in the last decade, universities are seeing a need to support its adoption and implementation from a strategic perspective. Policies and practices that enable and even encourage blended learning can strengthen a university's commitment to improve student learning as well as in crease side benefits such as access, flexibility, and cost effectiveness. While many studies have investigated more in general the quality and the effectiveness of the blended learning approach, very few studies provide guidance for institutions in higher education [54]. One of the most famous institutional framework has been developed in 2012 by Graham and colleagues: the framework aims to identify and provide details about issues that administrators should recognize in order to guide their institutions towards successful adoption and implementation of blended learning. Aiming both to a better understanding of the process underlying the adoption of a blended learning approach, and to provide support during its implementation, the Authors have identified key markers related to institutional strategy, structure, and support (Table 1):

- *Strategy*: it includes issues regarding the overall design of blended learning. A well-defined institutional direction, the creation of a task force, a clear policy, the resources' availability and time, for example, may help to define "if' and "how" blended learning may help the institution to meet its mission and goal [11, 55].
- *Structure*: it encompasses issues relating to the technological, pedagogical, and administrative elements facilitating the creation of a blended learning environment. The development of the infrastructure and internal guidelines, as well as the policies definition regarding ownership and accessibility of materials

Table 1 Blended learning implementation categories

Categories	Sub-categories	Description
Strategy	Purpose	The goals that universities intend to achieve implementing blended learning should be clearly identified. In literature, three general purposes for blended learning adoption have been identified: (a) enhanced pedagogy, (b) increased access and flexibility, and (c) improved cost-effectiveness and resource use
	Institutional advocacy	Advocacy is required among administrators, faculty, and other institutional personnel
	Definition	The creation of an institutional definition of blended learning can facilitate several objectives, which include distinguishing blended learning courses from other delivery methods for scheduling purposes, providing students with clear and reliable expectations regarding blended learning courses, and developing appropriate support strategies
Structure	Infrastructure	The establishment of the necessary technological infrastructure is central to the success of blended learning implementation
	Scheduling	The coordination and a clear communication of the scheduling of blended courses it is necessary for each semester
	Governance	Institutions should determine who approves the development of BL courses and who owns intellectual property rights to materials created for them
	Evaluation	A culture of systematic self-improvement is necessary. Using an evaluation system also quality and effectiveness of blended learning can be identified
Support	Professional development	Faculty members need to develop new technological and pedagogical skills to teach in a blended format. Faculty must have the technological skills necessary to design and maintain the online portions of each course pedagogical skills are necessary to fully investigate the wide variety of instructional methods unique to blended learning
	Technical and pedagogical support	Faculty members need continued assistance as they incorporate blended instructional design principles and practices into their. Students likewise require technical assistance in accessing course materials, engaging with course content. Support may occur in person or by telephone, via instant messaging or e-mail, or on a website containing tutorials and other instructional materials, preferably using multiple methods
	Institutional incentives	Several incentives may be used to support blended learning adoption by faculty members: to release more time to redesign courses, learn new technologies, and obtain necessary equipment; to increase the weight of blended learning courses in workload calculations, or allowing faculty to hire teaching assistants; to provide financial incentives (workload compensation, BL implementation stipends, or financing for technological equipment); to consider blended learning implementation in matters of tenure and promotion

available in the online environment and—finally—a systematic evaluation of satisfaction and success of a new blended course in terms of teaching, learning, technology, and administration may increase the chances of a successful blended learning implementation [11, 51, 56–58];

- *Support*: it involves issues relating to the manner in which an institution facilitates faculty implementation and maintenance of its blended learning design. The pedagogical and technological development of the actors involved in the creation and use of a blended learning approach and the design of an incentive system are recognized as critical factors for blended learning implementation [58, 60, 62].

Evidences for these three areas of consideration can be identified and differentiated across three stages of institutional adoption/implementation:

- *Awareness-exploration* (stage 1): the institution has not yet adopted a strategy regarding blended learning, but administrators are aware of and show limited support for individual faculty exploring ways in which they may employ blended techniques in their classes.
- *Adoption-early implementation* (stage 2): the institution adopts a blended learning strategy and experiments with new policies and practices to support its implementation.
- *Mature implementation-growth* (stage 3): the institution has well established blended strategies, structure, and support that are integral to its operation.

One of the most critical factors for the progression through these three stages is represented by faculty engagement in the adoption and implementation of the new teaching methods. Particularly, faculty satisfaction play a role in blended learning effectiveness and vice versa. System theory supports the notion that change made to one part of a system affects all other parts of the system [60].

Faculty satisfaction can be defined as the perception that teaching online is effective and professionally beneficial (definition provided by the American Distance Education Consortium). Bolliger and Wasilik [16] point out that faculty satisfaction is a "complex issue that is difficult to describe and predict" (p. 105).

In existing literature, factors influencing faculty satisfaction tend to be classified as intrinsic versus extrinsic, motivating versus inhibiting, and/or promoting satisfaction versus promoting dissatisfaction [59–61]. Cook et al. [59] classified factors as intrinsic or extrinsic and investigated the impact those factors had in contributing to the motivation or inhibition of experienced online faculty to continue teaching in the online education system. Intrinsic factors included desire to help students, opportunity to try something new, intellectual challenge, personal motivation to use technology, overall job satisfaction, the ability to reach a broader student audience, and the opportunity to improve teaching. Extrinsic factors included release time, support and encouragement from institution administrators and departmental colleagues, merit pay, monetary support, technical support provided by the institution, workload concerns, and quality concerns. This study showed that intrinsic factors positively contribute to ongoing and increased motivation to participate in the online education while failure to adequately address extrinsic factors can be found to contribute to greater inhibition to participate in the online education. Giannoni and Tesone [61] used a similar classification. Their findings indicate that a mix of both intrinsic (i.e. personal satisfaction, teaching development, professional prestige, intellectual challenge, and recognition) and extrinsic factors (time, technical support, monetary issues, job security, and promotion) contribute to faculty satisfaction.

Various factors exist that help to describe and define the faculty experience of online education [62–68]. However, according to Bollinger and Wasilik [16] these factors can be categorized into three groups: (a) student-related, (b) instructor-related and (c) institution-related. The access to higher education for a more diverse student population [68], the interactions with students [63, 64, 68] are—for example—factors belonging to the first group. The second group of factors influencing faculty satisfaction include self-gratification, intellectual challenge, and an interest in using technology [66]. This environment provides faculty with professional development opportunities and research and collaboration opportunities with colleagues [64–68]. In the last group, it is possible to include values and policies that support the faculty, workload issues, time for course development, compensation, a reward system for promotion and tenure [64, 67, 68] and, finally, policies that clarify intellectual property issues [62, 65, 67, 68].

Summarizing, the point is made that a successful distance education program is reliant upon a dedicated and committed distance faculty. A positive perception of distance education and satisfaction with the distance-learning environment are likely contributors to that success. Faculty satisfaction is a complex idea; it is an interaction of conditions related to the students, the institution, the department and even an instructor's own experiences and attitudes. Faculty who feel well-supported by their institutions, who have, for example, adequate technical and pedagogical support, and adequate professional development opportunities are reported to be more satisfied with online teaching overall [69].

Starting from this framework the empirical analysis of our research—presented in the following sections—has a twofold purpose. Firstly, using the case study of UNIPV, the adoption of a blended learning approach is analyzed, identifying the main features of the several categories (Table 1) used to understand the institutional strategy, structure, and support markers. The analysis of these three conceptual dimensions is conducted for two of the three stages of institutional adoption/implementation of blended learning: the "awareness and exploration" phase and the "adoption-early implementation" phase.

Secondly, a survey is conducted aiming to explore one of the most critical factors for the progression through these two stages: the faculty engagement and satisfaction in the adoption and implementation of the new teaching methods. The goal is to understand what are the main factors affecting satisfaction of faculty involved in a blended learning experience in order to identify some opportunity to both change and improve something in the chosen strategy, in the infrastructure or in the categories of the support makers.

4 Method

Since only limited empirical research on how higher education institutions deal with the adoption of blended learning has been found an explorative approach has been chosen. Particularly, the research being reported in this paper involved the case study of UNIPV engaged in the delivering of blended learning courses since 2008.

Other scholars used the case study approach to examine blended learning in higher education institutions [70, 71]. Among the others, the case study conducted by Taylor and Newton [71] at an Australian university is very useful to examine learning practices in an institution faced with the challenges of delivering both on-campus and distance learning programs—as for UNIPV.

In this study, a single case is used, which is an appropriate way of establishing the field at the early stages of an emerging topic [72]. Moreover, the single case study approach is normally preferred when an inductive approach can be adopted, using theory to explain empirical observations and also to inform refinements and extension of the theory [73–75].

The case study presented in this article aims to explore and to understand the methodology used to implement a blended learning approach in training programs. In particular, drawing on the conceptual framework provided by Graham and colleagues [20] we investigated how the blended learning is implemented within the Italian UNIPV. According to our exploratory approach, we selected UNIPV as an exemplar case study [75], with unique circumstances. In particular, in UNIPV, the project on blended learning begun prior to the regulatory intervention by Italian legislation. In 2013, in fact, there are two relevant facts for distance education in Italian context. On the one hand, the Decree n. 47/2013 clearly stated the conditions according to which a course of studies can be defined "blended". Furthermore, on September 2013 the triennial plan (2013–2015) for Universities presented by the Italian Ministry of Education, Universities and Research (MIUR) stated that one of the main objectives was the improvement of services provided to students: the promotion of distance education moving in this direction was one of the suggested actions by the Minister. In this setting, we analyzed four different building blocks in order to understand both how blended learning has been implemented and how faculty perceived this new learning approach: (a) strategy; (b) structure; (c) support; (d) faculty satisfaction.

The information gathered during this research relates to the results of both the *exploration* phase, which began in 2008 and was completed in late 2014, and the *adoption/implementation* phase, which began in 2015 and it is still ongoing. From a methodological point of view, data and information collection period is particularly significant for our analysis, since it allows us to better define the nature and the relevance of the collected information. The longitudinal approach used in the observation of the project development led to the analysis of context, groups, and individuals dynamics, concerning the implementation of the blended learning approach. To improve validity and reliability [75], of our finding and conclusions, we collected data from different sources. In relation to the three conceptual dimensions of analysis (*strategy, structure* and *support*), a triangulation was carried out between documental information and interviews. The documents helped understanding the relevance given to the different phases and practices, the modes of interaction between actors and the technologies adopted for blended learning. All information gathered provided also evidence on both the process of internal communication and the role of people involved in trialing and implementing blended learning. The interviews were conducted with some of the key organizational actors involved in the blended learning implementation process. The interviews were conducted to ensure that the case study is "bounded" [75] and to guarantee that the conclusions of this study are based upon specific observations [76]. Thanks to a collaborative analysis process between academics and organization technical staff, the case study description has improved and the construct validity has increased [75].

Finally, in relation to the *faculty satisfaction*—the last dimension of analysis—a survey was conducted on the entire population of instructors involved in blended learning (46 instructors) who taught a blended learning course during the academic years 2015–2016 and 2016–2017. Faculty members involved in blended learning courses were contacted via email and invited to participate in the study. The survey is composed by 13-items and it took approximately 5 min. Participation was voluntary and participants were assured of confidentiality of results. Of the 46 questionnaires that in this first stage were delivered, 38 were returned, this represent a response rate of approximately 83%. Our respondents include both Full (31.6% of the sample) and Associate (44.8% of the sample) Professors, Researchers (10.5%), and, finally, professor with a temporary appointment for a given course (13.1%). As with any survey of a particular and small group, cautions needs to be exercised in generalizing study findings.

The survey has a total of 15 questions including 13 questions with a 4-point Likert scale, ranging from 1 strongly disagree to 4 strongly agree. The items were taken from the scale on *online faculty satisfaction survey* (OFSS) developed by Bolliger and Wasilik in 2009. In this study we use only some items of the OFSS scale and they are grouped in three subscales: (a) student related issues (Cronbach's $\alpha = 0.52$), (b) instructor-related issues (Cronbach's $\alpha = 0.92$), and (c) institutional-related issues (Cronbach's $\alpha = 0.89$) [16].

5   The Case Study of the University of Pavia: Findings and Discussion

UNIPV is one of the oldest universities in Europe. It was founded in 1361 and has 13 faculties. Today the University boasts 25,000 students, both from Italy and from overseas. It offers study programmes at all levels: Bachelor's degrees, single-cycle Masters degrees, research degrees, specialty schools and level I and II Masters degrees.

UNIPV is in a way unique not only because of its prestigious historical origins and top quality achievements, but also due to its leading and promoting role in the so-called "Pavia System" characterized by 20 colleges and residences where thousands of students can live and study. In this frame, the project for the implementation of a blended learning in UNIPV begun in 2008. Since the beginning of 2015, following the triennial plan for the Universities promoted by MIUR, UNIPV presented a project for the implementation of blended learning approach in five course programmes. This project has been funded by the Italian Ministry and the work began with the establishment of a working group composed by the Pro-rector for didactics, the Delegate to ICT, the Head of the Information System Area and the Head of the Digital Learning and Innovation Service.

Summarizing, to obtain insights about the blended learning adoption from the awareness and exploration phase to the early implementation phase, we identified an institution at the adoption and early implementation stage that received a fund in 2015 to facilitate blended learning development.

5.1 Phase 1 (2008–2014): The Exploration Stage

The first step toward the blended learning adoption in UNIPV is moved in 2008 with the promotion of an experimental project involving 50 students and 7 single courses delivered by the Faculty of Pharmacy.

Looking for the *strategy* dimension, improved pedagogy, access and flexibility, cost effectiveness and the intention to increase the student-instructor relationship outside the classroom are the main purpose declared by UNIPV. The starting idea was to support traditional courses by creating an interactive digital environment where teachers, tutors, and students could share educational materials, create new ones, meet and deepen, ideally, what they did during their lessons. The primary purpose for adopting blended learning was to improve student learning outcomes. In addition, UNIPV noted cost-effectiveness as another important driver for attracting additional students or increasing the student retention. The way in which blended learning approach was put into practice depends on institutional advocacy, individuals who actively promoted blended learning and organized adoption efforts. In this experimental phase the Head of the Digital Learning and Innovation Service in collaboration with all the staff of the Service, and the President of the Faculty of Pharmacy were the main blended learning advocates. However, already at this stage emerged the relevant role of faculty members: faculty was one of the major drivers in implementing blended learning. Finally, the definition provided for blended learning was derived by Italian Legislation and included the combination of online and face-to-face instruction.

The analysis of UNIPV *infrastructure* evidenced how UNIPV focused on enhancing its technological infrastructure to facilitate online education. The creation of a "new" interactive digital environment called KIRO was very useful to share resources and experiences; at the same time, it represented a "place" where students could meet and where the relationship between students and tutors could be improved. However, UNIPV did not systematically identify blended courses in their course catalogs. The Faculty of Pharmacy allowed individual instructors informed students on the first day of class if a course was blended: in sum UNIPV did not create a systematic protocol for indicating all blended learning courses. Furthermore, in this first stage governance and evaluation practices were not clearly identified.

Finally, the focus on the last dimension of analysis (*support*) evidenced that incorporating the use of the digital platform (KIRO) into face-to-face instruction required no additional professional, technological or pedagogical support, since the instructors were not learning new technological skills and were "well-versed" in face-to-face instruction.

5.2 Phase 2 (2015–Today): The Adoption/Early Implementation Stage

The activities programmed for the experimental phase concluded approximately in December 2014. In 2015—after the fund obtained by MIUR—UNIVP completely redesigned the implementation of the blended learning approach. Currently, the service related to blended learning is supported by 18 instances of the Learning Management Systems Open Source Moodle: the access is guaranteed to 12,000 students and 550 instructors. In general, the main activities to promote the integration of blended learning in traditional learning consisted in the live recording of the traditional lessons through a mobile recovery, the work of post-production on the video and—finally—the uploading of the videos on thematic channels of a video streaming manager (VIMEO).

The blended learning approach is implemented in 6 course programs (Table 2): the diversity among course programs allows to better achieve the objectives defined for the project. For each course program, lessons have been recorded for at least 30% of CFUs in the study plan. UNIPV chose to adopt "vertical" video detection model: for each course program a number of single courses were identified: the final sum of the CFUs assigned to each single course corresponds to the 30% of CFUs delivered by the entire course program.

The evidences collected for this second stage showed a more complex frame for the three dimensions of analysis. The investigation about the *strategy* dimension revealed that the purposes UNIPV reported are aligned with those reported in the literature: pedagogical improvement, increased access and flexibility, and cost effectiveness. Blended learning adoption objectives seemed to be aligned also with institutional goals. Furthermore, the choice to implement blended learning only at the second cycle level (according to the Italian Higher Education Systems) allowed to implementers to consider different purposes for adopting Blended Learning. For example, administrators, tasked with the financial success of the institution, may

Table 2 Blended learning in UNIPV: the state of art

	Academic year 2015–2016	Academic year 2016–2017
Registered videos (total number)	682	385
Registered hours (total number)	1100	600
Course programmes (number)	6	6
Single courses (number) – in English language – in Italian language	13 10	9 10
Single course registered for each course programme – Communication, innovation, multimedia – Physics – International business and economics – Economics, finance and international integration – Civil engineering – Musicology	5 6 6 4 6 5	3 2 4 3 3 4
Access (number of views)	20.069	128.000

focus on increasing enrollment and retaining students, while faculty members may focus on specialized and highly differentiated course contents. In addition, focusing on students—the choice to implement blended learning in second cycle level allowed to provide this new training method to students who knew the existence of KIRO platform, its centrality for teaching activities and its services (how to use it). In the adoption phase the personnel working in the Digital Learning and Innovation Service, and the faculty members were the only blended learning *advocates*. It is possible to conclude that UNIPV should encourage advocacy at multiple institutional levels due to the distinct contributions provided by department administrators, faculty resource centers, faculty members, students and technical-administrative staff.

Adequate technological *infrastructure* during blended learning adoption is required. For this reason UNIPV adopted new technologies to facilitate BL adoption: 7 moving recovery for live recording, Films with Operator in Presence, 3 recovery Extron SMP 351, Nilox cameras, lavalier microphones, notebook for managing recoveries, 3 Macintosh for postproduction and software for postproduction. In addition, the use of Microsoft Surface were offered to all faculty members. The opportunity to link the surface to the board permitted to look and to use the Surface as an interactive whiteboard (on which to record slides, compose charts, write, etc.). Single courses and the timeline of the project are clearly scheduled at the beginning of each academic year, blended learning are finally approved by instructors before publication, no other approval is required.

Finally, a great number of initiatives are realized to provide *support* to the blended learning implementation. Firstly, UNIPV offered professional development to faculty adopting blended learning. In 2016 UNIPV created an online blended learning training program: the program consisted of 26 online training units that provided instructors with as little or as much training as they needed. In addition UNIPV provided presentations, seminars, or webinars to small groups of faculty members or even individual teachers. UNIPV offered also robust technological and pedagogical support systems: a central coordination center oversees all the technical-methodological aspects and reaches the periphery through a network of collaborators (Kiro Manager) operating at the departmental level to provide support. A help desk service was created to support both users and online instructors.

5.3   The Faculty Satisfaction

Table 3 provide the descriptive statistics for each item used to measure faculty satisfaction. The descriptive statistics reveal that the average scores are relatively high for items connected to both student and instructor subscale suggesting that most of the respondents are satisfied of the "new" way to interact with students.

Although most of the variables present a moderate degree of variability, the creativity required to an online instructor in terms of the resources used for the online course ($M = 2.58$, $SD = 0.793$), the higher workload perceived when teaching an online course as compared to the traditional one ($M = 2.61$, $SD = 0.790$) and the ability to provide better feedback to online students ($M = 2.21$, $SD = 0.741$) produced the greatest degree of heterogeneity in

Table 3 Means and standard deviation of scores

Subscale	Item	M	SD
Student	The level of my interactions with students in the online course is higher than in a traditional face-to-face class	2.11	0.658
	I am able to provide better feedback to my online students on their performance in the course	2.21	0.741
	My online students are more enthusiastic about their learning than their traditional counterparts	3.00	0.615
	My online students are actively involved in their learning	2.97	0.600
	I appreciate that I can access my online course any time at my convenience	3.00	0.658
	It is valuable to me that my students can access my online course from any place in the world	3.24	0.542
Instructor	I have to be more creative in terms of the resources used for the online course	2.58	0.793
	My students use a wider range of re-sources in the online setting than in the traditional one	3.45	0.555
Institution	I have a higher workload when teaching an online course as compared to the traditional one	2.61	0.790
	I am concerned about receiving lower course evaluations in the online course as compared to the traditional one	1.71	0.515

responses. The increased access (M = 3.24, SD = 0.542), the use of a wider range of resources in the online setting than in the traditional one (M = 3.45, SD = 0.555) and the concern about course evaluation (M = 1.71, SD = 0.515) produced the greatest degree of homogeneity in responses.

Moreover, the survey includes two items that are considered general satisfaction questions. Here instructors indicated their levels of agreement or disagreement with the statements 'I look forward to teaching my next online course' and 'I am more satisfied with teaching online as compared to other delivery methods'. The means for these items were 2.41 (SD = 0.686) and 2.54 (SD = 0.730), respectively.

The results of the study confirm that the students, the instructor, and the institution are important in the measurement of perceived faculty satisfaction. The student factor seems to be the most important factor influencing satisfaction of online faculty, which is encouraging because it leads us to believe that many online instructors are student centered. Mean scores show that participants felt most strongly about questions in this particular subscale. Student-related issues that were most valued by respondents include providing flexible and convenient access to courses. These are some of the issues related to faculty satisfaction mentioned by the Sloan Consortium [68]. Additionally, the majority of faculty believed that their online students are actively involved in their learning, participate at a good level, and communicate actively with the course instructors. These results are encouraging and reassuring for faculty who are either considering to move or expand their online course offerings or who are pressured by administrators to participate in distance education. Not surprisingly, instructor-related issues directly impact instructor satisfaction but were less important than student-related issues. Finally, institution-related issues seem to be less important to online faculty. The majority (52.63%) of respondents agreed or strongly agreed that they have a higher workload when teaching an online course. These findings are consistent with the literature that points out online instructors invest more time than instructors who teach face-to-face [64, 77–79].

6 Conclusions and Next Steps

This article examined an Italian case study of blended learning adoption in which the higher education institution transitioned between the blended learning stages of awareness/exploration and adoption/early implementation. We identified patterns and distinctions regarding university's strategy, structure, and support decisions during that transition. One of the most important finding include the strategic need to develop blended advocates at multiple institutional levels in order to establish a shared implementation vision, obtain necessary resources, and attract potential adopters. In addition, institutions need to better define blended learning structure for potential adopters. Some improvements is required also on the infrastructure in order to facilitate the integration between online and face-to face learning.

The application of this conceptual framework is important from a practical viewpoint when introducing blended learning into higher education as planners and implementers will consider the readiness to adopt, the blended learning options available and how their impact will be assessed before the implementation occurs. This provides a more holistic approach to the implementation of blended learning options would like to suggest to evaluate the impact of the blended learning approach during its design rather than as an afterthought after implementation.

Future research could determine the nature of strategy, structure, and support patterns during the transition between adoption/early implementation and mature implementation/growth. Research might also examine institutional adoption stages and markers from differing perspectives, including faculty, student, or support staff viewpoints. This case study showed that UNIPV begin implementing BL with a small group of initial adopters and anticipate scaling their efforts; future research could identify core factors that need to be considered during institutional scaling. Examples of such issues could include physical and technical infrastructure needs and the continued use of incentives to facilitate faculty adoption.

Finally, as with many exploratory studies, several limitations should be taken into account. First, the results are derived from a single higher education sector organization. It is thus not possible to predict the extent to which the results can be found in universities using a blended learning approach in Italy. On this point, a next step of the research is to increase the number of case in order to compare different approaches for implementing blended learning. Moreover, the findings are limited to a small number of respondents and no attempt are be made, in this research phase, to generalize the obtained results to the wider Italian higher education sector faculty members. Further research will attain an increase in the breadth and depth of the content, both through the involvement of other Universities, and through the analysis of the students' satisfaction.

References

1. Sher, A.: Assessing the relationship of student-instructor and student-student interaction to student learning and satisfaction in web-based online learning environment. J. Interact. Online Learn 8, 102–120 (2009)
2. Adeoye, Y.M., Oluwole, A.F., Blessing, L.A.: Appraising the role of information communication technology (ICT) as a change agent for higher education in Nigeria. Int. J. Educ. Adm. Policy Stud. 5, 177–183 (2013)
3. Garito, M.A.: L'Università nel XXI Secolo tra Tradizione e Innovazione. McGraw-Hill Education, Milano (2015)
4. Garito, M.A.: A strategy for Europe in the age of the knowledge society: building new knowledge networks among traditional and distance universities. New internet-based contents for a global labour market. In: Proceedings of the 2013 EADTU (European Association of Distance Teaching Universities)—Transition to Open and On-line Education in European Universities, Paris (2013)
5. Maeroff, G.I.: A classroom of one: how online learning is changing our schools and colleges. Palgrave MacMillan, New York (2003)

6. Aggarwal, A.K., Bento, R.: Web-based education. In: Aggarwal A. (ed.) Web-based learning and teaching technologies: opportunities and challenges, pp. 2–16. PA: Idea Group, Hershey (2000)

7. Pittinsky, M.S.: The wired tower: perspectives on the impact of the internet on higher education. Pearson Education, Upper Saddle River, NJ (2003)

8. Tan, H.Y., Neo, M.: Exploring the use of authentic learning strategies in designing blended learning environments a Malaysian experience. J. Sci. Technol. Policy Manage. **6**, 127–142 (2015)

9. Wade, R.: Pedagogy, places and people. J. Teach. Educ. Sustain. **14**, 147–167 (2012)

10. Harris, P., Connolly, J., Feeney, L.: Blended learning: overview and recommendations for successful implementation. Ind. Comm. Train. **41**, 155–163 (2009)

11. Garrison, D.R., Kanuka, H.: Blended learning: uncovering its transformative potential in higher education. Internet High. Educ. **7**, 95–105 (2004)

12. Wong, L., Tatnall, A., Burgess, S.: A framework for investigating blended learning effectiveness. Education + Training. **56**, 233–251 (2014)

13. Wilbur, S.: Creating a community of learning using web-based tools. In: Hazemi, R., Hailes, S., Wilbur S. (eds.) The digital university: reinventing the academy, pp. 73–83. Verlag, London (1998)

14. Arbaugh, J.B.: What might online delivery teach us about blended management education? Prior perspectives and future directions. J. Manage. Educ. **38**, 784–817 (2014)

15. Wu, J., Liu, W.: An empirical investigation of the critical factors affecting students' satisfaction. EFL Blended Learn. 4, 3 (2013)

16. Bolliger, D.U., Wasilik, O.: Factors influencing faculty satisfaction with online teaching and learning in higher education. Distance Educ. **30**, 103–116 (2009)

17. Sloan Consortium: Quick guide: pillar reference manual. Author, Needham, MA. Retrieved from http://www.sloanc.org/publications/books/dprm_sm.pdf (2002)

18. Selim, H.M.: Critical success factors for e-learning acceptance: confirmatory factor Models. Comput. Educ. **49**, 396–413 (2007)

19. Webster, J., Hackley, P.: Teaching effectiveness in technology-mediated distance learning. Acad. Manag. J. **40**, 1282–1309 (1997)

20. Graham, C.R., Woodfield, W., Harrison, J.B.: A framework for institutional adoption and implementation of blended learning in higher education. Internet High. Educ. **18**, 4–14 (2012)

21. Christo-Baker, E.: Distance education leadership in higher education institutions: explored within theoretical frameworks of organizational change and diffusion of innovations theory. In: Cantoni, L., McLoughlin C. (eds.) Proceedings of World Conference on Educational Multimedia, Hypermedia and Telecommunications, AACE, Chesapeake, VA, pp. 251–256, (2004)

22. Graham, C.R., Robison, R.: Realizing the transformational potential of blended learning: comparing cases of transforming blends and enhancing blends in higher education. In: Picciano, A.G., Dziuban C.D. (eds.) Blended learning: research perspectives, pp. 83–110. Sloan-C, Needham, MA (2007)

23. Tshabalala, M., Ndeya-Ndereya, C., Van der Merwe, T.: Implementing blended learning at a developing university: obstacles in the way. Electron. J. e-Learn. **12**, 101–110 (2014)

24. Bliuc, A.M., Goodyear, P., Ellis, R.A.: Research focus and methodological choices in studies into students' experiences of blended learning in higher education. Internet High. Educ. **10**, 231–244 (2007)

25. Drysdale, J.S., Graham, C.R., Spring, K.J., Halverson, L.R.: An analysis of research trends in dissertations and theses studying blended learning. Internet High. Educ. **17**, 90–100 (2013)

26. Graham, C.R.: Blended learning systems: definition, current trends, and future directions. In: Bonk, C.J., Graham C. R. (eds.) Handbook of blended learning: global perspectives, local designs, pp. 3–21. Pfeiffer Publishing, San Francisco, CA (2006)

27. Ocak, M.A.: Why are faculty members not teaching blended courses? Insights from faculty members. Comput. Educ. **56**, 689–699 (2011)

28. Rovai, A.P., Jordan, H.M.: Blended learning and sense of community: a comparative analysis with traditional and fully online graduate courses. Int. Rev. Res. Open Distance Learn. **5**, 1–13 (2004)
29. Jones, N.: E-CollegeWales, a case study of blended learning. In: Bonk, C.J. Graham, C.R. (eds.) Handbook of blended learning: global perspectives, local designs, pp. 182–194. Pfeiffer Publishing, San Francisco, CA, (2006)
30. Jones, N., Chew, E., Jones, C., Lau, A.: Over the worst or at the eye of the storm? Educ. Train. **51**, 6–22 (2009)
31. Garnham, C., Kaleta, R.: Introduction to hybrid courses. Teach. Technol. Today, 8–6 (2002)
32. ANVUR: Linee guida per l'accreditamento periodico delle sedi delle università telematiche e dei corsi di studio erogati in modalità telematica, (2014)
33. Ho, A., Lu, L., Thurmaier, K.: Testing the reluctant professor's hypothesis: evaluating a blended-learning approach to distance education. J. Publ. Aff. Educ. **12**, 81–102 (2006)
34. Vaughan, N.: Perspectives on blended learning in higher education. Int. J. E-Learn. **6**, 81–94 (2007)
35. Edginton, A.: Blended learning approach to teaching basic pharmacokinetics and the significance of face-to-face interaction. Am. J. Pharm. Educ. **74**, 1 (2010)
36. Napier, N.P., Dekhane, S., Smith, S.: Transitioning to blended learning: understanding student and faculty perceptions. J. Asynchronous Learn. Netw. **15**, 20–32 (2009)
37. Garrison, D.R., Vaughan, N.D.: Institutional change and leadership associated with blended learning innovation: two case studies. Internet High. Educ. **18**, 24–28 (2013)
38. Beggs, T.A.: Influences and barriers to the adoption of instructional technology. In: Proceedings from Mid-South Instructional Technology Conference, Murfreesboro, TN (2000)
39. Zhou, G., Xu, J.: Adoption of educational technology: how does gender matter? Int. J. Teach. Learn. High. Educ. **19**, 140–153 (2007)
40. Chen, B.: Barriers to adoption of technology-mediated distance education in higher education institutions. Q. Rev. Distance Educ. **10**, 333–338 (2009)
41. Mtebe, J.S., Raisamo, R.: Challenges and instructors' intention to adopt and use open educational resources in higher education in Tanzania. Int. Rev. Res. Open Distance Learn. **15**, 249–271 (2014)
42. Ngimwa, P., Wilson, T.: An empirical investigation of the emergent issues around OER adoption in Sub-Saharan Africa. Learn. Media Technol. **37**, 398–413 (2012)
43. Findik, C., Ozkan, S.: A model for instructors' adoption of learning management systems: empirical validation in higher education context. Turkish Online J. Educ. Technol. **12**, 13–25 (2013)
44. Swan, G.: Examining barriers in faculty adoption of an e-portfolio system. Australas. J. Educ. Technol. **25**, 627–644 (2009)
45. McCann, A.L.: Factors affecting the adoption of an e-assessment system. Eval. High. Educ. **35**, 799–818 (2010)
46. Buchanan, T., Sainter, P., Saunders, G.: Factors affecting faculty use of learning technologies: implications for models of technology adoption. J. Comput. High. Educ. **25**, 1–11 (2013)
47. Lin, C., Huang, C., Chen, C.: Barriers to the adoption of ICT in teaching Chinese as a foreign language in US universities. ReCALL **26**, 100–116 (2014)
48. Butler, D.L., Sellbom, M.: Barriers to adopting technology for teaching and learning. Educause Q **25**, 22–28 (2002)
49. Humbert, M.: Adoption of blended learning by faculty: an exploratory analysis. In: McCuddy M.K. (ed.) The challenges of educating people to lead in a challenging world, pp. 423–436. Springer, Dordrecht, The Netherlands (2007)
50. Oh, E., Park, S.: How are universities involved in blended instruction? Educ. Technol. Soc. **12**, 327–342 (2009)
51. Graham, C.R.: Emerging practice and research in blended learning. In: Moore M.J. (ed.) Handbook of distance education, pp. 333–350. Routledge, New York, NY (2013)
52. Oliver, M., Trigwell, K.: Can "blended learning" be redeemed? E-Learn. Dig. Media **2**, 17–26 (2005)

53. Sharpe, R., Benfield, G., Francis, R.: Implementing a university e-learning strategy: levers for change within academic schools. Res. Learn. Technol. **14**, 135–151 (2006)
54. Halverson, L.R., Graham, C.R., Spring, K.J., Drysdale, J.S.: An analysis of high impact scholarship and publication trends in blended learning. Distance Educ. **33**, 381–413 (2012)
55. Niemiec, M., Otte, G.: An administrator's guide to the whys and hows of blended learning. J. Asynchronous Learn. Netw. **13**, 19–30 (2009)
56. Battaglino, T.B., Haldeman, M., Laurans, E.: The costs of online learning. In: Finn, C.E., Fairchild D.R. (eds.) Education reform for the digital era, pp. 55–76. Thomas B. Fordham Institute, Washington, DC (2012)
57. Wallace, L., Young, J.: Implementing blended learning: policy implications for universities. Online J. Distance Learn. Adm. **13**, 7 (2010)
58. Maguire, L.: The faculty perspective regarding their role in distance education policymaking. Online J. Distance Learn. Adm. **12**, 1 (2009)
59. Cook, R., Ley, K., Crawford, C., Warner, A.: Motivators and inhibitors for university faculty in distance and e-learning. Br. J. Edu. Technol. **40**, 149–163 (2009)
60. Giannoni, D., Tesone, D.: What academic administrators should know to attract senior level faculty members to online learning environments. Online J. Distance Learn. Adm. **6**, 1 (2003)
61. Schifter, C.: Faculty participation in asynchronous learning networks: a case study of motivating and inhibiting factors. J. Asynchronous Learn. Netw. **4**, 15–22 (2000)
62. Durette, A.: Legal perspectives in web course management. In: Mann B.L. (ed.) Perspectives in web course management, pp. 87–101. Canadian Scholars' Press, Toronto, Canada (2000)
63. Fredericksen, E., Pickett, A., Shea, P., Pelz, W., Swan, K.: Factors influencing faculty satisfaction with asynchronous teaching and learning in the SUNY learning network. J. Asynchronous Learn. Netw. **4**, 245–278 (2000)
64. Hartman, J., Dziuban, C., Moskal, P.: Faculty satisfaction in ALNs: a dependent or independent variable? J. Asynchronous Learn. Netw. **4**, 155–177 (2000)
65. Palloff, R.M., Pratt, K.: Lessons from the cyberspace classroom: the realities of online teaching. Jossey-Bass, San Francisco (2001)
66. Panda, S., Mishra, S.: E-learning in a mega open university: faculty attitude, barriers and motivators. Educ. Media Int. **44**, 323–338 (2007)
67. Simonson, M., Smaldino, S., Albright, M., Zvacek, S.: Teaching and learning at a distance: foundations of distance education. Allyn & Bacon, Boston (2009)
68. Sloan Consortium: Faculty satisfaction. SloanCWiki, Needham, MA (2006)
69. Tabata, L., Johnsrud, L.: The impact of faculty attitudes toward technology, distance education, and innovation. Res. High. Educ. **49**, 625–646 (2008)
70. Motteram, G.: Blended' education and the transformation of teachers: a long-term case study in postgraduate UK higher education. Br. J. Edu. Technol. **37**, 17–30 (2006)
71. Taylor, J.A., Newton, D.: Beyond blended learning: a case study of institutional change at an Australian regional university. Internet High. Educ. **18**, 54–60 (2013)
72. Eisenhardt, K.M.: Building theories from case study research. Acad. Manag. Rev. **14**, 532–550 (1989)
73. Berry, A., Loughton, E., Otley, D.: Control in a financial services company (RIF): a case study. Manage. Account. Res. **2**, 109–139 (1991)
74. Otley, D.T., Berry, A.J.: Case study research in management accounting and control. Manage. Account. Res. **5**, 45–65 (1994)
75. Yin, R.K.: Case study research–design and methods. Sage Publications, Thousand Oaks, CA (1994)
76. Maxwell, J.A.: Qualitative research design: an interactive approach. Sage, Thousand Oaks, CA (1996)
77. Bender, D.M., Wood, B.J., Vredevoogd, J.D.: Teaching time: distance education versus classroom instruction. Am. J. Distance Educ. **18**, 103–114 (2004)
78. Conceição, S.C.O.: Faculty lived experiences in the online environment. Adult Educ. Q. **57**, 26–45 (2006)
79. Spector, J.M.: Time demands in online instruction. Distance Educ. **26**, 5–27 (2005)

Virtuality in E-Internships:
A Descriptive Account

Debora Jeske and Carolyn M. Axtell

Abstract Computer mediation has enabled virtual teams to collaborate across time and geographic boundaries. In addition, virtual or e-internships emerged about a decade ago. The advances in both computer mediation and human computer interaction have facilitated this development. The current paper examines the degree of virtuality found in 138 e-internship reports, focusing specifically, the percentage of interactions that takes place face-to-face compared to virtually in these internships. Half of our sample ($n = 79$) worked entirely virtual in that their interactions were computer-mediated and not face-to-face for more than 90% of their time. Most e-interns were part of a virtual team as well ($n = 109$). A third of our participants ($n = 40$) were exposed to a different culture by either working with people from another culture or working for an organization in a different country. Their contribution to the organization in terms of feedback and input was also noteworthy, as more than half of those in largely virtual settings nevertheless indicated they engaged in contextual performance—assisting their organization by volunteering, helping others, sharing information and resources. In addition, more than 90% were willing to commit to another e-internship or virtual career. This suggests that the experience and reliance on computer interactions even in temporary situations can have positive effects, where gains are not only task specific, but generate higher level benefits for e-internship providers in turn.

D. Jeske (✉)
University College Cork, Cork, Republic of Ireland
e-mail: d.jeske@ucc.ie

C. M. Axtell
University of Sheffield, Sheffield, UK
e-mail: c.m.axtell@sheffield.ac.uk

© Springer International Publishing AG, part of Springer Nature 2019
A. Lazazzara et al. (eds.), *Organizing for Digital Innovation*,
Lecture Notes in Information Systems and Organisation 27,
https://doi.org/10.1007/978-3-319-90500-6_17

219

1 Introduction

The research on virtual work has provided important insight into distributed team functions, team design, and the conditions under which knowledge sharing, communication-based group efforts and cooperation is likely to succeed [1–3]. The emergence of e-internships (also known as virtual internships) has the potential to expand this area of research, while also bringing in new complexities, such as college-to-work transitions, higher education concerns about quality assurance, and career-decision making. In this paper, e-internships are defined as partially or completely computer-mediated internships [4] that require minimal or no in-person interactions. In most cases, such e-internships will involve interns and supervisors working from different geographic locations or potentially in diverse time zones (see also [5, 6]). Work is accomplished via online tools and software that supports collaboration on projects and facilitates knowledge exchange and meetings [7]. The popularity of these internships is increasing in numerous countries as virtual work arrangements and blended learning approaches become more commonplace in the workplaces and higher education institutions in Europe, Australasia and the Americas [7]. In addition, their update by smaller and medium enterprises rapidly increases as they discover the benefits of such arrangements for their own learning and development [8]. However, no specific statistics are available as e-internships are organized by organizations rather than higher education institutions (but see trends, [7]), which may not be recorded and reported in the same way as internships organized by higher education institutions.

The current paper aims to provide insight into how virtual these e-internships actually are, and explores their collaboration with teams as well as their contribution to their employers. We consider the concept of resource dynamics and job crafting to understand some of the complexities in the design of, experience, and benefits of e-internships.

1.1 *Open Research Questions*

While a number of studies have been conducted with virtual teams featuring regular employees and traditional internships, work on e-interns is only at the beginning. How internship relationships function may also be dependent on the degree to which interns are virtual. Virtuality can be defined in terms of the degree to which teams use virtual tools in order to manage and execute processes, the informational value gained by these tools, and the synchronicity of team interactions [9, 10]. In the words of Liao [11]: 'How individuals are distributed and the extent to which virtual communication tools are employed are important determinants of team virtuality.'

Virtuality, as discussed by Kirkman and Mathieu [9], can exist in co-located teams that have the option to also meet face to face. Orhan [12] also believes that virtuality is not a concept that is particular to virtual teams alone due to the wide-spread use computer-mediated communication in the modern workplace. This means virtuality is not necessarily at the opposite end of the continuum from traditional face to face interactions in team settings. In the context of e-internships, the use of tools to overcome separation of space and time will be essential to success—which makes the degree of virtuality interesting in terms of how this is achieved and the outcomes that more or less virtual arrangements such as these may generate. Given the relative recency of e-internships, the following papers focuses on a number of knowledge gaps. In the following section we outline the current literature and the research questions that are the focus of this paper.

Virtuality in E-internships. The more virtual the internship, the higher will be the amount of computer-mediated interaction between the intern and their supervisor. That said, greater virtuality does not necessarily imply a qualitative difference in terms of the exchanges that are taking place. Kirkman and Mathieu [9] took the perspective that 'teams are less virtual to the extent that their direct (e.g., communications) or indirect (e.g., contributing to and accessing knowledge bases) exchanges with each other resemble those that would occur if mediating technologies were not employed.' However, the degree to which internships are more or less virtual may depend on the degree to which employers have designed them to be more virtual. At present, it is not clear how virtual an e-internship would have to be for it to be an e-internship rather than a normal traditional (face to face) internship. For example, some e-internships require one or two on-site visits (e.g., at the beginning and the end) but most of the work and interaction takes place on line. This suggests that the dichotomy between traditional and virtual internships may need to replace by a tripartite categorization: traditional internships involving 100% on-site presence, semi-virtual internships that may require at least one on-site visit, and entirely or 100% virtual internships that never require on-site visits. In addition, some interns may also shape virtuality via their preferences to work from home when possible. This means interns might also contribute to their own work environment and thus influence the degree of virtuality in their e-internships.

Interns, like employees, can influence their own experience by selecting the type of internships they seek, but also reaching out to others and proactively shaping the degree to which they interact with others virtually (leading to more engagement and online interaction). As a result, interns may participate in how virtual their internships are through their selection decisions but also their own influence on how interactions are organized and run. It may be difficult to determine the precise dynamics behind virtuality without longitudinal or multi-stakeholder analyses, which is the next step in this research. Learning about virtuality in e-internships is the first stage to identify the reliance on computer mediation. This raises the following question:

RQ1: How 'virtual' are e-internships?

Team Work. Virtual teams have become established in many organizations due to the digitization of work processes and more collaborative (and international) nature of work [9]. Some effort has been made to identify unique knowledge, skills and abilities that support virtual team performance [9]. Experimental research on teams working in virtual environments has shown that such interactions promoted shared understanding compared to text-based chat situations, which in turn contributed to consensus, satisfaction and perceived cohesiveness in these teams [13].

However, it is unclear whether or not e-intern are also part of virtual teams, linking the existing constellation of distributed teams to e-interns. Having access to such teams may ensure that access to support is greater than when interns are not working with virtual teams. This again influences the potential role of e-internships working in combination with other e-interns or employees. To understand these dynamics, the next stage is to examine the extent to which e-interns work in teams as this activity has usually been viewed as highly personalized and individual experiences. Fact is that e-interns are likely to be part of at least a dyad (i.e., their relationship with their supervisor), even if not necessarily a larger team. Access to structure and support from others may matter in other ways. More support and access to help may be important to overcome the potential perception of being isolated [14] or separated from the employers' main office, issues that has been observed in teleworkers [7].

In a sample of sales people working remotely, Kirburz [15] found no significant relationship between role of work resources such as autonomy, feedback, access to information and interaction with supervisors and job performance. Instead, factors such as the quality of the goal setting approach as well as task interdependence may be key aspects facilitating effective virtual team work [16]. Team work may be more likely the more interdependent the tasks are, and the more help newcomers (e.g., e-interns) may need to succeed in their roles. This makes access to communication structure and access to help an important aspect of team work. However, we do not know to what extent these factors play a role in virtual teams that include e-internships. Furthermore, it is unclear to what degrees e-interns are working in teams or simply with one supervisor. Depending on the team-based or individual nature of the experience, e-interns may perform at different levels, tackle more or less complex tasks, and gain different insights through work, peer interactions, mentors and so on. This leads us to the second research question of interest:

RQ2: Do e-interns work in (cross-boundary) teams?

Organizational benefits. E-internships may generate a number of benefits, both for individuals and organizations. Skill and competence developments are often important outcomes [17]. Interns have reported improved communication skills, greater perceived employability, and greater knowledge about one's career options [16]. In the case of organizations, e-internships may represent a good means for organizations to assess potential candidates for employment—either for virtual careers or regular on-site positions. When e-interns work in teams with other e-interns, their knowledge and resource sharing may positively contribute to their performance, offsetting the costs of organizing such e-internships. This means interns may provide added value to the organization—regardless of whether or not they are part of a team.

Previous research has demonstrated that telecommuting is linked to both task and contextual performance [18]. Organizational and work conditions may promote contextual performance, while personal initiative has also been linked to contextual performance [19]. This makes contextual performance particularly relevant to e-internships due to the computer-mediated, often task-oriented and virtual nature of the experience. Contextual performance can generate synergy and a sense of connection and thus positively influence both the task performance and the relationship between all involved (e.g., the interns, their teams and supervisors). And in contrast to organizational citizenship behaviors, contextual performance does not require necessarily as much contact with organizational representatives and more opportunity to engage in discretionary behavior. As a result, we would like to consider the following research question, focusing on the individual contribution of e-interns:

RQ3: Do e-interns exhibit contextual performance contributions?

Answering these three research questions will set the starting point to review notions of virtuality and a means to identify the possibilities inherent in e-internships, rather than focusing on the potential costs associated with setting and supporting such internships. This positivist stance is also reflected in the focus of our analysis.

2 Methods

2.1 Procedure and Participants

Recruitment involved a snowball technique where the researchers contacted organizations providing e-internships and e-interns known to the researchers. Notices about the e-internships were also posted on two internship portals. Participation was voluntary, anonymous, required consent from every individual and not remunerated. In order to ensure that we collected data from e-interns, all participants had to confirm that they had been or currently were e-interns. To clarify what we meant, we provided the following definition of e-internships on the participant information sheet: 'This survey is targeted at all those who have completed (or are currently completing) an e-internship/virtual internship. Such internships are also known as: virtual internships, e-internships, work from home internships, telework internships. That is, such internships involve the intern working entirely or mostly from home (or other location away from the organization's official location). As a result, most interactions and communication will have been computer mediated.' All participants needed to confirm their status as e-interns before they were able to proceed. Following consent, participants were asked about their experience (hours, virtuality, remuneration, location, industrial sector). Further information was collected about virtuality in terms of the teams they worked with, satisfaction with communication, and also their feedback to their employers (related to contextual performance, such as discretionary effort not required for task completion). We further asked about the extent to which e-internships included training or mentoring opportunities. This was followed by demographics.

The participants were recruited in two different rounds as part of a larger data collection effort. The survey was started by 171 participants. We retained only those cases that provided information about the degree to which their e-internship involved face-to-face interaction, resulting in a dataset with 137 participants (76 males and 61 females, 1 missing value). The age ranged from 17 to 50 (1 missing value). The large majority ($n = 103$) were studying for a degree (or vocational certificate) at the time of the e-internship.

2.2 Measures

The survey included a number of questions to assess the characteristics of both e-internships and the participants themselves.

1. **Virtuality**. This was assessed using several questions. First, we asked the percentage of interactions that took place face-to-face Second, we asked about their work location (the percentage spend working from home or some other location of their choice). And third, participants were asked what amount of time they spend working from home during their office. Finally, we asked whether or not the interns were the only member of their team to work virtually (dichotomous response options, either Yes or No).
2. **Communication Satisfaction**. Given the nature of the e-internships, we also considered the satisfaction of our participants with the communication structure (access to help). Communication may be particularly relevant when the e-internship involves teamwork—and therefore tasks that require more communication and organization to successfully complete the set tasks. Response options ranged from (1) *very unsatisfied* to (4) *very satisfied*. We also include a response option called "not applicable" for those who did not have any support and felt unable to report on communication structure and access to help. Some e-internships focus on independent projects that require minimal support, particularly when the e-intern is highly skilled or experienced, reducing their need for access to help. When *not applicable* was collected, the case was excluded from the analysis (7 cases).
3. **Background Information on E-internship**. The survey included questions on location of the e-internship providers, company size, organization type (profit, not-for-profit, government) and remuneration. Other variables of interest included year of completion of the e-internship, current e-internship status (as some e-interns completed their internships in the past) and working hours.

We also enquired about the role that e-interns occupied as part of their e-internship. The open response options were subsequently coded. The participants were also asked to indicate if they received training or mentoring. Training was not defined but mentoring was defined along the description by [20]. Accordingly, mentoring was described as a personal, helping relationship between a mentor and a mentee/protégé. This process may focus on the mentee's need for support, professional development and growth and varying degrees of support. The response options were dichotomous (*Yes/No*).

4. **Cultural Diversity**. One question pertained to the potential cross-boundary team composition. This question was relevant to all those participants who worked in virtual teams. This item stated the following: "Some e-internships require e-interns to work for a company in a different country or with individuals from different cultures". Responses were dichotomous (*Yes* or *No*).

5. **Contextual Performance**. All participants were asked three questions [21, 22]. Each item started with "Did you have the opportunity to" followed by the item stem: (a) "Volunteer to extra activities?", (b) "help and cooperate with others?", and (c) "Share job related information, knowledge, and experience with other co-workers?". Answering options included *Yes* or *No*.

6. **Career Interests**. Organizations and e-interns may benefit from e-internships as this experience may increase their interest in virtual careers or the option to work for the company (potentially remotely) in the future. Two open-response questions assessed the interest in e-internships and virtual careers. The open response options were individually coded as either affirmative (e.g., when the answers were *yes, sure*) or negative (e.g., *no*).

7. **Demographics**. This included age, gender, and student status.

3   Results

3.1   General Descriptives

Geographic and Organizational Diversity. The information from e-internship suggested significant geographic dispersion of e-internships (that is, the location of the office where their supervisor was based). We did not ask whether or not the e-internship was supervised by somebody at the national or regional headquarter of the organization. Our participants worked with organizations in locations such as India ($n = 109$), the USA ($n = 10$), Ireland ($n = 4$) and Australia ($n = 3$). Other countries included Brazil, France, Nigeria, Uganda, the United Arab Emirates, and the UK (each $n = 1$). The e-internship providers included for-profit organizations ($n = 102$), several non-profits ($n = 22$) and government agencies ($n = 8$). A third ($n = 40$, 29%) worked with individuals from other cultures (because their colleagues or organization came from different cultures). Almost half of the sample included e-interns in marketing roles ($n = 59$), but also programming ($n = 7$), writing ($n = 6$), content design ($n = 22$) and various analytical and admin roles. This suggests that the e-internships tend to predominate in areas linked to IT, marketing and web design.

Experience of E-internships. Overall, more than 80% ($n = 99$) worked more than 50% of their time during the e-internship in their home. At the time of the survey, only a quarter of participants had started the e-internship in the last two weeks ($n = 33$). All others had either completed or were still completing the e-internships. The large majority had completed their e-internships between 2013 and 2015 ($n = 111$). Up to a third ($n = 53$, 38.4%) worked up to 10 h a week, another third ($n = 41$, 29.7%) up to 20 h a week, and the remainder up to 30 ($n = 27$, 19.6%), or even 40 h ($n = 12$, 8.7%). A minority worked even more hours ($n = 5$, 3.6%). This suggests that a good number of participants worked full time hours during their internships. Internship length varied from up to 6 weeks ($n = 46$, 33.3%), up to 12 weeks ($n = 59$, 42.8) and in some cases from 3 to 12 months ($n = 29$, 21.0%). A number of e-interns reported that they had completed more than one e-internship ($n = 25$).

3.2 Research Questions

RQ1: How 'virtual' are e-internships? Around half (57.2%) of the sample ($n = 79$) spend a very limited time interacting in person with others, suggesting fully virtual internships. Similarly, only a very small number spend more than 70% interacting with others face-to-face (Table 1). Relatively equal number of participants received training or mentoring opportunities regardless of their degree of virtuality. While these results do not provide us with an indication of the significance of the differences (the cell sizes were too small to run comparative statistics), the results provide a first overview of the degree of virtuality in e-internships. The participants who were unpaid also tended to be more virtual (see overview of percentages in Table 1). For example, more interns with less than 10% face-to-face interaction tended to not be paid ($n = 61$) than paid ($n = 15$). The proportion of payment increased the more face-to-face contact individuals had in their e-internships (Table 2).

Table 1 Degree of virtuality and amount of training/mentoring offered to e-interns

Percentage face-to-face	Frequency	Percent	Training yes(no)	Mentoring yes(no)
less than 10%	79	57.2	46(33)	47(32)
10–30%	26	18.8	7(19)	17(9)
30–50%	17	12.3	6(11)	13(4)
50–70%	9	6.5	5(4)	8(1)
70–90%	5	3.6	0(5)	3(2)

Table 2 Degree of virtuality and extent of virtual team membership

	Only one in virtual team?		
Percentage	Yes	No	Frequency
Less than 10%	8	66	74
10–30%	3	19	22
30–50%	2	13	15
50–70%	1	8	9
70–90%	2	3	5
Total	16	109	125

RQ2: To what extent are e-interns working in virtual teams. An important consideration is the extent to which e-interns may also work together with others, in different locations. As the findings suggest, the large majority ($n = 109$) of participants worked in teams that included other team members who worked virtually. This is important as it may also means the infrastructure is geared towards more computer-mediated interactions to facilitate the effectiveness of all working online. Of the 127 participants for whom we had computed communication satisfaction, we found that those who worked with others virtually ($M = 3.24$, $SD = 0.78$) reported slightly lower, not higher satisfaction compared to those who did not work with virtual teams ($M = 3.59$, $SD = 0.79$). The group difference was approaching significance ($p < 0.054$). The overall satisfaction tended to the higher end of the spectrum, as the maximum score was 4.00 ($M = 3.20$, $SD = 0.70$).

RQ3: How does virtuality relate to contextual performance of e-interns? Contextual performance was of interest as we wanted to examine the extent the e-interns would not only complete their tasks. We asked participants whether they volunteered for extra activities; help or cooperate others; or share job related information, knowledge, and experience with other co-workers (Table 3). The

Table 3 Degree of virtuality of interns and their contextual performance

Contextual performance	Response options	Percentage of your interactions that was face-to-face (in person)					
		Less than 10%	10–30%	30–50%	50–70%	70–90%	Total
Volunteering	Yes	51	11	9	5	3	79
	No	26	13	8	4	2	53
	Total	77	24	17	9	5	132
Helping out/ cooperating	Yes	47	13	11	6	3	80
	No	30	12	6	3	2	53
	Total	77	25	17	9	5	133
Sharing information etc.	Yes	42	16	11	6	3	78
	No	35	9	6	3	2	55
	Total	77	25	17	9	5	133

extent to which individuals show evidence of contextual performance may depend on their ability to tell when such contributions are warranted. Even though many individuals rated high on the percentage of virtual rather than face-to-face interactions, a surprising number of participants provided feedback to their employers. Sharing information was lower compared to the other activities, potentially because the interns may have difficulty identifying which information, knowledge and experience would be helpful.

4 Discussion

The emergence of e-internships and their increasing popularity across different continents produces new research questions. While the research on virtual work and teams can produce helpful guidance, the experience of both e-interns and internship providers may be subject to the influence of many different aspects. In contrast to many distributed teams, e-interns are more likely to be students (as noticed also in our sample), have less experience in work settings, and may need more support during their e-internships than individuals working in established distributed teams with significant work and/or technical experience. In recognition of these developments, the current work considered the characteristics of e-internships to date, capturing some of the emerging themes. Specifically, we asked how 'virtual' e-internships are (RQ1), learn more about the extent to which e-interns work in virtual teams (RQ2), and any evidence about students engaging in contextual performance regardless of the virtuality of their e-internship (RQ3). We summarize our results and consider existing work in this area.

Our examination of virtuality (RQ1) showed that over half of the participants experienced a largely virtual work experience (spending less than 10% of their time face-to-face). This did not, however, appear to change access to training and mentors. Individuals who had training or mentoring were not more or less likely to be virtual. The descriptive patterns suggest that even in highly virtual internships, organizations provided mentoring and/or training options. The results indicated that a large number of individuals received training and mentoring, although the present research did not provide in-depth information on how these opportunities arose (as in offered by supervisors or requested by e-interns).

E-internships are, essentially, placements to support the transition from college to work. Supporting learning will be essential during this process. Supervisors can support and also foster internship crafting and designating post holders responsible for the outcome of this behavior (see also work by [23] on customizing job content), thus ensuring that e-interns also self-evaluate and reflect on how they shape their own e-internship. Our results thus confirm that many e-internships are almost entirely virtual. However, it is unclear if virtuality is driven by the task or circumstances. Orhan [12] proposed that virtuality can be construed as two-dimensional. He proposed that virtuality depends on the amount of face-to-face interaction/contact in teams and the degree of dependency. Our results do not provide any means to test if the provision of training and mentoring in e-internships was a tool to support inter-dependent working (in terms of coordination, collaboration, and task performance). However, dependency may be an important variable to consider to understand when e-internships involve teams or just dyads, and the degree to which training and mentoring will be available.

The second research question focused on the likelihood with which e-internships worked alone or with others who were virtual (RQ2). Our descriptives suggest that e-interns were also more likely to be working with others who were also virtual. The findings concerning RQ2 are interesting when we consider the link with training and mentoring (in reference to RQ1). Working in teams may increase the complexity of the tasks being completed, a possibility that we had no means to assess. In addition, those working on their own may have been more skilled which increased their independence. However, those working with others may have needed more training—leading to a steeper learning curve and thus potentially a more pronounced need for help. In the context of e-internships, such access to support may be more difficult to obtain right away due to temporal differences (a possibility that may be worth exploring in future research). Also considered in the section on team work (RQ2), participants reported relatively high communication satisfaction. Satisfaction with communication may be difficult to ensure in virtual teams and samples such as ours, where the majority worked with individuals in different countries or from different ethnic backgrounds. Schaubroeck and Yu [10] had also proposed that geographic and cultural differences may play a role in virtual teams. Yet, in our sample, we noted that working virtually did not, by default, require collaborations across countries or with colleagues from different cultures.

The third research question also considered the extent to which individuals would engage in contextual performance (RQ3). A large number of e-interns showed evidence of engaging in volunteering, helping others, and information sharing. E-interns that are supported to craft their job are better able to continuously fulfil, acquire or create work. This may set the stage for contextual performance as well. If the communication and support structures can be combined effectively, interns may also find it easier to adopt these knowledge practices. This may set the stage for both task and contextual performance. The research on distributed teams has already explored coordinated knowledge practices in distributed teams [24]. These include work coupling (this involves recognizing dependencies between individuals sharing work), the building of social capital (gained, for example, via networking and relationship building), and recognition of geographic and temporal differences (spatio-temporality; [24]). These recommendations have also been echoed in other work [14], which similarly emphasized the importance of trust, cooperation, information sharing, but also coordination to avoid isolating individuals, produce satisfaction and maintain performance in virtual teams. This suggests that the commitment to e-interns may also result in additional dividends in the form of contextual feedback and performance, going above and beyond task-based performance alone.

4.1 Implications

Our results may provide starting points for practitioners. We focus on the gains that organizations may obtain here, but also the human resource strategies that could support effective e-internship (teams). The fact that e-interns contributed to the organization via their suggestions (contextual performance) suggests that their virtuality is not necessarily an impediment. Even virtually, e-interns may gain insights that, despite of and possibly because of their potentially peripheral structural involvement with the employers, could provide the e-internship provider with useful insight on how to optimize their structure and resources to support virtual working. The link to virtual career preferences is also promising and suggests e-internships may be a good way to identify those candidates who may be particularly suited to working in virtual settings (some guidelines are already available in [7, 8, 25]).

A key criteria for success seems to be member competence and careful (team/ e-intern) selection. The degree to which an e-intern works with a virtual or traditional (location-bound) team may not be as important as their potentially independent ability to manage and utilize various tools to complete their tasks effectively (or task virtuality, [12]). Careful selection of the right candidates may be beneficial in other ways as well. It may increase the likelihood that e-interns are effective and satisfied. It may also ensure that teams are successful by ensuring all team members are competently managing the interdependencies, the socioemotional and task-related challenges that arise [20]. Recruiting the right interns to analyze, interpret, lead on and make decisions in virtual settings [26] will very likely also contribute to the success of e-internships.

Observing the trends of the last few years, we expect that e-internship are likely to become more acceptable, following the adoption observed for virtual work arrangements and simulated learning exercises. A number of factors may support or inhibit this development. First, new means to accredit e-internship similar to e-learning may encourage the adoption of such internship schemes. This trend is supported by efforts to design such internships within educational settings [25]. Second, emerging technological means and a multitude of different internship portals enable internship providers to meet and connect with potential interns world-wide. Third, more and more small and medium enterprises become aware of the opportunities that the e-internships present, particularly since they often lack the space and the human resources to recruit interns to their main sites [7, 8]. Countries such as India and the USA are prime locations where geographical distance and entrepreneurial spirit support e-internship growth. And fourth, many careers require individuals to engage in international collaborations. This makes e-internships more attractive. Lastly, the computer-mediated nature of such internships may enable certain groups to take these up more than traditional and thus location-based internship (e.g., due to financial, geographic or other constraints related to care responsibilities, issues related to various disabilities or mobility). This means e-internships can facilitate both diversity and inclusion at work, which may support organizational as well as individual learning [7, 8].

4.2 Limitations

The current paper provides a descriptive overview of the characteristics of e-internships. At the same time, the nature of the analysis was limited, in part because we needed to balance the benefits of long response scales (instead of dichotomous response options) against the potential drop-out rate and length of the survey.

Other limitations also apply. The reports were based on self-reports of students and their respective learning experience [4], which may affect the reliability of their responses (e.g., estimates of time spend working virtually). That said, most e-interns in our experience are given specific tasks and hours for an often limited number of weeks and months. On-site visits are not necessarily a frequent occurrence. These circumstances should enable them to make a more educated guess about the time spend working virtually. Second, given the age span observed in our sample, students may not be the only group worthy of study. Self-selection bias may have played a role in terms of who participated and who selected e-internships in the first place.

Furthermore, no information was available from the supervisors about their perceptions, which might be relevant to disentangle how the interests of different stakeholders drive and shape how e-internships are implemented (in terms of the technologies, tools, and supervision practices that are put in place). Third, we found some evidence that many e-interns experienced such e-internships. However, we did not have the means to explore the in-depth effects of geographic dispersion and the demands or implications for computer-mediated contact preferences and procedures.

4.3 Future Research

The paper outlined a number of potential avenues worthy of more research. For the sake of brevity, we focus on a short number examples here. Leadership skills and the willingness to delegate authority were not explored in our study, but may be worth future consideration. Especially in virtual teams, it may be important to be able to step back and avoid top-down instruction and authority-driven decision-making. This is also in line with the abilities identified in [26] that recognizes leadership and decision-making as key aspects for virtual teams. Shared leadership has also been shown to relate to team cohesion (in student-based traditional teams, [27]), while cohesion as well as leadership have been linked to performance (in professional virtual teams, [17]).

While we asked if individuals worked with others who were working virtually, the current paper did not investigate specific team type or designs. This is an underrepresented area of research [3] and worth further consideration. And lastly, it has yet to be determined to what extent (unclear) expectations, differing cultural and workplace norms shape performance in e-internships. A number of authors have outlined research propositions and frameworks on virtuality, culture and teamwork [10, 28] which provide further starting points for research in this area.

Acknowledgements We gratefully acknowledge the support of the many internship providers, e-interns, college ambassadors and administrators who gave us permission to post announcements for our study on their internship sites in India and the USA.

References

1. Bélanger, F., Allport, C.D.: Collaborative technologies in knowledge telework: an exploratory study. Inform. Syst. J. **18**, 101–121 (2008). https://doi.org/10.1111/j.1365-2575.2007.00252.x
2. Bosch-Sijtsema, P.M., Fruchter, R., Vartiainen, M., Ruohomäki, V.: A framework to analyze knowledge work in distributed teams. Group Org. Manage. **36**, 275–307 (2011). https://doi.org/10.1177/1059601111403625
3. Gibbs, J.L., Sivunen, A., Boyraz, M.: Investigating the impacts of team type and design on virtual team processes. Hum. Resour. Manage. Rev. ePub. (2016). https://doi.org/10.1016/j.hrmr.2016.12.006
4. Jeske, D., Axtell, C.M.: e-Internships: prevalence, characteristics and role of student perspectives. Internet Res **24**, 457–473 (2014). https://doi.org/10.1108/IntR-11-2012-0226
5. van Dorp, K.-J.: A premier European platform for clearing e-internships. Br. J. Edu. Technol. **39**, 175–179 (2008). https://doi.org/10.1111/j.1467-8535.2007.00731.x
6. van Dorp, K.-J., De Egana, A.H.C.A., de los Monteros, A.H.E.: Virtual internship arrangements for development of professional skills and competences. Commun. Cogn **44**, 33–52 (2011)
7. Jeske, D., Axtell, C.M.: Global in small steps: e-internships in SMEs. Org. Dyn. **45**, 55–63 (2016). https://doi.org/10.1016/j.orgdyn.2015.12.007
8. Jeske, D., Axtell, C.M.: How to run successful e-internships: a case for organizational learning. Develop. Learn. Organ.: Int. J. **30**, 18–21 (2016). https://doi.org/10.1108/DLO-09-2015-0073
9. Kirkman, B.L., Mathieu, J.E.: The dimensions and antecedents of team virtuality. J. Manag. **31**, 700–718 (2005). https://doi.org/10.1177/0149206305279113
10. Schaubroeck, J.M., Yu, A.: When does virtuality help or hinder teams? Core team characteristics as contingency factors. Hum. Res. Manage. Rev. ePub. (2016). https://doi.org/10.1016/j.hrmr.2016.12.009
11. Liao, C.: Leadership in virtual teams: a multilevel perspective. Hum. Res. Manage. Rev. ePub. (2016). https://doi.org/10.1016/j.hrmr.2016.12.010
12. Orhan, M.A.: Extending the individual level of virtuality: implications for task virtuality in virtual and traditional settings. Adm. Sci. **4**, 400–412 (2014). https://doi.org/10.3390/admsci4040400
13. Schouten, A.P., van den Hooff, B., Feldberg, F.: Virtual team work: Group decision making in 3D virtual environments. Commun. Res. **43**(2), 180–210 (2013). https://doi.org/10.1177/0093650213509667
14. Cogliser, C.C., Gardner, W., Quinn Trank, C., Gavin, M., Halbesleben, J., Seers, A.: Not all group exchange structures are created equal: Effects of forms and levels of exchange on work outcomes in virtual teams. J. Leadersh. Organ. Stud. **20**, 242–251 (2013). https://doi.org/10.1177/1548051812472370
15. Kirburz, K.: A closer look into remote work: examining resources within remote work arrangements with outcomes of job performance and work-family conflict. Dissertation

submitted to the University of South Florida. Available at: http://scholarcommons.usf.edu/etd/6275 (2016)

16. Hertel, G., Konradt, U., Orlikowski, B.: Managing distance by interdependence: goal setting, task interdependence, and team-based rewards in virtual teams. Eur. J. Work Organ. Psychol. **13**, 1–28 (2004). https://doi.org/10.1080/13594320344000228

17. Saafein, O., Shaykhian, G.A.: Factors affecting virtual team performance in telecommunication support environment. Telematics Inform. **31**, 459–462 (2014). https://doi.org/10.1016/j.tele.2013.10.004

18. Gajendran, R.S., Harrison, D.A., Delaney-Klinger, K.: Are telecommuters remotely good citizens? Unpacking telecommuting's effects on performance via i-deals and job resources. Pers. Psychol. **68**, 353–393 (2015). https://doi.org/10.1111/peps.12082

19. Speier, C., Frese, M.: Generalized self efficacy as a mediator and moderator between control and complexity at work and personal initiative: a longitudinal field study in East Germany. Hum. Perform. **10**, 171–192 (1997). https://doi.org/10.1207/s15327043hup1002_7

20. Han, S.J., Beyerlein, M.: Framing the effects of multinational cultural diversity on virtual team processes. Small Group Res **47**, 351–383 (2016). https://doi.org/10.1177/1046496416653480

21. Borman, W.C., Motowidlo, S.J.: Expanding the criterion domain to include elements of contextual performance. In: Schmitt, N., Borman, W.C. (eds.) Personnel Selection in Organizations, pp. 71–98. Jossey-Bass, San Francisco (1993)

22. Lee, Y.-H., Yang, L.-S., Wan, K., Chen, G.-H.: Interactive effects of personality and friendship networks on contextual performance. Soc. Behav. Pers. **38**, 197–208 (2010). https://doi.org/10.2224/sbp.2010.38.2.197

23. Hornung, S., Rousseau, D.M., Glaser, J., Angerer, P., Weigl, M.: Beyond top-down and bottom-up work redesign: customizing job content through idiosyncratic deals. J. Organ. Behav. **31**, 187–215 (2010). https://doi.org/10.1002/job.625

24. Franssila, H., Okkonen, J., Savolainen, R., Talja, S.: The formation of coordinative knowledge practices in distributed work: towards an explanatory model. J. Knowl Manage. **16**, 650–665 (2012). https://doi.org/10.1108/13673271211246202

25. Ruggerio, D., Boehm, J.: Design and development of a learning design virtual internship program. Int. Rev. Res. Open. Distrib. Learn. **17**, 1–16 (2016)

26. Krumm, S., Kanthak, J., Hartmann, K., Hertel, G.: What does it take to be a virtual team player? The knowledge, skills, abilities, and other characteristics required in virtual teams. Hum. Perform. **29**, 123–142 (2016). https://doi.org/10.1080/08959285.2016.1154061

27. Mathieu, J.E., Kukenberger, M.R., D'Innocenzo, L., Reilly, G.: Modeling reciprocal team cohesion–performance relationships, as impacted by shared leadership and members' competence. J. Appl. Psychol. **100**, 713–734 (2015). https://doi.org/10.1037/a0038898

28. Kramer, W.S., Shuffler, M.L., Feitosa, J.: The world is not flat: examining interactive multidimensionality of culture and virtuality in teams. Hum. Res. Manage. Rev. ePub. 1–17. https://doi.org/10.1016/j.hrmr.2016.12.007 (2016)

Part IV
Organizing for Digital Innovation

Designing e-Business for SMEs: Drawing on Pragmatism

Paolo Depaoli and Stefano Za

Abstract Investments in information technology related to the e-business adoption represent often crucial decisions for small and medium sized enterprises (SME). Therefore e-business design and implementation are key factors in minimizing risks and in promoting valuable outcomes. However, there is an inclination in the IS literature to adopt approaches and models that have been criticized for their techno-centric and mechanistic character. Here a pragmatist perspective is adopted "that allows for conceiving of technological and social aspects of work practices in an integrated way" (Alonso-Mendo et al in Eur J Inf Syst 18(3):264–279, 2009 [1, p. 40]). Given that e-business is distinguished by different levels of information exchanges among both the actors of the firm and its suppliers and customers, the paper proposes an interaction-based model to orientate both entrepreneurs' choices and designers' research and practice.

1 Introduction

Background. Despite its ups and downs, the fact that the global economy has been recovering from the worst crisis in decades has led international organizations to study the key growth drivers of small and medium sized enterprises (SMEs), given that these form the majority of the world's economic organizations and are fundamental to job creation and social cohesion. Financial inclusion and skill development and training are at center stage [23, 24]. Competence growth in information and communication technology (ICT) is included in a vast array of entrepreneurial, managerial, social, and technical skills that all need to be developed [2]. Digital transformation is considered by policymakers to be a source of business

P. Depaoli (✉)
Sapienza University of Rome, Rome, Italy
e-mail: paolo.depaoli@uniroma1.it

S. Za
LUISS Guido Carli, University, Rome, Italy
e-mail: sza@luiss.it

© Springer International Publishing AG, part of Springer Nature 2019
A. Lazazzara et al. (eds.), *Organizing for Digital Innovation*,
Lecture Notes in Information Systems and Organisation 27,
https://doi.org/10.1007/978-3-319-90500-6_18

237

opportunities with major societal impacts. SMEs are considered to be slower than larger firms in adopting digital technologies both because of a lack of awareness of the positive outcomes thereof and because of an inadequate skill level concerning these technologies [28].

Aims. In this context, the authors of this paper have started an IS design research process: (i) to develop the awareness of small business owners on the information technology related issues; (ii) to stimulate consultants to consider the entanglement of organization and technology [26] rather than having their primary focus on technology; (iii) to contribute to the design research literature in the information systems field by proposing a model to explain "interaction" as a key variable in the SMEs approach to e-business; (iv) to suggest policymakers to better support holistic (rather than technology centered) approaches to develop SMEs competitiveness through digitization.

Theoretical underpinnings. The research process is based on pragmatism because it is an approach well suited to investigate the intertwining of inquiry, work-practices, and strategizing [9], i.e. the aims of the research. Here we draw on the work of Göran Goldkuhl and Pär Ägerfalk who have relied on this philosophy to deal with the IS field by means of research, projects and publications [7, 8, 10]. Our research is based on the following four key concepts developed by these two authors in [10]: (i) "in communication and other direct interaction between actors, the social character is obvious" (p. 31); (ii) this also means that the use of an IT artefact must be social, since there can be no such use without the exploitation of signs" (ibid); (iii) the main functioning of IT artefacts within a work practice is as "instruments for social action" (p. 36) (iv) "… we can view IT artefacts in a work practice as: (1) technological artefacts with physical properties, (2) semiotic artefacts affording communication and interpretation, and (3) social instruments used to responsively express actors' beliefs, values, and intentions." (p. 36).

Methodology. Social actions are taken to be the core of the analysis of SMEs. The analysis concerns the actions (and interactions) performed by the actors within the relevant work practices with (or without) the support of IT artefacts so that the firm objectives are achieved. The research process adopted is the following. First, three SMEs were explored to identify the key issues concerning interactions supported by IT artefacts (exploring e-business practices). Second, the literature on e-business design is searched and commented upon (analyzing present knowledge). Finally, we propose a model to facilitate the design and decision making of SMEs concerning their level of involvement with e-business. This is also the structure of the paper.

2 Exploring Small Firm Business and e-Business Practices

Based on a substantial business history (over ten years), a significant number of customers, and employing ten or less people, three cases were identified on the institutional data used by the authors for their ongoing research. The purpose was to gain a first understanding of the main work practices, of the interaction levels among actors and of the IT artefacts that support them. Here, because of space constraints only one case is described and concerns a small software house ("Softer"). The other two firms (one is a restaurant and the other is active in real estate development) show attitudes towards ICTs which are similar to Softer's: the role of an ICT artefact becomes meaningful (and worth investing in) only in the light of the relevant work practices and of the interaction levels among actors they support.

In order to guide the analysis, three areas of interaction among internal (the entrepreneur, employees) and external (clients and suppliers) actors were identified in an ideal-type small firm: a 'core interaction area' where internal actors interact among themselves to carry out activities, an 'output interaction area' where internal actors engage customers, and an 'input interaction area' where connections with suppliers are managed. This classification chimes with the one provided by Kim et al. [17]: the business-to-employee-to-business space (for the business organiza- tion, its employees and its partners such as suppliers and distributors), the business-to-employee-to-consumer space (for business organization, employees and consumers), and the business-to-employee-to-employee space (for business orga- nization and its employees).

Exploring e-business in a small softer house: "Softer". This firm provides ICT training and software development services. Launched in the early 2000s, its initial focus was on training (partner of Sun and then Oracle). After five years Softer started to develop proprietary software applications (first for B2B then for B2C) using the innovative technologies taught in its courses, with the dual aim of enhancing its teaching activities and of pursuing new business opportunities. In 2010, Softer decided to base its development activities and training on Apple, with a growing interest in mobile apps. Presently the firm employs a total of six people (developers and instructors) plus a part-time accountant and an accountancy con- sultant to prepare the financial statements (a 'cloud' application developed inter- nally serves both of them).

The owner personally manages key client sales, leveraging his technical and teaching expertise. He assigns the smaller potential clients (especially for the mobile apps market) to five part-time sales agents paid on a commission basis. Two types of interaction take place in the Output Interaction Area: (i) the owner's interaction with the key clients and sales agents (the latter use an e-calendar for their business appointments); (ii) the instructors' interaction with the students. The for- mer consists of face-to-face meetings, phone calls and e-mail correspondence; the latter work in the classrooms organized at the clients' premises. Products and services are showcased on the company's website and on the pages of the most visited social networks (e.g., Facebook, Google+). The Core Interaction Area is where the new training courses and the new software are developed. The traditional white board is the main driver of employees' interaction, on which these latter post different coloured sticky notes with information on the matters discussed in the daily meetings; video conferences are used occasionally to bring agents or external colleagues into the discussion. The Agile approach taken by Softer means that the software it develops is organized by weekly objectives so the firm perceives no need for a shared calendar or planner. The e-mail is used to track exchanges of information and two servers support software versioning and document and file-sharing. The employer is the main actor in the Input Interaction Area, responsible for managing relations with Apple and other corporations that might be interested in a business agreement and hardware and software procurement, using the telephone and the e-mail or sometimes the Internet. However, small orders for specific needs can be placed by the employees so long as the supplier is known and reliable.

The Softer case attests that, despite the firm having the appropriate ICT competences the owner finds face-to-face interaction to be more effective than innovative cooperative work tools: its business aims often call for resolving installation, management and updating issues.

3 Searching Knowledge on e-Business Design for SMEs

Investments in technology represent often crucial decisions for small and medium sized enterprises (SME), especially for their potentially large impact on firm competitiveness [12]. At the same time, investments in IT, related to the e-business adoption, are resulted in tangible financial benefits in customer development and e-marketing [15]. Hence, the e-business implementation management have a critical role in order to achieve positive outcome minimizing risks [14].

The literature shows a broad range of e-business definitions. Some equate it to e-commerce [5, 20, 29], while other ones [21, 34] rank e-commerce as merely one stage of the e-business stage model proposed or analyzed. In this paper, we follow [31, 32, 35] who define e-business to be where "economic value creation and information technology (IT) come together and enable inter-organizational connectivity". However, different from these latter authors, we replace the term 'connectivity' with the term 'interaction' to better convey the organizational nature of the exchanges. On the whole the IS studies identify several common factors and show that the implementation of an e-business model is primarily customer-driven, with smaller firms positioned at the early stages of the adoption sequence [18]. Improvements in competitive positioning have been observed when e-business investments are coherent with the SME's environment, strategic objectives and technology management capabilities [30]. The level at which a firm has already incorporated e-business into its traditional operations is an important and decisive factor that spurs the scholars to advise adopting a maturity or stage (the two terms are used interchangeably in the literature) model to evaluate future e-business investments [4, 21, 29, 34]. In fact, while e-business can potentially keep competitive pressure in check, reduce costs and improve performance [25], project implementation often suffers delays or failures [16, 20]. Thus, SMEs looking to invest in full-fledged e-business are offered stage models to serve as roadmaps.

The aim of these models is to give the firms a yardstick with which to measure the specific conditions of each step of their digital journey and to identify the relative barriers and/or facilitators [29].

A growing number of authors have questioned whether the use of stage models by SMEs is appropriate, claiming that these are not only too generic, i.e., incapable of responding to the diverse nature and needs of each firm, but also lack the support of empirical evidence [1]. Moreover, other research suggests that there may be no sequential path to e-business adoption after all [19]. Martin and Matlay [21] argue that the stage model-based approach is misdirected and likely to fail. According to Zheng [35], stage models (e.g., that of Willcocks et al. [34]) are more relevant and useful for large firms rather than SMEs. Indeed, such models do not take account of the variety and uniqueness of smaller firms. As Taylor and Murphy [32] argue, the maturity models take exclusively a technological approach to the adoption of e-business. Moreover, the models often assume a sequential and progressive engagement with e-business information technology. Given the business diversity of SMEs, we need to improve our understanding of how these firms recognize and develop business opportunities generally, and not just the ones that might or might not be associated with a particular set of technologies [32]. Indeed, Levy et al. [19] argue that e-business adoption cannot be modelled as a sequential process precisely because SMEs might decide to implement only certain Internet applications, in line with their growth and business value goals. Also Zheng et al. [35] argue that e-business adoption by SMEs depends mainly on their strategic focus, on the owner's knowledge of IT opportunities and on customer pressure, rather than on the requirements of a specific stage.

In short, the fact that SMEs tend to adopt technology in a discontinuous way, taking a non-linear, stage-by-stage progression path [6], means it is necessary to build more realistic models to surpass that mechanistic view.

4 Proposing an Interaction-Based Model for Designing Ebusiness

The principal aim of the proposed model is to support an e-business design-research endeavour by representing a map of the main interactions connecting the diverse actors so that an appropriate mix of ICT and non-ICT supported actions can be identified. The model (see Fig. 1) is meant to highlight five aspects: (1) integrating interaction, (2) marrying technology to the organization, (3) newly defining e-business, (4) integrating interaction intensity, and (5) dividing interaction into the three ideal-typical areas introduced in the description of "Softer".

Integrating interaction. It refers to the need of integrating the digital and the non-digital modes of interaction used by the individuals, teams and units of an organization to communicate internally and externally in the pursuit of the firm's business objectives. The concept of interaction is indeed relevant in organization

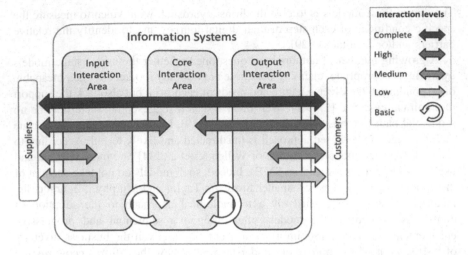

Fig. 1 The interaction-based development model for e-business

theory which uses different approaches to shed light on the question of coordination and integration. Van de Ven et al. [33] tackle coordination mechanisms at the unit level, interdependence and unit size to conclude that the use of group coordination is higher and more effective when the unit size is smaller and uncertainty and interdependence are higher. Grandori and Soda [11] state that repeated sequential communications, decisions and negotiations need to take place in order to maintain long-term cooperation. This emphasizes the crucial dimension of 'interaction' in SMEs, the cornerstone for developing their relationships (based on cooperation and trusting attitudes) with other organizations and individuals (partners, suppliers, clients, institutions).

Marrying technology to the organization. The model marries technology to the acts of organizing and communicating and, specifically, for the achievement of the firm's goals. That is, an existing business model can only be improved on if the focus is "redirected away from ICT as an end in itself towards ICT as a means to an end, i.e., realizing business opportunities, generating profits and creating wealth" [32].

Newly defining e-business. Building the model on the view that technology is not an end in itself but a complement to the business and organizational activities allows for a redefinition of e-business as the pursuit by the relevant internal and external actors of different levels of (digitally supported) interaction with the aim of exchanging information and knowledge significant for improving the work practices engaged in the pursuit of the objectives of the organization.

Integrating interaction intensity. Taking into account potentially different levels of technically feasible and organizationally rewarding interaction involving diverse types of actors, the model emphasizes not only the number of actors and 'areas' involved in the interaction processes, but also the intensity of their interactions. For example, a 'low' level of interaction identifies a situation where only one party to the exchange has access to the information or knowledge and has no or little power to intervene on either the content or the method of interaction (as for example in website brochures for customers). At the other end of the scale, the 'complete' level of interaction encompasses most of the relevant actors (employees, suppliers, customers, public administrations and so on) that a firm has to deal with in the pursuit of its business and which might play an active role in its processes (as for example in supply chain management systems when the firm is a link in the value chain).

Dividing interaction into three areas. At this point of our discourse, we can better specify the meaning of the three ideal-type areas introduced in section two above to describe Softer's e-business. The key interaction areas of the model are defined as follows: the 'input interaction area' (where the SME relates to individuals and organizations that supply intermediate goods and services); the 'output interaction area' (the management of customer relations); and the 'core interaction area' in which the firm's processes transform the relevant inputs into significant outputs. The higher the number of actors and the degree of active participation, the more complex the technical and organizational implications become. Conversely, it is not unusual to find that one individual (i.e. the owner) manages all supplier and client activities of the smaller firms (i.e., both input and output interaction areas).

The five levels of the proposed model do not represent a sequence but the interrelated actions undertaken by a firm to design and implement e-business. The actions may be subject to change over time because entrepreneurs tend to change their objectives, in line with the evolution of the business environment and advanced ICT becoming available. The time factor and the non-sequential nature of the interaction levels of the (non-linear) model better reflect how an SME may want to go about its business. Typically, it maintains a flexible approach to adapt its level of interaction to the opportunities that arise with different partners.

5 Concluding Remarks

The model proposed in this paper aims to facilitate the design and decision making of SMEs concerning their level of involvement with e-business. It is a supportive rather than a prescriptive model. According to Levy and Powell [19] 'SMEs are unlikely to follow a stages model' because entrepreneurs decide to 'adopt Internet' on the basis of the expected business value rather than on a given maturity level. With its interpretive and supportive design the proposed non-linear model aims at guiding business owners and advisors in implementing an SME e-business strategy that effectively meets business needs. Even though it is developed to better support the design of the process of digitization of smaller firms, the proposed model is actually an enterprise model for SMEs based on interaction levels: the main supportive literature is cited in the subsection 'integrating interaction' above. In these concluding remarks, its usefulness in complementing other approaches is briefly shown by reference to the work of Osterwalder and Pigneur [27] and to the Viable System Model literature [3, 13]. The first authors are concerned with the identification of the key components of a business model, which constitute their Business Model Canvas, and with the iterative process that allows for an appropriate model to be built. They warn entrepreneurs not to stop at their initial business model but to "iteratively adapting [it] in response to customer feedback" (p. 71)—which indeed underlines the role of the 'output interaction area' in this paper. Of the complex architecture and evolution of systems that are viable, that is "capable of independent existence" explained by Beer [3], one basic rule is of interest here: the way a system, with its subsystems, interacts with its environment is key to his viability (paraphrased, ibid p. 14). Within the systemic approach, Hoverstad and Ward [13] highlight the interactive and generative character of organizations: "organisations have multiple purposes which are emergent properties of the system. For us to understand how the organisation works as a system, we need to be able to model multiple purposes, how these interact and how they have been generated by the system, are being generated currently and are likely to be created in the future." (p. 4). In this paper, the proposed model is non-linear exactly because it acknowledges the fact that the interactions of the firm both within itself, among its subsystems, and with its environment generate emerging needs and purposes; these may give rise to novel levels of interaction and digitization. Finally, Hoverstad and Ward (ibid. p. 5), drawing on the work of Humberto Maturana [22] on structural coupling, underscore that the identity itself of a system (e.g. an individual, a firm) can be viewed through the relationships it engages with other entities: "When one system is an important part of the environment of another system and vice versa the second system forms an environmental element for the first, clearly when one system changes the other will tend to change too."... "The definition of identity then is by reference to the key relationships the system has with its environment." In the model proposed in this paper the importance of mutual influence among actors (actually 'systems') is in fact acknowledged in the subsection 'integrating interaction intensity' above depicting four possible interaction levels (low, medium, high, and complete) in the relationships engaged by an SME.

In sum, the 'levels of interaction' of the proposed model are 'markers' that enable an entrepreneur (and the designer) to make sense of prior experiences and/or to design and select the e-business solution appropriate for an organization and its objectives. Further, the model is not subject to a preconfigured set of technologies: it is not dominated by the "how" and the "where" of infrastructure and application management. Thus, the firm can adopt the kind of technology better suited to support a chosen level of interaction. The successful management of the selected technology is based on the identification of the appropriate mix of competences either available in-house or to be contracted externally. Policy makers can use the proposed model to sidestep the technological bias when assessing the current state of play of e-business development in the SME universe and, hence, to aid the formulation of the actions needed to support the SMEs in developing a digitally oriented business.

This paper has summarized the results of the first part of the research concerning the design of e-business and SMEs. In the next steps the experience of other enterprises from different industries will be collated and the make/buy alternatives in digital technologies competences will be investigated.

References

1. Alonso-Mendo, F., et al.: Understanding web site redesigns in small- and medium-sized enterprises (SMEs): a U.K.-based study on the applicability of e-commerce Stage Models. Eur. J. Inf. Syst. **18**(3), 264–279 (2009)
2. Ashurst, C., et al.: The role of IT competences in gaining value from e-business: an SME case study. Int. Small Bus. J. **30**(6), 640–658 (2011)
3. Beer, S.: The viable system model: its provenance, development, methodology and pathology. J. Oper. Res. Soc. **35**(1), 7–25 (1984)
4. Chaston, I., et al.: The internet and e-commerce: an opportunity to examine organisational learning in progress in small manufacturing firms? Int. Small Bus. J. **19**(2), 13–30 (2001)
5. Daniel, E., Wilson, H.: Adoption of e-commerce by SMEs in the UK. Int. Small Bus. J. **20**(3), 253–270 (2002)
6. Fillis, I., et al.: A qualitative investigation of smaller firm e-business development. J. Small Bus. Enterp. Dev. **11**(3), 349–361 (2004)
7. Goldkuhl, G.: From action research to practice research. Australas. J. Inf. Syst. **17**(2), 57–78 (2012)
8. Goldkuhl, G.: Meanings of pragmatism : ways to conduct information systems research. In: Proceedings of the 2nd International Conference on Action in Language, Organisations and Information Systems (ALOIS), pp. 13–26 (2004)
9. Goldkuhl, G.: Pragmatism vs interpretivism in qualitative information systems research. Eur. J. Inf. Syst. **21**(2), 135–146 (2012)
10. Goldkuhl, G., Agerfalk, P.J.: IT artifacts as socio-pragmatic instruments: reconciling the pragmatic, semiotic, and technical. Int. J. Technol. Hum. Interact. **1**(3), 29–43 (2005)
11. Grandori, A., Soda, G.: Inter-firm networks: antecedents, mechanisms and forms. Organ. Stud. **16**(2), 183–214 (1995)
12. Grant, K., et al.: Risky business: perceptions of e-business risk by UK small and medium sized enterprises (SMEs). Int. J. Inf. Manage. **34**(2), 99–122 (2014)
13. Hoverstadt, P., Ward, A.: Defining identity by structural coupling in VSM practice. In: UKSS International Conference, Oxford, UK (2010)
14. Janssen, W., et al.: Business process engineering versus e-business engineering: a summary of case experiences. In: Proceedings of the 36th Annual Hawaii International Conference on System Sciences, 2003, p. 9. IEEE (2003)
15. Johnston, D.A., et al.: Does e-business matter to SMEs? A comparison of the financial impacts of internet North American SMEs. J. Small Bus. Manag. **45**(3), 354–361 (2007)
16. Kapurubandara, M., Lawson, R.: SMEs in developing countries need support to address the challenges of adopting e-commerce technologies. In: 20th Bled eConference, pp. 485–499 (2007)
17. Kim, H.D., et al.: Building web 2.0 enterprises: a study of small and medium enterprises in the United States. Int. Small Bus. J. **31**(2), 156–174 (2011)
18. Levenburg, N.M., Magal, S.R.: Applying importance-performance analysis to evaluate E-business strategies among small firms. E-service J. January 2005, 29–48 (2005)
19. Levy, M., Powell, P.: Exploring SME internet adoption: towards a contingent model. Electron. Mark. **13**(2), 173–181 (2003)

20. Magal, S.R., et al.: Towards a stage model for e-business adoption among SMEs: preliminary results for manufacturing and service firms. In: AMCIS 2008 Proceedings (2008)
21. Martin, L.M., Matlay, H.: "Blanket" approaches to promoting ICT in small firms: some lessons from the DTI ladder adoption model in the UK. Internet Res. 11(5), 399–410 (2001)
22. Maturana, H.: Autopoiesis, structural coupling and cognition: a history of these and other notions in the biology of cognition. Cybern. Hum. Knowing. 9(3–4), 5–34 (2002)
23. OECD: Financing SMEs and Entrepreneurs 2013: An OECD Scoreboard. OECD Publishing (2013)
24. OECD: Skills Development and Training in SMEs, Local Economic and Empoyment Development (LEED). OECD Publishing (2013)
25. Oliveira, T., Martins, M.F.: Firms patterns of e-business adoption: evidence for the European Union-27. Electron. J. Inf. Syst. Eval. 13(1), 47–56 (2010)
26. Orlikowski, W.J.: Sociomaterial practices: exploring technology at work. Organ. Stud. 28(9), 1435–1448 (2007)
27. Osterwalder, A., Pigneur, Y.: Aligning profit and purpose through business model innovation. In: Palazzo, G., Wentland, M. (eds.) Responsible management practices for the 21st century, pp. 61–75 (2011)
28. Probst, L., et al.: Digital transformation scoreboard 2017: evidence of positive outcomes and current opportunities for EU businesses (2017)
29. Rao, S.S., et al.: Electronic commerce development in small and medium sized enterprises: a stage model and its implications. Bus. Process Manag. J. 9(1), 11–32 (2003)
30. Raymond, L., Bergeron, F.: Enabling the business strategy of SMEs through e-business capabilities: a strategic alignment perspective. Ind. Manag. Data Syst. 108(5), 577–595 (2008)
31. Robeiro, F.L., Love, P.E.D.: Value creation through an e-business strategy: implication for SMEs in construction. Constr. Innov. Inf. Process. Manag. 3(1), 3–14 (2003)
32. Taylor, M., Murphy, A.: SMEs and e-business. J. Small Bus. Enterp. Dev. 11(3), 280–289 (2004)
33. Van De Ven, A.H., et al.: Determinants of coordination modes within organizations. Am. Sociol. Rev. 41(2), 322–338 (1976)
34. Willcocks, L., et al.: Moving to e-business. Random House Business Books, London (2000)
35. Zheng, J.: Small firms and e-business: cautiousness, contingency and cost-benefit. J. Purch. Supply Manag. 10(1), 27–39 (2004)

Different Strategies for Different Channels: Influencing Behaviors in Product Return Policies for Consumer Goods

Ferdinando Pennarola, Leonardo Caporarello and Massimo Magni

Abstract One more time the online channel differs from the offline one. Our study on the product return strategies in the retail industry shows that even if more expensive for online retailers, product return policies are more generous and perceived as lenient by consumers. Our measures were collected in the Italian jeans retail industry, with a comparative study done on firms active on both channels and representing more than 50% of the overall industry sales. The impossibility to serve the customer at a distance and the need to strategically boost online sales are becoming a serious trap for online retailers.

1 Introduction

After your shopping, either online or in store, seemingly pleased of your purchases, you might experience something has gone wrong. Looking at the item bought, you might realize that the color was not as expected, the size was not fitting well or you simply recognize the fact the item was the result of an impulsive purchase. As consequence, you could decide to return the good in order to re-invest your money in something else. Doubtless, this is an important moment in the customer-retailer relationship. This moment can be considered a real test for retailers, and its failure can really make customers feel tricked and, as consequence, ruin the business.

As reported in many cases, and confirmed by scholars in the current debate on return policies, the possibility to return a product is very important for customers. Scholars demonstrated that product return policies can be perceived by consumers

F. Pennarola (✉) · L. Caporarello · M. Magni
Università Bocconi, Milan, Italy
e-mail: Ferdinando.pennarola@unibocconi.it

L. Caporarello
e-mail: Leonardo.caporarello@unibocconi.it

M. Magni
e-mail: Massimo.magni@unibocconi.it

© Springer International Publishing AG, part of Springer Nature 2019   247
A. Lazazzara et al. (eds.), *Organizing for Digital Innovation*,
Lecture Notes in Information Systems and Organisation 27,
https://doi.org/10.1007/978-3-319-90500-6_19

as positive quality signal of the retailers [28] and as a risk reliever during the purchasing process [27]. Furthermore, Janakiramana, Syrdalb and Freling recently [14] demonstrated that lenient return policies increase, at the same time, the consumers' attitude to purchase again and the customers' attitude to return the product. Nevertheless, the effect on the former seems greater.

Looking at how important return policies are for customers, a question rises spontaneously: why should retailers put in practice restrictive return policies, with the risk of losing customers and ruining their business? The answer is related to the costs of these return policies. In fact, indulgent return policies can be very expensive for retailers: a research on US offline mass merchandisers suggested that negative profits are often associated to product return rates higher than 20% (of what has been sold) [23]. These costs have been reported by the literature to be associated to three main factors:

- high processing costs related to the reintegration of the returned product in the companies' stores or warehouses [14];
- the low-salvage value of the returned products [14];
- return frauds [11].

Moreover, it is important to underline that these costs are considerably greater for online retailers than for offline ones [7, 10]. On one side, online retailers are usually affected by higher processing costs for the reintegration of returned items [10]. On the other side, also due to the impossibility to physically inspect the product before the purchase [27], items bought online are returned more often compared to items bought in offline stores. This difference is demonstrated by the gap between the average product return rate (for the US market) in the online business (33%) and in the offline one (8.9%). As consequence, online retailers end up coping with higher processing costs related for the single return and more items returned. This structural disadvantage for the online business related to product return policies' costs, uncovers a research gap in the current literature debate. This gap concerns the difference in the nature of product return policies belonging to the online and the offline channel. In this paper, we investigated the phenomenon by looking at the case of the jeans manufacturing and retailing industry in Italy, with both a desk and a field study.

2 Theory and Hypotheses

2.1 The Notion of Reverse Logistics

According to the definition given by the American Reverse Logistics Executive Council, reverse logistics is "the process of planning, implementing, and controlling the efficient, cost effective flow of raw materials, in process inventory, finished goods and related information from the point of consumption to the point of origin for the purpose of recapturing value or proper disposal" [19, p. 17]. As a matter of facts, the reverse logistics process starts from final customers. The products they previously bought are returned and then recollected by the selling companies whose purpose is to manage properly their end of life [9]. In order to so, companies can apply different strategies and resort to different disposition channels:

1. they can undertake recycling actions in order to partially recover and reusing some parts of products disposed;
2. they can do re-manufacturing or refurbishment in order to try to resell these products to customers as brand-new;
3. they can repair these products for selling them in the second hand-market;
4. they can sell returned products by the pound and dispose them through liquidation auctions, for example.

Tonanont [26] illustrates a generic scheme of closed loop supply chain (the bundle of forward and reverse logistics processes of a company), which allows to understand how reverse logistics is integrated in the value chain of a company (Fig. 1).

In order to fully understand what the most important features of a closed loop supply chain are, the definition given by Guide and Van Wassenhove [12] results particularly useful. Based on this new definition, closed loop supply chain management is defined as "the design, control and operation of a system to maximize value creation over the entire life cycle of a product with dynamic recovery of value from different types and volumes of returns over time" [12, p. 10]. This definition is particularly important since it explicitly underlines what are the advantages for a firm in the implementation of an efficient closed loop supply chain (and consequently, the implementation of an efficient reverse logistics). The main opportunity for a company in this case, is to maximize the value of a product across its entire lifecycle.

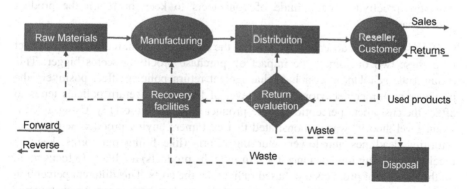

Fig. 1 A general scheme of closed loop supply chain

2.2 Value of Product Returns for Customers

It has been demonstrated that the existence of product return policies (companies' internal laws regulating products returns' occurrences) has a concrete value for customers. In particular, for those ones whose purchase of a certain product did not come with the satisfaction expected. Different roles have been attributed to such policies:

- they can be perceived by customers as a positive quality signal of the retailers [28];
- they have an important role of risk relievers for customers, during the purchasing process [27].

Concerning the latter, the possibility to give back the product once bought, makes customers less stressed during the purchasing process, lowering their perception of the financial and product risks associated to the purchase. This is particularly true for online transactions where customers are incapable to physically inspect products. Dholakia et al. [7] suggested that return policies are part of the overall value proposition provided by the retailer. In this sense, it is reasonable assuming that the increasing restrictiveness of such policies would eventually impact negatively this value proposition. This negative impact has, of course, its own risks, the largest of which is losing unsatisfied customers. In 2016, Janakiramana et al. [14] made an interesting study on the effectiveness of lenient return policies. In their publication, they addressed the following research question: "do lenient return policies increase product purchase more than product returns?"

In addressing the research question, they adopted a meta-analysis approach, synthesizing data from previous studies on how return policy leniency affects two main outcomes:

- purchase proclivity (the attitude of consumers to purchase);
- return proclivity (the attitude of consumers to keep or return the product purchased).

As results, it was observed that, even if the effects of lenient return policies affect both these two outcomes, the impact on purchase proclivity seems bigger. This brought the scholars to conclude that lenient return policies affect positively the purchase customer behavior. A high level of leniency in return policies tends to affect the customers perception of the product purchased, too [13]. Using a "construal level theory" was demonstrated that costumers buying products with longer returning deadlines and lower returning efforts (like filling out forms, keeping receipts or driving long distance for returning the products) are likely to focus more on the benefits of products purchased rather than the costs. This different perception leads eventually to a greater satisfaction of the product bought for the customers.

2.3 Cost of Product Returns for Retailers

Moving towards restrictive return policies in order to try to curb returns and drastically decrease returns rates is a big temptation for retailers. Returns can be very expensive for them for two main reasons [14]:

- the high processing costs related to the reintegration of the product in the companies' warehouses or stores;
- the low salvage value associated with returned merchandise.

A recent research about US mass merchandisers and nationwide chains publicised by Speights and Hilinski [23] suggests that product returns rates higher than 20% are often associated with negative operating profits for these offline players. A returned item causes the retailer to lose part of the profit margin on the original sales. The reduced margin is both determined by a lower expected sales price of the returned product (since, being the item not brand-new anymore, a markdown has been put onto its original price) and additional costs (like additional sales staff time for evaluating the conditions of the returned item, administrative and back office expenses). Furthermore, additional costs are not just related to legitimate product returns [11] but also to return frauds. In 2014, US retail Industry figures indicate that the total amount of merchandise returned was $ BL 284 and that the 3.8% of this figure ($ BL 10.8) can be estimated to be "return frauds" [25]. Speights and Hilinski [23] classified the most common types of return frauds and abuse schemes, offering also an overview of their estimated distribution in the US market [8, 15, 17].

2.4 Difference in Product Returns Facts Between Offline and Online Retailers

There is some consensus that product return rates associated to online retailers are higher compared to offline ones. In US, the average product return rate for online retailers was reported as high as 33% of all the products ordered, which is even more impressive if compared to the one of brick and mortar stores of 8.89% [25]. There is no evidence that the situation in Europe is radically different. As previously mentioned, the impossibility to physically check the products in online retailing, certainly contributes to this higher rate. Another big difference is the cost per item returned, related to the processing of these returns. Yet, the evidence suggests these costs are generally higher for online retailer than they are for brick and mortar stores [7, 10]. The reason at the bottom of this difference is in part due to the fact that brick and mortar stores can use existing physical sites to restock, quite immediately, the items returned [10]. Online retailers instead, often need to set distinctive returning facilities where temporarily restock returns, definitely increasing processing costs. Given the great importance of returning products in the online business, more restrictive return policies could negatively impact the ability to appeal and satisfy customers doing online shopping [18, 22]. An interesting fact is that, according to Stock [24], in the early days of e-commerce 40% of retail shoppers were not keen on buying online because of a higher perceived difficulty in returning the products. Even in more recent time (2010), this rate was said to persist [2]. Nevertheless, several factors among which web technologies [6], customers' reviews [21] and legislation (e.g. EU laws state that customers can return products for any reason within 14 days from the purchase) have contributed to decrease this rate [1, 3–5].

2.5 Main Factors in Product Returns Policies

A study conducted by Janakiramana et al. [14], based on an extensive research synthesis of the previous literature, described how return policies can be characterized by the level of leniency (or restrictiveness) of 5 main factors:

- *time leniency* (depending on the length of the period eligible for returning the product);
- *monetary leniency* (depending on whether the product is refund at 100% or less, for example in presence of restocking fees or shipping fees);
- *effort leniency* (depending on the level of effort required to customers for returning the product. For example: easiness of return process, original package or receipt required, forms fulfillment required);
- *scope leniency* (depending on whether the return is accepted for items which were in sale when purchased);
- *exchange leniency* (depending on whether the return is refunded through cash back or store credit).

2.6 Research Questions

Return policies are important both in online and offline retailing. Besides, the possibility to return a product bought online works as a financial risk reliever against the impossibility to physically inspect the product before the purchase [27]. So, if two identical return policies (same level of time, monetary, effort, scope and exchange leniency), belonging to two companies operating in different channels (offline and online), are considered, the online retailer's one should be even more appreciated by customers.

Because of the higher costs incurred, the online retailer should be less indulgent with his return policy. This might decrease that double digits product return rate which characterized the business (Janakiramana et al. [14] suggested that there is a positive correlation between a lenient return policy and customers' return proclivity). Nevertheless, this move could negatively impact the customer satisfaction and its purchase proclivity (the attitude of customers to purchase again). With that being said, the first research question surges spontaneously:

HP1: Are product return policies of online retailers more lenient than offline ones, even if the formers have higher returns-related costs?

Determining if online return policies are more lenient than offline ones will work as an empirical test for the thesis of Janakiramana et al. [14], which claims the existence of a positive correlation between return policy leniency and customer return proclivity (and so higher product return rates). In case of positive answer, it will mean that online retailers value more customers satisfaction rather than the financial burden associated to lenient return policies. Nevertheless, in order to really increase customers satisfaction and their purchase proclivity (the attitude of customers to purchase again), lenient return policies need to be perceived as such by customers, too. As consequence a second research question rises:

HP2: If product return policies of online retailers are more lenient than offline ones, are they perceived as such by customers, too?

3 Method

3.1 General Framework

We investigated the case by looking at the jeans manufacturing and retailing industry in Italy, selecting a sample of 4 companies that represent more than the 50% of items sold. All our sample companies operate both in the online channel (through e-commerce websites) and the offline one (through proprietary and franchised stores). We analytically compared the return policies of the two channels.

All the data regarding these companies' product return policies have been collected in different ways:

- for the online channel, the main sources of these information have been detailed companies' website pages, mystery shopping to test returns procedures and calls to customer service departments.
- for what concerns the offline channel, mystery shopping, in site clerks' interviews and calls to customer service departments have been used.

To answer the second research question, a general theory of measurement called Analytic Hierarchy Process (AHP) was adopted. This model is a mathematical framework, which "founds its widest applications in multi-criteria decision making, planning, resource allocation and conflict resolution" [20]. Raw data (or in other words, customers perceptions) were collected through an ad hoc web survey. The questions asked in the survey had the double purpose of:

- Understanding what are the factors (among time, monetary, effort, scope and exchange leniency) customers repute more important in a product return policy;

- Understanding how customers evaluate the relative performance of a firm which is performing differently from another with respect to each of the aforementioned factors.

AHP methodology allows you to take into account several factors at the same time, making pairwise numerical tradeoffs in order to reach a conclusion [20]. We used the AHP methodology at its full potential following a 3 steps approach: (1) criteria weights determination, (2) alternative weights determination, (3) global score calculation. These inputs were collected from customers using an ad hoc web survey; we collected 986 valid answers out of a sample of 1385. Our answers followed a stratification technique to ensure representativeness of company customers according to Nielsen market surveys. Each interviewed was asked to compare, pair-wise, each factor to the others and to assign a score from 1 to 9.

3.2 Sample Selection

We choose the jeans industry for three main reasons:

- The product return rate for the apparel category (grouping which includes jeans, too) is higher than the average of all the other product categories, both in online and offline channel;
- The jeans industry in Italy is a mature industry;
- The jeans industry in Italy (especially the economy segment) is not a fragmented one.

In such shrinking environment, customers tend to start to focus less on the benefit of the product alone and to move their attention on the price and services associated to the product [16]. This could mean, for example, customers might put more attention over product return policies. An industry breakdown including the most important players, their market shares and their sales absolute value is presented in Fig. 2.

We then chose Carrera, OVS, H&M and Zara. These four companies can be considered highly representative of the industry both in terms of market share and

Main players	Market Shares 2015 (%)	Sales 2015 (EUR million)	
Carrera SpA	15.2%	€	60.2
OVS SpA	15.2%	€	60.2
Hennes & Mauritz Srl	13.4%	€	53.1
Zara Italia Srl	8.9%	€	35.4
C&A Moda Italia Srl	1.3%	€	5.3
Others	46.1%	€	183.0
Tot	100%	€	397.20

Fig. 2 Italian economy jeans industry breakdown: main players

in terms of number. Altogether, their market share amounts up to 52.6% of the industry and four is considered a number big enough to be illustrative of the industry itself, and they all sell online and through stores.

4 Results

The following table summarizes the results (Fig. 3).

Two are the factors whose level of leniency is the same for the online and offline channels: this is the case for "Time Leniency" and for "Scope Leniency". In fact, regarding the former, the four companies selected do not show any difference, in terms of time period for returning the product, between the two channels. Carrera offers a 14 days window for returning the product regardless of the purchasing channel, while all the others offer 30 days. Concerning the "Scope Leniency" factor instead, all the four companies give customers the possibility to return products bought (online or offline) at discount or in sale. As far as the "Monetary Leniency" factor is concerned, the offline channel seems to be more lenient than the online one. This is due to the fact that two companies out of four require extra fees to customers for returning products they bought online. Indeed, Carrera requires its customers to pay the shipping fee for shipping back the online purchases they want to return. At same time, H&M requires customers to pay a restocking fee of Euro 2.95 for returning their online purchases. In both these two cases the reimbursed value to customers is less than 100% of the value of the product bought. This discrepancy comes from the difference between the refunded cost of the product

	Online Channel				Offline Channel				Most lenient policies (online/offline)
	Carrera	OVS	H&M	Zara	Carrera	OVS	H&M	Zara	
Time Leniency	14 days	30 days	30 days	30 days	14 days	30 days	30 days	30 days	Same leniency level
Monetary Leniency	Less than 100%	100%	Less than 100%	100%	100%	100%	100%	100%	Offline
Effort Leniency									Online
Possibility to return the product even without the original package or price tags	No	Yes	Yes	Yes	No	No	No	No	Online
Need to contact customer service before returning the product	Yes	Yes	No	Yes	No	No	No	No	Offline
Possibility to require a pick-up service for the product that has to be returned	No	Yes	Yes	Yes	No	No	No	No	Online
Possibility to avoid to specify the reason why returning the product	Yes	No	No	Yes	Yes	Yes	Yes	Yes	Offline
Possibility of easy and immediate access to companies' product return policies (e.g. links in the companies' websites homepages)	Yes	Yes	Yes	Yes	No	No	No	No	Online
Scope Leniency	Return for discounted items accepted	Return for discounted items accepted	Return for discounted items accepted	Return for discounted items accepted	Return for discounted items accepted	Return for discounted items accepted	Return for discounted items accepted	Return for discounted items accepted	Same leniency level
Exchange Leniency	Cash	Cash	Cash	Cash	Store credit	Store credit	Store credit	Store credit	Online

Fig. 3 Return policies comparison between the online and offline channels

and the extra costs sustained to return it. Finally, concerning the last two factors ("Effort Leniency" and "Exchange Leniency") the online channel seems to be more lenient than the offline one. Concerning the "Effort Leniency" factor instead, given the complex nature of the factor itself, the comparison between the two channels is made among its sub-factors:

- Possibility to return the product even without the original package or price tag: for this sub-factor, the online return policies are more lenient than the offline ones. None of the companies accept returning products bought offline without the original price tag attached.
- Need to contact customer service before returning the product: regarding this sub-factor, offline return policies are more lenient than online ones. In this case, customers do not need to contact anybody for returning products bought in offline stores: they just need to go directly to the store and drop the product.
- Possibility to require a pick-up service for product that has to be returned: concerning this sub-factor, online return policies are more lenient than offline ones. All these companies (except Carrera) provide this service for returning online purchases (not offline ones).
- Possibility to avoid specifying the reason why returning the product: for this sub-factor, offline return policies are more lenient than online ones. In fact, no questions are usually asked about the return reason during the physical returning process in offline stores. The same cannot be said for the online channel: companies' websites (except in the case of Carrera) explicitly ask customers the reason why they are returning their online purchases.
- Possibility of easy and immediate access to companies' product return policies: regarding this sub-factor, online return policies are more lenient than offline ones. As already specified in the previous chapter, no web page, booklet or brochure specifying the offline product return processes exist.

Since three out of five sub-factors are more lenient for online product return policies, the parent factor "Effort Leniency" can be said to be more lenient for the online channel.

Summing up, the result of the comparison follows:

- in case of two factors ("Time Leniency" and "Scope Leniency") the level of return policies leniency is exactly the same in the two channels (online and offline);
- for what concern one factor ("Monetary Leniency"), offline return policies are more lenient than online ones;
- regarding two factors ("Effort Leniency" and "Exchange Leniency") online return policies are more lenient than offline ones.

Since "it takes two to tango", it's important to verify whether clients perceive the same about the return policy. The inputs collected through the survey and elaborated according to the AHP are illustrated below. For the purpose of this paper we show the global scores only.

	Time Leniency	Monetary Leniency	Effort Leniency	Scope Leniency	Exchange Leniency	Final Score
Carrera Online	0.005	0.009	0.014	0.014	0.024	6.5%
Carrera Offline	0.005	0.057	0.012	0.014	0.003	9.1%
OVS Online	0.033	0.057	0.034	0.014	0.024	16.1%
OVS Offline	0.033	0.057	0.012	0.014	0.003	11.9%
H&M Online	0.033	0.007	0.062	0.014	0.024	13.9%
H&M Offline	0.033	0.057	0.012	0.014	0.003	11.9%
Zara Online	0.033	0.057	0.061	0.014	0.024	18.7%
Zara Offline	0.033	0.057	0.012	0.014	0.003	11.9%

Global Score Online	55.3%
Global Score Offline	44.7%

Fig. 4 AHP model: the "Global Score" calculation phase

Looking at the first matrix in Fig. 4, all companies' "Global Scores" referring to their online and offline channels can be observed. It is important to remember that each alternative's "Global Score" is the result of summing up all the alternative's marginal global score referring to the five different factors. Indeed, each marginal global score depends both on the relative performance of the alternative considered compared to the others and, at the same time, on the relative importance that customers attribute to the factor to which the marginal global score refers. With that being said, summing up all the "Global Scores" related to the companies' online channels against the offline ones (second small matrix at the bottom of Fig. 4), the second research question (if product return policies of online retailers are more lenient than offline ones, are they perceived as such by customers?) can be positively answered, too. Customers seem to perceive online product return policies as more lenient than offline ones.

5 Discussion and Lessons Learned

The first interesting insight from the analysis is that, while the leniency of product return policies of online retailers is higher than online ones, the difference in customers' perception about the relative level of return policies leniency is not as large as one might think. Looking at the "Global Scores" for online and offline channel in Fig. 4 (in the bottom left part of the figure), it can be immediately noticed how online product return policies are perceived as more lenient compared to offline ones, but not by a great extent (10.6% difference in terms of score). Considering the much greater financial burden that online companies (compared to offline ones) need to sustain to fuel customer satisfaction concerning product return policies, a much greater difference in terms "Global Score" would be desirable for the online channel. This may be a hint for the existence of room for improvement in return policies strategies; in particular, in terms of a better allocation of resources in specific areas. With this regard, a second important take away of this analysis is that, some "return policies optimization" strategies could be pursued by those online retailers willing to increase the leniency level of their return policies as perceived by their customers. In particular, online companies should understand what are the most important factors in return policies for their customers. Then, online retailers should understand if those factors that are less important for customers are also those ones which triggers important costs and expenses for the company. If this is the case, online players should modify their return policies in order to achieve a policy which represents a greater value for the customers and smaller financial burden for the company. The money saved from decreasing the level of return leniency related to the "Exchange Leniency" factor, could be potentially invested in other factors much more important for customers. Examples are the "Monetary Leniency" factor (which of course implies potential important financial burdens for the company as well) or the "Effort Leniency" factor. Concerning the latter, in particular, a possible "return policy optimization strategy" could be implemented. As a matter of facts, the presence of some of its sub-factors (like the possibility to avoid specifying the reason why retuning the product or the possibility not to contact customers service before returning the product), while it has a great value for customers, it does not really represent a direct cost for the company.

Limitations of our findings are linked to the nationality of the sample and the industry choice we made. Nevertheless, two major universal insights from this thesis can be pinpointed: (1) First, the awareness that different aspects of product return policies are valued differently by customers. (2) Second, companies operating both online and offline, with a clear prevalence of sales coming from the second channel, should really start thinking how to optimize their online return policies in order not to negatively impact their profitability in the future.

References

1. Bhutta, K.S., Huq, F.: Supplier selection problem. Supply Chain Manage. Int. J. 7(3), 126–135 (2002)
2. Bonifield, C., Cole, C., Schultz, R.: Product returns on the internet—a case of mixed signals. J. Bus. Res. 63(10), 1058–1065 (2010)
3. Choi, T.M.: Analytical Modeling Research in Fashion Business. Springer, Berlin (2016)
4. Chu, R.: What online Hong Kong travelers look for on airline/travel websites? Int. J. Hospitality Manage. 20(1), 95–100 (2001)
5. Dae-Ho, B.: The AHP approach for selecting an automobile purchase model. Inf. Manage. 38, 289–297 (2001)
6. De, P., Hu, Y., Rahman, M.: Product-oriented web technologies and product returns: an exploratory study. Inf. Syst. Res. 24(4), 998–1010 (2013)
7. Dholakia, R., Zhao, M., Dholakia, N.: Multi-channel retailing: a case study of early experiences. J. Interact. Mark. 19(2), 63–74 (2005)

8. Eisenhardt, K.: Building theories from case study research. Acad. Manage. Rev. **14**(4), 532–550 (1989)
9. Govindan, K., Soleimani, H., Kannan, D.: Reverse logistics and closed-loop supply chain: a comprehensive review to explore the future. Eur. J. Oper. Res. **240**, 603–626 (2015)
10. Grewal, D., Iyer, G.R., Levy, M.: Internet retailing: enablers, limiters, and market consequences. J. Bus. Res. **57**(7), 703–713 (2004)
11. Griffis, S.E., Rao, S., Goldsby, T.J., Niranjan, T.T.: The customer consequences of returns in online retailing: an empirical analysis. J. Oper. Manage. **30**, 282–294 (2012)
12. Guide, V.D., Van Wassenhove, L.N.: OR FORUM—the evolution of closed-loop supply chain research. Oper. Res. **57**(1), 10–18 (2009)
13. Janakiraman, N., Ordónez, L.: Effect of effort and deadlines on consumer product returns. J. Consum. Psychol. **22**(2), 260–271 (2012)
14. Janakiramana, N., Syrdalb, H.A., Freling, R.: The effect of return policy Leniency on consumer purchase and return decisions: a meta-analytic review. J. Retail. **92**, 226–235 (2016)
15. Kalton, G., Flores-Cervantes, I.: Weighting methods. J. Official Stat. **19**, 81–97 (2003)
16. Kasturi Rangan, V., Moriarty, R.T., Swartz, G.S.: Segmenting customers in mature industrial markets. J. Mark. **56**(4), 72–82 (1992)
17. Kish, L.: Methods for design effects. J. Official Stat. **11**, 55–77 (1995)
18. Liang, T., Huang, J.: An empirical study on consumer acceptance of products in electronic markets: a transaction cost model. Decis. Support Syst. **24**(1), 29–43 (1998)
19. Rogers, D.S., Tibben-Lembke, R.S.: Going Backwards: Reverse Logistics Trends and Practices. Center for Logistics Management, University of Nevada, Reno. Reverse Logistics Executive Council, Reno (1998)
20. Saaty, R.W.: The analytic hierarchy process-what it is and how it is used. Math Model. **9**(3–5), 161–176 (1987)
21. Sahoo, N., Srinivasan, S., Dellarocas, C.: The Impact of Online Product Reviews on Product Returns and Net Sales. Workshop on Information Systems Economics, Milan, Italy (2013)
22. Shim, S., Eastlick, M., Lotz, S., Warrington, P.: An online prepurchase intentions model: the role of intention to search. J. Retail. **77**(3), 397–416 (2001)
23. Speights, D., Hilinski, M.: Return Fraud and Abuse: How to Protect Profits. Accessed in Sept 10, 2016 from The Retail Equation: https://www.theretailequation.com/Retailers/images/public/pdfs/whitepapers/wpTRE4013WhitePaperReturnFraud101Feb2013.pdf (2013)
24. Stock, J.: Development and Implementation of Reverse Logistics Programs. Oak Brook, Illinois, US (1998)
25. The Retail Equation: Consumer Returns in the Retail Industry. Accessed in June 12, 2016 from The Retail Equation: http://www.theretailequation.com/Retailers/images/public/pdfs/industryreports/ir2014nrfretailreturnssurvey.pdf (2014)
26. Tonanont, A.: Performance Evaluation in Reverse Logistics With Data Envelopment Analysis. The University of Texas at Arlington, p. 2 (2009)
27. Van den Poel, D., Leunis, J.: Consumer acceptance of the internet as a channel of distribution. J. Bus. Res. **45**(3), 249–256 (1999)
28. Wood, S.L.: Remote purchase environments: the influence of return policy Leniency on two-stage decision processes. J. Mark. Res. **38**(2), 157–169 (2001)

A Cross-National Analysis of E-HRM Configurations: Integrating the Information Technology and HRM Perspectives

Eleanna Galanaki, Alessandra Lazazzara and Emma Parry

Abstract This study is based on a configurational approach and aims to provide systematic knowledge on which configurations of e-HRM adoption actually exist at the global level. We operationalised e-HRM configuration as a combination of the actual degree of technological presence and the degree to which the technology is used to enable HRM activities. The core research questions addressed in this paper are: Which configurational types exist in e-HRM adoption? Which contextual factors explain the emergence of a certain configurational type of e-HRM? We adopted an exploratory cross-national research design and performed a cluster analysis among 5854 companies operating in 31 countries. According to our findings four types of e-HRM configurations can be identified named "non-usage", "HR primacy", "Integrated e-HRM", and "IT primacy". In particular, the lack of cooperation between IT and HR departments generates hybrid e-HRM configurations and unsuccessful adoption. Moreover, organizational size, SHRM and competing in international markets contribute more to determine the actual type of e-HRM configuration. Our results suggest also that the effect of national policies triggering innovation on e-HRM configurations should be considered rather than broader geographical clusters.

1 Introduction

In recent years, advancements in electronic human resource management (e-HRM) resulting from the rapid development of the Internet have focused attention on e-HRM within the scholarly debate. The term "e-HRM" was first used in the 1990s

E. Galanaki
Athens University of Economics and Business, Athens, Greece
e-mail: eleanag@aueb.gr

A. Lazazzara (✉)
Department of Social and Political Sciences, University of Milan, Milan, Italy
e-mail: alessandra.lazazzara@unimi.it

E. Parry
Cranfield School of Management, Cranfield University, Cranfield, UK
e-mail: emma.parry@cranfield.ac.uk

© Springer International Publishing AG, part of Springer Nature 2019   261
A. Lazazzara et al. (eds.), *Organizing for Digital Innovation*,
Lecture Notes in Information Systems and Organisation 27,
https://doi.org/10.1007/978-3-319-90500-6_20

to reference Human Resource Management "transactions" conducted via the Internet [1] and refers to the "planning, implementation and application of information technology for both networking and supporting at least two individual or collective actors in their shared performing of HR activities" [2].

Although it is still a relatively new scholarly field, there is already a well-developed knowledge on the quantitative adoption of e-HRM [e.g. 3–6]. One of the drivers of the surge in the use of e-HRM over the past decades may be its administrative and strategic benefits since the adoption of e-HRM is expected to change the HRM configuration within companies [3, 7–10]. However, empirical evidence for the actual attainment of expected benefits, especially in terms of facilitating the strategic transformation of the HR function, is scarce [6, 10–12]. Therefore, several authors have questioned the appropriateness of a deterministic view of e-HRM as causing organizational change and suggested that e-HRM is the outcome of strategic choices on the part of HR functions [2, 13]. A large scale adoption of e-HRM technology does not necessarily imply organizational e-HRM effectiveness [14]. Recent literature suggests that the deployment of e-HRM can both be a precursor of strategic HRM and be preceded by the HR strategy as the successful implementation of IT solutions depends on strategic input of HRM. However, the outcomes of E-HRM depend on the broader context in which organizations exist [c.f. 14]. Therefore, understanding how e-HRM is adopted is more important than ever. In particular, research examining qualitative differences in e-HRM adoption aiming at understanding differences in the nature of e-HRM configurations is critical [16].

In order to answer the call for more empirical studies to inform the conceptualization of e-HRM adoption [6] we operationalised e-HRM configuration as a combination of the actual degree of technological presence and the degree to which the technology is used to enable HRM activities. We based our study on a configurational approach [e.g. 17, 18] in order to provide systematic knowledge on which configurations of e-HRM adoption actually exist according to the information technology and human resource management focus. Moreover, as recommended by Strohmeier and Kabst [16] we determine which factors drive the emergence of these configurations via our cross-national research design. Therefore, our research questions are:

- Which configurational types exist in e-HRM adoption?
- Which contextual factors explain the emergence of a certain configurational type of e-HRM?

Due to the embryonic state of the knowledge on this topic, we adopted an exploratory perspective in order to generate hypotheses on different e-HRM configurations. A cluster analysis among 5854 companies operating in 31 countries was conducted.

The remainder of the paper is organized as follows. We begin with a definition of key theoretical constructs and present types of e-HRM. Second, we describe the sample, the survey data and the analytical approach adopted in this study. Third, we report our results, present the discussion, outline implications and limitations, and describe possible next steps.

2 Theoretical Framework

2.1 E-HRM Typologies

E-HRM has traditionally been defined as an "umbrella term covering all possible integration mechanisms and contents between human resource management (HRM) and IT, aimed at creating value for targeted employees and managers" [19].

E-HRM may support particular HR activities and has a wide range of goals. In order to explore the multidimensionality of the concept, e-HRM research has lead to three main e-HRM typologies [16]. The oldest one is based on the criterion of information systems functions [20] and distinguishes an automational and an informational type [e.g. 21–23]. The first type aims to merely automate HR tasks while the second one aims to support and increase the quality of HR-related decision-making. The second typology distinguishes according to the corporate significance of e-HRM and identifies an operative and a strategic type of e-HRM [e.g. 24–26]. Operative e-HRM aims to improve administrative tasks by increasing efficiency and reducing costs. On the opposite, strategic e-HRM supports HR tasks with a direct impact on corporate strategic objectives and especially on firm performance. Finally, the most dominant typology in the e-HRM literature has been developed by Lepak and Snell [27], later followed by Parry and Tyson [11], which classified e-HRM into a three types—operational, relational and transformational—according to expected outcome. Operational e-HRM is aimed at improving efficiency or reducing costs by automating administrative HR tasks. Relational e-HRM allows managers and employees remote access to HR information, empowering them to perform HR tasks themselves and extending their ability to connect with other parts of the company and outside organizations. Lastly, transformational e-HRM allows people to communicate across geographical boundaries and share information, thereby playing a key role in supporting virtual teams and network organizations [11].

The three categorisations above are all conceptually derived. Recently, Strohmeier and Kabst [16] tried to advance systematic knowledge on different types of e-HRM use by empirically gaining e-HRM configurations. A configurational approach aims to identify patterns of characteristics and activities that occur together on the basis of different contextual conditions [e.g. 17, 18]. In their study Strohmeier and Kabst [16] acknowledged three types of e-HRM: (a) "non-users", not employing e-HRM; (b) "operational users", which aim is to reduce administrative burden; (c) and "power users", which combines operational, relational and transformational e-HRM. Moreover, they identified a set of contextual variables that is systematically associated with the three e-HRM types and their contribution to organisational success. However, this more advance taxonomy is based on HR activities supported by information technology, but has neglected the role of IT systems in realizing them not considering the concrete technologies and applications employed.

2.2 Information Technology and HRM Perspectives

Recently, a new definition of e-HRM as a set of 'configurations of computer hardware, software and electronic networking resources that enable intended or actual HRM activities (e.g. policies, practices and services) through coordinating and controlling individual and group-level data capture and information creation and communication within and across organizational boundaries' [15] emerged. This definition underlines the existence of multiple elements that need to be integrated in order to understand e-HRM features and characteristics. In particular, e-HRM has both an information technology and a human resource management focus [28]. The technological focus is more related to the degree of the physical presence of information technologies that allow HR activities, while the HRM focus is the degree to which e-HRM is used to enable HR activities [15]. However, most of the studies exploring e-HRM adoption have embraced the point of view of HRM or IT separately, not considering how HRM and IT change in response to one another or which e-HRM configurations emerge according to the prevailing focus. Indeed, much of the research on e-HRM has been published in the management, human resources, and industrial/organizational psychology literature [29] and often the centrality of technology in deploying and delivering HR related tasks and managing people has been overlooked. Moreover, the prevailing assumption is a universalistic approach according to which the degree of adoption of IT systems such as HRIS is an antecedent to the effective usage of e-HRM for HR purposes [30]. In other words, for a company to effectively integrate e-HRM into multiple HRM functions, a minimum level of e-HRM development is necessary. This suggests that the level of e-HRM sophistication and embeddedness within HR practices increases when the extent of e-HRM adoption (technical infrastructure) increases. This linear and universally generalizable relationship among the extent of e-HRM adoption and effective HRM usage does not take into account the variation in e-HRM within organizations, which represents variation in organizational capability to support "increasingly coordinated individual and group-level transactions that capture HR data, creates HR information and provides HR data access and information regardless of geographical constraints and organizational horizontal and vertical differentiation" [15].

  In order to disentangle the complex interaction between HRM and technology, we propose a new configuration model based on the type of technology and HRM activities performed by organizations.

3 Method

3.1 Sample and Procedures

The data employed in this study stem from the Cranet survey, one of the most representative large-scale international comparative surveys of HRM systems [31]. The survey provides comprehensive information about the HRM practices of organizations and uses the participating companies' HR directors as the key informants. Questionnaire back-translation, sampling criteria and data collection procedures were overseen by partner business schools and universities operating in each country (for a detailed description of the Cranet approach see [32]). Moreover, Cranet data have been extensively used in e-HRM research [e.g. 4, 5, 15, 16, 26, 27]

The 2014–2015 dataset covers 5854 organizations across 31 countries, i.e., Australia, Austria, Belgium, Brazil, Croatia, Cyprus, Denmark, Estonia, Finland, France, Germany, Greece, Hungary, Iceland, Indonesia, Israel, Italy, Latvia, Lithuania, Philippines, Russia, Serbia, Slovakia, Slovenia, South Africa, Spain, Sweden, Switzerland, Turkey, United Kingdom and the USA.

Of the companies examined, 3981(68% of sample) were in the trade and services sector, 1639 (28% of sample) were in the manufacturing sector, and only 234 (4% of the sample) were in the primary sector of the economy. The majority of the organizations were private (4098; 70%) and 16 organizations (28% of the sample) were multinationals. In 64% of the companies, the most senior person in HRM had a seat on the Board of Directors. The majority of the companies also involved HR people in business strategy development (Table 1).

Table 1 Descriptive statistics for the sample (N = 5854)

Variable	Mean	SD
IT for HRM	1.53	1.15
e-HRM usage	1.71	0.93
Organizational size (sizeln)	6.29	1.56
HRM position on the Executive Board	0.64	0.48
Strategic involvement of HRM	2.14	1.03
e-HRM outsourcing	1.02	1.35
Proportion of the workforce with a higher education	3.86	1.38
Global competition	3.26	1.35
Trend_market	3.38	1.02
Sector		
Private	70.13%	
Economic Sector		
Primary	3.73%	
Manufacturing	28.3%	
Trade & Services	67.97%	
Property		
MNC	28.02%	

3.2 The Study Variables

E-HRM variables. For determining different types of e-HRM configurations a set of binary categorical variables were employed. The first e-HRM variable, *extent of IT for HRM*, was measured as a formative measure of the degree of physical presence of information technologies that allow HR activities; it has a minimum of 0 and a maximum of 3. It was calculated by adding three categorical (yes/no) questions from the CRANET questionnaire: (a) Human resource information system or electronic HRM systems for HRM activities (HRIS); (b) manager self-service for HRM activities (manager self-service); and (c) employee self-service for HRM activities (employee self-service). The second e-HRM variable, *extent of e-HRM usage*, is a formative measure of the penetration of e-HRM in multiple HRM functions with a minimum of 0 and a maximum of 4. This variable was calculated by adding four categorical (yes/no) questions from the CRANET questionnaire: (a) the vacancy page on the company website as a recruitment method (e-recruitment); (b) online selection tests as the selection method (e-selection); (c) bottom-up or top-down electronic communication (e-communication); and (d) the use of computer-based packages/e-learning for career management (e-learning).

  E-HRM configurations context. In order to contextualise e-HRM configurations a set of variables that showed relevance in previous general e-HRM research [cf. 6] was employed.

  Organizational size was the natural logarithm of the total number of employees in the organization. *Global competition* was measured by asking the respondents to characterize the main market(s) for their organization's products or services based on a 5-point Likert scale (1 = "local", 2 = "regional", 3 = "national", 4 = "continent-wide", 5 = "worldwide"). A six-point scale was adopted to measure the *proportion of the workforce with a higher education/university qualification* and the *proportion of young employees* (1 = "0%", 2 = "1–10%", 3 = "11–25%", 4 = "26–50%", 5 = "51–75%", 6 = "76–100%"). *HRM position on the Executive Board* was measured via a categorical (yes/no) variable ("Does the person responsible for HR have a place on the board or equivalent top executive team?"). Moreover, the *strategic involvement of HRM* was measured via a 4-item Likert scale answering the question: "If your organization has a business/service strategy, at what stage is the person responsible for HRM involved?" (0 = "not consulted", 1 = "on implementation", 2 = "through subsequent consultation", 3 = "from the outset"). Finally, *e-HRM outsourcing* was measured via a 5-item Likert scale (0 = "not outsourced", 4 = "completely outsourced"). Company performance was measured in terms of *revenue* (one question asking how gross revenue had been over the previous three years on a 5-point scale ranging from 1- "So low as to produce large losses" to 5-"Well in excess of costs") and rate of *service quality, productivity, profitability, innovation stock market performance* and *environmental matters* compared to other organizations in the same sector (on a 5-point scale: "Poor or at the low end of the industry", "Below average", "Average or equal to the competitors", "Better than average", "Superior"). We also asked respondents to rate the *growth of the market* currently served by their organization (5-point scale ranging from 1-"Declining to a great extent" to 5-"Growing to a great extent").

3.3 Analysis

Consistent with an explorative configuration approach, cluster analysis with hierarchical Ward's distance was applied in order to see how companies are grouped according to their e-HRM application. This analysis identified 4 clusters, in two dimensions, IT for HRM and e-HRM usage (Fig. 1).

4 Results

According to the results of our analysis, four different e-HRM configurations emerged (Fig. 1). The first cluster represented the lowest degree of digitalization of the HR function. Of the companies examined, 26% (N = 1534) have not adopted e-HRM at all or have very low adoption rate. The second cluster denoted an

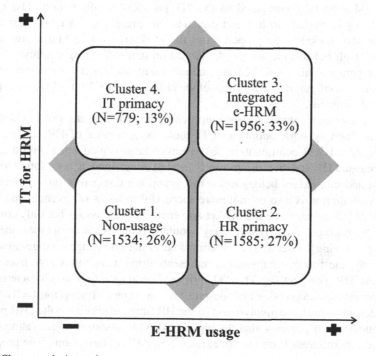

Fig. 1 Cluster analysis results

intermediate level of the HR function digital phenomenon with a greater emphasis on the HRM aspects than on the IT itself. Indeed, about 27% (N = 1585) of the sample denoted an HR primacy in the adoption of the e-HRM system. The third cluster grouped the largest number of organizations (N = 1956) since about 1/3 of the sample showed both an high emphasis on IT and HRM aspects in adopting e-HRM. Finally, only 13% (N = 779) of the companies belonged to the fourth cluster which is characterized by an IT primacy since the companies declared an high investment in IT for HRM but a very low usage for HR activities.

Regarding the contextual variables associated with the respective e-HRM configurations (Table 2), the "non-usage" configuration is characterized by a smaller organizational size and a low strategic orientation of the HR function compared to the other groups. Because of the low adoption rate the e-HRM outsourcing is very low. Companies belonging to the non-usage group are characterized by a low proportion of highly educated and young employees. In terms of performance and efficiency they are mainly competing at the local level (no multinational companies) and had the lowest stock market performance and in general worse performance than cluster 3.

The second cluster denotes an intermediate level of the HR function digital phenomenon with a stronger emphasis on the HRM side. The "HR primacy" configuration seems to be related to medium organizational size. Although the large extent of e-HRM adoption for HR activities, it is not characterized by a real HR strategy in e-HRM adoption. Indeed, the configuration does not present higher rate of SHRM especially compared to the "IT primacy" configuration. The e-HRM outsourcing is medium to low and organizations present a wider openness toward international markets. The proportion of the workforce with a higher education is not very high but this cluster has the largest presence of young employees among the four groups. This e-HRM configuration presents an higher revenue rate than the IT primacy configuration but is less efficient than cluster 3 on all the firm performance dimensions.

The third cluster stands for the comprehensive electronisation of HRM with an integrated and synergic adoption of IT tools for a number of HR activities. The "Integrated e-HRM configuration" is typical of large organization with a strategically oriented HR function. Employees' level of education has been found to be the highest and companies belonging to this group are competing on a global scale. This configuration is also overall more successful in terms of revenue, and also of profitability, innovation, stock market and environmental issues but only compared to the "non-usage" and "HR primacy" configurations. This companies operate in markets showing moderate growth compared to the non-usage configuration.

Finally, the fourth configuration represents firms more innovative from the IT than the HR perspective. The "IT primacy" configuration is characterized by medium organizational size and, despite the low extent of adoption for HR activities, denotes a strategic involvement of the HR function similar to the "HR primacy configuration". It presents also the highest e-HRM outsourcing rate (although not significantly different from the "Integrated e-HRM" configuration). The proportion

Table 2 Means and ANOVA for difference of means by cluster

Variable	Cluster 1 N = 1534		Cluster 2 N = 1585		Cluster 3 N = 1956		Cluster 4 N = 779		ANOVA F $\alpha = 0.05$	Pairwise comparisons with Bonferroni adjustment $\alpha = 0.05$
	Mean	SD	Mean	SD	Mean	SD	Mean	SD		
IT for HRM	0.51	0.50	0.59	0.49	2.67	0.47	2.56	0.50	✓	all 6
e-HRM usage	0.71	0.45	2.29	0.49	2.40	0.55	0.78	0.42	✓	all 6
Organizational size	5.75	1.34	6.12	1.43	6.83	1.64	6.34	1.57	✓	all 6
HRM position on the Executive Board	0.53	0.50	0.62	0.49	0.73	0.44	0.68	0.47	✓	all 6
Strategic involvement of HRM	1.94	1.13	2.09	1.03	2.31	0.93	2.13	1.01	✓	all but 4 versus 2
e-HRM outsourcing	0.76	1.27	0.93	1.30	1.21	1.36	1.23	1.48	✓	all but 4 versus 3
Proportion of the workforce with a higher education/university qualification	3.64	1.37	3.73	1.39	4.14	1.36	3.94	1.35	✓	all but 2 versus 1
Proportion young employees	2.53	1.00	2.67	0.94	2.59	0.92	2.52	0.91	✓	only 2 versus 1. and 2 versus 4
Global competition	3.12	1.31	3.19	1.33	3.47	1.36	3.13	1.41	✓	only 3 versus 1. 3 versus 2 and 3 versus 4
Revenue	3.79	1.07	3.93	1.02	4.10	0.99	3.79	1.14	✓	all but 4 versus 1 and 4 versus 2
Quality	4.00	0.83	3.96	0.90	4.00	0.91	4.05	0.86	–	none
Productivity	3.67	0.90	3.71	0.87	3.74	0.89	3.73	0.91	–	none
Profitability	3.40	0.95	3.49	0.96	3.60	0.96	3.51	1.03	✓	only 3 versus 1. and 3 versus 2
Innovation	3.41	1.03	3.51	1.01	3.63	1.00	3.52	1.01	✓	only 3 versus 1. and 3 versus 2

(continued)

Table 2 (continued)

Variable	Cluster 1 N = 1534		Cluster 2 N = 1585		Cluster 3 N = 1956		Cluster 4 N = 779		ANOVA F α = 0.05	Pairwise comparisons with Bonferroni adjustment α = 0.05
	Mean	SD	Mean	SD	Mean	SD	Mean	SD		
Stock_market	2.96	1.20	3.31	1.15	3.55	1.06	3.34	1.20	✓	all but 4 versus 2 and 4 versus 3
Environment	3.50	0.95	3.55	0.97	3.66	0.99	3.59	1.01	✓	only 3 versus 1. and 3 versus 2
Trend_market	3.31	1.06	3.39	0.98	3.45	1.02	3.34	1.06	✓	only 3 versus 1

of the workforce with a higher education is medium to high but it has an older age composition compared to the "HR primacy" type. This configuration is not serving an international market and seems not to specifically contribute to firm performance although it has the lowest stock rate among those adopting e-HRM and a lower revenue rate compared to the third cluster.

With regard to cross-national differences (Table 3), "non-usage" configuration is mainly located in Eastern Europe but also South Africa and Brazil while the "Integrated e-HRM" configuration is predominantly present in Western countries (i.e. Northern and Southern Europe, USA and Australia) and also some Asian countries (i.e. Philippines and Indonesia). The two intermediate configurations —"HR primacy" and "IT primacy"—do not show specific geographical differences although Western countries reporting high level of "Integrated e-HRM" configurations (e.g. Germany Switzerland, UK) and Eastern countries reporting high level of "non-usage" (e.g. Latvia, Lithuania, Russia) present a penetration level of the "HR primacy" configuration higher than 30%. In the same vein, Western countries reporting high level of "Integrated e-HRM" configurations show also a penetration level of the "IT primacy" configuration higher than 20% (i.e. Italy, Sweden and USA).

5 Discussion and Conclusion

Relying on a configurational approach [e.g. 17, 18], this paper aimed to provide systematic knowledge on e-HRM configurations according to the information technology and human resource management perspectives. Summarising the findings, the following propositions can be made:

P1: Four types of e-HRM configurations can be identified named "non-usage", "HR primacy", "Integrated e-HRM", and "IT primacy".
P2: Organizational size, SHRM and competing in international markets contribute more to determine the actual type of e HRM configuration.
P3: The lack of cooperation between IT and HR departments generates hybrid e-HRM configurations and unsuccessful adoption.
P4: The effect of national policies triggering innovation is more useful than broader geographical clusters in analysing different e-HRM configurations.

Interestingly, one out of three organizations are fully adopting e-HRM: both showing a high level of technological development and e-HRM usage for HR activities. Confirming previous research [cf. 6, 16] adoption is more wide-spread among large organizations and a strategic orientation of the HR function seems to be a prerequisite for such types of configuration [cf. 9]. The participation of the head of HR on the Board of Directors together with the involvement of the HR function in the development of the business/service strategy enhance the link between organizational and HRM goals. The alignment between IT investment and

Table 3 The four clusters by country

Country	Cluster 1 (%)	Cluster 2 (%)	Cluster 3 (%)	Cluster 4 (%)	Tota (%)
Australia	15	23	47	16	100
Austria	31	29	27	14	100
Belgium	11	24	55	10	100
Brazil	40	29	18	13	100
Croatia	45	30	19	6	100
Cyprus	28	21	38	14	100
Denmark	20	34	35	11	100
Estonia	34	34	25	7	100
Finland	14	29	46	11	100
France	11	21	55	13	100
Germany	19	40	33	8	100
Greece	37	27	24	12	100
Hungary	40	28	25	7	100
Iceland	27	32	30	11	100
Indonesia	14	36	47	3	100
Israel	42	12	27	19	100
Italy	16	12	45	27	100
Latvia	40	31	15	13	100
Lithuania	32	44	16	8	100
Philippines	27	31	33	9	100
Russia	38	33	25	4	100
Serbia	50	25	19	6	100
Slovakia	37	31	19	13	100
Slovenia	44	22	16	18	100
South Africa	37	30	17	16	100
Spain	19	24	45	12	100
Sweden	8	19	52	21	100
Switzerland	20	35	38	7	100
Turkey	21	17	48	15	100
United Kingdom	12	31	39	19	100
USA	15	20	42	23	100
Total	26	27	33	13	100
Total	1534	1585	1956	779	5854

e-HRM effective usage in larger organisations with a clear strategic orientation exceeds the contribution to organisational success of other configurations, especially the "non-usage" configuration and the one based on the HR initiative only. Moreover, although a European-wide study found that employees' level of education neither furthered nor hindered e-HRM adoption [5], our study showed that this has an impact especially for the integrated configuration but also for the "IT primacy" one. E-HRM requires a certain degree of technical knowledge and skills and higher education include basic IT skills and familiarization with electronic tools. Therefore, since this has been found to be positively associated with HRM innovation [33], IT skills of the employees are especially favourable to the full integrated adoption of e-HRM. Finally, organizations displaying an "Integrated e-HRM" configuration are usually operating in a global scenario whereas e-HRM facilitates collaboration and information sharing across geographical boundaries.

Although in the last four decades organizations have increasingly adopted e-HRM technology [6], one out of five organizations in the world are still displaying a "non-usage" configuration. The contextual characteristics of such configuration explain why for same organizations investing in e-HRM systems is not worthwhile and so they are less likely to adopt them. Usually companies do not adopt e-HRM when they don't reach that 'critical mass' in terms of number of employees, which would justify such a substantial investment by guaranteeing return on it. This result is in line with Strohmeier and Kabst' [16] findings, according to which "non-user" was predicted just by organizational size. Moreover, this configuration is characterized by a low level of strategic human resource management. One possible explanation is that since the HR function is not involved into the development of the strategic/business plan the value of e-HRM systems is not adequately supported. Another explanation could be that those companies lack an institutionalized HR function at all. In addition, these companies present low level of higher educated and young employees, therefore employers may view a potential lack of skills as a threat to successful implementation especially at the beginning of e-HRM adoption [34, 35]. This configuration is also characterized by very low organizational performance especially if compared to the "Integrated e-HRM" one. This means that organizations belonging to this cluster may be affected by budget limitations and lack the financial resources needed to invest in e-HRM systems [6]. The configurational approach takes into account not only the internal fit of configurational variables but also the external fit of configurational variables with contextual variables [e.g. 17, 18]. In this case it is also clear that the national business system affects the adoption of e-HRM since most of the countries showing high non-usage rate are Eastern European, which are characterized by lower gross domestic product and innovation rate. Surprisingly, a previous study by Strohmeier and Kabst [5] revealed that the chance of adopting e-HRM is higher in Eastern than Western business systems. However, that study addressed the overall adoption of e-HRM as a dichotomous measure (e.g., questions asking whether or not organizations have any e-HRM tools), so even if a certain degree of adoption may be present in Eastern countries, this does not imply a higher level of e-HRM sophistication or the extent of usage for HR activities. Consequently, the "non-usage" configuration seems to fit very well with major contextual conditions.

The view of "non-usage" and "Integrated e-HRM" configurations being opposite poles between not adopting or fully adopting e-HRM becomes slightly complicated when adding other two hybrid configurations deviating from this underlying continuum. According to Kossek et al. [36] communication and collaboration between

HR and IT units is crucial for successful e-HRM adoption nevertheless these units often have different priorities, culture and visions. The "HR primacy" and "IT primacy" configurations represent two intermediate level in e-HRM adoption—one being more HR-function and the other more IT department focused—and constitute an example of misalignment between the two units. Both configurations are characterized by medium size in terms of number of employees and both present a similar level of strategic orientation with the "IT primacy" configuration exceeding the "HR-primacy" one. The "HR primacy" configuration seems therefore to be the result of a kind of "bottom up" approach in e-HRM adoption whereas the HR function implement web-based tools based on social media and user-friendly logic in order to answer specific employees' needs without an alignment with broader organizational goals and the IT department. Indeed, given the higher level of internationalization, it could be the case that specific groups of employees need to communicate and share information across geographical boundaries, so e-HRM is adopted in order to support virtual teams and network organizations [11]. Moreover the highest presence of young employees which are more comfortable when interacting through technological systems then older employees makes this configuration particularly suited to meet the expectations of Gen Y employees [37]. On the opposite, the "IT primacy" is characterized by the lowest level of young employees but a higher employees' education level and a mainly local focus. In this case there seems to be incongruence between the needs of the HR function and the IT department since the level of technological development of the e-HRM tools is high but the actual usage for HR activities is low. Moreover, due to the highest e-HRM outsourcing, this may allow smaller organizations to adopt e-HRM without larger investments but may also represent a lack of resources and capabilities in-house or that e-HRM adoption is not part of the business strategy [38]. One or other configurations are also not successful in terms of performance, meaning that without a close collaboration between the IT and HR departments e-HRM adoption may not be successful.

In conclusion, despite several theoretical and practical limitations related to the configurational approach and type of data employed, our study aimed to provide a first exploration of e-HRM typology based simultaneously on the IT and HRM perspectives in order to stimulate future deeper understanding of e-HRM adoption. One reason for the lack of empirical evidence for the actual attainment of the expected benefits of e-HRM adoption [6, 10–12] may be related to the failure to consider different e-HRM configurations while analyzing the overall adoption. Therefore, as a next step of this exploratory research we aim to explore factors associated with the four e-HRM configurations in order to understand which factors influence the deployment of e-HRM configurations within organizations and to understand how companies may switch from one to the other. Moreover, according to the results of this preliminary analysis, due to the lack of significant differences among geographical cluster in e-HRM configurations (except for the non-usage one which seems to be peculiar or Eastern European countries) we argue that the effect of national policies supporting innovation should be analysed instead of considering geographical clusters as homogenous in influencing e-HRM adoption.

References

1. Lengnick-Hall, M.L., Moritz, S.: The impact of e-HR on the HRM function. J. Labour Res. **24**, 365–379 (2003)
2. Strohmeier, S.: Research in e-HRM: review and implications'. Hum. Resour. Manag. Rev. **17**, 19–37 (2007)
3. Florkowski, G., Olivas-Lujan, M.: The diffusion of human resource information technology innovations in US and non-US firms. Pers. Rev. **35**, 684–710 (2006)
4. Panayotopoulou, L., Galanaki, E., Papalexandris, N.: Adoption of electronic systems in HRM: is national background of the firm relevant? New Technol. Work Employ. **25**, 253–269 (2010)
5. Strohmeier, S., Kabst, R.: Organizational adoption of e-HRM in Europe: An empirical exploration of major adoption factors. J. Manag. Psychol. **24**, 482–501 (2009)
6. Bondarouk, T., Parry, E., Furtmueller, E.: Electronic HRM: four decades of research on adoption and consequences. Int. J. Hum. Resour. Manag. **5192**, 1–34 (2016)
7. Marler, J.: Making human resources strategic by going to the net: reality or myth? Int. J. Hum. Reosurce Manag. **20**, 515–527 (2009)
8. Ruel, H., Bondarouk, T., Looise, J.: E-HRM: innovation or irritation. An explorative empirical study in five large companies on web-based HRM. Manage. Rev. **15**, 364–381 (2004)
9. Marler, J.H., Fisher, S.L.: An Evidence-Based Review of E-HRM and Strategic Human Resource Management. Hum. Resour. Manag. Rev. **23**, 18–36 (2013)
10. Ruël, H.J.M., Bondarouk, T.V., Van der Velde, M.: The Contribution of E-Hrm to Hrm Effectiveness. Hum. Relations. **29**, 280–291 (2007)
11. Parry, E., Tyson, S.: Desired goals and actual outcomes of e-HRM. Hum. Resour. Manag. J. **21**, 335–354 (2011)
12. Hempel, P.S.: Preparing the HR profession for technology and information work. Hum. Resour. Manage. **43**, 163–177 (2004)
13. Haines, V.Y., Lafleur, G.: Information Technology Usage and Human Resource Roles and Effectiveness. Hum. Resour. Manage. **47**, 525–540 (2008)
14. Wright, P.M., Dunford, B.B., Snell, S.A.: Human Resources and the Resource-Based View of the Firm. J. Manage. **27**, 701–721 (2001)
15. Marler, J.H., Parry, E.: Human resource management, strategic involvement and e-HRM technology. Int. J. Hum. Resour. Manag. **5192**, 1–21 (2015)
16. Strohmeier, S., Kabst, R.: Configurations of e-HRM—an empirical exploration. Empl. Relations. 36, (2014)
17. Meyer, A.D., Tsui, A.S., Hinings, C.R.: Configurational approaches to organizational analysis. Acad. Manag. J. **36**, 1175–1195 (1993)
18. Short, J.C., Payne, G., Ketchen, D.J.: Research on organizational configurations: past accomplishments and future challenges. J. Manage. **34**, 1053–1079 (2008)
19. Bondarouk, T., Ruel, H.: Electronic human resource management: challenges in the digital era. Int. J. Hum. Reosurce Manag. **20**, 505–514 (2009)
20. Zuboff, S.: Automate-informate: the two faces of intelligent technology. Organ. Dyn. **14**, 5–18 (1985)
21. Ball, K.S.: The usage of human resource information systems: a survey. Pers. Rev. **30**, 677–693 (2001)
22. Broderick, R., Bodreau, J.W.: Human resource management, information technology, and the competitive edge. Acad. Manag. Perspect. **6**, 7–17 (1998)
23. Kovach, K.A., Cathcart, C.E.: Human resource information systems (HRIS): Providing business with rapid data access, information exchange and strategic advantage. Public Pers. Manage. **28**, 275–282 (1998)
24. Hussain, Z., Wallace, J., Cornelius, N.E.: The use and impact of human resource information systems on human resource professionals. Inf. Manag. **44**, 74–89 (2007)

25. Strohmeier, S., Kabst, R.: Evaluating major design characteristics of human resource information systems. Int. J. Bus. Inf. Syst. **9**, 328–342 (2012)
26. Teo, T.S.H., Soon, L.G., Fedric, S.A.: Adoption and impact of human resource information systems (HRIS). Res. Pract. Hum. Resour. Manag. **9**, 101–117 (2001)
27. Lepak, D., Snell, S.: Virtual HR: strategic human resource management in the 21st century. Hum. Resour. Manag. Rev. **8**, 215–234 (1998)
28. Thite, M., Kavanagh, M.J., Johnson, R.A.: Human resource information systems: Basics, applications, and future directions. Sage, Thousand Oaks, CA (2012)
29. Johnson, R.D., Lukaszewski, K.M., Stone, D.L.: Introduction to the Special Issue on Human Resource Information Systems and Human Computer Interaction. AIS Trans. Human-Computer Interact. **8**, 149–159 (2016)
30. Teo, T.S.H., Lim, G.S., Fedric, S.A.: The adoption and diffusion of human resources information systems in Singapore. Asia Pacific J. Hum. Resour. **45**, 44–62 (2007)
31. Brewster, C., Mayrhofer, W., Morley, M.: New Challenges for European Human Resource Management. Macmillan, Basingstoke (2000)
32. Brewster, C., Hegewisch, A., Mayne, L., Tregaskis, O.: Methodology of the Price Waterhouse Cranfield Project. In: Brewster, C., Hegewisch, A. (eds.) Policy and Practice in European Human Resource Management, pp. 230–245. Routledge, London (1994)
33. Kossek, E.E.: Human resources management innovation. Hum. Resour. Manage. **26**, 71–92 (1987)
34. Panayotopoulou, L., Vakola, M., Galanaki, E.: E-HR adoption and the role of HRM: evidence from Greece. Pers. Rev. **36**, 277–294 (2007)
35. Lazazzara, A., Ghiringhelli, C.: Strategic HRM and e-HRM adoption: an empirical study. In: Harfouche, A. and Cavallari, M. (eds.) The Social Relevance of the Organisation of Information Systems and ICT. Springer International Publisher
36. Kossek, E.E., Young, W., Gash, D.C., Nichol, V.: Waiting for innovation in the human resources department: Godot implements a human-resource information-system. Hum. Resour. Manage. 135–159 (1994)
37. Bissola, R., Imperatori, B.: The unexpected side of relational e-HRM. Empl. Relations. **36**, 376–397 (2014)
38. Insinga, R.C., Werle, M.J.: Linking outsourcing to business strategy. Acad. Manag. Exec. **14**, 58–70 (2000)

Company Reporting on Social Media: A Content Analysis of the Albanian Companies

Eldi Metushi[iD] and Andrea Fradeani[iD]

Abstract Social media represent an important tool for information dissemination and companies have widely accepted the potential benefits associated with their usage. In this regard, we analyze the social media reporting practices for a sample of 200 Albanian companies during one year. In specific, we focus on the content of the posts shared by the companies on their Facebook, Twitter and LinkedIn official pages. Our main objective is to understand the purposes of social media reporting activities of Albanian companies and whether there are differences in their disclosure practices compared to companies from the European Union (EU). This article demonstrates that less than half of the companies of the sample have at least one social media page and Facebook represents the social media most preferred by companies for their reporting initiatives, while LinkedIn the least preferred. In addition, we find that Albanian companies use social media mainly for marketing activities. When analyzing if there are specific variables that could explain company reporting activities on social media, we find that company sector, audience and sales might explain its activity on social media. This study adds to the existing literature by providing social media reporting activities from the perspective of a developing country planning to be part of the EU and thus implementing its promoted disclosure practices. In addition, our findings corroborate with previous studies analyzing the social media reporting practices mainly for EU and US companies.

E. Metushi (✉)
Canadian Institute of Technology, Tirana, Albania
e-mail: eldi.metushi@cit.edu.al

A. Fradeani
University of Macerata, Macerata, Italy
e-mail: andrea.fradeani@unimc.it

© Springer International Publishing AG, part of Springer Nature 2019
A. Lazazzara et al. (eds.), *Organizing for Digital Innovation*,
Lecture Notes in Information Systems and Organisation 27,
https://doi.org/10.1007/978-3-319-90500-6_21

1   Introduction

Corporate use of social media represents a new means of communication to stakeholders. Kaplan and Haenlein [1] define social media as "a group of Internet-based applications that build on the ideological and technological foundations of Web 2.0, and that allow the creation and exchange of User Generated Content". Nowadays these Internet-based applications have radically transformed company reporting practices due to the several benefits associated with their usage. In general, internet reporting has the advantages of lower costs, wider reach, frequency and speed [2]. In the case of social media, improved transparency, increased interactivity and information disclosed, and promotion of products and services are some of the benefits associated to their use [3–6]. Furthermore, the different characteristics of social media allow users to differentiate the type of communication and information. Stakeholders now can take an active part on social media by sharing the information disclosed by companies, being part of discussions, giving their opinions and sharing those with others, and consequently becoming important factors for the company strategy formulation and implementation.

Scholars [7, 8] have highlighted that the reasons behind social media use by companies are to be explained by the Stakeholder Theory, Legitimacy Theory, and Reputation Risk Management. The Stakeholder theory suggests that managers should consider the concerns of all the stakeholders in order to achieve their support and in line with this, the organization's management will undertake activities deemed important by their stakeholders and also report to them on these activities [9–11]. In this sense, the voluntary disclosure of financial, social and environmental information may be considered an important tool to reduce the information asymmetries existing between the organization and its stakeholders and thus increase corporate transparency [12, 13]. In turn, Legitimacy theory points out the existence of a social contract between company and society and managers will adopt strategies and also widely disclose the information showing the company's willingness to comply with society's expectations [14]. Finally, social media reporting may be also considered as a consequence of Reputation Risk Management [15]. The necessity to safeguard their reputation may push companies to use social media for reporting to stakeholders to show that their expectations are met. The failure of doing so, in turn, may have a negative impact on company's reputation and as a consequence manifest a decrease in revenues and ability to attract financial capital, and also a reduced appeal to current and potential employees [16].

Considering the benefits above mentioned and the increased use of social media by companies worldwide in this study we focus our attention on social media activities of the Albanian companies. In particular, the aim of this paper is to analyze whether the Albanian companies use social media and what is their main purpose of social media usage. To do this we use the metrics developed by Bonsón and Ratkai [7] to analyze the reporting practices on Facebook, Twitter and LinkedIn for a sample composed of 200 largest Albanian companies. We choose big companies because they may be more incentivized to increase their engagement on social media because they may bear the costs associated with this activity and also for the purpose to increase transparency and thus mitigate the information asymmetries existing between managers and stakeholders. In addition, voluntary disclosure on social media may help these companies to have a better access to funding opportunities, considering the issues related to the capital market in developing countries such as Albania.

To the best of our knowledge, this is the first study analyzing social media reporting activities from the perspective of a developing country such as Albania. Analyzing this particular environment is of importance because the European Commission is planning to further increase the number of states in the coming years and member states from the Balkan region are expected to join it. In this regard among the other requirements, companies need to adopt transparency practices promoted in the EU, and voluntary disclosure on social media represents an important mechanism for the transparency of the financial markets [17]. In addition, the results of this study could further contribute to the existing literature analyzing the companies' reporting practices on social media for non-marketing purposes in Europe and beyond [4, 18–21]. In fact, it is interesting to point out that all the studies analyzing the companies' use of social media consider companies from developed countries. Thus, it becomes interesting to observe whether these results will still hold for developing countries where it is expected that the capital market is still not yet developed. Furthermore, the fact that our sample represents companies from different industry sectors and data from three different social media makes our results more representative.

In the following section we discuss the literature review while in Sect. 3 will follow a description of our sample and the methodology used. In Sect. 4 we will show our results on corporate use of social media and finally, in Sect. 5 we provide the summary and conclusions.

2 Literature Review and Research Questions

2.1 Literature Review

Recently there has been an increasing focus by scholars on social media and they are found to have positive effects on company performance, communication effectiveness, stakeholder engagement, marketing strategies etc. A recent focus of the literature has been considering the social media adoption for accounting and auditing purposes [22]. Eschenbrenner et al. [23], focusing on Facebook and Twitter messages posted by public accounting firms during 2012, suggest that these firms mainly use social media to achieve business objectives such as Knowledge Sharing, Socialization and Onboarding, and Branding and Marketing. The authors when dividing the public accounting firms between Big 4 and second tier-firm find that the Big 4 firms pursue Knowledge Sharing objectives on Facebook and Twitter to a greater extent compared to second-tier firms. On the other side, the second tier firms pursue Socialization and Onboarding on Facebook and Branding and Marketing on Twitter to a greater extent than the Big 4 firms. Other researchers focus on the market impact of social media adoption by the S&P 1500 firms [5, 24]. They suggest that the trading volume increases after earnings news disclosed on social media [24] and that firms that are active on social media are highly valued by the market and have higher future financial performance [5]. In addition, Du and Jiang [5] further show that when social media engagement is higher firms report higher performance. Furthermore, social media represent an important tool for investor relation purposes [25]. Trinkle et al. [26] point out that investors' perception of the news on social media and their reaction to these news are also influenced by the comments attached to these news. The authors suggest that the reactions to good and bad news are symmetrical when comments are attached to the news disclosed and comments can change the valence of the news. Dorminey et al. [27], analyzing the effect of SEC approval of the firms' social media information dissemination, suggest a positive association of social media use and market reaction as measured by the trading volume and that this association is stronger following the SEC's guidance. Collecting the public tweets recorded between the period from February 28 to December 19th during 2008 to analyze the public mood, Bollen et al. [28] found a positive correlation with the Dow Jones Industrial Average over time suggesting a positive relationship between public mood as measure and the stock market. Furthermore, Blankespoor et al. [29] and Prokofieva [20], by using different samples, find that Twitter dissemination of corporate information help companies attract investors' attention and lower information asymmetries.

Thus far, scholars have widely analyzed the role of social media for marketing purposes. Hence, social media Websites are becoming increasingly popular and in the near future they are likely to evolve into primary online travel information sources [30]. In addition, companies use social media especially to interact with customers, increase brand awareness, customer engagement, promote sales and acquire new customers [31]. Furthermore, customer participation in online brand communities it is found to positively influence the customers' purchase frequency even though this is only true when the participation is moderate [32]. Similarly, social media usage is found to have a significant impact on brand equity [33]. The authors using a standardized online survey from three different industries suggest that while traditional media has a stronger impact on brand awareness the social media usage strongly influences brand image. Another interesting study that demonstrates the importance of social media for marketing purposes is also the study of Leung et al. [34], suggesting that when the customers' attitude towards the hotel's social media page is positive they will in turn show a favorable attitude towards the hotel brand. Social media activity is found to have also positive effects, on users' word of mouth and attitudinal loyalty Risius and Beck [35]. In addition, Xu and Wu [36] suggest that the more interactive the communicative process on Twitter has been during company crisis periods, the less crisis responsibility the company will bear and in addition, the more favorable the organizational reputation and customers' purchase intentions will be.

Furthermore, there is an extensive research focusing on the use of social media for stakeholder engagement. A part of these studies [3, 37, 38] investigate the reasons why stakeholders engage on social media activities. Lewis et al. [37] find that subgroups defined by gender, race/ethnicity, and socioeconomic status show different network behaviors and students sharing social relationships as well as demographic traits share also a significant number of cultural preferences. Analyzing the use of companies' social networks sites in China, Men and Tsai [3] find a medium level of public engagement with corporate social network pages and find that internet users in China mainly use these sites as a primary source of product, promotion and corporate information. In turn, considering only two types of stakeholders in Switzerland, politicians and digital natives, Ruehl and Ingenhoff [38] investigate their motives and level of engagement on corporate social media pages. The authors find that the two stakeholder groups differ in their motivations and behavior on using corporate social media pages. In fact, the authors point out that the digital natives prefer using Facebook to interact with companies while politicians prefer Twitter. YouTube is the social media platform less preferred by both groups.

On the other side, other studies investigate how companies use social media to engage stakeholders [6, 39, 40]. Schniederjans et al. [39] find financial performance enhancement opportunities for firms using social media for Impression management strategies. Similarly, Jiang et al. [6] suggest that communication managers recognize the importance of social media in prior-crisis environmental scanning, creating a credible on-line voice by providing timely accurate information to affected communities, and adopting social media in crisis engagement. However, contrary to the previous results, Manetti and Bellucci [40], when analyzing the use of social media for engaging stakeholders in sustainability reporting, find only a small number of organizations using social media for this purpose, and generally the level of interaction was low. Porter et al. [41], differently from the above, mentioned studies use two types of analysis, one to investigate the CEO's Twitter engagement and another one to explore their opinions about the social media. The authors find that in general senior managers remain slow in accepting social media engagement and legitimization and, contrary to the other studies mentioned above, they place a low credibility and value to social media.

In this study the attention is focused on the companies' reporting practices in Albania by analyzing their activities on Facebook, Twitter and LinkedIn. Previous studies have already analyzed the company reporting practices for European companies [4, 19, 42]. In general, using a content analysis to investigate the social media posts' content, these studies suggest generally positive outcomes between company activity on social media and stakeholder engagement. In addition they point out that companies have widely accepted the benefits of social media communication strategies and their importance for stakeholder engagement purposes. To the best of our knowledge, for Albania there are no previous studies analyzing the company reporting practices on social media. We find only the studies of [43, 44] which mainly focus on Digital Accounting and banks Internet financial reporting but no previous studies specifically focused on social media reporting activities.

2.2 Research Questions

As mentioned previously there is an increasing attention towards social media adoption as a communication tool for disclosure purposes by European companies. In this study we focus our attention on the level of social media adoption by the Albanian companies and try to understand how our findings compare with the results of previous studies on European companies. In addition, we also investigate the main purpose of social media usage for the companies of our sample and which is their most preferred social media. In line with previous studies, we also try to understand some of the determinants of company social media activity. Thus, we analyze whether company sector may influence its reporting activities on social media [17, 45, 46]. The reason is related to the fact that companies of specific sectors (for example Media sector or Retail sector) may have higher interests to use social media for their disclosure purposes compared to other sectors. In line with this, their disclosure practices may influence also the social media activity of other companies operating in the same sector. Thus, our first research question is as follows:

RQ1: Is company activity on social media influenced by the company's sector?

Moreover, according to [4, 19] company activity on social media may influence its audience as measured by the number of likes and followers for Facebook, and number of followers for Twitter and LinkedIn. It is expected that when the company is active on social media this will help to get more likes, shares and comments from its followers, and this in turn may influence others to follow the social media page of the company leading to a higher audience. Hence, our second research question is as follows:

RQ2: Is there any relationship between company social media activity and its audience?

Finally, we also consider whether there is a correlation between company social media activity and sales. Previous findings suggest a positive relationship between social media activity and company sales [4, 5, 32]. These studies suggest that higher social media activity will lead companies to achieve better stakeholder engagement and thus higher customer loyalty and positive attitudes towards company's product, which in turn will lead to increased revenues for the firm. Our third research question is the following:

RQ3: Does company's social media activity influence its sales?

3 Methodology

The sample chosen represents the 200 biggest companies operating in Albania as of March 2016. We found the full list of the companies in an article published by Monitor[1] journal. In Albania, there is no mandatory rule demanding companies to disclose their financial information, so for the sample chosen we had only the list of companies and their total sales as published in the article above mentioned. The number of companies distributed by sector is provided in Table 1. To classify the companies according to their sector we used the Industry Classification Benchmark.[2] As we may observe, there is a considerable variability of the number of companies per sector. The Retail, Construction and Materials, and Oil and Gas sectors are those most represented in the sample while there are only few companies from the sectors of Technology, Media, Basic Resources and Personal and Household products.

To collect the data on social media reporting activities we manually analyzed the official Facebook, Twitter and LinkedIn pages of the companies during a period of one year starting from March 1st, 2016. We used a content analysis to categorize the type of social media posts. For Facebook and LinkedIn posts, the metrics used represent those proposed by Bonsón and Ratkai [7].

However, as suggested by the authors, for Twitter we made few variations to these variables. Thus, for Twitter posts we analyzed the replies instead of the comments. In their study, Bonsón and Ratkai [7] categorize social media posts in Corporate Social Responsibility (CSR) information, marketing, customer support/ customer services and other. In turn, the CSR information is divided into four other categories represented by, environmental, social, financial and governance. Thus, we have a total of seven categories to divide our final social media posts.

4 Results

When analyzing the number of companies adopting a social media we find that 90 companies use at least one type of social media for their disclosure purposes. This represents 45% of the companies of our sample, and considering the fact that the social media used in this study are the ones mostly used by the companies for their disclosure purposes [4, 29] we think that this number is considerably low. Facebook (45% of the sample) is the social media mostly used, while for Twitter (22%) and LinkedIn (17%) it seems that companies do not prefer them for their disclosure

---

[1]For the full list of the companies, refer to the following article link: http://www.monitor.al/200-vip-e-2015-s-ekonomia-ne-udhekryq, last accessed 2017/09/14.

[2]Refer to the following link for the full structure of company sector classification: http://www.icbenchmark.com/structure, last accessed 2017/09/14.

Table 1 No. of companies
distributed by sector

Supersector	No. of companies
Banks	12
Basic resources	3
Construction and materials	36
Financial services	5
Food and beverage	5
Health care	9
Industrial goods and services	7
Insurance	4
Media	2
Oil and gas	28
Personal and household products	3
Retail	62
Technology	1
Telecommunication	6
Travel and leisure	10
Utilities	7
Total	200

purposes. It is interesting to point out that only 16 (8%) companies use all the three types of social media, suggesting that for the Albanian companies using just one social media is sufficient for their disclosure purposes.

4.1 Facebook

In Table 2 we report descriptive statistics on the content of the posts shared on Facebook by the companies of our sample. As we may observe, there are considerable differences in terms of how companies use Facebook for their disclosure purposes and also on the type of posts they share. In fact, in Table 2 it seems that companies use Facebook mainly for marketing activities. The second post content mostly shared on the company social media pages represents the category "Other".

As mentioned previously, this category includes every type of post content that cannot be classified in the other six categories. For the specific case, these posts represent pictures or quotes from well-known people that companies share on their social media page, and for which there is a considerable attention by the followers as measured by the posts' likes and comments. Even though more information is needed, we think that one explanation regarding the use of these posts is related with the purpose to engage the audience and increase brand awareness. Nevertheless, for both categories the median and the standard deviation suggest that there is a considerable variability on the number of posts shared by the companies for these two categories, and the results should be carefully interpreted. In addition,

Table 2 Descriptive statistics of Facebook activity

	Average	SD	Median	Min	Max
Governance	0.02	0.15	0	0	1
Environmental issues	0.32	1.4	0	0	13
Social/human res/career	1.22	4.7	0	0	35
Financial report/transparency issues	0.46	0.21	0	0	1
Customer supp/customer serv	0.93	1.58	1	0	15
Marketing/selling/products	115.05	926.5	1	0	8532
Other	11.2	81.05	1	0	730

interesting to point out is also the fact that according to the results in Table 2, companies of the sample do not prefer to use Facebook for disclosing information on their CSR activities. Another possible explanation could be also that companies may not be involved in CSR activities at all.[3]

4.2 Twitter

When analyzing the posts content for Twitter, the results seem comparable to the findings for Facebook. Thus, we still find that based on the posts average the companies use Twitter mainly for marketing purposes. Compared to Facebook, for Twitter the average of marketing posts by companies is higher. However, as it was the case for Facebook, the values of the standard deviation and the median suggest that these results should be carefully interpreted. In addition, the second largest post content shared on Twitter is "Other", the same as it was for Facebook (Table 3).

We think that in this case, another possible explanation could be related to the fact that the companies influencing the category of "Other" for Facebook may be the same for Twitter. Finally, only few companies share CSR activities on Twitter. In fact, for Twitter we show that for specific categories the average number of posts is zero, suggesting that these companies do not disclose any information for these categories during the period of our analysis.

4.3 LinkedIn

Table 4 reports descriptive statistics results for LinkedIn. We still observe that the highest average is for the marketing posts.

---

[3]In this regard, we rapidly controlled some of the companies' websites to see whether they disclose this information on Internet and we found similar results suggesting that most probably these companies do not involve in CSR activities.

Table 3 Descriptive statistics of Twitter activity

	Average	SD	Median	Min	Max
Governance	0	0	0	0	0
Environmental issues	0	0	0	0	0
Social/human res/career	0.8	4.3	0	0	27
Financial report/transparency issues	0	0	0	0	0
Customer supp/customer serv	0.8	3.2	0	0	15
Marketing/selling/products	246.9	1370.2	0	0	8632
Other	11.4	50.08	0	0	265

Table 4 Descriptive statistics of LinkedIn activity

	Average	SD	Median	Min	Max
Governance	0	0	0	0	0
Environmental issues	0.1	0.3	0	0	1
Social/human res/career	0.4	0.9	0	0	5
Financial report/transparency issues	0.03	0.2	0	0	1
Customer supp/customer serv	0.8	3.6	0	0	21
Marketing/selling/products	2.1	9.9	0	0	57
Other	0.2	0.9	0	0	5

This is a surprising result considering the purpose of LinkedIn as a social media aiming to facilitate professional networking. Compared to the other social media presented previously, we show that for LinkedIn the number of posts on average is considerably lower suggesting that Albanian companies are less active on LinkedIn. In addition, different from the previous results, in this case the second largest average is "Customer support/services". In fact, this result in not surprising considering that this category is more related with the main purpose of LinkedIn as a social media. Finally, in line with the above findings, LinkedIn seems to be not preferred for CSR reporting activities.

4.4 Statistical Analysis

Below we report the results of statistic analysis for a set of variables that may explain company activity on social media. The variables used were tested to assess the normality of their distribution, and because the variables were not normally distributed, as in [4, 19] we used non parametrical tests for our statistical analysis. In Table 5 we report the relationship between company social media activity and its sector to respond to our first research question. Based on the Kruskal-Wallis H-test results, we find statistically significant results for Facebook and Twitter activity of the companies suggesting that company activity on Facebook and Twitter is

Table 5 The relationship between company activity and its sector using Kruskal-Wallis H-test

Dependent	Independent	χ^2 results	df	Significance
Activity	Sector			
		36.275[a]	14	0.0009*
		34.569[b]	12	0.0005*
		9.480[c]	11	0.578

Notes *Significant at $p < 0.01$, [a]Facebook, [b]Twitter, [c]LinkedIn

influenced by its sector. However, the same cannot be said for company activity on LinkedIn. The results suggest that there is no relationship between company activity on LinkedIn and its sector.

Furthermore, in Table 6 we report the results of our statistical analysis to respond to the other research questions. For Facebook, the variable "Audience" represents the sum of the number of followers and likes that the company's Facebook page has, while for Twitter and LinkedIn this represents the number of followers of the company's social media page.

As we may clearly observe, for all the three types of social media, the Spearman's correlation coefficient reports that the relationship between company activity on social media and its audience goes from moderate (Facebook) to strong (Twitter and LinkedIn). Thus, company activity on social media may help the company increase its number of followers and thus achieve wider reach and stronger engagement with its stakeholders.

Table 6 The relationship between company activity, revenues and audience using Spearman's correlation

Variable	Sales	Activity	Audience
Activity	0.273[a]		
	(0.009)* 0.136[b] (0.403) 0.091[c] (0.616)		
Audience		0.411[a]	
		(0.0001)* 0.701[b] (0.0000)* 0.617[c] (0.0001)*	
Sales			0.099[a] (0.356)
			0.167[b] (0.305) 0.240[c] (0.178)

Notes *Significant at $p < 0.01$, [a]Facebook, [b]Twitter, [c]LinkedIn

For the third research question, we find a week to moderate Spearman's correlation coefficient (0.273) only for the relationship between company Facebook activity and sales. In line with previous studies, the results suggest that Facebook activity helps companies increase their sales. We find that the activity on Twitter and LinkedIn does not influence company sales.

In addition, we tested whether there is a relationship between the number of social media used and company sales. The result of the Spearman's correlation coefficient was 0.191 and significant at $p < 0.01$ (sig. 0.0068) level, suggesting a week to moderate relationship. Thus, even the number of social media used by companies for disclosure purposes and stakeholder engagement helps them increase their sales.

Overall, our results suggest that Albanian companies do not have a strategy for social media communication and companies use social media mainly for marketing purposes. As it is the case for other countries, Facebook and then Twitter are the social media mostly used [4, 24, 29]. We also find some relevant differences when comparing our results with those of previous studies in Europe [4, 19, 47]. Thus, considering that our sample represents the biggest companies operating in Albania, we find that less than half of the companies of the sample use at least one social media. In addition, we observe considerably low average percentages for the other posts contents compared to the findings of the studies previously mentioned. However, when analyzing some of the variables that could explain the social media communication strategies of the Albanian companies our findings, at least for Facebook and Twitter, corroborate with those of previous studies.

5 Conclusions

In this study we assess the social media practices of the Albanian companies. Social media represent an important tool for stakeholder engagement and in this study we analyze whether Albanian companies recognize this benefit. We focus on Facebook, Twitter and LinkedIn, and using a content analysis to evaluate the content of the posts shared by the companies, we find interesting results.

Thus, despite the fact that social media benefits are widely recognized we find that less than half of the Albanian companies have at least one social media page. Moreover, we show that Facebook (45%) is the most widely used social media followed by Twitter (22%) and LinkedIn (17%). In addition, only 8% of the companies use all the three social medias, suggesting that usually one social media fits the disclosure purposes of the companies. Furthermore, using a content analysis to categorize the content of the posts shared by companies on their social media pages, we show that the main purpose of social media usage is for marketing. This becomes more interesting considering the fact that we report the same findings even for LinkedIn, which represents a professional business social media and thus it is used mainly for other purposes. Finally, when using statistical analysis to explain the company activity on social media, we show that for Facebook and Twitter the industry sector may explain company activity on social media. In addition, we also show that company activity on social media may play an important role for the company in increasing its audience. In fact, using Spearman's correlation coefficient we find that this relationship is significant and goes from moderate to strong for all the three social medias analyzed. When analyzing the relationship between company social media activity and sales we find that this relationship is significant only for Facebook, suggesting that Facebook activities may help companies increase their sales. We also find that the number of social medias used by companies for their disclosure purposes positively affects also their sales, as showed by the statistically significant Pearson's correlation coefficient.

This study represents the very first study analyzing the social media disclosure practices for the companies of a developing country such as Albania. Albania is aiming to be part of the EU in the coming years, and for this purpose company disclosure practices are expected to converge towards those of EU practices. We show that Albanian companies use social media mainly for marketing purposes and according to our descriptive statistics they do not have a communication strategy on social media. Comparing our results with the findings of previous studies in Europe [4, 19, 47], similarities are observed only with regard to the main purpose of social media reporting, which we found that it was done for marketing purposes. In fact, with regard to the number of companies with a social media and the CSR disclosure activities on social media, we observe differences compared to the studies above mentioned and thus, we suggest that companies should do more in this regard considering the importance of social media as a communication tool and their role in increasing firms' transparency. Furthermore, this research extends the metrics developed by Bonsón and Ratkai [7] to Twitter and LinkedIn. In line with the authors' suggestions, for Twitter and LinkedIn we made few modifications to these metrics to better assess the company audience and activity. Finally, our findings especially those related to the relationship between company activity, audience and sales could be taken into consideration by companies for further planning to increase their audience or sales through social media communication strategies.

As per the limits, we think that the main limitation is related to the considerable variability of our results that do not allow us to have a final conclusion on the social media disclosure practices of the Albanian companies. In addition, another limit of the study is related to the few company data available for our statistic analysis. In fact as we mentioned previously, there are no mandatory requirements for the Albanian companies to publicly disclose their financial information. This obliged us to limit our statistical analysis only to available data such as those related to company sales and sector. We suggest that further research should focus on other variables that could better explain company need for social media disclosure. In addition, the sample represents also companies that operate in international markets. It may be interesting in further studies to analyze whether there are differences in the social media disclosure practices between these two types of companies. Finally, another interesting research could be that explaining why the companies of our sample use LinkedIn mainly for marketing purposes despite its different purpose as social media. In this sense questionnaires sent to companies' social media managers could better explain their LinkedIn communication strategies.

References

1. Kaplan, A.M., Haenlein, M.: Users of the world, unite! The challenges and opportunities of Social Media. Bus. Horiz. 53(1), 59–68 (2010)
2. Debreceny, R., Gray, G.L., Rahman, A.: The determinants of Internet financial reporting. J. Account. Public Policy 21(4–5), 371–394 (2002)
3. Men, L.R., Tsai, W.H.S.: Beyond liking or following: understanding public engagement on social networking sites in China. Public Relat. Rev. 39(1), 13–22 (2013)
4. Bonsón Ponte, E., Carvajal-Trujillo, E., Escobar-Rodríguez, T.: Corporate Facebook and stakeholder engagement. Kybernetes 44(5), 771–787 (2015)
5. Du, Q., Fan, W., Qiao, Z., Wang, G., Zhang, X., Zhou, M. (2015). Do Facebook activities increase sales? In: AMCIS 2015 Proceedings. Retrieved from http://aisel.aisnet.org/amcis2015/e-Biz/GeneralPresentations/33
6. Jiang, H., Luo, Y., Kulemeka, O.: Social media engagement as an evaluation barometer: insights from communication executives. Public Relat. Rev. 42(4), 679–691 (2016)
7. Bonsón, E., Ratkai, M.: A set of metrics to assess stakeholder engagement and social legitimacy on a corporate Facebook page. Online Inf. Rev. 37(5), 787–803 (2013)
8. Rivera-Arrubla, Y.A., Zorio-Grima, A.: Integrated reporting, connectivity and social media. Psychol. Mark. 33(12), 1159–1165 (2016)
9. Freeman, R.E.: Strategic Management: A Stakeholder Approach. Cambridge University Press (2010)
10. Jensen, M.C.: Value maximization, stakeholder theory, and the corporate objective function. J. Appl. Corp. Finance 14(3), 8–21 (2001)
11. Guthrie, J., Petty, R., Ricceri, F.: The voluntary reporting of intellectual capital: comparing evidence from Hong Kong and Australia. J. Intellect. Capital 7(2), 254–271 (2006)
12. An, Y., Davey, H., Eggleton, I.R.C.: Towards a comprehensive theoretical framework for voluntary IC disclosure. J. Intellect. Capital 12(4), 571–585 (2011)
13. Michelon, G., Parbonetti, A.: The effect of corporate governance on sustainability disclosure. J. Manag. Gov. 16(3), 477–509 (2012)
14. Deegan, C., Rankin, M., Tobin, J.: An examination of the corporate social and environmental disclosures of BHP from 1983–1997: A test of legitimacy theory. Acc. Auditing Accountability J. 15(3), 312–343 (2002)
15. Bebbington, J., Larrinaga, C., Moneva, J.M.: Corporate social reporting and reputation risk management. Acc. Auditing Accountability J. 21(3), 337–361 (2008)
16. Fombrun, C.J., Gardberg, N.A., Barnett, M.L.: Opportunity platforms and safety nets: corporate citizenship and reputational risk. Bus. Soc. Rev. 105(1), 85–106 (2000)
17. Bonsón, E., Escobar, T.: Digital reporting in Eastern Europe: an empirical study. Int. J. Acc. Inf. Syst. 7(4), 299–318 (2006)
18. Barnes, N.G.: The Fortune 500 and Social media: a longitudinal study of blogging, Twitter and Facebook usage by America's largest companies. http://www.umassd.edu/media/umassdartmouth/cmr/studiesandresearch/2010F500Final.pdf. Last accessed 2017/09/14 (2010)
19. Bonsón, E., Bednarova, M., Escobar-Rodríguez, T.: Corporate YouTube practices of Eurozone companies. Online Inf. Rev. 38(4), 484–501 (2014)
20. Prokofieva, M.: Twitter-based dissemination of corporate disclosure and the intervening effects of firms' visibility: evidence from Australian-listed companies. J. Inf. Syst. 29(2), 107–136 (2015)
21. Tao, W., Wilson, C.: Fortune 1000 communication strategies on Facebook and Twitter. J. Commun. Manag. 19(3), 208–223 (2015)
22. Debreceny, R.S.: Social media, social networks, and accounting. J. Inf. Syst. 29(2), 1–4 (2015)
23. Eschenbrenner, B., Nah, F.F.-H., Telaprolu, V.R.: Efficacy of social media utilization by public accounting firms: findings and directions for future research. J. Inf. Syst. 29(2), 5–21 (2015)

24. Jung, M.J., Naughton, J.P., Tahoun, A., Wang, C.: Corporate Use of Social Media. Unpublished paper, Northwestern University (2014)
25. Ramassa, P., Di Fabio, C.: Social media for investor relations: a literature review and future directions. Int. J. Digit. Acc. Res. **16**, 117–135 (2016)
26. Trinkle, B.S., Crossler, R.E., Bélanger, F.: Voluntary disclosures via social media and the role of comments. J. Inf. Syst. **29**(3), 101–121 (2015)
27. Dorminey, J.W., Dull, R.B., Schaupp, L.C.: The effect of SEC approval of social media for information dissemination. Res. Acc. Regul. **27**(2), 165–173 (2015)
28. Bollen, J., Mao, H., Zeng, X.: Twitter mood predicts the stock market. J. Comput. Sci. **2**(1), 1–8 (2011)
29. Blankespoor, E., Miller, G.S., White, H.D.: The role of dissemination in market liquidity: evidence from firms' use of Twitter™. Acc Rev. **89**(1), 79–112 (2014)
30. Xiang, Z., Gretzel, U.: Role of social media in online travel information search. Tour. Manag. **31**(2), 179–188 (2010)
31. Tsimonis, G., Dimitriadis, S.: Brand strategies in social media. Mark. Intell. Plann. **32**(3), 328–344 (2014)
32. Wu, J., Huang, L., Zhao, J.L., Hua, Z.: The deeper, the better? Effect of online brand community activity on customer purchase frequency. Inf. Manag. **52**(7), 813–823 (2015)
33. Bruhn, M., Schoenmueller, V., Schäfer, D.B.: Are social media replacing traditional media in terms of brand equity creation? Manag. Res. Rev. **35**(9), 770–790 (2012)
34. Leung, X.Y., Bai, B., Stahura, K.A.: The marketing effectiveness of social media in the hotel industry: a comparison of Facebook and Twitter. J. Hospitality Tourism Res. **39**(2), 147–169 (2015)
35. Risius, M., Beck, R.: Effectiveness of corporate social media activities in increasing relational outcomes. Inf. Manag. **52**(7), 824–839 (2015)
36. Xu, J., Wu, Y.: Using Twitter in crisis management for organizations bearing different country-of-origin perceptions. J. Commun. Manag. **19**(3), 239–253 (2013)
37. Lewis, K., Kaufman, J., Gonzalez, M., Wimmer, A., Christakis, N.: Tastes, ties, and time: a new social network dataset using Facebook.com. Soc Netw. **30**(4), 330–342 (2008)
38. Ruehl, C.H., Ingenhoff, D.: Communication management on social networking sites: stakeholder motives and usage types of corporate Facebook, Twitter and YouTube pages. J. Commun. Manag. **19**(3), 288–302 (2015)
39. Schniederjans, D., Cao, E.S., Schniederjans, M.: Enhancing financial performance with social media: an impression management perspective. Decis. Support Syst. **55**(4), 911–918 (2013)
40. Manetti, G., Bellucci, M.: The use of social media for engaging stakeholders in sustainability reporting. Acc. Auditing Accountability J. **29**(6), 985–1011 (2016)
41. Porter, M.C., Anderson, B., Nhotsavang, M.: Anti-social media: executive Twitter "engagement" and attitudes about media credibility. J. Commun. Manag. **19**(3), 270–287 (2015)
42. Escobar-Rodríguez, T., Bonsón-Fernandez, R.: Facebook practices for business communication among fashion retailers. J. Fashion Mark. Manag. Int. J. **21**(1), 33–50 (2017)
43. Lamani, D., Cepani, L.: Internet financial reporting by banks and insurance companies in Albania. Rom. Econ. J. **14**(42), 159–174 (2011)
44. Perri, R., Allko, D.: Business reporting language: a survey of Albanian companies and institutions. Czech J. Sci. Bus. Econ. **4**(4), 39–49 (2015)
45. Ettredge, M., Richardson, V.J., Scholz, S.: The presentation of financial information at corporate web sites. Int. J. Acc. Inf. Syst. **2**(3), 149–168 (2001)
46. Boritz, J.E., Timoshenko, L.M.: Firm-specific characteristics of the participants in the SEC's XBRL voluntary filing program. J. Inf. Syst. **29**(1), 9–36 (2015)
47. Bonsón, E., Flores, F.: Social media and corporate dialogue: the response of global financial institutions. Online Inf. Rev. **35**(1), 34–39 (2011)

The Usage of Social Networking Technology. The Case Study City of Naples Facebook Account

Benedetta Gesuele and Alberto Celio

Abstract This study aim is to understand the diffusion of networking technologies by Italian municipalities. Using the case study methods, we try to explore the official Facebook page in order to highlight the municipalities Facebook activities on social media to promote interconnectivity between government and its stakeholders. Above all, we would answer to two research questions: (1) how the municipalities use a social media? (2) What type of contents they disclosure using these tools? During the research, we supervise the City of Naples Facebook account to highlight the municipalities behavior on social media and the content mainly disclosure by municipalities through the social media.

1 Introduction

In the last decades, the great diffusion of electronic government (e-government) and of the information and communications technology (ICTs) tools help governments in information provision and service delivery. New technologies, as social media, promote interconnectivity between government and its stakeholders (citizens, companies, employees, and others) as well as to encourage decentralization, transparency, and internal and external accountability [1]. The alternative communication tools become the growing force for public transparency and accountability key drivers for good governance [2]. The social media usage in the public sector, especially in the municipalities, facilitate access to information, openness, transparency, the engagement of citizens, and have been effective tools to promote public goals and improve the public value creation [3–5].

B. Gesuele (✉)
ACRI, Associazione di Fondazioni e Casse di Risparmio SpA, Rome, Italy
e-mail: benedetta.gesuele@acri.it; benedettagesuele@gmail.com

A. Celio
Department of Business and Economics, Parthenope University, Naples, Italy
e-mail: alberto.celio@uniparthenope.it

© Springer International Publishing AG, part of Springer Nature 2019
A. Lazazzara et al. (eds.), *Organizing for Digital Innovation*,
Lecture Notes in Information Systems and Organisation 27,
https://doi.org/10.1007/978-3-319-90500-6_22

293

In Italy, during the last time, many municipalities have added to their official websites (mandatory disclosure) also several social media to communicate with citizens, as additional form of on line communication (such as Facebook, Twitter, and YouTube).

Our study focuses on Web 2.0 applications, as Facebook, usage by municipalities. This study aim to contribute to this research gap by investigating the Facebook usage by a municipality in term of contents disclosed and impact of them on citizens. Using the case study method, we explore the Facebook account activity of Naples, a city in South of Italy.

In this case, we chose to investigate the behavior of Naples on Facebook because Naples is one of the most populous cities in the South of Italy and, in line with previous major studies, the face to face interaction between local administrators and citizens could be very hard [6]. For this reason, the social networking technologies could represent the good communication tools to reduce the distance between municipalities and their stakeholders [7].

We focus on Facebook because is the social media that dominate the web and it is commonly used applications by local governments.

The structure of this paper is as follows. In the next section, we introduce the theoretical background on social media usage by municipalities. In Sect. 3, we outline the research methodology and then we describe the analysis of the results (Sect. 4). Finally, in Sect. 5 we discuss findings and present limitations, conclusion and practical implication.

2 The Social Networking Technologies: Theoretical Background

The development of social media is bringing new ways for government to communicate with citizens. These applications provide new possibilities for community leaders, elected officials and government service providers to be in touch with each other [8]. Social media refers to "a group of Internet-based applications that build on the ideological and technological foundations of Web 2.0, and that allow the creation and exchange of User Generated Content" [9]. At the simplest, Web 2.0 is the technical platform where social media applications born to exchange user-generated content [4]. These tools donate services like blogs, microblogs, media (audio, photo, video, text) sharing, and social networking, promoting creation and support of social interaction, collaboration, and exchange of information between users [9]. Today, there are several social media platforms different from each other to achieve any goal relate to the successful communication [10] for example Facebook, Pinterest, Instagram and Youtube allow people to share with other users' text, picture, video, and music (e.g., Facebook, Twitter, Youtube).

To date the number of users has increased and social media be transformed into elements very important for public administrations to create synergies between government and people, for disseminating government information, and co-creation value for citizens. The increasing of social media has led scholars to analyze the social media's impact on e-government, for more clarification see Magro's work 2012 [11].

Magro's [11] review pointed that in 2010 there was a large number of research on social media and e-government and that the central themes in literature linked to social media policy and strategy [4], case studies [12], and social media use in disaster management [13]. Another key issue emerged from Magro's review was the relationship between success and social media in e-government [14], however the utility of social media was mined usefulness in government [15]. In fact, Magro shown that: "The 'best' way to use social media in government is a nebulous and subjective problem that does not lend itself to a single set of guidelines for every task, country, agency, citizen, and government" [11].

Many authors affirmed that the opportunities provided by Web 2.0 applications for government are connected to transparency and accountability [2, 3, 7, 10, 22], through dissemination information to the citizens [4]; improvement of policy making [6], by increasing opportunities to participate and collaborate in decision making or voting [4]; improvement of public services [6]. However social media can increase management issues such as loss of control [14], low propensity to citizen participation [10, 16], privacy and security issues [7], communication issues [4].

Picazo-Vela affirms that government policies to ensure the success of social media must aim for a proper updating of laws and regulations [4]. Development of social media application is divided in three levels: central, regional, and local government. We focused on social media usage by municipalities because their rising diffusion as an additional form of e-disclosure. This analysis is based on previous study like a survey of Norris and Reddick on social media adoption of local governments (e.g., Facebook, Twitter, and YouTube) in the United States [17]. It outlined that the social media have improved the relationship between municipality and citizen and two-thirds of local governments had adopted at least one social media.

Bonsón points out that most local governments use social media but the participation of citizens is very limited [6].

Klang and Nolin studied the use of social media by Swedish political parties to improve interaction between municipality and citizens [18].

3 Research Method

This study aim is to understand the diffusion of networking technologies by municipalities. Therefore, the research questions that guided this study are (1) how the municipalities use a social media? (2) What type of contents they disclosure using these tools? Using the case study method, we try to explore the official Facebook Municipality Account to highlight the its Facebook activities on social media to promote interconnectivity with principal stakeholders. During the research, we supervise the City of Naples Facebook account to highlight the municipalities behavior on social media and the mainly contents disclosure used its. We choose this municipalities because it is one of bigger (in term of number of inhabitants) in Italy. The years under investigation is 2015. Following we describe the research context and then we focus our attention on the single research questions.

3.1 The Research Context

In Italy, in the last decades, the regimentation about e-disclosure become more and more complex and predominant, for e.g. the legislative decrees 150/2009 and 33/2013 are the laws related to mandatory public disclosure. At the same time, the government regulation enhances the importance of external control and performance goals, in fact the legislative decree 150/2009 proposed the extend control on municipalities' activities in order to improve performances. Starting from this reform, the local government discloses some information on their activity, such as objectives, organization, performance indicators and data about resources spent to deliver public services. In 2013, the legislative decree 33 established the mandatory disclosure to publish on the website by municipalities. At the same time, many municipalities are starting to use the social media to improve the citizens-public administration trust relationship. In particular, we focus our attention on Naples. It is one of the most populous cities in the South of Italy and, in line with previous major studies the face to face relation is very hard [5, 9, 13]. For this reason, the social networking technologies could represent the good communication tools to reduce the distance between municipalities and their stakeholders [10].

4 Data Analysis

In this section, we describe the analysis to explain the research questions.

4.1 How the Municipalities Use a Social Media?

To explore the Municipality activity using social networking we observe the City of Naples Facebook account behaviors during the year under investigation. The City of Naples is one of bigger city in Italy, for this reason the face to face interaction between citizens and public manager is very complex [5, 6, 8]. The introduction social networking tools, as Facebook, are getting facilitate the interaction and the disclosure information. Thanks these instruments to enhance the relationship between the municipality manager and citizens, in fact citizens can receive more type of information and, moreover, they can transfer their opinion about the municipalities managers activities, above all in real time. During the 2015, the Naples Official Account received 3560 number of like and its activity seem very great, in fact it published 12,990 posts and 1594 users talking about it (Table 1).

In the second phase, we choose to analyze the basic Fb account activity in the last six months of the year to comprehend the Account behaviors in term of post frequency (Table 2). For Practical reasons, we choose to analyze the post published only in the last six months of years.

According to previous studies [19]. We explore the municipality activity in order to understand the regularity of post published and we analyze the timing of posts by municipality as Posting Time. First of all, we identified the posts published during the working days and in the off days. Secondly, defining the range of hours when the posts are published, we consider four time slots: (1) from 8:00 to 12:00, (2) from 12:00 to 16:00; (3) from 16:00 to 20:00 and (4) beyond 20:00. The following table describe the Posting time for the municipality investigated during the last six months of the 2015, the values are expressed as value % (Table 3).

The findings show that the great part of posts is published during the working day (83.97%). During the second and the third slots time (from 12:00 to 16:00 and from 16:00 to 20:00 there are the major number of post published. We underline that there are posts published beyond the 20:00.

4.2 What Type of Contents They Disclosure Using These Tools?

In the second research steps, we chose to analyze the type of contents disclosure, considering the major previous studies [20, 21] we classified the content published into 4 categories, such as co-design (1), local events (2), local public services (3), and provision of information (4). Co-design category represents all content published that refers the citizens' participation to political municipalities life such as municipality councils or city council meetings [21, 22]. Local events contain the contents regarding on artistic, cultural and sportive events organized by municipalities or in the municipalities area by other organizations. The other category Local public services regard the information on public services as transport, security, energy etc.... all information can be considered "of public utilities". The last category regarding on the information, that is contents by which local

Table 1 Naples Facebook account basic activity

	NLikes	Post published	Photo	Post with like	Comment by users	Comment by municipality	Talking about
Fb account	3605	12,990	41	11,636	1404	110	1594

Table 2 Naples Facebook account activity: posts

Month	Days	Total post	Average post in a Day
December	31	138	4,322,580,645
November	30	105	3,323,457,797
October	31	120	3,612,903,226
September	30	107	3,433,333,333
August	31	70	2,161,290,323
July	31	95	2,967,741,935
June	30	126	3,966,666,667
Total		761	

Table 3 Naples Facebook account: posting time

Month	Posting time %					
	Off day/working day		Time in a day			
	Total post in off day	Total post in working day	From 8:00 to 12:00	From 12:00 to 16:00	From 16:00 to 20:00	Beyond 20:00
December	10.14	86.96	9.42	42.03	45.65	2.90
November	12.38	81.90	7.62	49.52	37.14	5.71
October	0.00	93.33	5.00	39.17	49.17	6.67
September	8.41	87.85	3.74	55.14	37.38	3.74
August	21.43	74.29	10.00	54.29	31.43	4.29
July	20.00	76.84	7.37	50.53	38.95	3.16
June	13.49	80.95	15.87	33.33	45.24	5.56
Total	11.43	83.97	8.54	45.20	41.66	4.60

governments offer to citizens' information such as weather forecast, traffic information etc. [19, 20, 22]. The following table shows the categories identifies using an excel application for account selected (Table 4).

The table shows that municipalities analyzed uploaded contents related to local events (55.18%), local events (24.92%), local public services (14.38%), and co-design (5.52%) categories.

4.3 Which Type of Impact the Social Media Have on Citizens?

In order to observe the citizens' perception about municipalities activities on Facebook we use a survey and engagement metric system.

We construct a simply survey that is posted by Public Relation Office on Facebook page on 25 March 2015. The survey was available only for one day on Official Municipality Facebook page. Fifty persons responded to the survey.

Table 4 Post category

| Month | Post category solo status % value | | | |
| | (1) | (2) | (3) | (4) |
	Co-design	Local events	Local public services	Provision of information
December	8.16	62.24	15.31	14.29
November	5.38	52.69	16.13	25.81
October	1.00	67.00	22.00	10.00
September	5.43	53.26	11.96	29.35
August	16.28	41.86	0.00	41.86
July	3.75	41.25	28.75	26.25
June	4.35	57.61	0.00	38.04
Total	5.52	55.18	14.38	24.92

Considering the exiguous number of replays, in the following research phase, we observe the municipality' Facebook activity considering its based activity.

4.4   The Survey

The survey is composed by 15 questions. They can be divided in two groups; from 1 to 7 they investigate about the profile of replays, the other part investigates about the citizens perception of social media. During this study, we are chosen to focus our attention on a group of questions regarding the consultation of Facebook page and the citizens' perception. The survey results show that: the 42% of replays consult often (more 4 ways and less 8 in one day) the municipality Facebook page (the 8% of replays consult the page more 8 ways in one day; the 20 consult the page from 2 to 4 ways and the 30% of replays consult the page less 4 ways in a week); the 66% of replays consider the Facebook municipality page easy to consult (only 2% of replays consider the page hard to consult and the other part of replays consider the page is quite easy to consult). The replays perceive the official municipality Facebook page as e-democracy instrument, namely the 48% of them. Only the 16% of replays don't perceive this tool as e- democracy instrument, the remainder of respondent has not an opinion. Considering the poor information that we collect using the survey we measure the ability of municipality to catch the citizens attention using three specific engagement measure consolidate in previous major literature.

5   Findings, Conclusion, Limits and Practical Implication

The municipality investigated communicates with its stakeholders using the official Facebook Account. Firstly, results have shown that the main communication topics between local government and citizens are local events and provision of information. Local public service and co- design are less important. These results are, in accordance with previous researches, that are investigated the same topic [19, 20, 22]. Respect other previous researches we chose the topics identified are smaller as number, we justified this type of results considering that we analyze only one case study. The topic major discussed on line is local events, considering this evidence we argue that in this way the local administration, (which manage the account) can highlight the good made activities and in this way, enhance its social image and improve the citizens participation. The co-design seems to have less importance, we justified these results considering the cultural and political context.

Moreover, the time when the account usually used (not office time or in off day) shows that it might be appropriate to have a staff who should devote exclusively to interaction with citizens through Facebook.

The case study is able to describe only one fact and, considering the type of phenomena, we aren't able to generalize the results. For the second part of the research, the number of replays is exiguous considering the number of fans of page and the city population, but we justified this limit considering the exiguous time that the survey was available online.

References

1. La Porte, T.M., de Jong, M., Demchak, C.C.: Public organizations on the world wide web: empirical correlates of administrative openness. In: Proceedings of the 5th National Public Management Research Conference, College Station, TX (1999)
2. Bonsón, E., Torres, L., Royo, S., Flores, F.: Local e-government 2.0: social media and corporate transparency in municipalities. Gov. Inf. Q. 29(2), 123–132 (2012)
3. Bertot, J.C., Jaeger, P.T., Hansen, D.: The impact of polices on government social media usage: issues, challenges, and recommendations. Gov. Inf. Q. 29(1), 30–40 (2012)
4. Picazo-Vela, S., Gutiérrez-Martínez, I., Luna-Reyes, L.F.: Understanding risks, benefits, and strategic alternatives of social media applications in the public sector. Gov. Inf. Q. 29(4), 504–511 (2012)
5. Oliveira, G.H.M., Welch, E.W.: Social media use in local government: Linkage of technology, task, and organizational context. Gov. Inf. Q. 30(4), 397–405 (2013)
6. Bonsón Ponte, E., Escobar Rodríguez, T.: A survey on voluntary disclosure on the internet: empirical evidence from 300 European union companies (2012)
7. Bertot, J.C., Jaeger, P.T., Hansen, D.: The impact of polices on government social media usage: issues, challenges, and recommendations. Gov. Inf. Q. 29(1), 30–40 (2012)
8. Kavanaugh, A.L., Fox, E.A., Sheetz, S.D., Yang, S., Li, L.T., Shoemaker, D.J., Xie, L.: Social media use by government: from the routine to the critical. Gov. Inf. Q. 29(4), 480–491 (2012)
9. Kaplan, A.M., Haenlein, M.: Users of the world, unite! The challenges and opportunities of social media. Bus. Horiz. 53(1), 59–68 (2010)
10. Metallo, C., Gesuele, B.: Determinants of Twitter adoption in local governments: empirical evidence from Italy. Int. J. Aud. Technol. 3(2), 79–94 (2016)
11. Magro, M.J.: A review of social media use in e-government. Adm. Sci. 2(2), 148–161 (2012)
12. Cottica, A., Bianchi, T.: Harnessing the unexpected: a public administration interacts with creatives on the web. Eur. J. ePractice 9, 82–90 (2010)
13. Yates, D., Paquette, S.: Emergency knowledge management and social media technologies: a case study of the 2010 Haitian earthquake. Int. J. Inf. Manage. 31(1), 6–13 (2011)

14. Ferro, E., Molinari, F.: Making sense of Gov 2.0 strategies: "no citizens, no party". JeDEM-eJournal eDemocracy Open Gov. **2**(1), 56–68 (2010)
15. Landsbergen, D.: Government as part of the revolution: using social media to achieve public goals. In: Proceedings of the 10th European Conference on e-government, pp. 243–250 (2010)
16. Anttiroiko, A.V.: Innovation in democratic E-governance: benefitting from web 2.0. Citizens E-Government: Eval. Policy Manage. **110** (2010)
17. Norris, D.F., Reddick, C.G.: Local e-government in the United States: transformation or incremental change? Public Adm. Rev. **73**(1), 165–175 (2013)
18. Klang, M., Nolin, J.: Disciplining social media: an analysis of social media policies in 26 Swedish municipalities. First Monday, **16**(8) (2011)
19. Cvijikj, I.P., Michahelles, F.: Online engagement factors on Facebook brand pages. Soc. Netw. Anal. Min. **3**(4), 843–861 (2013)
20. Sobaci, M.Z., Karkin, N.: The use of Twitter by mayors in Turkey: tweets for better public services? Gov. Inf. Q. **30**(4), 417–425 (2013)
21. Lin, M.F.G., Hoffman, E.S., Borengasser, C.: Is social media too social for class? A case study of Twitter use. TechTrends **57**(2), 39 (2013)
22. Gesuele, B., Metallo, C., Agrifoglio, R.: What do local governments discuss in social media? An empirical analysis of the Italian municipalities. In: Blurring the boundaries through digital innovation, pp. 297–306. Springer International Publishing (2016)

Author Index

© Springer International Publishing AG, part of Springer Nature 2019
A. Lazazzara et al. (eds.), *Organizing for Digital Innovation*,
Lecture Notes in Information Systems and Organisation 27,
https://doi.org/10.1007/978-3-319-90500-6

Printed in the United States
By Bookmasters